W9-DHU-739

Reference Guide for Consumers

Reference Guide for Consumers

by

Nina David

R. R. BOWKER COMPANY
A Xerox Education Company
New York & London, 1975
XEROX

Published by R. R. Bowker Co. (A Xerox Education Company)
1180 Avenue of the Americas, New York, N.Y. 10036

Printed and bound in the United States of America

Library of Congress Cataloging in Publication Data

David, Nina.
Reference guide for consumers.

Includes indexes.
1. Consumer education—Bibliography. I. Title.
Z5776.C65D4 [TX335] 016.64073'0973 75-12912
ISBN 0-8352-0768-4

To Michael

CONTENTS

Preface ix
How to Use This Book xi

I. **Multimedia Materials** 1

II. **Organizations** 191
U.S. Federal Agencies 191
Private Organizations 202
U.S. State, County, and City Agencies 212
Canadian Agencies 259

III. **Newspapers** 264
U.S. Newspapers 264
Canadian Newspapers 277
Syndicated Columnists 277

Directory of Publishers 279
Author Index 291
Title Index 307
Subject Index 325

PREFACE

In the past few years, the consumer movement has emerged from relative obscurity, shedding its faint aura of idiosyncrasy, to become one of the most important and legitimate concerns of the day. Following such headline-making books as Ralph Nader's classic, *Unsafe at Any Speed*, the needs of consumers have begun to be felt in the marketplace. The publishing field has responded by producing an ever-increasing number of books educating consumers in many fields, such as, managing money, buying a car, and shopping for furniture. Magazines and films devoted to these issues have begun to proliferate. Grass roots organizations have sprung up across the country. National, state, and local governments are passing consumer legislation and setting up consumer agencies. Newspapers feature "Help" and "Action" columns and services.

This book aims to pull together the many varied sources of consumer information, evaluate the multimedia material, and present the whole in a form for ready reference.

Almost all materials included in *Reference Guide for Consumers* have been submitted for review by private organizations, publishers of books, pamphlets and magazines, and film distributors. The only exceptions were a small number of books which were either unavailable or which certain publishers refused to furnish. I have tried to look at these books in the library; in a few cases this was not possible. Within this framework, I have attempted to review all books published between 1960 and June 1974, and in print at the time of research. A few publishers sent materials published in the summer and fall of 1974. Films were considered from 1965, although there is little of real merit before the 1970s. Filmstrips were looked at, but not reviewed. It is the opinion of this reviewer that the medium itself is static and didactic. While filmstrips may have some use in certain classroom situations, so much better material is available in other media that filmstrips are not essential to the well-rounded collection. All bibliographic material has been checked and is correct as of summer 1974.

Books, pamphlets, magazines, and films were chosen that would aid consumers in getting the most value and protection in the marketplace, in buying the best goods, and in obtaining the best services. It is hoped that this information will result in time and money saved in buying new products and in conserving those items already purchased.

Organizations that provide protection, information and/or legal redress have been included. Only major private groups (with a few exceptions) have been described. While the list of U.S. state, county, city, Puerto Rican, and Canadian government organizations was up to date as of June 1974, new agencies are forming constantly. Information on all organizations, public and private in this book, was obtained from questionnaires sent in July and September 1974. For organizations which did not respond to a request for information, basic data only: name, address, telephone number, and head of organization has been inserted for the reader's convenience.

In the section listing newspapers with consumer action columns and services, only those newspapers answering a questionnaire sent in October 1974 were incorporated in the book.

It is my hope that libraries will use the first section of *Reference Guide for Consumers* to build their consumer collections and the last two sections to direct patrons to sources of help and further information concerning consumer affairs.

I wish to thank Mr. Francis Pollock, Editor of *Media & Consumer* for his assistance in furnishing me with a list of consumer journalists; Mr. Erasmus J. Struglia, Director of Staff and Information Services at Consumers Union, for putting his library collection at my disposal; and Ms. Rochelle Alper and Ms. Constance Piellucci of the Telephone Reference Division of the Brooklyn Public Library, for their help in checking sources. Special thanks to my editor, Ms. Patricia Glass Schuman, for her advice and encouragement.

How to Use This Book

Arrangement

Reference Guide for Consumers is arranged in three key parts: an annotated bibliography of multimedia materials, a detailed listing of consumer organizations, and a listing of newspapers and columnists frequently dealing with consumer problems.

In Part I, "Multimedia Materials," numbered annotated entries within each subject are listed in alphabetical order (generally by author, but occasionally by title). A magazine is designated by an asterisk (*); a film by a dagger (†).

In Part II, "Organizations," arrangement is alphabetical for U.S. federal agencies and for American and Canadian private groups. *Subagencies are filed beneath their parent organization.* It is geographic by state, for state, county, and city agencies (including Puerto Rico), and by province for Canadian agencies.

In Part III, "Newspapers," listings are in alphabetical order by city within each U.S. state and Canadian province; syndicated columnists follow alphabetically.

Cross-References

Cross-references in Part I refer readers to other relevant subjects within this section and/or pertinent organizations in Part II. The latter cross-references are suggestive, covering major areas only. There are also cross-references within the text of the annotations which quickly refer the user to entry numbers of books discussed.

Consumers wanting information, advice, or aid on a particular topic should:

1. read all annotations in Part I under a particular subject, e.g., Frauds;
2. check *see also* references when appropriate, e.g., Automobiles—Frauds; Consumer Protection; Medical Care—Frauds; Real Estate—Frauds;
3. check pertinent organizations in Part II, e.g., U.S. Federal Agencies—Federal Trade Commission; U.S. Postal Service;
4. read all material in their own *state*, *county*, and *city* (if American) or *province* (if Canadian).

Indexes

There are three indexes in *Reference Guide for Consumers:* an author index, a title index, and a subject index. These indexes list *by entry number only* all books, pamphlets, magazines, and films annotated in Part I.

I. MULTIMEDIA MATERIALS

All materials are arranged within each subject area in alphabetical order by main entry. In most cases, books and pamphlets are listed by author. Occasionally, they are listed by title, as are all magazines and films. Magazines are marked by asterisks (*); films by daggers (†).

AIRPLANES

For pertinent organizations see Part II, U.S. Federal Agencies—Civil Aeronautics Board.

1. Griffin, Al. **So You'd Like to Buy an Airplane!** Macmillan, 1970. 330 pp. $7.95.

Griffin, an airplane flyer and owner, has written the only book in this field, a once-over-lightly review of planes, from single engines to jets. Eight categories of aircraft are listed in ascending order of gross weight: single engines—fixed gear, light twins, heavy twins, turboprops, etc. Approximately one page of information is devoted to each model. Each section concludes with "Best of Class" (Standards). In effect, the standards and descriptive material leave it up to the reader to decide which plane to buy; Griffin does not recommend any models, although he makes critical comments about each one. He also shows prospective flyers the pitfalls of taking instruction from unlicensed teachers, the best way to get proper training, pass the exams, and save money in the process, e.g., buy a plane rather than rent one. A very good chapter, "Aero Economics," deals with specific banks and bankers that finance loans for planes, ways to bargain with dealers, a breakdown of the costs of running a plane, the value of flying clubs (several people owning a single plane), and figures which "prove" that, if used enough, some planes cost less to run than new cars.

ANNUITIES

See also Insurance, Life; Pensions; Retirement

2. *Maloney, Richard F., ed. "Annuities from the Buyer's Point of View," **Economic Education Bulletin,** vol. 13, no. 8 (1973): 1–15. $1 per issue.

The article gives a brief, but very clear, description of different types and functions of annuities and how to choose a company and a contract. Other sources of retirement income are also covered: Social Security, savings and investments, pension plans, and life insurance. Showing how annuities fit into the total retirement picture, Maloney points out that annuities, which offer fixed sums of income for life, have historically returned less money for living due to inflation. To offset inflation, he suggests that annuities be purchased along with high-grade common stocks. Noting that annuities can greatly increase total income available over a lifetime (as opposed to living off principal and possibly outliving one's investments), he also suggests that it is not in a buyer's best interest to put all monies into these funds. A chart showing the returns from 39 companies on installment refund annuities and 38 companies on straight life annuities helps consumers choose which company to buy from.

APPLIANCES

See Household Equipment and Furnishings

AUCTIONS

3. De Forrest, Michael. **How to Buy at Auction.** Simon and Schuster, 1972. 224 pp. $6.95.

A basic guide with easy-to-follow instructions, its seven chapters point up the economy and fun of it all: how to find auctions in the country and in the city, ten points by which to gauge the relative honesty of an auctioneer, how and when to inspect and attend auctions, chances of getting a treasure, tactics of bidding and withdrawing a bid, how to claim a purchase. Personal anecdotes, interspersed throughout, make the book pleasant as well as informative reading.

4. Rubin, Leona. **How to Defend Yourself at Auctions.** Westover, 1972. 191 pp. $5.95.

Rubin begins with basics, i.e., explaining what an auction is, defining auctioneering terms (e.g., "knocked down," "buyer's privilege"). She describes different types of auctions in the United States and Europe, how to find them, where to find the objects listed in the catalogs, how to bid, bidding styles, prices to bid, signals and traps (e.g., how to spot shills and touts), the role of the auctioneer, what to try for—and what to avoid. Antiques, wines, autographs, art—objects generally considered good buys for investment—are covered in depth, but she does not ignore other areas of collectibles. Chapters end with humorous, but down-to-earth advice and are reinforced by humorous illustrations. A fine layout enhances reading ease.

AUTOMOBILES

See also Insurance, Automobile

5. Car/Puter. **Autofacts 1973.** Cornerstone Library (Simon and Schuster, dist.), 1973. 188 pp. Paper, $1.50.

Car/Puter is a Brooklyn, New York firm that sells most new cars and light trucks for $125 above dealer costs. *Autofacts* is a listing of 1973 prices for these American cars and trucks along with the dealer freight costs. It notes each automobile model and all its optional equipment, with columns for "Cost to Dealer" and "Manufacturer's Suggested Retail Price." A pricing form, to be used to add up the cost of a car or to order a personalized computerized printout from Car/Puter is included. The cost for the printout is $7.50. Since Cornerstone does not publish annually, its value is limited. The book can still be of help, however, for consumers who wish to use Car/Puter's services or who want a general indication of dealer markups on car parts.

6. **†Consumer Education: Buying an Automobile.** AIMS Instructional Media Services, 1973. Color. Sound. 16 mm. 14 min. Sale $190. Rent $20.

The film deals with the dos and don'ts of car buying. A teenage boy sees an ad in the paper for a used car and goes over to look at it. The boy then goes to a bank to talk about a loan, to an insurance company to find out about rates and costs, and to a mechanic in a diagnostic center to check out the car. The point is made that buyers should shop for a particular car: one they can afford to buy and maintain. Intended mainly for high school students, it is a good film which does not talk down to its audience.

7. Consumer Guide. **Auto Test. Automobile Buying Guide. Automobiles. Previews.** Annuals. Publications International. Paper $1.95 ea. Pocket Books. $1.95 ea.

Four times a year Consumer Guide publishes information on automobiles. *Previews,* in June has the least value. It is simply drawings and preliminary reports on the forthcoming crop of cars. *Automobiles,* the November issue, has prices for all new cars and some preliminary recommendations. The two important issues are the *Automobile Buying Guide,* published in January, which functions as an annual, and *Auto Test,* published in March. *Automobile Buying Guide* has further tests of the cars as well as prices and a listing of accessories. *Auto Test* combines listings of the cars with test ratings, suggested retail prices, discount prices, and best-buy recommendations. The March 1974 issue had the results of Consumer Guide tests on auto gas mileage. They showed higher gas mileage than the Environmental Protection Agency tests. Another report discussed how optional equipment affects fuel economy and how to improve mileage. For consumers, the issues to buy are either *Auto Test* or *Automobile Buying Guide*.

8. Groves, C. E. **How to Buy Cars at Top Discount.** Arco, 1970. 150 pp. Paper $1.65.

Outdated in much of its theory, *How to Buy Cars at Top Discounts* is solid on learning to deal with salesmen, finance agencies, and automobile advertising. Groves suggests offering about $200 above dealer costs to the new car dealer, and then trading in the old car to the dealership at fair value. He shows how to compute wholesale prices and why it is easier (and cheaper in the long run) to trade in rather than sell the old car. Groves describes the questionable sales techniques and advertisements of car salesmen, e.g., take-overs, lowballing and highballing, and explains how to deal with them. Sections on financing costs are good, but the chapter on resale values is outdated, and the one on car servicing is suspect. The author feels that "lemons" are a thing of the past and that a good relationship with a serviceman will take care of all problems. He is against foreign cars, stating that they are cheap because they are cheaply built. A brief chapter points up the pros and cons of leasing. "A Thumbnail Guide" containing 52 questions and answers in random order summarizes the major points of the book.

9. Markovich, Alexander. **How to Buy a New or Used Car.** (Popular Science Car Owner's Take Along Library). Popular Science (Dutton, dist.), 1971. Paper $5.95 (five-volume set).

Generally conventional advice is offered without the hyperbole too often found in books of this type. Material covers buying a new or used car, bargaining with dealers, and financing the purchase. In one useful chapter, Markovich offers his opinion on the need for different pieces of optional equipment. He is in favor of small V-8 engines, disc brakes, and four-door cars, but is against automatic headlight dimmers, tinted glass, or power-assisted brakes. A checklist of these points and 1971 prices of optional equipment is included. The author suggests buying an affordable, comfortable car for which service is readily available. Used cars should be bought at a new car dealer's lot. A good section notes which car defects should be fixed before selling or trading in and which should not, e.g., upholstery should be mended, the car should be waxed, but not painted. For checking out a used car, Markovich offers a list of items by category, and within the category by defect. For each defect, he assigns a point score, e.g., leak under automatic transmission: 250 points; misaligned trunk: 15 points. If the car scores high, you don't want it. A short book, but to the point.

10. **Money Management: Your Automobile Dollar.** Illus. Money Management Institute, Household Finance Corp., 1971. 36 pp. Paper 25¢. Quantity orders discounted.

A no-nonsense pamphlet that covers costs and tips on buying, operating, and maintaining a car. Material on buying new and used cars includes a very good list of tests "on the lot" and "on the road" for the used car, expenses of standard and optional equipment (including safety devices), and auto insurance (not often covered even in books). Financing, expenses of maintenance and operation, tips for efficient and safe driving, and places to get service are also discussed.

11. Sifarkis, Carl. **175 Money Saving Tips for Every Car Owner.** Tower, 1970. 149 pp. Paper 95¢.

Errors in spelling and printing abound in this poorly proofed and edited book; even the author's name appears differently on the title page and on the cover. The title is also misleading: this is actually a conventional (though somewhat sensationally presented) general book on auto buying and maintenance. Chapters deal with buying new and used cars, warranties and guarantees, financing and insurance, and tips on tire and auto repairs and service frauds. Some useful tips include buying the octane suggested by the manufacturer or a lower octane if the car still runs well, getting replacement tires that are the same as the originals, learning simple auto maintenance, and when buying a used car, to get one two–three years old in a good, though not popular make. As a whole, the book suffers from poor presentation.

12. Till, Anthony. **What You Should Know before You Buy a Car.** Award, 1967. 156 pp. Paper 75¢.

Till, a car salesman and dealer, has written this book as if he were teaching auto sales fraud. Some of the more dishonest techniques include lowballing the customer (offering a deal at a price too good to be true) and calculating the total cost of a car on an adding machine with extra figures already in the machine. He explains financing and urges customers to pay cash or finance new and used cars through banks. When buying used cars, he suggests buying a real "cheapie" direct from a new car dealer, and a good, medium-priced car from an independent dealer with a clean lot and book value prices. An eye-opening chapter gives explicit pointers on learning to distinguish the ex-taxicabs and police cars on a lot. Chapters on how to read and understand new and used car advertisements (almost as good as in Groves, *see* entry 8) are also lessons in fraud and deception. The moral of it all is that it is impossible to get a car for less than it is worth—and most times, the customer will be taken for a ride.

13. Weiss, Mark. **501 Valuable Tips and Free Materials for Motorists.** Books for Better Living, 1974. 160 pp. Paper $1.25.

A strange compendium of the practical and the useless, further marred by the constant use of capital letters and exclamation points, e.g., BUYING A USED CAR FROM A RENTAL FIRM!, or FEDERAL SPECIFICATIONS FOR BATTERIES!, and STOP AUTO THEFT! FREE FACT SHEET ON THE ELECTRONIC PROTECTOR—AUTO GUARD! These three headings highlight the good and bad points of this marginal book. The first gives solid advice on the bargains that may be gotten from rental agencies; the second suggests sending for a government booklet listing specifications and brand names; the third tells consumers to send for promotional material from the manufacturers and implies (without any evidence) that the product is good. Weiss covers buying and maintaining new and used cars; auto, tire, and safety supplies; leasing; insurance; and financing; and he throws in the names and addresses of various government consumer protection agencies across the country along with a short and very poor list of free films for drivers.

AUTOMOBILES—COMPLAINTS

See also Consumer Complaints

14. Nader, Ralph, Ralf Hotchkiss, and Lowell Dodge. **What to Do with Your Bad Car: An Action Manual for Lemon Owners.** Grossman, 1971. 175 pp. $8.95. Paper $2.95.

This is a partial outgrowth of *Unsafe at Any Speed* (*see* entry 24), helping motorists pick safe, defect-free cars, and offering advice on coping with lemons. Besides explaining how cars work and what can go wrong with them, the authors note safety features (chassis frames, rear window defrosters and wipers) and hazards (fully tinted windows) that should be considered before purchase. They suggest that buyers should try to get dealers to accept their Customer New Car Order Form and New Vehicle Warranty which protect rather than strip buyers of rights. The "action" section, "What to Do When You Get a Lemon" features model complaint procedures for use against dealers and manufacturers. Owners are advised to send letters to company presidents, directors, congressmen, government officials such as the chairman of the Federal Trade Commission and the director of the National Highway Safety Bureau, and are shown legal methods of redress: individual, class action, and small claims suits. The authors suggest imaginative ways of getting attention: personalized bumper stickers, entering the lemon in an auto show, sending it to the president of the company. They stress that leverage comes from working with consumer groups, such as the Automobile Protection Association and the Consumer Education and Protection Association. Appendices include a model consumer organization complaint letter and home and business addresses of the presidents and directors of the major auto companies.

AUTOMOBILES–FRAUDS

See also Frauds

15. Randall, Donald A., and Arthur P. Glickman. **The Great American Auto Repair Robbery: A Report on a Ten-Billion Dollar National Swindle and What You Can Do about It.** Charterhouse, 1972. 283 pp. $7.95.

The first part of this two-part book details auto repair frauds, and the second offers advice on owner protection. The authors point out that some swindles can be traced to ineptitude, lack of training, and lack of licensing and standards and other swindles, to larceny. They show how consumers are charged for unnecessary, nonexistent, or repeat repairs; warn against using repair shops that quote flat-rate manual fees (as any good mechanic can better the time by at least 50 percent); stress the need to describe car symptoms to service managers (instead of guessing at the problem), and urge motorists to shun shops suggested by insurance claims agents. A recap of each chapter concludes with suggestions on "What You Should Do" to beat the rackets, e.g., patronize specialty shops used by fleet owners or independent general repair shops where the owner is one of the mechanics. Tips on saving money include reading the owners manual, getting proper maintenance checks, keeping batteries, tires, wheels, oil, et al., in functioning condition. The authors feel that the best way to save operating money is to buy small cars that change styles infrequently. They take the government to task for not pressing antitrust suits against large auto companies (General Motors in particular) and urge consumers to pressure Congress into passing legislation to license and train auto mechanics and provide fair warranties. Useful for making complaints are the addresses of state commissioners of motor vehicle departments, insurance departments, motor vehicle inspection agencies, and consumer protection agencies, as well as auto and tire manufacturers and insurance companies. Suggestions for other actions include making "lemon" signs to put on cars, placing ads in newspapers, picketing dealers and/or repair shops, and above all, being persistent. Similar in many ways to *How to Get Your Car Repaired* (*see* entry 17) and *What to Do with Your Bad Car* (*see* entry 14), but all three are valuable and should be consulted.

16. Randall, Donald A., and Arthur P. Glickman. **The Great American Auto Repair Robbery.** Cassette recording. Narrated by Moses Gunn. Voice Over Books, 1973. 90 min. $6.95.

A condensation narrated by Moses Gunn, this cassette recording highlights the major ideas and most of the summaries of the book. Since *The Great American Auto Repair Robbery* is filled with facts, figures, and dates, some of the material is difficult to follow on cassette. Also, Gunn's presentation tends to get monotonous and lacks dramatic appeal. For those commuters and other car owners who regularly listen to tapes and cassettes, it can be used profitably while traveling.

AUTOMOBILES–MAINTENANCE AND REPAIRS

For pertinent organizations see Part II, U.S. Federal Agencies–Department of Transportation, National Highway Traffic Safety Administration; *Private Organizations*–Automobile Protection Association.

17. Carlson, Margaret Bresnahan, and Ronald G. Shafer. **How to Get Your Car Repaired without Getting Gypped.** Harper & Row, 1973. 278 pp. $5.95; paper $1.50. Barnes & Noble. Paper $1.95.

Carlson was formerly a research associate at the (Nader) Center for Auto Safety; Shafer is a reporter for the *Wall Street Journal,* writing on consumer issues. Theirs is a clear and concise book teaching basic auto mechanics to the uninformed in order to save them time, money, and anguish. The authors highlight common auto frauds and come-ons, such as a $75 transmission job or the use of phantom parts. A checklist of what to do when the car won't start and a chapter on deciphering common trouble signs are by themselves worth the price of the book. The latter explains what certain noises signify and how to know when and what is wrong with various parts of the car. In addition, charts show the costs of keeping up a car over a ten-year span and how to determine when the costs of fixing a car are too high to warrant keeping it. When a car is to be repaired, the best place for the work to be done is the local independent garage dealer. New car dealerships should be used only for parts on a warranty, and specialty shops (transmission or muffler shops) should be avoided unless the problem is very obvious. Work orders *without blank spaces* should be authorized by owners in writing. For those who do not get their cars properly repaired, or who feel abused in other ways, methods of complaint and legal redress are explained. The authors, in collaboration with Consumers Union, are compiling ratings on repair shops across the country. They invite all motorists to participate in the program by filling out and sending in the questionnaire at the back dealing with local shops.

18. †**Consumer Education: Maintaining an Automobile.** AIMS Instructional Media Services, 1973. Color. Sound. 16 mm. 11 min. Sale $150. Rent $15.

Stressing preventive maintenance and educated car ownership, the film, intended primarily for teens, makes its points well. It begins by showing a young woman buying car supplies to use at a do-it-yourself garage. She checks plugs, changes oil, etc. The narrator explains the difficulties–and necessity–of finding reputable service stations which stand behind their work and offers pointers for keeping down costs: have all prices stated before work begins; any job errors must be corrected promptly and without charge; on major repairs, get more than one estimate as well as a written guarantee on defects and workmanship. The film also explains the need to contact the Better Business Bureau and local consumer agencies when services are poor.

19. Lee, Albert, and John D. Weimer. **How to Get Good and Honest Auto Service.** Warner Paperback, 1973. 230 pp. Paper $1.50.

A very good buy, this deals with auto maintenance and repairs, including the problems of untrained mechanics and unsavory business practices. Lee likes diagnostic centers that do not do repairs, most independent neighborhood service and gas stations, and even speciality stores (transmission and muffler shops) when a problem is obvious. He warns against bargains, as they may cost you your life. An excellent idea is to take an automotive course and do your own repair work, particularly at the new fix-it-yourself garages where you can rent a stall and tools. A chapter on whom to and where to complain "if you get took" is too short, but does have addresses of manufacturers' and distrubuters' customer relations departments. The bulk of the book is devoted to teaching motorists to spot problems: to understand the repair process (including parts); to know how much repairs should cost (charts cite costs in different cities throughout the country), and to determine the possibility of fixing it yourself. In the concluding chapter, "Trouble Shooting," symptoms and causes of problems are listed in neat columns for ready reference.

20. Olney, Ross R. **How to Keep Your Car Running, Your Money in Your Pocket, and Your Mind Intact.** Regnery, 1973. 176 pp. $8.95.

Intended for persons with little or no knowledge of auto mechanics, Olney's text tells what to do when something goes wrong and how to know if new parts are necessary. One chapter describes "How It All Works, Simply Put"; five others show what can go wrong with each major component of a car: engine, transmission, drive shaft and rear end, tires, wheels and suspension, brakes, and such miscellaneous items as radio, fuse panel, horn, clock, windshield wipers and blades, cigarette lighter, air conditioner, heater, and defroster. Olney describes, locates, and explains the function of each, then launches into the heart of the book, "What to Do If . . ." He tells how to spot signs of trouble for each part and what to expect if the part must be changed or fixed. While similar to the excellent chapter "Common Trouble Signs" in *How to Get Your Car Repaired . . .* (*see* entry 17), this book deals with the problems in more depth. The last chapter explains how to develop a good relationship with a neighborhood service station: buy gas, oil, grease, and service and set up a record of sales. Olney feels that these stations, affiliated with large oil companies, are the ones more likely to honor reasonable complaints. He recommends a driver's survival kit: spare tire, spare fuses, flares, jumper cables, flashlight, and tire chains. A good book, its only drawback is its price.

21. Till, Anthony. **What You Should Know before You Have Your Car Repaired.** New American Library, 1970. 160 pp. Paper $1.

Showing the kinds of service that can be expected at different types of repair stations, Till takes manufacturers to task for insisting on volume sales and for untrained mechanics. Thus, new car dealerships produce shoddy repair work at best, but generally replace parts rather than repair them and charge flat-rate fees which run twice as high as necessary. Franchised stores that deal with specific parts, e.g., transmissions and mufflers, cannot be judged as a group. He suggests learning about individual reputations, since many dishonest mechanics hide behind a franchise name. Till scores diagnostic analysis centers that do repairs for producing fraudulent results leading to unnecessary work. He finds large independent garages are generally honest, as are small one- and two-person garages. Till also has kind words for gas station operators who have servicemen on call for repairs seven days a week. Small places also tend to repair rather than replace (a less costly procedure). Frequently, they get replacements from wrecking lots—and save owners bills for both labor and parts. Till points out that good maintenance will cut down on repairs. He notes the limitations on new car warranties and the need to understand them before buying. A good chapter deals with accidents, body repairs, and insurance claims. An excellent piece of advice is to have a low-priced Polaroid camera in the car at all times to be able to record an accident. An appendix lists flat rates by hours and costs; a glossary lists automotive terms.

22. Weissler, Paul. **How to Buy Services and Parts for Your Car.** (Popular Science Car Owner's Take Along Library). Popular Science (Dutton, dist.), 1971. Paper $5.95 (five-volume set).

Weissler has divided his book into two sections: buying services and buying parts. For general service he suggests using a local gasoline station at which you are known and which uses credit cards (giving you up to two months to pay the bills). He explains labor and parts costs and highlights good and bad services. For example, during an engine tuneup, spark plugs should be replaced, not cleaned, and the ignition should not be timed for power (it shortens spark plug life and can cause engine ping). On exhaust systems, he points out that since anyone can install a muffler easily and quickly, it is best to have the local service station do it. Other services cover brakes, major engine and transmission work, the cooling system, tire repairs, and paint jobs. Tips on buying tires, shock absorbers, batteries, spark plugs, engine oil, oil filters, and new, used, and rebuilt parts are covered in the second section. Weissler doesn't specify brands, but offers general suggestions, e.g., for a normal car, it is best to buy belted bias-ply tires at a tire store, new batteries at a discount house, and used batteries (for an old car) at a wrecking yard.

AUTOMOBILES—SAFETY

For pertinent organizations see Part II, U.S. Federal Agencies—Department of Transportation, National Highway Traffic Safety Administration; *Private Organizations*—Automobile Protection Association; Center for Law and Social Policy; Center for Science in the Public Interest; Public Interest Research Group.

23. Center for Auto Safety. **Small on Safety: The Designed-In Dangers of the Volkswagen.** Grossman, 1972. 180 pp. $6.95

A Nader group research report that takes up where *Unsafe at Any Speed* (*see* entry 24) leaves off, it highlights the shortcomings of the Volkswagen. According to the group, it is the most dangerous car on the road. They say that although some defects have been corrected since 1968, these have been only half-way measures, and the danger of death or serious injury is still great. Hazards include the windshield, seat tracks and back, doors that open on impact, and the gas tank's location. The VW microbus they consider "the most dangerous four-wheel vehicle of any type designed for highway use." They stress the danger from its side-wind sensitivity and poor handling qualities, and they warn the public to avoid the car at any price.

24. Nader, Ralph. **Unsafe at Any Speed: The Designed-In Dangers of the American Automobile.** Rev., expanded ed. Grossman, 1972. 417 pp. $7.95. Bantam. Paper $1.95.

This updated version of the 1965 classic that helped launch the consumer movement includes the original text, a 77-page preface with information on developments "Since Unsafe at Any Speed," and appendixes that include an 18-point safety hazard car check, a California resolution on auto pollution, the National Traffic and Motor Vehicle Safety Act of 1966, a partial list of safety-related defect investigations and several appendixes relating to the accident-prone Corvair. The text consists of a long discussion of the hazards of that car; the lack of concern for auto safety shown by manufacturers in general and by General Motors in particular; engineering concern for styling at the expense of safety; the Society of Automotive Engineers, which controls motor vehicle standards (and is controlled by the auto companies); the "traffic safety establishment," which consists of self-interest auto groups, and the relationship between auto pollution and smog. In the preface Nader notes that accidents have not been reduced with seat belts, that cars are not being built safer, that knowledge of cars with specific long-term defects is not being disseminated, and that there is a real need for traffic safety groups and for government to provide such information and to move for strict safety standards.

AUTOMOBILES—USED

25. Friedman, Gil. **How to Buy and Sell a Used Car in Europe.** Yara, 1972. 24 pp. Paper $1.50.

Friedman's pamphlet was published in 1972—so prices are no longer accurate, although the basic situation has not changed. According to the author, the best place to buy a used car is in Germany, where there is a glut of cars on the market, particularly Volkswagens. Friedman explains the procedures necessary for buying the car, including, in some countries, the need for getting an International Driving Permit. He lists addresses of German auto flea markets and suggests universities and U.S. army bases as good places for bargains, along with police and post office auctions. The author explains how to get a car inspected and registered, how to sell it in Europe or ship it to America. The appendix has pictures of various classified auto ads in German and translations of the ads. In many ways, this is a simplified, stripped-down version of Wilkes's *How to Buy a Used Volkswagen in Europe . . .* (*see* entry 32).

26. Jackson, Charles R. **How to Buy a Used Car.** Chilton, 1967. 90 pp. $2.75.

Former car salesman and manager Charles Jackson has written a book that too often mimics the advertising and sales techniques he is out to expose. But since over 20 million used cars are sold each year, many people would do well to read this book or one like it (*How to Buy a New or Used Car, see* entry 9; *What You Should Know before You Buy a Car, see* entry 12). Jackson stresses three things to shop for: good mechanical condition, reasonable price and low (preferably no) finance charges. He suggests going to different lots for comparison shopping, asking to see good cars, and returning to bargain on price and trade-in after the car has been checked out by a reliable repairman. When buying, put at least 30 percent down (including taxes and motor vehicle fees), or you may find yourself saddled with usurious interest and finance charges, your furniture as collateral, and your house and car repossessed. Jackson feels it is best to buy from a franchised new car dealer in a high-income area where residents are likely to take good care of their cars and frequently trade in and/or up for status. (These dealers do not want used cars cluttering up their lots.) He also states that big luxury cars are the best used car buys. Written well before the energy crisis and increase in gasoline prices, this last advice is best disregarded.

27. Lee, Albert. **The ASC Guide to Best Buys in Used Cars.** 1974 ed. Bantam, 1973. 370 pp. Paper $1.95.

The book is based on the results of a questionnaire on the frequency of repair records and body integrity of all American cars built between 1967 and 1973, as well as on a comparison of the cars in terms of seating room in front and back, luggage space, turning diameter, and gasoline mileage (with regular fuel). The questionnaire was sent to approximately 6,000 members of the Automotive Service Council of America (ASC; formerly known as the Independent Garage Owners Association, IGO). The author lists the October 1973 price for each car, and shows how to determine current price. (A radically changed auto market has drastically affected prices, and his rules no longer apply uniformly.) Lee also explains when to buy a used car (December is best); where to buy (from a new car dealer); how much to pay (as much as possible without having to finance the purchase); how to finance if necessary (from a bank, not a car dealer); how to spot a stolen car (new paint without signs of an accident, new locks and ignition, etc.), and how to check the car for defects. The book would be very helpful if published annually, which unfortunately it is not. The annual *Buying Guide Issue* of *Consumer Reports* (*see* entry 65) lists frequency of repair records for domestic and foreign cars based on consumer responses, and its data may well be as valid as the garage owners and body repairmen's reports.

28. ***N.A.D.A. Official Used Car Guide.** National Automobile Dealers Used Car Guide Co., 1961– . Monthly. $13.

Known in the trade as the Blue Book, this is the listing of used car prices (the average retail, trade-in, and loan value) that is referred to by car buyers and sellers and by banks. Prices generally go back seven years, i.e., the value of models from 1967 through 1974 are given in the 1974 issues. Foreign cars are listed from the date of their first importation into the United States, if imported after 1967. While prices do not take into account body and mileage of an individual car, car buyers are advised to look at the current N.A.D.A. guide before they trade in or shop for a used car.

29. Pagino, Edmond J., Jr. **Car Purchase and Maintenance.** (The Consumer Education Series). Pendulum, 1973. 85 pp. Paper $1.25.

Designed for the "young consumer," i.e., the high school student, this text covers auto purchasing and maintenance in a concise, yet informative manner which should prove a useful adjunct to teachers of driver education courses. The first chapter, "Your Automobile Decision," is particularly good, pointing up differences in insurance and maintenance costs as well as differences in purchase prices of various styles and sizes of automobiles. Other chapters dealing with buying and financing new and used cars, insurance and liability, and operating and maintenance costs are also good. A checklist of items to look for to avoid buying a lemon is reprinted from Nader's *What to Do with Your Bad Car* (*see* entry 14). In addition, this booklet discusses driving and safety features, driving skills and laws, and ways to avoid auto repair gyps.

30. Stone, Bill. **So You're Going to Buy a Used Sports Car.** Sports Car Press, 1967. 111 pp. $2.95.

A short, informally written guide on the mechanics of purchase for prospective buyers of used sports cars, it covers determining choice of car and model, checking it out, finding an honest seller, financing the purchase, and repairing the car. Even though information on cars from 1967 on is lacking, this is the only book devoted exclusively to used sports cars and is worth looking at. Some suggestions are obvious yet practical. For example, discussing the desire to buy a sports car in the first place, the author stresses the need to get one that suits the buyer's personality. A list of the 22 top used sports car choices notes special values in different models of the same car. This material particularly would be greatly enhanced by updating, but for anyone interested in models produced before 1967, it is still helpful. Two chapters show how to test the car on the lot and on the road. A checklist with photographs is very handy, e.g., a picture of worn pedals and an odomoter showing low mileage indicates fraud. Stone points up the differences between car failings that are cheap and/or easy to fix and those that are difficult and/or expensive. How to fix the car, sources of used parts (lists of junkyards, where to write for auto repair manuals, etc.) conclude the book.

31. †**Tommy's First Car.** FilmFair Communications, 1972. Color. Sound. 16 mm. 11 min. Sale $145. Rent $15.

A film which won the red ribbon (second prize) at the 1973 American Film Festival sponsored by the Educational Film Library Association (EFLA), it is devoted entirely to checking out a used car to make sure it is a good buy free of defects. We see a teenage boy and his father at a used car lot; the man shows his son how to determine safety and value. They look at such features as paint, tires, and upholstery; check the lights, brakes, wheels, etc.; take the car for a test drive and bring it to a trusted mechanic for his opinion. All done nicely without talking down to the film's intended audience of young, first-time car owners.

32. Wilkes, John. **How to Buy a Used Volkswagen in Europe, Keep It Alive and Bring It Home!** Illus. by Inge Vogt. Ten Speed, 1973. 146 pp. $6.95; paper $3.

Devoted entirely to buying, driving, maintaining, and shipping a used Volkswagen from Europe to the United States and covering much of the same information as *How to Buy and Sell a Used Car in Europe* (*see* entry 25) this book has much more detail and clarity. In addition to listing the best cities in Germany to make the purchase, the author also suggests places in other countries: London, Amsterdam, Paris, and provinces, and American Express offices everywhere. Prices are listed for all of Europe. Wilkes explains how to recognize various European models of the VW, how to determine the car's condition prior to purchase, how to register it in urban and rural areas, how to maintain and repair it, and gives rules for driving in various countries: speeds, border crossings, etc. A good chapter tells how to ship the car to the United States: converting it to American specifications, picking it up at the port of entry, registering it, and so on. Appendices cover how to get insurance in Europe; how to determine a VW's model, year, and type of engine, and how to read German classified ads and bulletin boards. Also included are lists of auto clubs and authorized VW service agencies throughout Europe and a glossary of automotive terms in English, German, French, Italian, Dutch, and Swedish. While there is not much need to buy the hardcover edition, the paperback is an excellent buy.

BANKING SERVICES

See Savings and Thrift

BANKRUPTCY

See also Credit; Debt

33. Burger, Robert E., and Jan J. Slavicek. **The Layman's Guide to Bankruptcy.** Van Nostrand Reinhold, 1971. 100 pp. Paper $4.95.

A very clear and easy to understand guide to bankruptcy. The authors explore the seven most common reasons for going bankrupt: credit mania, divorce, sudden medical bills, prolonged unemployment, business failure, lawsuits, and poverty. They explain personal (straight) bankruptcy, business bankruptcy, and Chapter 13—the Wage Earner Plan (debt consolidation in which all debts are eventually paid—usually within two to three years). Examples of all forms necessary for each are included, with detailed instructions on filling them out and filing them. An order blank for complete sets of forms is included at the back of the book. A rather unclear chapter deals with exemptions allowed under bankruptcy, but this and the lack of an index are the only things wrong with the book. The authors have included one appendix, which lists the locations of all federal bankruptcy courts, and another, a glossary. One of the book's best features is its presentation of the material in a fair, nonpreaching manner, allowing each person who may be facing bankruptcy to decide whether to choose personal bankruptcy or debt consolidation—and providing the means to do either easily.

34. Meyers, Jerome I. **Wipe Out Your Debts and Make a Fresh Start.** Chancellor Press, (Dell, dist.) 1973. 255 pp. $8.95; paper $3.95.

Meyers, a practising trial lawyer in New York City, has written a practical guide for the debt-ridden. As he points out, bankruptcy is a constitutional right, and one which individuals paying out more than 20 percent of their income for back debts should consider in preference to debt consolidation under Chapter 13—the Wage Earner Plan. Meyers uses real and fictitious cases and quotes judges and referees in bankruptcy courts on the advantages of becoming a bankrupt. He explains when one spouse is responsible for the other's debts, when gifts and transfers of property may be made between them, and when and where real and personal property can be exempt from surrender. Fraudulent transfers and payments, nondischargeable debts, and fraudulent acts which cause the denial of bankruptcy are covered. An important chapter concerns proper court procedure for the potential bankrupt. The author shows when it is economical to use a lawyer and when one can go it alone. He details psychological as well as economic reasons for bankruptcy and Chapter 13 shows how to fill out the forms for each. Appendixes list U.S. district courts, Homestead Exemption Laws, personal property exemptions, life insurance exemptions and federal exemptions, plus sample Homestead Declaration forms and a glossary. Some of the text gets rather technical, but anyone faced with debts will do well to read the book.

35. Rutberg, Sidney. **Ten Cents on the Dollar or the Bankruptcy Game.** Simon and Schuster, 1973. 183 pp. $6.95.

Basically, an outline-exposé of business bankruptcies, there is little in this for the individual. In itself, the book has merit, as it gives practical advice for those in grave financial difficulties in business who are faced with the prospect of bankruptcy.

36. Sullivan, George. **The Boom in Going Bust: The Threat of a National Scandal in Consumer Bankruptcy.** Macmillan, 1968. 215 pp. $5.95.

In spite of its title, a good part of this book is devoted to explaining the mechanics of declaring bankruptcy, filing for consolidation of debt under Chapter 13—the Wage Earner Plan, and going into receivership. Sullivan traces the history of bankruptcy laws through the ages and focuses on U.S. legislation. He is concerned with the growing number of persons declaring individual bankruptcies, but seems more concerned that they are not using Chapter 13, which he prefers. Sullivan feels that filing for Chapter 13 teaches money management and helps the individual keep a feeling of self-respect. He concedes that only those with sufficient earning power can use Chapter 13 successfully, and only if the plan does not exceed 36 months and take more than 25 percent of the earned income. In spite of his preference, he does give information on how to file for straight bankruptcy, explains which debts are dischargeable, when to get a lawyer, and different court procedures. As one of his reasons for prefering Chapter 13, Sullivan points out that not only can it salvage a credit rating to some extent, but can also help get a job, since people who file under

13 are not bankrupts, just debtors, and the question of bankruptcy is often asked on employment applications.

BICYCLES

37. Ballantine, Richard. **Richard's Bicycle Book.** Illus. by John Betchelor. Ballantine, 1972. 249 pp. Paper $1.95.

Dedicated to "bicycle maintenance and enjoyment," this very good buy explains the basics of bicycle construction, how to chose a bike, maintain it, and keep it from being stolen. With diagrams as clear as the text, the author shows which features to look for in each type of bike. He names brands and gives general price ranges in each category. Before taking delivery, Ballantine suggests a test drive, among other things. Stores that sell bikes and parts by mail and an incomplete list of good bicycle stores are also noted.

38. Complete Bicycle Book: Buyer's Guide. Petersen Publishing, 1972. 240 pp. $3.95.

While the *Complete Bicycle Book* contains some advice on how to buy bicycles and what to look for in judging a proper bike fit, there is little in it for the would-be purchaser. The buying guide itself is a bicycle catalog, arranged by type of bike, with a picture of each one, and a short description of frame, wheels, handlebars, brakes, and saddle. No attempt is made to evaluate the equipment. Not recommended.

39. Consumer Guide. **Bicycle Test Reports.** Annual. Publications International. Paper $1.95. Doubleday. $1.95. Popular Library. $1.50.

Each year, *Bicycle Test Reports* rates and ranks all types and price ranges of bicycles: from those for the two- to five-year-olds to ten-speed adult bikes costing over $250. In addition, the report rates track, tandem, and folding bicycles, adult tricycles, exercisers, and accessories (locks, chains and cables, lights, safety equipment, luggage carriers, child carriers, touring bags, etc.). Information about all major manufacturers and distributers is supplied. There are chapters on bicycle care, maintenance, and safety as well as information on how to find, and buy, a bike that fits. The bikes are judged within categories and, where there are great price differences, within a price range, e.g., under $100 (for a ten-speed bike), $100–$149, $150–$249, over $250.

40. Henkel, Stephen C. **Bikes: A How-to-Do-It Guide to Selection, Care, Repair, Maintenance, Decoration, Safety, and Fun on Your Bicycle.** Illus. Chatham Press. 1972. 96 pp. $4.95.

This everything-you-want-to-know-about-bicycles is charmingly illustrated and lightheartedly written, and once a person is hooked on the sport, it will add to the fun. The book has a good section on buying new and used bikes and tips on buying for the young (beginning) child rider. Henkel discusses which accessories to buy—and which to stay away from. He includes charts of gear ratios, for gauging the right frame size by leg length and height, average prices of bicycles and parts in early 1972, and lists of accessories for safety, convenience, and comfort. Henkel also talks about bicycle games, bike repair and maintenance, how to ride, touring and luggage, and more. A bibliography is also included.

41. Humphrey, Clifford C. **Back to the Bike.** Illus. by Keith Halonen. 101 Productions, 1972. 96 pp. Paper $2.95.

This practically written and delightfully illustrated book with an ecological point of view tells how to select and maintain a bicycle and its rider and about "The Bicycle As an Alternative Means of Transportation." "Selecting Your Bike" discusses different types of bicycles for different types of riding, basic differences between bikes, which to buy, accessories, a list of new products, and selected price lists. "Maintenance of the Rider" explains how to ride, how to adjust the bike, safety precautions, clothing, and theft protection. The information is always sensible and to the point. As a general bicycle book, this one is definitely one of the best.

CAMERAS

See Photographic Equipment

CAMPING EQUIPMENT

42. Colby, C. B. **Today's Camping: New Equipment for Modern Campers.** Coward, McCann & Geoghegan, 1973. 48 pp. $3.86.

Intended as an introduction to camping gear, this book gives readers a minimum of information. Material on each type of gear is condensed into one paragraph, and roughly 3–6 models of each type are pictured on facing pages. The reader is then expected to send for equipment catalogs, read books on camping, and speak to other campers. In any event, this book is of little use to consumers wishing to make intelligent purchases. Not recommended.

43. Consumer Guide. **Camping and Backpacking Equipment Test Reports.** Annual. Publications International. Paper $1.95.

Camping and Backpacking Equipment Test Reports annually provides "complete coverage of equipment for all aspects of camping under canvas" plus several articles that relate to new innovations or fashions. While some articles are more general in nature than others, the editors include listings of "Best Buys" (frequently divided by price category) on many of the items. In the 1974 annual, ratings and best buys were appended to articles on tents, stoves, lanterns and heaters, coolers and jugs, sleeping bags, and backpacks and frames. Brand-name recommendations of a more general type involved grills and accessories, camp food and cookware, campwear, miscellaneous gear, such as insect repellents, first-aid kits and survival gear, camping trailers, and bicycle camping. In addition, articles on maintaining and packing camp gear and learning the basics of camp housekeeping were also included. Particularly useful for the beginning camper who must buy a great deal of equipment, it is also helpful for anyone wishing to read about the latest in gear.

CARPETS

See also Household Equipment and Furnishings

44. Franses, Jack. **European and Oriental Rugs for Pleasure and Investment.** Illus. Arco, 1970. 176 pp. $5.95.

Franses, a London rug dealer and expert, manages to impart a great deal of information on valuable Oriental and European carpets in a relatively short space. He believes that good carpets make excellent investments as long as they are cared for and renovated properly whenever necessary. (*See* entry 45, *Check Points on How to Buy Oriental Rugs*, for an opposing view.) Ten rules for judging a rug before buying include asking the dealer to show all repairs, finding out whether the dealer will buy the carpet back some time in the future at a higher price, checking colors for vegetable and aniline dyes, checking borders, etc. The author also lists seven keys to carpet identification: design, knot, dyes and color significance, wool and patina, side cords, end fringes, and weft. Twenty-six countries and more than 120 weaving centers are covered. A rather general history of carpets in each of the countries is also included.

45. Jacobsen, Charles W. **Check Points on How to Buy Oriental Rugs.** Illus. Charles E. Tuttle, 1969. 208 pp. $10.75.

A leading American authority on the subject provides these checkpoints, on everything from buying new and used Oriental rugs to buying at auctions and used rug sales. Jacobsen is against buying from anyone other than a reputable dealer (like himself). He does not think rugs should be bought as investments, as prices are already inflated. He is against buying cheap rugs. He shows how to pick rugs that will appeal to the eye and to the pocketbook, how to care for them, and how to restore them if necessary. The author continually refers to his other writings and past predictions, and spends a bit too much time congratulating himself on being right so often. In spite of this, his book is a detailed and knowledgeable discussion on what to look for in buying and caring for good rugs, and should be consulted by anyone considering their purchase, particularly if investment is the prime motivation.

46. Schlick, D. P. **Modern Oriental Carpets: A Buyer's Guide.** Illus. by Yvonne J. Schlick. Charles E. Tuttle, 1970. 139 pp. $5.

Schlick covers the present-day output of Persian, Turkoman, Pakistani, Indian, Caucasian, Chinese, and Turkish rugs. In a short chapter dealing with carpet characteristics and another concerning the "Economics of Oriental Carpet Buying" he discusses the five basic characteristics which determine price: pile, design, borders, foundation, and backing. To these, he adds a sixth feature: the carpet factor. This is Schlick's computation for each carpet country of the "cost of living, wages paid to weavers, and quality of the finished product" that make it possible to judge a carpet's cost. He then shows how these factors are added up. A table of pricing information on 38 different types of carpets is also included. Although the prices are as of 1967, the system will still work, since relative costs of living are basically unchanged. This chapter alone makes the book worthwhile. The author's wife, Yvonne J. Schlick, has illustrated the book with 16 undistinguished black-and-white photographs of workers, mosques, and museums and 38 beautiful color photographs of Oriental carpets.

CLOTHING

See also Stores and Services. *For pertinent organizations see Part II, U.S. Federal Agencies*—Department of Agriculture, Agricultural Research Service—Conservation, Research and Education; Department of Agriculture, Extension Service; Federal Trade Commission; *Canadian Agencies—National Agencies*—Department of Consumer and Corporate Affairs.

47. Money Management: Your Clothing Dollar. Illus. Money Management Institute, Household Finance Corp., 1972. 38 pp. Paper 25¢. Quantity orders discounted.

An overview of the subject, the publication takes up buying and taking care of clothes for men, women, and children as well as clothes for everyone: footwear, sweaters and knitwear, furs, and accessories. The pamphlet also includes choosing patterns and fabrics, the wardrobe budget, and clothes care. Nothing new here, but it is presented in an intelligent and straightforward manner, useful for classrooms. Charts provide space for taking a wardrobe inventory and for making spending plans for clothing purchases and services: cleaning, alterations, etc.

COLLECTING

Note: Each area of collection and many subspecialties have their own price guides. Consumers interested in learning about a particular topic can consult Dorn's *The Insider's Guide to Antiques, Art and Collectibles* (*see* entry 48) for a basic bibliography on many topics. Certain publishers specialize in price guides to a variety of collectibles, and writing for their catalogs is a good idea. One publisher specializing in this material is Wallace-Homestead, with many guides on different types of jewelry, glass, and memorabilia. R. R. Bowker's *Subject Guide to Books in Print* lists price guides under individual subjects, e.g., "Bottles," "Glass Fruit Jars," "Numismatics—Collectors and Collecting." Under the general heading of "Collectors and Collecting" in the *Subject Guide* will be found all books on the subject, including such general price guides as Kovel's *Complete Antiques Price List*, which is updated regularly. The best advice in consulting these guides is to make sure the merchandise you are considering corresponds in quality to that described in the books and the prices are current.

48. Dorn, Sylvia O'Neill. **The Insider's Guide to Antiques, Art and Collectibles.** Doubleday, 1974. 334 pp. $7.95.

Dorn presents the art of buying and selling art, antiques, and collectibles. She lists 20 items that contribute to value: age, beauty, condition, rarity, fashion, workmanship, etc., and explains how prices are determined, why prices and price guides are more useful to sellers than to buyers, why it is poor business to use the guides in a transaction, and how prices are inflated. She also discusses different markets and buyers—from pickers to prestigious dealers—and notes some pros and cons of buying from private individuals (the possibility of a good price versus questionable ownership, poor restoration, fakes, or even unrealistic prices). Dorn devotes considerable space to rules for buying at auction, including the dicta never to bid on uninspected items, always to add into cost the price of repairs, never to get carried away by the bidding, and if cheated, to scream. "Selling Possessions Successfully" summarizes much of the previous material, and includes ways to advertise, promote, and price goods and how to determine profits. The second half of the book is a sketchy rundown of 44 areas of collecting that encompasses carnival and depression glass, comic books, pornography, and works of nature as well as the more usual stamps, coins, fine art, and furniture. Dorn notes a few guidelines for collecting, buying, and occasionally selling each, and lists the best books on each topic (if they exist). The bibliography will be very useful to beginning collectors, and the book itself can be a help to all.

COMPLAINTS

See Consumer Complaints

CONDOMINIUMS

See also Houses—Buying; Landlords and Tenants. *For pertinent organizations see Part II, U.S. Federal Agencies*–Department of Housing and Urban Development, Housing Production and Mortgage Credit—Federal Housing Administration.

49. Karr, James N. **The Condominium Buyer's Guide: What to Look for—and Look Out for—in Resort, Residential and Commercial Condominiums.** Fell, 1973. 203 pp. $9.95.

The author, who is involved with the development of resort condominium communities, writes mainly about metropolitan and suburban residential condominiums, but includes resort and commercial ones as well. Prospective buyers would do well to heed his advice. For each category, Karr lists points to consider before purchase and spells out benefits and drawbacks of different types of offerings. He suggests doing a simple market study of location, price, neighborhood, zoning, sales activity, and prospective purchasers for the development as a whole, and he shows how to check purchase and sales agreements, master deeds, unit deeds, bylaws, and regulations and how to determine how well the buildings will be managed. Design features to look for include project image or attractiveness, amenities, common facilities, and parking. Most critical of all are financial arrangements (obligations and benefits of ownership), so buyers are urged to investigate all cost sheet data. Three key questions to ask are: What tax bracket has the developer used in his calculations to arrive at a tax savings? How have yearly real estate taxes been calculated? and Has the lender agreed to the mortgage terms in the cost sheet? For resort condominiums that will be rented, he shows how to add in such factors as costs of renting, cash flow, and return on investment. Appendices give examples of all legal documents noted in the text, state statutes and regulatory requirements, a model Federal Housing Authority Condominium Statute, depreciation calculations and mortgage payment tables.

50. Sheldon, Roy. **Know the Ins and Outs of Condominium Buying.** Exposition, 1973. 78 pp. $4.

Published by a vanity press, this is a slight, awkwardly written booklet by a retiree living in a Florida condominium. Within a framework of moralities and social judgments, Sheldon obliquely discusses the financial side of condominium buying. He points out that since many residential condominiums are in low-cost-of-living areas, more people can afford them than realize. He discusses different types of residential condos from single family to luxury highrises, services that can be expected from each, and costs for such services. Information on owner versus developer management does not deal directly with abuses in the system by the latter. A good chapter covers buying new as opposed to resale units. The author also has some practical material on moving—what to take and what to leave behind. For serious buyers, *The Condominium Buyer's Guide* is recommended (*see* entry 49).

51. Stover, William R. **What You Should Know before Buying a Condominium.** Trend Publications, 1972. 30 pp. Paper $1.

Most of this pamphlet is designed to help prospective condominium buyers understand the provisions of Florida's Condominium Act. The author also gives a brief history of the condominium, defines it, notes its advantages, and points up obligations of ownership, e.g., an owner must help to operate the facility in cooperation with other members of the association. Material on finding the right section of the state in which to live, deciding on a single house or apartment, and checking out the neighborhood and actual house is sketchy. A glossary of condominium terms, an index to the law, and the Florida Condominium Act complete the contents.

52. Vogts, Alfred. **How to Buy a Condominium.** Hurricane House (Trend Publications, dist.), 1969. 48 pp. $3.95.

Written with the retiree in mind, a useful but overpriced pamphlet on choosing the "good" condominium. Vogts defines "condominium," shows what to look for in the "Declaration of Condominium," and how to select a condominium that has regulations to suit each owner. For example, for those wishing to rent, renting privileges are desirable; for those who live in the condominium year round, the noise of vacationers may be disturbing. The author notes advantages and disadvantages to single story, garden apartment, and high-rise homes, e.g., the ground floor may be noisy, but it is practical for the infirm if elevators are not working; upper floors have better views and seem cleaner. Vogts stresses the need to find out about the operation, management, rules, and regulations of a condominium. He warns against property and recreational facilities that are owned by the developer and leased to the association, rising maintenance charges, easements, changes in the Declaration of Condominium, etc. Short chapters explain how to organize and operate a condominium, the function of the manager, and pitfalls of buying for a profit motive and of moving into "key jobs" (having to accept the place as is). The California, Arizona, and Florida Condominium acts (as of 1969) are included.

CONSUMER COMPLAINTS

See also Automobiles–Complaints; Consumer Protection; Consumer Protection–Directories. *For pertinent organizations see Part II, U.S. Federal Agencies*–Department of Health, Education and Welfare, Office of Consumer Affairs; *Private Organizations*–Center for Study of Responsive Law; The Consumer Protection Center; Consumers Education and Protective Association.

53. Charell, Ralph. **How I Turn Ordinary Complaints into Thousands of Dollars: The Diary of a Tough Customer.** Stein and Day, 1973. 192 pp. $6.95.

Not a diary, but a series of anecdotes showing how Ralph Charell managed to gain satisfaction from companies, great and small, who took his money and gave shoddy service and/or merchandise in return. Charell relates the incidents lightheartedly and succinctly and offers his experiences for other put-upon consumers in their fight to make companies sit up and take notice of legitimate complaints. Charell won a rebate from Consolidated Edison, moving and buy-out money from his landlord, out-of-pocket expenses from the telephone company, and free merchandise from major stores as compensation for harassment, poor service and/or quality. The author advises patience, humor, and perseverance in the quest for satisfaction. Suggestions, often wry, such as writing complaints on the most expensive stationary one can afford and filing a complaint before the event, should delight as well as help consumers.

54. Rosenbloom, Joseph. **Consumer Complaint Guide.** Annual. Macmillan. $8.95; paper $2.95.

The immediate success of the *Consumer Complaint Guide* seems to have convinced the author to produce this book annually. The 1974 edition has information on safeguards that consumers can expect, e.g., guarantees and warranties, major consumer laws, fraudulent and/or unethical sales practices (material which can be found in substantially the same form in earlier editions). In discussing how and to whom to complain he explains, in an abbreviated manner, the proper form of a complaint letter and procedures for complaints; names of "Help" and "Action" services of some local radio and TV stations, and addresses of all local Better Business Bureaus, a few industry and trade associations, and some federal agencies charged with protecting the consumer. State, county, and city consumer agencies are also listed, but without any text explaining their functions. The main body of this book is an A–Z listing of over 7,600 manufacturers and suppliers, along with the names of a top executive for each firm. Previous editions also had many listings of service industries, such as public utilities, transportation services, and electric and gas companies, which are now deleted. The 1973 edition, entitled *Consumer Action Guide,* can be consulted for those addresses. The strong point of this book lies in the names and addresses of people to whom to complain rather than in the mechanics of complaining.

55. **Telegripe Complaint Kit.** Infact Systems, 1971. 29 pp. 32 envelopes. Paper $1.29.

A clever, ready-to-use package prepared for the disgruntled consumer, the *Kit* consists of 29 pages of instructions: why one should complain, to whom (presidents of corporations and directors of agencies are best), how to refine a general complaint into a specific one, and very good sample complaint forms. Thirty-two self-mailing envelopes, similar to aerograms, with the forms printed on them, carbon paper for copies, and a record-keeping chart showing the status of complaints complete the package. Consumers who have used the *Kit* say they get excellent responses, probably because it looks like a telegram, and people tend to give them greater attention than if they were simple letters.

56. White, Jack, Gary Yanker, and Harry Steinberg. **The Angry Buyer's Complaint Directory.** Wyden, 1974. 292 pp. $7.95; paper $3.95.

The best all-purpose complaint guide. A directory of organizations is supplemented by one chapter entitled "Your Guide to Complaining," another "Operating Tips," and a third "Form Letters." The first tells how to learn about consumer rights, how to file a complaint by letter and telephone, and the value of sending carbon copies to persons and institutions sympathetic to your claim. The authors have included basic material on what to expect from federal, state, and local agencies, as well as from trade and industry associations; how to take a case to small claims or civil court, and how citizens groups can help you and you can help them. Special emphasis is given to the Consumer's Education and Protective Association (CEPA). "Operating Tips" is a practical guide for dealing with department stores, utilities, landlords, banks and credit companies, doctors, auto dealers, et al. Twelve form letters are included for use in typical situations, ranging from a complaint about a faulty repair to reporting a violation of the law. The bulk of the text is a listing of organizations: federal agencies handling 36 problems ranging from unfair advertising practices to missing mail and race discrimination; 32 trade and professional groups; state, regional, and local groups subdivided by specific types of complaints, and a listing of all small claims courts with claim limits, fees, etc.

CONSUMER EDUCATION

See also Consumer Protection *and specific subjects, e.g.*, Food; Medical Care. *For pertinent organizations see Part II, U.S. Federal Agencies*—Department of Agriculture (all agencies); Department of Health, Education and Welfare, Office of Consumer Affairs; General Services Administration, Consumer Information Center; Government, Printing Office; *Private Organizations*—Chamber of Commerce of the United States; Consumer Federation of America; Consumers' Association of Canada; Consumers Education and Protective Association; Consumers' Research Inc.; Consumers Union of United States, Inc.; The Cooperative League of the USA; Council of Better Business Bureaus; L'Institut de Promotion des Intérêts du Consommateur; *State, County, and City Agencies,* and *Canadian Agencies.*

57. Better Business Bureau. **Consumer's Buying Guides: How to Get Your Money's Worth.** Barnes & Noble, 1973. 205 pp. Paper $2. Award. Paper $1.25. Benjamin Co. Paper $1.50 (100 copies minimum order).

Useful, if elementary, guide for those at the beginning level of consumer awareness, written by the Better Business Bureau, with an unsurprising emphasis on benefits gained from using its services. It covers the basic areas of intelligent buying and offers specific guidelines for consideration before purchasing household appliances, furniture, carpeting, homes, autos, food, clothing, and insurance. It also covers buying some rather unusual items: home improvements (siding, landscaping, lumber, lawn sprinkler systems, driveways, water softeners) as well as funerals, home study courses, and book and magazine subscriptions. Approximately one page is devoted to each subtopic, e.g., dishwashers, cooperatives and condominiums, contracts and guarantees, earning money at home, so only the highlights are touched on. Each chapter ends with tips summarizing most of the preceding advice. The bureau is quick to point out frauds and schemes in advertising, sales, and services at all levels and suggests contacting it or other organizations before buying or investing. A list of all cities in which the BBB operates throughout the world is appended.

58. ***Canadian Consumer.** Sandra Thomspon, ed. Consumers' Association of Canada, 1963–. Illus. 6 issues a yr. $5.

This is the Canadian equivalent of *Consumer Reports* and *Consumers' Research Magazine* (*see* entries 65 and 68). Consumers' Association of Canada tests and rates a variety of Canadian merchandise (e.g., housewear, clothing, home accessories, and equipment) for quality, durability, safety, and cost and makes recommendations (acceptable, unacceptable). It reports on consumer legislation–the June 1974 issue detailed the provisions of Canada's Consumer Packaging and Labelling Act proclaimed on March 1, 1974. Other regular features include questions and answers on Canadian real estate, "Current Concerns," which discusses legislative and regulatory programs, and a "Consumers Speak" section. The magazine also highlights activities of the CAC main office and local chapters. Its value cannot be overstressed, as it reports on Canadian consumer protection and rates Canadian merchandise–both activities not covered by American publications. A French-language edition, *Le Consommateur Canadien*, is also available.

59. ***Changing Times: The Kiplinger Magazine.** Robert W. Harvey, ed. The Kiplinger Washington Editors, Inc. 1947– . Illus. Monthly. $7.

Dedicated to showing consumers how to save money and get the best value from products and services, much of the advice is useful, although too often overstated and/or oversimplified. Articles average one-four pages and are written in a chatty, informal style. *Changing Times* does not rate products by brand name (although brand names may be mentioned). Automobile information includes price, mechanical specifications, weight, and dimensions. Each year, the December issue lists all American cars, April issue, most foreign ones. The cars are not evaluated. Articles featuring books and magazines on different subjects, e.g., books for handicrafters, 50 useful government publications, etc., are often included. These are frequently older or standard texts being brought to the reader's attention. Articles on taxes are included in the issues from January through April. Material also covers travel and vacations, health, insurance, investments, gyps and frauds, money management, food, household equipment, recreation, sports, and hobbies, and some government activities. "Newscheck" (updating earlier trends and events), "Your Questions Answered," and "Things to Write For" are regular features. An index by broad subject area is published in the December issue and cumulates articles for the year.

60. ***The Consumer Educator.** Fred T. Wilhelms, ed. National Association of Secondary School Principals, in cooperation with the Council of Better Business Bureaus. 1972– . Monthly (10 issues a yr.; September–June). $2 with dues.

For the classroom teacher or curriculum administrator, each four-page issue is designed to show how business (often the Better Business Bureau) is attempting to improve consumer practices and information. The January 1974 issue focused on low-income consumers and noted a few teaching resources, e.g., filmstrips "for youthful consumers" and business firms. The February 1974 issue evaluated some consumer resource materials and provided a short article on truth and accuracy in advertising. It suggested class activities, such as monitoring television spots. "Consumer's Corner" lists paperbacks, periodicals, and free Better Business Bureau fact booklets of interest to consumers. While many of the suggestions are good, the newsletter tends to overemphasize the BBB. Teachers should be able to find better material elsewhere.

61. ***The Consumer Gazette.** Bill Wolf, ed. United Consumer Service Corp., 1973. Illus. Bimonthly. $4.95.

This is an 80-page bimonthly compendium of some good consumer articles mixed with "current product sample offers, discount coupons, premiums and other valuable benefits from America's leading companies." Unfortunately, the advertising tends to get in the way of the information and is, at times, even at cross-purposes. For example, while a May/June 1974 article points out that sugar's "detrimental effects on the body [include] tooth decay, heart disease, diabetes, hypoglycemia and other ailments," three pages later, the consumer is offered a seven-cent discount to buy a Health Toffee Bantam Bar. Some information is simply behind the times, e.g., the March/April 1974 issue noted Betty Furness as New York City Commissioner of Consumer Affairs—a post held by Elinor Guggenheimer since January of that year. There are really many excellent articles in each issue, as well as fine features, e.g., the May/June 1974 issue discussed "How to Translate Your Insurance Policy into English," "The Cost of Dying," and "Gazette Pediatrician." But when is an article legitimate and when are the editors subtly pushing an advertiser's product? *Consumer Gazette* proves that huckstering does not mix with consumer interest. Not recommended.

62. Consumer Guide. **Best Buys & Discount Prices.** Annual. Publications International. Paper $1.95.

Similar in intent to Consumers Union *Buying Guide Issue* and Consumers' Research *Handbook of Buying Issue* (*see* entries 65 and 77), *Best Buys & Discount Prices*, published each January, features and rates products by brand name, model number, and price. It also summarizes much of the information found in other publications produced by Consumer Guide, e.g., *Product Report, Automobiles,* and *Photographic Equipment Test Reports* (*see* entries 63, 7, and 433). The emphases here are on listing discount and/or low prices of items in relation to their average retail prices as well as on determining best buys in each group of products. The guide's coverage of consumer goods ranges from automobiles, stereo equipment, TVs, and radios to air conditioners, photographic equipment, and appliances for the home and personal care. Like many other Consumer Guide materials, this one is available through other publishers, e.g., Pocket Books ($1.95) and Doubleday. Doubleday's version, entitled *Ratings & Discount Prices,* and costing $2.50, includes CG information on bicycles, guns, and camping and fishing equipment.

63. Consumer Guide. **Product Report.** Annual. Publications International. Paper $1.95.

One of Consumer Guide's many publications, *Product Report* contains nothing not listed in *Best Buys & Discount Prices* (*see* entry 62). As the price for both volumes is the same, and *Best Buys* has reviews on many more products, *Product Report* is not recommended.

64. ***Consumer Information: An Index of Selected Federal Publications of** Consumer Interest. General Services Administration–Consumer Information Center, 1970– . Quarterly. Free.

The index lists "approximately 250 . . . consumer-oriented publications on how to buy, use, and take care of consumer products." Subjects covered are appliances and household furnishings; autos: budget and finance; child care; clothing, fabrics, and laundering; consumer education and protection; energy conservation and environmental protection; food; health; housing; landscaping, gardening, and pest control; older Americans; recreation, travel, and leisure activities. At least five publications are listed in each subject area; about half the publications are free, while prices for the rest generally range from 25¢ to 85¢, with only ten costing $1 or more. Though the index provides just a sampling of the dozens of reports, bulletins, pamphlets, and annuals prepared by the various federal agencies, this listing can lead interested consumers to other material on the same subject. The Spanish-language version, *Información para el Consumidor*, lists the federal publications for consumer interest that are published in Spanish.

65. ***Consumer Reports.** Consumers Union of United States, Inc., 1936– . Illus. Monthly. $10 (includes **Buying Guide Issue**, December).

Consumer Reports is probably the best-known and one of the most respected consumer magazines in the country. The bulk of its articles are reports of impartial laboratory tests evaluating brand-name consumer products (from automobile air bags and air conditioners to water repellent finishes and exterior wood stains). The magazine is also dedicated to providing standards for manufacturers to adhere to and government agencies to enforce. Product ratings range from "acceptable" to "intermediate" to "not acceptable." Check-rated are those items of high quality which are far superior to other products in their class; "best buys" are products high in quality and relatively low in price. The auto issue is published each April, but cars are rated throughout the year. Monthly features include "Docket Notes," which tell of government actions in enforcing consumer protection laws; record reviews of approximately ten classical records (in stereo); movie reviews, which summarize both critics' choices and those of *CR* readers, and "Work in Progress," which notes future articles. A monthly cumulative index lists articles of major interest of the preceding 11 months. Highly recommended. The subscription price includes the annual *Buying Guide Issue*, (published each December), but that issue is available alone for $2.65. It contains summaries of evaluations of the present year plus some of previous years not yet updated. In addition, it also includes some general consumer information, e.g., material on government agencies, consumer credit and credit cards, explanations of guarantees and warranties, and tips on moving. The December 1973 guide contained over 2,000 ratings by brand and model. Useful by itself or in conjunction with the monthlies.

66. **The Consumer's Handbook of Better Living.** Award, 1970. 351 pp. Paper $1.25.

Various sections of *Consumers All: The Yearbook of Agriculture, 1965* (*see* entry 100), are contained in this volume published in 1970. Nowhere do the publishers mention the source or date of their information. "Houses," "Plants," "Outdoors," and parts of "Furnishings," "Equipment," and "Safeguards," are included. The cost is low, but consumers should know that the information is from 1965 and that better, more recent material is available.

67. ***Consumers Index to Product Evaluations and Information Sources.** Pierian, 1974– . Quarterly. $25.

This recent addition to consumer literature is devoted to indexing "comparisons and evaluations of all manner of consumer goods and services . . . ." The range is too broad. Besides covering such consumer topics as household goods, sports and recreational equipment, food, beverages, tobacco products, drugs, cosmetics, investments, finances, and security and related services, it also includes furnishings and equipment for schools, libraries, and businesses, and such subtopics as "sex, pregnancy, birth control, and VD." Under the subtopic noted are indexed articles on abortions ("Implications of Legalization") and on sex ("Your Sex Life and How It Affects the Way You Sleep"). Over 100 periodicals are indexed (including five from England and one each from Australia and France; their value to American consumers is questionable). General discussion and survey articles are indexed, as well as specific products which are listed by brand name and model number. *Consumers Index* plans to include digests of consumer books and articles in future issues.

68. ***Consumers' Research Magazine.** F. J. Schlink, ed. Consumers' Research, Inc. 1927– . Illus. Monthly. $8 (includes *Handbook of Buying Issue*, October).

Formerly known as *Consumer Bulletin*, this is the oldest consumer magazine (and organization) in the country. A majority of its articles are brand-name ratings and reports of impartial laboratory tests. Ratings range from "A. recommended" to "B. intermediate" to "C. not recommended." Some products, such as air conditioners and heating equipment, are given provisional recommendations each year, but are never actually rated. Many other articles explaining how to judge quality do not include brand ratings. In 1974 such articles have dealt with toys, fishing tackle, and a sensible weight-loss plan. *Consumers' Research* emphasizes health, safety, and foods, but tests other types of products as well, ranging from air cleaners and calculators to wrist watches and open-end wrenches. Monthly features include a major editorial dealing with a topic of consumer interest (e.g., the Consumer Product Safety Commission or saving money at the supermarket); a record review listing high-quality classical records; movie reviews (with age suitability) summarizing critical opinion from 11 review sources; "Consumers' Observation Post" noting news items; readers' questions with editorial replies, and occasional reviews of books on consumer-interest topics. A cumulative (monthly) index lists articles from the last 12 issues. Highly recommended. (*See also* entry 77.)

69. Denenberg, Herbert S. **The Shopper's Guidebook to Life Insurance, Health Insurance, Auto Insurance, Homeowner's Insurance, Doctors, Dentists, Lawyers, Pensions, Etc.** Consumer News, 1974. 160 pp. $3.50.

Twenty-three *Shopper's Guides* put out under the auspices of the Pennsylvania Department of Insurance have been collected and edited. Many were written by Denenberg when he was commissioner of the department. Taken as a whole, the material provides an enormous amount of practical information on how to get the best insurance and professional help. (For names of individual guides and their annotations, check under *A Shopper's Guide to . . .* in the title and author indexes. In terms of advice on getting the most value for the money, this book must rank as one of the best. Highly recommended.

70. Dowd, Merle E. **How to Live Better and Spend 20% Less.** 2nd ed. Parker Publishing, 1972. 264 pp. $6.95.

This is very similar to Dowd's money management advice in *How to Get Out of Debt and Stay Out of Debt* (*see* entry 179) plus his prediction that consumers could spend 20 percent less following his advice. (True only if consumers are extremely wasteful in the first place.) The advice is mired in arithmetic: each cost-cutting step is added and totaled and presented to readers in terms of percent of monies saved. The book is so arranged that spectacular (over 20 percent) saving hints are boxed, set off by exclamation marks, and more. Some obvious but practical hints: eating less (serving smaller portions) will cut food bills; staying healthy will reduce medical costs; paying back loans quickly will reduce total debts; buying used books and gifts in advance and traveling off-season will lower recreation costs. Dowd insists that buying specials will save consumers up to 25 percent. Even more questionable is the author's presentation of a "family spending plan" which shows how to plan for short- and long-term expenses. This is standard budgeting information, and Dowd offers it as his unique contribution and the special feature of the book.

71. Fargis, Paul. **Consumer's Handbook.** Hawthorn, 1967. 306 pp. $6.95.

A direct copy of *Consumers All* (*see* entry 100), with a few of the more outdated articles deleted, this is more expensive than the original. Another copy, *The Consumer's Handbook of Better Living* (*see* entry 66), costs only $1.25. This version is not recommended.

72. Ferguson, Mike, and Marilyn Ferguson. **Champagne Living on a Beer Budget: How to Buy the Best for Less.** Putnam, 1968. 271 pp. $5.95.

An effort to teach consumers the art of living better and more enjoyably while spending less, this book is written in a breezy, let's-have-fun style that matches its philosophy. The focus is not bargain hunting for necessities but for luxuries, although the former is covered to some extent. For example "A Loaf of Bread a Jug" not only discusses food bargains but also how to buy good wines cheaply. "His and Hers—Gilding the Lily" suggests shopping at outlet, sample, surplus, or designer resale stores for top brand-name clothes at budget prices. "Santa Baby" deals with the art of gift buying. "Fun and Games, Small Sprees, and Fat Splurges" advocates dine-out clubs at night, lunching at good restaurants by day, wine-making at home, season tickets to sports events, concerts, and the theater. "Let the Rest of the World Go Buy" illustrates the value of renting—cars, clothes, furniture, sewing machines, sports equipment. Other preciously labeled chapters, "The Castle," "Sticks and Stoves," and "Wheels," cover the home, furnishings and appliances, and automobiles, along with hints on cutting costs during pregnancy, infant and child care, insurance, etc. Some material is dated, e.g., airline travel bargains, but by and large, most of the ideas still work.

73. Fitzsimmons, Cleo. **Consumer Buying for Better Living.** Wiley, 1961. 546 pp. $10.25.

While the copyright is 1961 and statistics need revision, the material in this college-level text on consumer buying by the professor and head of Purdue University's Home Management and Family Economics Department is such that almost nothing is outdated and the value of the book remains high. Fitzsimmons analyzes the problems involved in purchasing goods: those that are the same for all commodities and those that are specific for certain goods. She discusses different types and functions of markets, consumers and how they buy, the demand for goods and how it is met, and consumer-oriented agencies and organizations. She covers buying food, housing, clothing, equipment, and household furnishings; home maintenance and operating services; health, transportation, recreation, protection, as well as buying a lifestyle. Fitzsimmons deals with emotional as well as economic factors in analyzing the choices consumers (should) make. "Guides for Thinking" are included within each chapter as well as review questions and problems, and references to other sources. More scholarly than most other books on the subject, it is intended primarily for the student of home economics and family finance.

74. Fletcher, Adele Whitely. **How to Stretch Your Dollar.** Rev. ed. Benjamin Co., 1972. 123 pp. Paper $1.50 (100 copies minimum order).

In her discussion of basic and practical ways to "stretch the dollar" Fletcher covers food, clothing, houses and appliances, cars, savings, insurance, education, and entertainment. The best chapters deal with food and clothing. Shopping tips in supermarkets include learning the best buys in all stores in an area, and buying sale items only if they are useful. Information on the clothing dollar explains how to recognize quality, when to stock up on sale items, e.g., stockings in summer. She points out that it is unnecessary to buy expensive clothes for children as they prefer casual clothes, and outgrow the outfits quickly. Each chapter concludes with "Points to Remember" summarizing the most practical advice. A 1970 edition is available in pocket-size for 50¢ (100-copy minimum order), also from the Benjamin Co; it is good for promotional material, and can be used in the classroom from junior high and senior high to adult education classes.

75. Gale, Ella. **$$$ and Sense: Your Complete Guide to Wise Buying.** Award, 1965. 283 pp. Paper 75¢.

Gale's book remains a good source for those interested in spending money wisely. She emphasizes the value of reading labels and why they are sometimes not helpful or are missing altogether. She explains when it is best to shop at discount stores, save and redeem trading stamps, shop by brand name, buy extravagances and gifts, and how to deal with door-to-door salespeople, spot legitimate sales and bargains, and use credit wisely. Chapters on food and clothing are somewhat outdated by Truth-in-Packaging, unit pricing (in some cities), permanent labels, and—naturally—prices. But in all chapters, including those on buying furniture, home appliances and bedding, Gale appends a practical checklist of tips to ensure the best value for the shopping dollar. Material on housing covers only the pros and cons of buying a new versus an older home, but the checklist is again concise and useful. A good, if somewhat abridged, list of stains and stain-removing formulas is included.

76. Gordon, Leland J., and Stewart M. Lee. **Economics for Consumers.** 6th ed. Van Nostrand Reinhold, 1972. 719 pp. $10.95.

Providing concepts of consumer economics and consumer protection for college students, the book's sections cover running the marketplace, forces influencing consumer demand, intelligent shopping, and consumer protection efforts by sellers and government. Most of the information is very practical, e.g., discount stores may save money, but comparison shopping is necessary on every item to be sure; trading stamps usually drive up prices, but in some cases they may save consumers money; promotional games are unethical and should be banned. Material on brands, prices, and quality makes clear that price and quality frequently have little relationship to each other. The authors discuss such standard topics as savings and investments and buying houses, automobiles, and insurance. Unusual topics cover emotional needs and financial costs of burials, marriages, and other ceremonial celebrations that have become economic rites (Mother's Day, graduations). Practical review questions and projects complete each chapter. The text well justifies its long history (the first edition appeared in 1939) and can be used with high school students and the general public too.

77. ***Handbook of Buying Issue.** Consumers' Research, Inc. Annual. Paper $2.95.

Called the *Consumer Bulletin Annual* until 1973, the *Handbook* is now the regular October issue of *Consumers' Research Magazine* (*see* entry 68). Articles are excerpted from those appearing in the previous monthlies of the current year, and from older issues if the editors feel the material still has current interest and value. The *Handbook*, like the regular issues of *Consumers' Research*, includes both brand-name evaluations and articles of a more general nature. Useful by itself or in conjunction with its 11 companion monthlies.

78. Jelley, Herbert M., and Robert O. Herrmann. **The American Consumer: Issues and Decisions.** McGraw-Hill, 1973. 502 pp. $7.96. Student Activity Guide $3.28.

This is high-school level material divided into sections on money management, wise buying, and consumer issues (problems and solutions). Older editions appeared in the 1950s as *Consumer Living* and in the 1960s as *Consumer Economics*; the latter is still available and not recommended (*see* entry 104). This edition, by Jelley and Herrmann, university teachers of business education and agricultural economics, respectively, allows for full clarification of consumer problems and does not talk down to its audience. The best material deals with spending money intelligently. Home, cars, insurance, furnishings, clothing, recreation, appliances, and more are handled with enough depth to give students an awareness of the pros and cons of issues, e.g., term versus cash value insurance, good and bad features of health insurance, when appliances are economical and when not. Budgeting and income planning show the importance of tailoring plans to individual goals and needs and how it can be done easily. The main drawback of the book is that it still assumes the male to be the prime buyer and decision maker. Consumer history, current problems, and the responsibilities of consumers, government, and business are also covered. Questions and activities complete the text.

79. King, John W. **Save Money and Grow Rich.** Lyle Stuart, 1968. 288 pp. $4.95.

An A–Z listing of everything and anything from abstracts to zoos, King threw together this mishmash and offers short paragraphs on each, all supposedly designed to save the consumer money. "Addresses" suggests preaddressing envelopes to people you write to often; "zoos" (trip to) suggests bringing your own peanuts, lunches, and snacks; following yoga will save many health bills and result in a longer, happier life. On the last, King suggests a particular book to write for. This one is not recommended.

80. Kinney, Jean, and Cle Kinney. **How to Get 20 to 90% Off on Everything You Buy.** Parker Publishing, 1966. 255 pp. $6.95; paper $1.95.

The Kinneys, apparently very successful examples of their own skill at saving, cannot decide for whom they are writing. While many of their money-saving ideas are geared to comfortable homeowners, a lot of advice is for city dwellers in general and New Yorkers in particular. Aside from such almost useless suggestions as renting your three free bedrooms on an upper floor (to live rent-free), buying designer clothes in Paris just before the new shows (when discounts are greatest), and choosing cruises wisely, some very practical advice is proffered, e.g., trading goods and services rather than buying. On the whole, the book promises much more than it delivers. As of September 1973, it was in its fourteenth printing "completely updated to reflect current economic conditions." In spite of the Kinney book's success, *Champagne Living on a Beer Budget* (*see* entry 72), similar in intent, is the better buy.

81. Klein, David, and Marymae Klein. **Supershopper: A Guide to Spending and Saving.** Praeger. 175 pp. $5.95.

In short chapters, clear prose, and solid, down-to-earth advice directed at more than 40 million teenagers who collectively spend over $20 billion a year, the Kleins show how to find part-time and seasonal (summer and Christmas) work, how to pay taxes (if necessary), different ways to save and invest, and they concentrate on teaching how to spend money wisely. They discuss the negative aspects of advertising and of buying unnecessary brand-name items. An interesting chapter deals with saving the environment, e.g., conserving electricity, buying soda in returnable bottles, using vegetable garbage as plant mulch. Other segments are devoted to buying items of particular interest to teens: typewriters, hi-fi equipment, musical instruments, clothes, bikes, and motorcycles, to name a few. The final chapter deals with how and when to return merchandise and lists channels of complaints when all else fails.

82. Linder, Bertram L., and Edwin Selzer. **You the Consumer.** Sadlier, 1973. 190 pp. $5.52; paper $3.72.

For high school students with low reading levels, the book's chapters deal with consumers, advertising, credit, buying wisely, budgets, saving and investment, automobiles, homes, etc. The format is attractive, but the content suffers from a once-over-lightly approach that glosses over many problems. The chapter on buying insurance, for example, does not allow students the opportunity to make value judgments on best buys and is also blatantly sexist (particularly for a text with a publication date of 1973). On the other hand, certain chapters are good. These include "Advertising and the Consumer," "Comparison Shopping," and "Reading Labels."

83. Margolius, Sidney. **The Consumer's Guide to Better Buying.** Rev. ed. Pocket Books, 1972. 436 pp. Paper $1.25.

One of the standards in the field since its original publication in 1942, Margolius's consumer guide is probably the best available. Whatever the subject, Margolius packs more straightforward information into less space than most other writers. "Guide to Best Values" covers consumer ignorance and fraud, how to stretch the dollar, and 12 shopping principles to produce better purchasing power. "Sources for Savings" has one of the best discussions found in any book on buying in chain, discount, and department stores, specialty shops and supermarkets, through cooperatives, and by mail. "The Guide to Values" explains what to look for when buying clothing, home furnishings and rugs, home appliances, televisions and audio equipment, life and health insurance, auto and property insurance, medicines, toiletries, cosmetics, home cleaning aids, cars, food, and housing, including ways to cut and keep down housing costs. "Managing Your Own Money," on money management and credit, rounds out the coverage of better buying. In each section, Margolius names local as well as national brands and stores and gives typical values to look for and bad buys to avoid. Eminently practical and usable.

84. Meyer, Martin J. **Martin Meyer's Moneybook.** (Books for Better Living). Simon and Schuster, 1972. 224 pp. $8.98.

A combination of *Dont't Bank On It!* (*see* entry 489) and *Credit Cardsmanship* (now called *How to Turn Plastic into Gold*); (*see* entry 172). In this volume, Meyer summarizes the material, calls these banking and credit card schemes "money keys," and italicizes them. The last few pages concern themselves with "Found Money Keys," time-worn ideas for conserving money which Meyer says will save thousands of dollars each year. The ideas include buying drugs generically (to save about $200); using a small car (to save $400–$800 on operating and maintenance costs); staying at low-cost motels; buying less, and using vegetable scrapings and leaves in soups (instead of throwing them out). Marginal.

85. Money Management Booklet Library. Illus. Money Management Institute, Household Finance Corp., various dates. 12 booklets. Paper $3 the set. Quantity orders discounted.

The 12 pamphlets cover the range of money management concerns, stressing spending plans throughout: managing credit, reaching financial goals, spending by children, and getting the best in food, clothing, housing, home furnishings, appliances, automobiles, health, recreation, savings, and investment. The pamphlets are revised periodically, and all are on a level appropriate for anyone of high school age and up. A teacher's guide is available with the set. The pamphlets (all good) are annotated separately. (For individual titles see *Money Management* in the title index.)

86. Money Management: Your Shopping Dollar. Illus. Money Management Institute, Household Finance Corp., 1972. 32 pp. Paper 25¢. Quantity orders discounted.

This pamphlet provides a very good explanation of shoppers' roles as purchasing agents, customers, and citizens. For the first role, shoppers must determine spending values and goals and develop shopping skills: read and keep labels, warranties, and guarantees; shop and compare brands and stores; deal only with reputable sellers; read and understand contracts before signing. General buying guides to goods and services cover food, clothing, major appliances, as well as doctors, bankers, accountants, drycleaners, barbers, beauticians, household help, etc. It details customer rights and citizen obligations: communicate likes and dislikes; follow shopping etiquette; learn about quality standards, such as seals and labels; use services of local stores and understand their methods of operation. An excellent checklist spells out advantages and disadvantages of different shopping facilities: retail stores, cooperatives, department stores, specialty shops, discount stores, mail-order shops, vending machines, door-to-door sellers. Some of this information repeats material from other Money Management Library pamphlets, but it is a good buy individually or as part of the series.

87. ***Moneysworth**. Betty Fier, ed.-in-chief. Avant-Garde Media, 1970– . Fortnightly. $5.

Published 26 times a year, this started out as an eight-page (or less) newsletter, but it is now a tabloid. It continues to try to cover anything and everything for consumers that is or will be making news. A March 19, 1974 article (written when *Moneysworth* was still in its old format) found fake meat a good buy, and conducted a taste test of various brands of soy and wheat protein substitutes. The issue also explained the Keogh Plan for the self-employed and how to select stereo speaker systems (with brand-name ratings). April 1, 1974, told how to give a haircut; pointed out some (not very esoteric) tax deductions, such as false teeth, eyeglasses, carfares to the doctor, bad debt write-offs, income averaging; what to expect from a hearing test and a brand-name evaluation of hearing aids. Unfortunately, one of the newsletter issues of *Moneysworth* also devoted four of its eight pages to advertising a new book it published on legal advice, while another devoted three pages to pushing the legal adviser and the magazine itself. Although buying the periodical may lead to occasional savings, consumers would do well to spend their money elsewhere.

88. National Observer. **The Consumer's Handbook: 100 Ways to Get More Value for Your Dollars.** Dow-Jones, 1969. Vol. 1, 162 pp. Vol. 2, 205 pp. Paper $1.95 ea.

The book's articles, reprints from *The National Observer*, updated where necessary and ranging in length from one to five pages, are designed to educate consumers to cost-conscious methods of buying products and services. Guidelines for purchase as well as for determining need are set forth. Brands are rarely mentioned and more rarely compared, although there are some exceptions, e.g., children's encyclopedias. Volume 1 contains 55 articles and over 90 hints haphazardly arranged (with index); volume 2 has 56 articles and over 60 hints arranged by broad subject areas: automotive, education, health and safety, food and household, investing, and recreation and hobbies. A seventh category, "Miscellaneous," completes the book. Subjects range from discussions of whether to lease a car (volume 2) or reupholster furniture (volume 1) to new services, such as lawn maintenance companies, and products that shockproof rugs (volume 2). Other topics range from finding a doctor, dentist and lawyer (volume 1) to looking for values in coffee, tea, and bourbon (volume 2).

89. **138 Ways to Beat the High Cost of Living.** Channing L. Bete, 1971. 15 pp. Paper 25¢. Quantity orders discounted.

A useful compilation on how to stretch one's money, the pamphlet shows how to make a budget and offers tips for saving on food (use "money-off" coupons, buy economy cuts of meat, cook meats at lower temperatures for less shrinkage); transportation (buy gas and oil at fill-it-yourself stations, buy a car with manual transmission), and clothing (sew your own; avoid fashion fads; launder without too much detergent, as detergents weaken material). Other tips include saving money on recreation, furniture and appliances, and shelter. While its simple wording and illustrations make the pamphlet particularly useful for adult education classes, it may be referred to by any consumer looking for helpful tips.

90. Oppenheim, Irene. **The Family as Consumers.** Macmillan, 1965. 318 pp. $6.50.

An overview of the subject, somewhat drily presented, it needs updating for accuracy. Oppenheim, assistant professor of home economics at New York University and a past president of the Council on Consumer Information, stresses emotional, social, and economic needs as factors in consumer decisions. Using the family as the basic consumer group, she explains its role in spending for food, transportation, housing, clothing, leisure, and insurance, as well as in getting credit, in saving, and in investing. The section on budgeting has information on planning daily expenditures, assessing a budget, and the values of wise purchasing (including shopping calendars of sales and monthly price cuts). Chapters of special interest deal with the problems of teenagers and senior citizens: their place in society as well as their roles as consumers. Footnotes, bibliographic sources, charts, and graphs abound, all of which need updating and revision.

91. Poriss, Martin. **How to Live Cheap but Good.** Illus. by Charles C. Hefling, Jr. (American Heritage) McGraw-Hill, 1971. 319 pp. $6.95: paper $3.95.

Writing for young people "with high tastes and low income" on their own for the first time, Poriss maintains that common sense and a sense of humor are prerequistites for learning the art of living "cheap but good." The guide is predominently concerned with housing: finding a room, apartment, or house; moving into it; furnishing, maintaining, and repairing it, and moving away. Other chapters deal with saving money on utilities, on auto and appliance repairs, on books and writing materials, on clothing, and on health care. Although anyone can follow his advice, Poriss assumes the reader will be someone with a roommate; indeed he devotes space to the art of finding one and the etiquette of living with one or more (of the same or opposite sex). Tips on moving are excellent: how to rent U-Hauls, trailers, and trucks; how to pack and move each piece of furniture (remove drawers from chests, pack each lampshade separately). Material on food is as basic as explaining the uses of various utensils, shopping, menu planning, and storage and freezing tips. Lively and humorous illustrations are particularly helpful in elucidating the material on home repairs. Will appeal mainly to those with little cash and lots of energy, but the advice is sound and can be followed successfully by others.

92. Raines, Margaret. **Consumers' Management.** Charles A. Bennett, 1973. 343 pp. $8.72.

Older editions were entitled *Managing Livingtime*, a more accurate indication of the book's contents than the present title. Raines concentrates on home management, and the book is more suibable for a course in home economics than in consumer management. Material for consumers, i.e., purchasing food, clothing, housing, and credit and managing money, looks as if it had been supplied by manufacturers and advertisers. It is not only old-fashioned in style, it is also old-fashioned in emphasis. For example, chapters deal with clothing "glamour," wedding plans, and study time. Not for students in a consumer education class. Not recommended.

93. Randall, Robert W. **Consumer Purchasing.** (The Consumer Education Series). Pendulum, 1973. 86 pp. Paper $1.25.

Consumer Purchasing is one of a nine-part educational series for high school students. Even though some of its material is not as up to date as its copyright suggests, it is, overall, well chosen and relevant to its audience's interests: how to get college loans, how to shop for a first car, etc. Conventional chapters deal with Truth-in-Lending and the cost of credit, food and other supermarket values, furniture, appliances, and clothing (including care and use). Good ones cover different types of insurance (health, property, life, etc.), advertising games, and buying services. Each chapter contains a glossary, questions, and actions for students.

94. Saunders, Rubie. **Smart Shopping and Consumerism.** Illus. by Gail Owens. Watts, 1973. 63 pp. $3.95.

A consumer education resource for young teenagers, it concentrates on the essentials as applied to that group. Short chapters discuss the value of budgeting (and learning how to do so painlessly); shopping for food, clothing, and credit, and learning to save. Of particular interest to teens: buying mail order records; shopping for cosmetics; eating out and tipping in restaurants. Saunders stresses proper manners when going into stores and includes advice against shoplifting. Information is very sparse (each chapter contains only a few pages) and illustrations seem designed for the youngest teens. But by and large, Saunders gets her points across without didacticism and her brevity can be considered a plus with this audience. The price of the book, however, is too high for its size. *Supershopper* (*see* entry 81), while written for a slightly older audience, is preferred. This is a reasonably acceptable second choice.

95. Scaduto, Anthony. **Getting the Most for Your Money: How to Beat the High Cost of Living.** McKay, 1970. 241 pp. $6.95.

Scaduto provides practical, easy-to-follow information (replete with tabular material): wise buying begins with planning ahead, doing comparison shopping, and knowing when sales are held, and Scaduto includes a month-by-month chart of 95 different sale items. Nine chapters describe in detail methods for saving money on food, clothing, household expenses, automobiles, recreation, college expenses, insurance, and health. To cut food costs he advises buying in season, buying the store brand, comparing different forms of the product for price (fresh, frozen, and canned), and buying for nutrition. When purchasing an appliance, he suggests looking first at the cheapest no-frill model, and then carefully adding on the other wanted features. On automobiles, he suggests bargaining for the cost of accessories, buying in the fall when new models arrive, and getting a full-size standard model as a used car. A very well-arranged no-nonsense book.

96. Schoenfeld, David, and Arthur A. Natella. **The Consumer and His Dollars.** 2nd ed. Oceana, 1970. 365 pp. $6. Finegan, Marcella E. **The Consumer and His Dollars: Workbook and Study Guide.** Oceana, 1972. 88 pp. Paper $1.50.

Suitable for young students and for an adult education audience, it traces, in simplified style, the roles of consumers in the economy and of government and private agencies in safeguarding consumer laws and legal rights. It also provides information on how to "spend dollars with sense" on food, clothing, automobiles, appliances, furniture, credit, housing, insurance, investing, and saving. Other material covers how to budget wisely, the taxpayer and taxation, and how to recognize and avoid frauds, quackery, and deception. A glossary and an unrevised bibliography (taken from the first edition) are included. Although the textbook contains questions at the conclusion of each chapter, the publisher has added a workbook and study guide to accompany it.

97. ***Service: USDA's Report to Consumers.** Lillie Vincent, ed. U.S. Department of Agriculture, 1963– . Monthly. Free.

Normally a four-page newsletter issued monthly, recent issues were reduced to two pages or came out bimonthly. This was due to increased duties on the part of the editor who expects the situation to straighten out shortly. *Service*, designed for those "who report to the individual consumer rather than for mass distribution" notes books, pamphlets, films, slides, et al., available from the Department of Agriculture, and gives tips on food, cooking, health, diet, nutrition, and gardening, i.e., everything that comes under the responsibility of the department. For example, in the combined February–March 1974 issue, one article stressed the need for a balanced diet, another both told of USDA scientists who have produced vegetables with more nutritional value than their present-day counterparts and gave a "Spring Food Preview" of foods and prices. The two-page April 1974 issue had a very interesting article on the exotic foods we import (such as ginseng and pickled pimentos), noted that a new USDA slide set on the food stamp program was available for purchase, listed pamphlets for purchase on buying used furniture and sewing machines, and told of a protein-rich candy being developed by USDA scientists that is nutritional as well as tasty. Good for libraries and for schools (below the college level) with consumer education and home economics courses.

98. Shortney, Joan Ranson. **How to Live on Nothing.** Rev. ed. Pocket Books, 1971. 336 pp. Paper 95¢.

Praised by the editors of *The Whole Earth Catalog*, this book does not quite explain "how to live on nothing," but it does its best. Shortney, who lives on a Pennsylvania farm, emphasizes do-it-yourself, making do, and doing without. She has recipes for rye-kernel coffee, dandelion salad, and the like. Her chapter on clothes, heavy on salutes to Salvation Army outlets, explains how to make new garments from old: a child's slip from a man's shirt, a bolero from a suit jacket, and how to care for clothes so they will last. The author covers buying furniture at country auctions, buying old houses that need repairs, conserving fuel and keeping warm (proper dressing to cut wind and reduce heat dispersal). There is a nice section on gifts that utilize talent and little money, e.g., lending out services, be it for babysitting or ironing, as well as making food and clothing. Vacationing in your home territory for free at museums and parks or camping in state and national recreational areas are some other suggestions. Shortney has a rather extensive list of folk medicines with their uses and recipes. She urges exercise and weight control to stay healthy, and explains proper dental hygiene for healthy teeth. Other material covers government benefits, willing your body to science, getting a free education, and more. She concludes with a listing of 100 items that have second lives, from chalk ends for shining metal to pretzel tins for preserving woolens.

99. Troelstrup, Arch W. **The Consumer in American Society: Personal and Family Finance.** 5th ed. (McGraw-Hill Series in Finance). McGraw-Hill, 1974. 678 pp. $10.95.

Originally published in 1952 as *Consumer Problems* and subsequently as *Consumer Problems and Personal Finance*, this latest edition includes such topics as the working wife and mother and the consumer movement: regulation and legislation at the federal and state level, consumer groups in the United States and abroad. Information is provided on food labeling and open dating; communal living; mobile home and condominium buying; costs of health care, drugs, and health insurance; automobile hazards; costs of repairs and low quality of work, etc. Material is recent, with easy-to-read charts and graphs, and covers all topics one expects in a consumer education text at the college level. The best aspect of the book is its ability to look at a topic and point out areas of consumer concern, e.g., "Consumer Protection: The Federal Government and the Consumer" and "Consumer Protection on the State and Local Levels: Consumer Justice—Conclusions." Appendix A: "Ways to Save Money from Marriage to Retirement" is a summary of consumer tips on buying food, housing, transportation, clothing, and personal and medical care. Appendix B: "Federal Agencies Serving the Consumer" lists major agencies, but does not spell out their duties in detail. While generally excellent in content, the writing is often pedantic, particularly in the introductory chapter, "The Consumer in Our Society."

100. U.S. Department of Agriculture. **Consumers All: The Yearbook of Agriculture, 1965.** 1965. 496 pp. $5.65.

A basic, if somewhat pedestrian and outdated overview of the consumer world, it covers the purchase, use, and/or preparation of food, furnishings, household equipment, houses, finance, insurance, health, accident prevention, gardening, landscaping, recreation, and clothing. Signed articles average four–six pages; the list of contributors covers seven pages. Everything, even the most basic of concepts, is explained. Food articles include tips on cooking outdoors, menu planning from foreign cuisines, and information on school lunches. Selecting and refinishing furniture, planning and using fireplaces, paneling walls, and laying floors are among the articles in the furnishings section. On finance, information is given about mortgages, credit, and family budgets. Safety covers accidents and their prevention in the home, fire protection, help in disasters, health services, etc. Landscaping, gardening, country vacations, handicrafts, wildlife, and nature study are also discussed. Broad coverage, easily read, this is useful for the beginning reader in the field.

101. U.S. Department of Agriculture. **Handbook for the Home: The Yearbook of Agriculture, 1973.** 1973. 388 pp. $5.70.

An introduction to the ways families can live fully, securely, satisfyingly—and economically. While much of its general material (on budgets, buying insurance, home decorating and maintenance) can be found in other books (in a more lively presentation), there is enough here to make this publication worthwhile to consult. This includes information on buying a second (vacation) home, on sewage and water considerations, on new developments in home building and methods of home construction. Checkpoints to look for when buying large and small appliances, luggage, clothes for the aged and the handicapped, and vacations are also valuable. A section on evaluating a local community's services to the individual and to the family is unique in a book of this type. Typical of Department of Agriculture yearbooks, this one is composed of many short articles, most of which deal only with the obvious, but are useful nonetheless.

102. Warmke, Roman F., et al. **Consumer Economic Problems,** 8th ed. South-Western, 1971. 665 pp. $6.68.

Objective and straightforward, but it is, unfortunately, a dull high school text on economics, economic theory, and consumer education. The consumer education material covers money management (including investment and credit), insurance, housing (particularly private housing), advertising, and legal and social protection for consumers. Better material is available, e.g., *The American Consumer* (*see* entry 78).

103. †**Why Do You Buy?** Journal Films, 1972. Color. Sound. 16 mm. 9½ min. Sale $125. Rent from University of Illinois at Champaign, $6.25.

"A look at the modern consumer and a few of his hang-ups," the film introduces viewers to teenagers Mildred Maximum and Frank Frontlash. The narrator explains that they—and we—buy to gain love and affection, status, and the approval of friends. It shows that our cars tell a great deal more about us than just the fact that we (may) need transportation. Mildred is shown buying an ugly, but fashionable raincoat; Frank, a useless encyclopedia. The film ends with the two of them, and many others, waiting on line to return their unwanted goods. At times funny, its point is belabored and somewhat overlong even at nine and a half minutes. The film won the blue ribbon at the 1973 Educational Film Library Association (EFLA) Festival in the category of consumer affairs.

104. Wilhelms, Fred T., Ramon P. Heimerl, and Herbert M. Jelley. **Consumer Economics,** 3rd ed. McGraw-Hill, 1966. 495 pp. $8.36.

Superseded in content and approach by *The American Consumer* (*see* entry 78), this text should be removed from the market. The format is poor, the material is presented with a once-over-lightly approach, and the writing style is guaranteed not to hold the teenagers' attention. For schools using this text, the best sections cover consumer testing laboratories and their procedures and wise buying habits and principles.

105. Williamson, Ellen. **Spend Yourself Rich.** Doubleday, 1970. 322 pp. $6.95.

A trivial book telling the wealthy how to spend money enjoyably, including ways to raise horses, dress glamorously, and (for widows) how to catch a second mate. Sections on investing in art, jewelry, and land display little insight and less practicality. Not recommended.

106. Wingate, Isabel B., Karen R. Gillespie, and Betty G. Addison. **Know Your Merchandise.** 3rd ed. McGraw-Hill, 1964. 672 pp. $8.96.

Although suggested for the use of consumers as well as retailing students, *Know Your Merchandise*, written by three teachers of retail management, is aimed primarily at those who will be working in "well-stocked department stores." Some of the material is completely outdated; other information needs revision. In the past, the authors have revised the text about once every ten years; a new edition may be planned. Half the merchandise covered here is textiles: their makeup, uses, advantages, and disadvantages. The rest includes plastics, rubber, paints, paper and stationery, furs, leather, shoes, gloves, jewelry, soaps and cosmetics, foods, glassware, tableware, furniture, etc. Some of the information is too brief to be of any value, e.g., sections on furniture, jewelry, household utensils. Other material is marred by extraneous editorial comment, e.g., minks are vicious and bloodthirsty. The authors stress use and durability; price and brands are not discussed. There is little of a critical nature in the text.

CONSUMER EDUCATION—BIBLIOGRAPHIES

107. **Consumer Education: A Bibliography.** Bibliographic Services Division, Sasketchewan Provincial Library, 1973. 18 pp. n.p.

An A–Z listing by author of 86 books on consumer education that were available in the Saskatchewan, Canada, libraries in 1973. Since many of the books listed are no longer in print, it cannot be used as the basis of building a similar collection in another small library. Very limited in value outside of Saskatchewan.

108. U.S. Office of Consumer Affairs and New York Public Library. **Consumer Education Bibliography.** 1971. 192 pp. Paper $1.

These very brief annotations of more than 4,000 books, pamphlets, booklets, periodical articles, audiovisual aids, and teaching materials on consumer interests and education prepared by the Office of Consumer Affairs in cooperation with the New York Public Library are arranged by broad subject areas and listed alphabetically by title. Access to information is limited. The bibliography consists mainly of annotations of articles and pamphlets. When the material is of possible interest to children or young adults, such information is noted. A special section, "Children's Books," contains annotations of books on such subjects as career guidance, business and industry, health and safety, and hobbies and sports. Age level is specified for each book.

CONSUMER EDUCATION–STUDY AND TEACHING

For pertinent organizations see Part II, U.S. Federal Agencies–Department of Health, Education and Welfare, Office of Consumer Affairs; *Private Organizations*–American Council on Consumer Interests; American Home Economics Association; Home Economics Education Association.

109. Charters, Margaret. **Consumer Education Programming in Continuing Education.** (Publications in Continuing Education. Occasional Papers, no. 34). Syracuse University, Publications in Continuing Education and ERIC Clearinghouse on Adult Education, 1973. 36 pp. Paper $1.75.

Charters provides an analysis of the need for consumer education programs in continuing education. She defines consumer education as education of the citizen-consumer with decision-making responsibilities in the public, individual, and family domains. Charters concentrates on adult education material for the poor and undereducated. She has looked at much of the available literature and summarized its findings. The 66-book and pamphlet bibliography will be of great value to anyone involved in similar programming.

110. A Guide for Evaluating Consumer Education Programs and Materials. American Home Economics Association, 1972. 23 pp. Paper. Free.

The association defines consumer education as the preparation of the individual in skills, concepts, and understanding necessary to achieve the most satisfaction and uses of resources. A series of scales have been devised for evaluating programs and material which can double as criteria for developing the programs and materials. "Objectives" of the curriculum measure social significance, human values, communication of content, specificity of behavior aspect, and intellectual difficulty. "Content" is evaluated in terms of objectivity, organization, conceptualization, difficulty level, timeliness, credibility, focus, and relevancy. "Learning Experiences" measures the maturity level of the learner, variety, sensory and thought stimulation, relevancy and learning feedback. "Evaluation Materials and Procedures" has ten criteria including continuity, comprehension, and validity. "Educational Materials" has 18 criteria ranging from relationship to objectives, relevancy, and timeliness to physical appearance, packaging, and cost. The scales are on a continuum from excellent to poor. In addition, each section suggests specific content and/or objectives.

111. HELPs (Home Economics Learning Packages). American Home Economics Association, various dates. Paper $2 ea.

HELPs are prepared by classroom teachers and cover various subjects and performance levels. Each one must be judged individually as their quality varies. For example, *Read the Label* (eighth grade, complexity level intermediate), on foods and nutrition, and *Be an Able Label Reader* (grade 12, intermediate), on textiles and furs, are both good; but *Values and Goals Have Strings on Your Money* (senior high, intermediate), on money management, is not. Other *HELPs* deal with credit (*Buy Now, Pay Later*), fibers (*Be Fiber-Wise for Good Fabric Buys*), and convenience foods (*Let's Consider Convenience Foods*). Each packet has two parts: one for teachers and the other for students. The first outlines the lessons and materials and provides test answers. The student section lists learning objectives and gives pretests, lessons, and readings. Students can work individually or in groups using the material. A complete package costs $2; the student section costs $3 in lots of ten.

112. **†On Your Own.** FilmFair Communications, 1972. Color. Sound. 16 mm. 23¼ min. Sale $300. Rent $30.

In this documentary study of a high school consumer education class in California the students are shown discussing various aspects of consumer education, home economics, and "bachelor survival" and seen checking out buys in supermarkets, working in stores for vocational training, and providing consumer information to the community. At the end of the term, they sum up what they have learned from the classes. Sponsored by the Department of Vocational Education, Bureau of Home Education, and the Chancellor's Office of the California Community Colleges, the film offers teachers an overview of consumer education curricula and benefits, but has less value for students taking such courses.

113. U.S. Office of Consumer Affairs. **An Approach to Consumer Education for Adults.** 1973. 37 pp. Paper 55¢.

Suggested Guidelines for Consumer Education: Grades K–12 (*see* entry 114) was published in 1970. This 1973 pamphlet is highly recommended. It is designed to help educators establish and organize consumer education programs for adult students beyond the high school level. Special sections are devoted to the needs of special groups: low income, elderly, rural, blacks, Spanish speaking, Indians. The authors have suggested content areas and potential resources. The latter include aids to teaching adults on an individual basis, aids to teaching adult education courses, texts and bibliographies, consumerism studies, and periodicals. They have also listed organizations devoted to consumers and to adult education. A partial directory of federal agencies and a list of bibliographic sources for further information complete the pamphlet.

114. U.S. Office of Consumer Affairs. **Suggested Guidelines for Consumer Education: Grades K–12.** 1970. 58 pp. Paper $1.05.

Still the best and most comprehensive guide for consumer education below the college level, *Suggested Guidelines* is intended for use by teachers, administrators, supervisory personnel, and curriculum planners for developing their own consumer education programs and relating them to learning resources in the community. The booklet shows how such courses can be implemented within the existing curriculum framework and also defines course topics and areas of study. Government agencies serving the consumer are also listed, and an extensive, 16-page bibliography of multimedia "instructional resources" is particularly useful.

CONSUMER ORGANIZATIONS

See Consumer Protection—Directories

CONSUMER PROTECTION

See also Consumer Education *and specific subjects, e.g.*, Automobiles—Frauds; Food—Adulteration and Protection; Product Safety. *For pertinent Organizations see Part II, U.S. Federal Agencies; Private Organizations; State, County, and City Agencies*, and *Canadian Agencies*.

115. Aaker, David A., and George S. Day, eds. **Consumerism: Search for the Consumer Interest.** 2nd ed. Free Press, 1974. 460 pp. $10.95; paper $5.25.

Readings on consumerism designed primarily for managers and students of business, the articles are taken from a variety of sources and represent a spectrum of opinion, although omitting the sensational, the overly partisan, or the superficial. Part I gives historical and current perspectives on consumerism; Part II deals with the availability of information prior to purchase; Part III, with the transaction itself; Part IV, with the postpurchase experience; and Part V, with broadening the perspective, e.g., ecology and social issues in advertising as they relate to consumers. Many of the articles are taken from business and law journals, are written by persons favorable to business, and are intended for school use by business students. There are also articles by consumer advocates, such as Ralph Nader, Senator Warren Magnuson and Philip Schrag, giving balance to the collection. A good text for school use; discussion questions are appended to each section.

116. ***ACCI Newsletter.** Monthly (9 issues a yr.; September-May). **Consumer Education Forum.** 3 issues a yr. **The Journal of Consumer Affairs.** Gorden E. Bivens, ed. 2 issues a yr. American Council on Consumer Interests. $2.50 ea.

The official publications of the American Council on Consumer Interests, the $10 annual dues include subscriptions to all three periodicals. *The Journal of Consumer Affairs* is a scholarly publication written by college teachers and intended primarily for the membership of the council. Articles average 10–15 pages and are replete with charts, graphs, and other tables. Two Summer 1974 articles discussed the Federal Trade Commission's consumer protection activities and food shopping in supermarkets. Lengthy reviews of consumer-related books are a regular feature. Not for the general consumer, but for professionals and students of consumer affairs. The four-page *Consumer Education Forum* is, as its name implies, a chatty exchange of ideas and activities for use in consumer education classes below the college level. The four-page *ACCI Newsletter* contains short summaries of federal, state, and international consumer actions as well as an annotated list of recent consumer resource materials.

117. Berger, Robert, and Joseph Teplin. **Law and the Consumer.** (Justice in America Series). Houghton Mifflin, 1974. 102 pp. Paper $1.84.

The authors provide information on laws on advertising, credit, contracts, and breach of contracts, in addition to a few guidelines on how consumers can help themselves. They explain certain laws, e.g., Truth in Lending, written contracts, implied promises, and fair bargains, and give examples of each as well as safeguards against false advertising and fraudulent sales contracts. Each section includes a few important consumer cases with a discussion on how and why the state or federal courts decided them. The book is aimed at the junior high school student, and each chapter is interspersed with questions and classroom assignments. Written in an intelligent manner, it is nicely documented and attractively presented and should hold the student's attention.

118. ***CAN: Consumer Action Now.*** Linda Stewart, ed. Consumer Action Now, 1970– . Illus. Monthly. $5.

The offical newsletter of Consumer Action Now, a volunteer consumer group based in New York City, each four-page issue deals with one topic and covers it in depth. Over the years, issues have been devoted to air pollution and cars, water pollution, solid wastes, additives in breads and other foods, dangers in toys and household cleaning products, no-fault insurance, how to fight city hall, and over-the-counter drugs. Articles on the OTCs cover the psychological push to pills in our culture, a very good explanation of the similarities and differences between brand-name and generic drugs, and a drug dictionary that notes popular OTCs, lists their ingredients, brand names, and prices, and points out dangers from use. Writing and illustrations are excellent, and occasionally even humorous. The newsletter provides a great deal of practical information on a variety of subjects of interest to consumers everywhere, and it does so at a very low cost. Highly recommended.

119. ***Caveat Emptor: The Consumer Protection Monthly.*** Robert L. Berko, ed. Caveat Emptor, 1971– . Illus. Monthly. $5.95.

This 24-page monthly is a strange compendium of sensational headlines and stories, reprints from news sources and other magazines, and solid articles by respected consumer advocates (e.g., Ralph Nader, Herbert Denenberg, Michael Jacobson), all printed on cheap newsprint and hideously illustrated. A good article by Senator Barry Goldwater on why Congress should repeal Social Security earnings limitations and another by Herbert Denenberg on pensions (both in the May 1974 issue) must be contrasted with such sensational articles as "Death from O-T-C Laxatives" and "Safety Tips for Streakers" in the June 1974 issue. Monthly features include "Hazardous Products" and "Frauds of the Month." In spite of the good features, the format, headlines, and editing are so poor that it is difficult to recommend the magazine, and it may be considered only as secondary material.

120. ***Consumer Close-Ups.*** New York State College of Agriculture, Life Sciences and Human Ecology, Cooperative Extension, Consumer Education, 1968– . Monthly. Individual copies free, 100 copies, $1.25.

Each two–four page issue of *Consumer Close-Ups* is devoted to one topic. The May 27, 1974, issue discussed credit and defined credit bureaus and credit ratings and explained how a systematized credit reporting system works. The June 24, 1974 issue was on the Federal Trade Commission, and it explained the purposes of the FTC, its method of regulation, and its operations. The newsletters, free to home economists and others who can show professional need, can be used with junior and senior high school and adult education classes, as well as with consumer self-help groups.

121. ***Consumer New$week.** Arthur E. Rowse, ed. Consumer News, 1967– Weekly. $15.

Formerly *U.S. Consumer*, the four-page newsletter features "news you can use from the Nation's Capital." It stresses government action (or inaction), with cover stories usually filling page 1. The July 8, 1974, issue highlighted the relationship of early sugar diets in rats to high cholesterol levels in adulthood as well as a chart of electric appliances, their average wattages, and their use of kilowatts per year. The Nixon administration view of the consumer as the cause of inflation, a Federal Trade Commission suit against Sears, Roebuck for bait and switch tactics, and a report of some unsafe intrauterine devices (IUDs) were in the July 15, 1974, edition. The newsletter also notes cases before courts in various states and in Washington and significant actions of consumer groups around the country. For use by consumer action groups and schools, rather than by individual consumers wanting to save or stretch their dollars.

122. Corr, Francis A. **Government Services for Consumers.** (The Consumer Education Series). Pendulum, 1973. 76 pp. Paper $1.25.

In spite of its title, there is very little information in this booklet that deals with "Government Services for Consumers." Instead, there is information on worker protection (including unions), filing and determining income taxes, etc. One chapter deals very generally with government protection agencies and another with how consumers can protect themselves. All in all, not very useful.

123. Driscoll, James G. **Survival Tactics: Coping with the Pressure of Today's Living.** Dow-Jones, 1973. 253 pp. Paper $2.95.

A collection of articles which ran in Driscoll's *National Observer* column, "Survival Tactics," some of them show how individuals have fought against and beaten the system, others describe cases that still have not been decided in the courts, and many deal with people in a lighthearted mood "coping with pressure." They range from stories of a commuter suit against the Baltimore & Ohio Railroad for stopping commuter service to reader suggestions for improving auto repair services and reducing frauds to a fish store owner's battle to win a proper credit rating. One article is about football wives, another describes a contest to determine whether watermelon cools one off better than does a hard drink, a third deals with ways to enliven hospitals and nursing homes (and pair them companionably with orphanages and schools). The book is arranged by very broad subject categories, there is no index, and information on a given subject is difficult to find. But most of the columns are fun to read and many offer interesting and novel methods of coping.

124. Drury, Treesa Way, and William L. Roper. **Consumer Power.** Nash, 1974. 245 pp. $6.95; paper $3.95.

The emphasis here is on getting consumers to use their power to effect change. Well-intentioned, loaded with good material, it is nonetheless poorly arranged, and the missing index makes information retrieval particularly difficult. Drury and Roper, both consumer activists, discuss six major areas of concern: auto safety, food purity, advertising, health care and insurance, buying a home and moving, and atomic power plants. One chapter concerns common myths that harm consumers, e.g., that the Food and Drug Administration assures the efficacy of all prescription medicines, or that the Toy Safety Act certifies all toys on the market hazardfree. The last two chapters deal with steps consumers can take to fight back and to organize action groups. Tips are inserted midchapter, information on individual suits are used to "prove" that individuals can effect change, and so on. "How to Fight Back" haphazardly covers suggestions for making buying power count, how and when to write or complain to government and industry, how to sue and get legal help, successful court cases, tips on buying food and clothing and on how to buy cars. Regarding buying cars, the authors are against it in today's market and offer tips for keeping the old one. "How to Organize for Consumer Action" is well arranged and informative. Appendices list state consumer agencies and attorneys general, a few national consumer organizations and state groups, and a very short bibliography.

125. ***FDA Consumer.** Food and Drug Administration, Office of Consumer Affairs, 1971– . Illus. Monthly (10 issues a yr). $5.30.

Offering advice to consumers on how to use products safely and on scientific developments and new regulations of the Food and Drug Administration, it covers all products under the jurisdiction of the department: food, drugs, medical devices, cosmetics. Many of the well-written articles are signed. Not surprisingly, the articles tend to back up current FDA positions, e.g., "A Primer on Food Additives" provides a short history of the FDA and its laws and states that consumers need not fear for their safety; additives and chemicals are approved only after the most stringent tests. A supplement, *FDA Consumer Memo*, is also provided. Recent issues of the one-page flyer have covered brochures available from the FDA and information on how to report "mislabelled, insanitary or otherwise harmful" products to the department. Regional offices are also listed.

126. Fortune Magazine Editors. **Consumerism: Things Ralph Nader Never Told You.** (Perennial Library). Harper & Row, 1972. 113 pp. Paper 95¢.

Six essays which deal with phosphate controversy, toy safety, food additives, auto safety, appliances and servicing, and packaging and waste, that appeared in *Fortune* magazine in the first half of 1972. While the editors note arguments on both sides of each issue, they are obviously on the side of the manufacturer and/or packager. There are few suggestions for the consumer, but guidance can be picked up between the lines, e.g., buying a product is a vote for it; boycotting expresses consumer displeasure. Multifaceted problems in consumer controversies are highlighted, e.g., "Tempest in Toyland" notes that marbles and baseball bats are probably the two most dangerous toys, but no one is trying to ban them; that there is no consensus on whether children are harmed by commercials, and no one knows how they can be protected. The editors feel that the newly created Major Appliance Consumer Action Panel (MACAP) will help reduce consumer dissatisfaction, that recycling of products has drawbacks, and that some packaging reduces pollution. (On the last they point out that plastic wrap results in less spoilage in lettuce and grapes.) Definitely against headlong intervention in the marketplace, the arguments here are somewhat similar to Peterson's in *The Regulated Consumer* (*see* entry 142).

127. Fuller, John G. **200,000,000 Guinea Pigs: New Dangers in Everyday Foods, Drugs, and Cosmetics.** Putnam, 1972. 320 pp. $7.95

Updating the 1933 classic, *100,000,000 Guinea Pigs* by Arthur Kallet and F. J. Schlink, it covers many of the same subjects, often denounces the same manufacturers and brands. Fuller's thesis is that the situation today is worse than it was in 1933: modern science and technology having brought more hazards and greater dangers (dangers so great that they more than overshadow problems, such as poor quality and outrageous prices for goods and services). His book deals with toys, drugs, mouthwashes, food, and more. He documents dozens of cases of unsafe drugs sold and prescribed when "ethical" pharmaceutical firms were aware of the probabilities of cancer, prenatal deformities, and drug dependencies, or when carelessness led to botulism and skin diseases. Fuller recounts the disasters of mercury in fish, insecticide poisonings, death from hexachloraphene, and he denounces the FDA for its stand on cyclamates and saccharin as well as for allowing so many additives and preservatives on the GRAS (Generally Regarded as Safe) list. He states the case well for tougher laws and tougher enforcement as the only ways to safeguard consumers.

128. Gaedeke, Ralph M., and Warren W. Etcheson. **Consumerism: Viewpoints from Business, Government, and the Public Interest.** Harper & Row, Canfield Press, 1972. 401 pp. Paper $5.95.

The consumer movement, presenting many of the best arguments and viewpoints of buyers, sellers, and consumer advocates, this collection is keyed to 12 introductory college textbooks as a source of supplementary readings for business students. Articles cover the history and major issues of consumerism here and abroad, government's role in protecting consumers (existing programs, proposed legislation and consumer representation within government), and the business response (meeting the challenge of stricter product standards and better self-regulation). Appendices include a three-page list of significant U.S. consumer protection legislation from 1872 to 1971, some consumer bills introduced into the 92nd Congress (1971–1972) without specifying which, if any, of the bills became law, and a list of important government-financed consumer activities in nine western European countries and in Canada. Although many of the articles are reprinted from business journals, such as the *University of Washington Business Review*, the *Akron Business and Economic Review*, and *Sales Management*, articles are also presented from consumer-oriented sources, such as Ralph Nader's *Unsafe at Any Speed* and the *Final Report of the National Commission on Product Safety*.

129. Herndon, Booton. **Satisfaction Guaranteed: An Unconventional Report to Today's Consumers.** McGraw-Hill, 1972. 342 pp. $8.95.

Commissioned by the Montgomery Ward Company to show off their best side. While most of this poorly written book is both elementary in approach and extremely self-congratulatory, one chapter, "The Challenge of the Consumer," is a fairly straightforward explanation of sales, price reductions, and ways to get the best prices and values. Herndon discusses standard brands versus private labels, gives an account of the fight to promote permanent labeling information on garments, and explains the pros and cons of credit, service, and repair warranties. On Consumers Union ratings, the position of Montgomery Wards seems to be that CU is correct when it rates the company high and mistaken in its testing procedure when it rates the company low. A valid criticism is that frequently CU will test an old model instead of the newest one or not rate major manufacturers at all. The book itself must be read carefully, but it is one of the few written entirely from a manufacturer's and seller's point of view. As such, it acts as a counterpoint to much of the current consumer literature.

130. Leinwald, Gerald, ed. **The Consumer.** (Problems of American Society). Washington Square, 1970. 190 pp. Paper 75¢.

Part of a series intended for use as a text in urban schools, this book highlights the problems facing consumers. Part 1, an overview of the subject, focuses on the plight of the poor, e.g., higher prices, shoddy merchandise, swindles, the need for learning how to budget, how to use credit, and how to read labels wisely. The negative aspects of advertising, such as creating needs for new products and dissatisfaction with old ones are noted. A few consumer agencies and organizations are also listed. Part 2 consists of 15 readings excerpted from a variety of sources, e.g., the *Wall Street Journal, Unsafe at Any Speed* (*see* entry 24), *The Medicine Show* (*see* entry 188), *$$$ and Sense* (*see* entry 75), *The Innocent Consumer vs. the Exploiters* (*see* entry 134). The readings highlight such problems as consumer gyps, false advertising, shoddy merchandise, life on a welfare allowance, and having to budget on a restricted income. Questions for further discussion follow each selection.

131. Lewis, James, ed. **The Consumer's Fight-Back Book.** Award, 1972. 154 pp. Paper 95¢.

Exposes the frauds and swindles, shoddy merchandise, and poor services that cost American consumers over $200 billion a year and gives tactics for fighting back. In the home, consumers are advised to be wary of the telephone company, home appliance repairmen, and mail and telephone swindlers. Credit cards and easy credit leading to debt are a second major area of concern. Consumers are shown how to fight creditors and how to get bank loans and insurance. Retail auto-buying schemes, and frauds perpetuated by auto repair persons and auto tire dealers are likewise detailed. Commenting on the sorry state of medical and dental services, the writers think that little can be done other than to get good professional help in the first place. *The Consumer's Fight-Back Book* is best when highlighting corrupt practices and services and showing how and where to complain. Too often it can lead readers to think that all complaints get action, and that all legitimate cases are resolved in favor of the consumer.

132. McClellan, Grant S., ed. **The Consuming Public.** (The Reference Shelf, vol. 40, no. 3). Wilson, 1968. 219 pp. $4.50.

Short articles chosen with care and intelligence, presenting a spectrum of views on various facets of the consumer problem, its sections are entitled "The Citizen as Consumer," "The Role of Government as Protector," "Business and Consumer Protection," "Consumer Concerns," and "Consumer Interest Movement." Articles are reprinted from sources as varied as *Consumer Reports*, the *New York Times, Congressional Digest, Fortune, Vital Speeches of the Day, Harvard Business Review,* and *Newsweek.* Some of the material is dated, and some (with hindsight) is shown to have been overly optimistic. Nonetheless, this is interesting reading.

133. Magnuson, Warren G., and Jean Carper. **The Dark Side of the Marketplace: The Plight of the American Consumer.** Prentice-Hall, 1968. 240 pp. $5.95.

Senator Magnuson, chairman of the Senate Commerce Committee, and Jean Carper, formerly editor of the National Safety Council's magazine, *Family Safety*, have coauthored this book dealing with the flagrant misconduct and frauds carried out in the name of business. There are stories of deceptive practices in selling and advertising, of victimization of the poor beyond their understanding or financial means, of betrayal of consumers by manufacturers of shoddy and dangerous products, and a discussion of business and morality (the selling of quack medicines and medical devices, attempts to produce a safe cigarette). The book is filled with case after case highlighting the immorality of manufacturers and salespeople and the lack of protection afforded consumers who think they are safe from physical and economic abuse. Written in 1968, some of the worst practices have been outlawed, but most of the material is as true today as it was then.

134. Margolius, Sidney. **The Innocent Consumer vs. the Exploiters.** Trident, 1967. 240 pp. $6.95.

As its title implies, this book shows the many ways in which consumers are cheated by virtue of their naiveté. Methods range from high interest charges on credit cards and small loans to garnishment of wages, repossessions of merchandise, and inflated prices for packaging, convenience foods (often with little nutritive value), supermarket expenses, and advertising costs. Consumer expert Margolius exposes fraudulent home improvement practices and overcharges as well as referral plan hoaxes. (The latter are plans in which those who buy certain products are promised bonuses for referring others who buy. The bonuses are rare, but the installment contracts are valid and prices are high.) Deceptive pricing practices: exaggerated list prices, contest "winnings," buying "repossessed" goods, and bait selling are detailed. The high costs of brand-name drugs and (inadequate) mail order health insurance are also covered. Margolius points up the low quality of goods in general and stresses the need for safety, performance, identity standards, and quality grading. The concluding chapter is devoted to those few consumer protection laws and methods of legal redress available in 1967. This situation has changed somewhat for the better since then, but Margolius's thesis is still valid. Appendices list major consumer organizations and Better Business Bureaus.

135. Margolius, Sidney. **The Responsible Consumer.** (Pamphlet no. 453). Public Affairs, 1970. 20 pp. Paper 35¢. Quantity orders discounted.

In his discussion of consumerism and protection and problems of consumers, Margolius points out that although most states have established consumer agencies, and the federal government has passed laws, the agencies often have no policing powers, and the problems remain. Advances are also noted, e.g., toy safety standards, reductions in the number of sizes on consumer items, such as soaps and jellies, and the drug amendment to the Food, Drug and Cosmetic Act. He discusses credit costs, and includes a calendar of annual sales for wise shopping. Margolius stresses the need for consumers to be aware of their rights and aware of the laws, to band together in consumer groups, and to spend money wisely as well as to earn it well. A few sources of help and information are listed, ranging from state and federal agencies (insurance departments, the Federal Trade Commission) to private organizations, such as credit unions, cooperatives, labor unions, and Better Business Bureaus.

136. ***Media & Consumer.** Francis Pollock, ed. Media & Consumer Foundation, 1973– . Illus. Monthly. $12.

The nonprofit public service *Media & Consumer* was started by a grant from Consumers Union in 1973. Its 16 pages are a compilation of reprints or highlights of consumer-oriented news stories and broadcast transcripts ("Clip Service"); evaluations of the news media ("Journalism Review"); articles on "Consumer Action" taken by individuals and groups, and columns, letters, and editorials from the media ("Commentary"). Each issue features several articles of one–two pages and dozens of shorter ones. The April 1974 issue highlighted what readers can do about school bus safety, how to rate creditors by collection clout, and how to compute bank interest. The May 1974 issue exposed censorship in the news media and vocational schools as "fast buck" businesses, and explained how to evaluate nursing homes. *Media & Consumer* provides readers with a wealth of lively, well-written information from sources as diverse as *Sports Illustrated, Sales Management,* the *Baltimore Sun,* the *Wall Street Journal,* and the *Boston Globe.* It is undoubtedly the best new consumer periodical on the market. Highly recommended.

137. Murray, Barbara B., ed. **Consumerism—the Eternal Triangle: Business, Government and Consumers.** Goodyear, 1973. 469 pp. Paper $5.95.

These readings (many of them from such business periodicals as the *Wall Street Journal, American Economic Review,* and *Journal of Marketing*), dating mainly from the 1970s, are, for the most part, serious attempts at highlighting the problems of consumerism; emphasizing the relationship between business, government, and consumers in their social, economic, and marketing aspects, and offering constructive solutions. Arrangement is by subject: the role of the Federal Trade Commission as the single most important enforcement agency of consumer legislation; the need for changing credit and lending laws, the value of the Truth-in-Packaging Law; warranties and product liability; problems of low-income groups in the marketplace. Well researched and thorough in coverage, *Consumerism* would be an excellent supplement to college-level consumer courses.

138. Nader, Ralph, ed. **The Consumer and Corporate Accountability.** Harcourt Brace Jovanovich, 1973. 375 pp. Paper $4.95.

Utilizing excerpts and reports from magazines, newspapers, books, government hearings, testimonies, etc., that touch on all aspects of business and the consumer, it deals specifically with the problems of corporate accountability to make the public aware of the dimensions of "corporate irresponsibility" and to push for citizen action. The book is divided into sections with such titles as "Corporate Disregard for Life," which includes material on cigarette advertising, automobile hazards, and flammable clothes for children, and "Truth versus Profits in Advertising," with information on drug companies peddling dangerous drugs and the nutritionless cereals sold to children. Other sections deal with "Compulsory Consumption," "Consumer Waste and Frustration" (supermarket overcosts and waste, infringement of privacy) "The Regulatory-Industrial Complex" (traces the strands that bind business and government), "Dissent from Within" (material on people who did not go along with the system), and "The New Accountability: An Agenda for Action." Suggestions include controlling monopolistic prices, deterring business crime, federal "chartering" for firms engaged in interstate business that would involve policing and enabling provisions, corporate disclosure, etc. Should be read in the classroom as well as in the home, to provide as wide an audience as possible.

139. Nader, Ralph, Peter J. Petkas, and Kate Blackwell, eds. **Whistle Blowing: Report of the Conference on Professional Responsibility.** Grossman, 1972. 302 pp. $6.95. Bantam. Paper $1.95.

Speeches by keynote speakers Ralph Nader, Senator William Proxmire, business reform advocate Robert Townsend, and Professor Arthur S. Miller of the National Law Center at the January 30, 1971, conference comprise the first section of the book. They describe the function of whistle blowing and the ethics and legality of the persons who blow the whistles. Section 2 focuses on 12 famous cases, among them A. Ernest Fitzgerald and the cost overrun of the Lockheed C-5A, Dr. Jacqueline Verrett and cyclamates, William Stieglitz and federal auto safety standards, and the Colt Firearms Company workers and the Colt M-16 rifle. It shows what happened to the causes they espoused and, in many cases, the punishments the individuals received. Section 3 suggests changes that must be made in corporations, government, and law to protect employees trying for change. It suggests strong professional societies and labor unions to protect individuals, responsive corporate structures, ombudsmen, civil service reform, and laws to protect the employee as well as the employer. "Strategies for Whistle Blowers," section 4, explains when and how to blow the whistle ethically, legally, and effectively. Appendices include codes of ethics of chemists, engineers, lawyers, and doctors and a model draft of an "Employee Rights and Accountability Act" for the future safeguarding of persons involved in whistle blowing.

140. ***OCA Consumer News.** Ed Riner, ed. Office of Consumer Affairs, Department of Health, Education and Welfare, 1970– . 24 issues a yr. $4.

Issues highlight federal consumer activities, report on product safety, and note proposed legislation and issued standards and regulations. One four-page issue (August 1, 1974) featured the Consumer Product Safety Commission's bicycle safety standards plus regulations on bikes by the Department of Transportation and recommendations by the National Highway Safety Advisory Commission and the Federal Highway Administration. Other articles in the same issue dealt with safe canning of fruits and vegetables, electrical brownouts, and warnings on brands of spray shampoos and pesticide aerosols. The *OCA Consumer Register* is a one-page supplement which summarizes the most recent items of consumer interest that appear in the *Federal Register.* It cites the regulations or standards in the *Federal Register,* refers to news articles in past issues of *Consumer News*, and explains where consumers can send comments, notifications, or inquiries.

141. ***Of Consuming Interest.** Jane S. Wilson, ed. Federal-State Reports, 1967– . Weekly. $72.

Consumer information "for those who supply consumer goods and services," the four-page newsletter covers federal, state, county, and municipal agencies, court decisions, laws and legislation (proposed, pending, and passed), consumer advocates and lobbies, and industry-related information on consumer affairs. There even are reports on materials available to consumers, e.g., the October 2, 1974, issue reported on a 72-page *Prescription Price Book* published by Osco Drug, Inc., covering 95 percent of all prescription prices in its 17-state drug chain. The material is presented in an impartial manner—so consumers as well as suppliers could use the newsletter to stay abreast of current events. The price, however, puts it out of reach except through libraries.

142. Peterson, Mary Bennett. **The Regulated Consumer.** (Principles of Freedom Series). Nash, 1971. 271 pp. $7.95.

Peterson, conservative author of the *Wall Street Journal* column "Reading for Business," feels that government regulation is interventionist and against the interests of the consumer. As an economist, she believes in "benign" regulation, that is, setting standards and codes. All else is against competition and therefore against consumers. Here she explores the problems arising from seven federal agencies: Food and Drug Administration, Antitrust Division of the Justice Department, Federal Trade Commission, National Labor Relations Board, Interstate Commerce Commission, Civil Aeronautics Board, and Federal Communications Commission. She quotes consumer advocates, such as Nader and others, who have written books damning these regulatory agencies. Peterson's thesis, however, is that the consumerists, although well-meaning, are looking in the wrong place for help. She feels business and industry should regulate itself, and that competition, the keystone of the free enterprise system, will keep the marketplace healthy. She also thinks that too much energy has been spent in defending the consumer against deceptive practices. Citing the cyclamate and thalidomide blunders, court cases against the electrical manufacturing companies for price fixing, and more, Peterson says most of our regulatory laws are anticonsumer and should be repealed.

143. †**The Poor Pay More.** National Educational Television (Indiana University—Audio-Visual Center, dist.), 1967. B&W. Sound. 16 mm. 60 min. Sale $200. Rent $9.15.

A feature of NET's "Journal," *The Poor Pay More* graphically illustrates how those in ghetto neighborhoods are preyed upon by fraudulent salespeople and discriminated against by utilities and stores. A community action group, Massive Economic Neighborhood Development (MEND), catches a door-to-door salesman misrepresenting a food-freezer plan. An attorney shows how local supermarkets raise prices when welfare checks come in and use ghetto stores as dumping grounds for old and/or inferior foods. The telephone company is shown discriminating against people who live in poor neighborhoods (by insisting on deposits not asked of people living in other neighborhoods). The film uses real people. It was filmed in New York City and names national as well as local stores as culprits. The need to change the system as well as to educate the poor is stressed.

144. Ramparts Magazine with Frank Browning. **In the Marketplace: Consumerism in America.** Harper & Row, Canfield Press, 1972. 245 pp. Paper $2.95.

A collection of well-researched, carefully written, thought-provoking articles from books and magazines detailing the machinations of various businesses, media, and government agencies which work against consumers and provide poor, fraudulent, or nonexistent products, services, and regulations. Part 1 includes articles by Ralph Nader on cars, Jessica Mitford on the Famous Writers School, and Larry Luce on gasoline additives. The three chapters in the second section deal with passenger trains and the Interstate Commerce Commission, the American health crisis and the Health Policy Advisory Committee, and the mental health industry. Part 3 exposes the advertising, television, and radio industries for creating our current unnecessary consumer needs.

145. Ross, Donald K. **A Public Citizen's Action Manual.** Grossman, 1973. 237 pp. $5.95; paper $1.95.

An extremely practical (Nader-sponsored) action manual with blueprints to correct inequities in the consumer society by banding together in Nader-like groups, it stresses the necessity of local citizen action for local change. "Projects to Protect the Consumer" includes ways to reform the Automobile Association of America, evaluate pension funds, survey bank interest rates, and detect and correct fraudulent repair rackets. "Some Prescriptions for Better Health Care" details projects to promote toy safety, fight noise, lower prescription drug prices, enforce the Occupational Safety and Health Act, and make Blue Cross and Blue Shield consumer advocates. "Shifting the Tax Burden" shows how to determine whether local industries and citizenry are being assessed fairly—and how to repair the inequities. "Making Government Responsive" explains how to judge legislators, form citizens lobbies, hold hearings, investigate government agencies, evaluate government inspection programs, and improve small claims courts. "Fashioning the Tools of Citizenship" discusses specialized action groups and clubs, shows how to mobilize students and how to form such groups. For each project, the author outlines past (mostly successful) activities and explains how to adapt the approach to new situations. A very practical suggestion is to write to the original group and get their material. Highly recommended.

146. Sanford, David. **Who Put the Con in Consumer?** Liveright, 1972. 166 pp. Paper $2.95.

Offers more than it delivers, and while it documents many of the abuses of the marketplace, it does so in a manner more lighthearted than its subject warrants. Chapter headings, which are not indicative of actual content, also detract from the book. On the plus side, Sanford takes aim at food conglomerates whose goal is profits at the expense of the nation's health and pocketbooks, the tobacco industry and the U.S. government for allowing tobacco advertising, television executives for general timidity on consumer safety and advertising aimed at children, landlords whose leases and actions are unconscionable but legal, and manufacturers who produce shoddy merchandise and worthless guarantees. "Politics in the Marketplace" pokes fun at people who boycott goods out of principle (e.g., grapes) as well as at outmoded laws (e.g., those prohibiting the sale of nondefense items to unfriendly nations). The author is against laxness in government, wanting more laws with stronger teeth and a tougher Office of Consumer Affairs. Sanford feels the best recourse for consumers who buy shoddy merchandise and/or service and get no satisfaction is to take to the picket lines, and he lists rules for picketing taken from *What to Do with Your Bad Car* (*see* entry 14).

147. Schrag, Philip G. **Counsel for the Deceived: Case Studies in Consumer Fraud.** Pantheon, 1972. 200 pp. $5.95.

Personal recollections of Philip Schrag, New York City's first official Consumer Advocate. He documents six cases of consumer fraud, showing the inequities in laws that protect sellers rather than buyers, the exhausting legal work required to get cases to court, and the pitifully few remedies consumers have. Schrag and his lawyers, working as defenders of consumer rights under Bess Myerson, New York City's first Commissioner of Consumer Affairs, had to resort to highly suspect methods themselves to try to win some measure of relief for victims of consumer fraud. He cites cases of "lifetime shopping services," false appliance repairs, misleading advertising, and magazine subscription gyps, and shows that even with airtight cases, buyers are often out cash and service and sellers go unpunished. The ethics of the department, i.e., using deception to fight deception, is discussed. Schrag points out that courts and laws cannot solve consumer fraud, and he feels that consumer education is of limited value. His strongest recommendations are consumer class actions and neighborhood arbitration tribunals as well as corporate self-policing and executive accountability. This book will leave readers discouraged, as it highlights the ineffectiveness of even strong consumer laws and departments.

148. Solomon, Goody L. **The Radical Consumer's Handbook.** Ballantine, 1972. 174 pp. Paper $1.25.

Solomon, who was executive editor of the Office for Consumer Affairs, U.S. Department of Health, Education and Welfare, is a long time advocate of consumer causes. Her book is a philosophical expression of "radical consumerism" and a blueprint for consumer action. Despite its name, "radical consumerism" encompasses a rather conservative desire for "fairness in the marketplace, and an end to . . . economic waste"—i.e., an end to immoral and/or criminal practices through strong policing of the marketplace, an agency created to speak for consumers, grievance-solving mechanisms (consumer class actions), and a knowledgeable public. Her blueprint for action consists of learning to seek redress for personal grievances, organizing for strength, and buying wisely. Solomon offers "gripe tactics": methods of complaint to businesses and trade associations and federal, state, and local governments, along with names, addresses, and telephone numbers. A guide to small claims courts is reprinted from the October 1971 *Consumer Reports.* Solomon explains how to use the law and points up the need to strengthen existing laws. Chapters on group power highlight past accomplishments of consumer groups, group tactics, and a list of private organizations to contact and/or join. A short chapter on becoming a "knowing consumer" (learning how to buy wisely) completes the book.

149. Winter, Ralph K., Jr. **The Consumer Advocate Versus the Consumer.** (Special Analysis No. 26). American Enterprise Institute for Public Policy Research, 1972, 16 pp. Paper $2.

This is a succinct and provocative analysis of consumer ideology, possibilities for change, and reasons why (in the opinion of the author) the cure—more regulatory agencies and more regulations—would be worse than the disease. Winter, professor of law at Yale University Law School, and ardent proponent of laissez-faire, feels that the creation of a Consumer Protection Agency is an admission of failure by all agencies designed to regulate the marketplace. He asks why the public should feel that a new agency would be any better, and who would police the new agency.

CONSUMER PROTECTION—DIRECTORIES

For pertinent organizations see Part II, Private Organizations—Center for Study of Responsive Law.

150. Directory of State and Local Government and Non-Government Consumer Groups. Consumer Federation of America, 1973. 29 pp. Paper $2.

This directory lists the name, address, telephone number, and head of state and local government and private groups in the United States, Puerto Rico and the Virgin Islands. Although the Consumer Federation of America compiled most of the data in 1973, the information is still reliable.

151. Sprecher, Daniel, ed. **Directory of Government Agencies Safeguarding Consumer and Environment.** 5th ed. Serina, 1974. 119 pp. Paper $5.95.

Arranged by subject, this directory lists the federal and state officials responsible for assistance, advice, action, and information in 16 areas of consumer and environmental concern. Of these, nine pertain to consumers: automobile safety, consumer protection, food and drugs, insurance, land sales, meat and poultry surveillance, movement of household effects, pesticide regulations, and weights and measures. The names, addresses, and telephone numbers of key personnel are listed. Frequently, regional and district officers of federal agencies are also noted. Jurisdictional maps of various U.S. agencies are included, such as the Marketing and Consumer Service of the Department of Agriculture and the Food and Drug Administration of the Department of Health, Education and Welfare. Updated fairly regularly, the directory fulfills a useful, if limited, function.

152. Thomas, Sarah M., and Bernadine Weddington. *A Guide to Sources of Consumer Information.* Information Resources, 1973. 177 pp. $10.50.

This guide is ostensibly to sources of information for the consumer: books, directories, documents, periodicals, and indexes published since 1960, and including organizations on the private as well as governmental levels. The authors admit that many items have been overlooked and many are included that should have been omitted. They state that "no effort has been made to judge the quality of the material listed." This is evident from the inclusion of the *New York Times Magazine*, *Drug and Cosmetic Industry*, and *Cosmopolitan* in the periodicals section, National Restaurant Association and the Neighborhood Cleaners Association under private organizations, and much more. Not recommended.

153. Trzyna, Thaddeus C., ed. **Directory of Consumer Protection and Environmental Agencies.** Academic Media, 1973. 627 pp. $39.50.

According to the editors, 194 pages are listings of organizations "concerned with the right of the consumer . . . to safety, freedom of choice, adequate information, sources of redress, quality, and integrity." They run the gamut from national, state, and local governmental agencies to national and local private organizations. Of the 901 listings, 117 are devoted to the purposes, key personnel and addresses of local Better Business Bureaus, over 100 to state environmental health and sanitarian associations (better listed in the second half of the book with other environmental agencies), and private groups, such as the National Cable Television Association (which represents the interests of some 1,100 operating cable TV systems) and the Federal Bar Association (an organization of attorneys now or formerly in federal service). Had the editors not found the need to lengthen the book unnecessarily, they would have performed a better and more useful service. Information on each organization lists name, address, telephone number, key personnel, purposes, activities, and publications, if any. Not really worth the price.

154. U.S. Office of Consumer Affairs. **Directory of State, County, and City Government Consumer Offices.** 1974. 44 pp. Paper $1.10.

The latest compilation of state, county, and city consumer offices reported to the Office of Consumer Affairs. On the state level, this includes consumer protection agencies, consumer advisers to governors, and offices of the attorneys general concerned with consumer interests. For each listing, the name, address, and telephone number of the person in charge is given. When branch offices exist, these are listed too. A chart of the administrative locations of state consumer offices is included.

155. U.S. Office of Consumer Affairs. **Forming Consumer Organizations.** 1972. 32 pp. Paper 35¢.

An excellent guide specifically designed for people wishing to organize into consumer groups; that is, while the steps shown on how to form groups, set up bylaws, and define standing and special committees are general enough to be of use to any group, there is also material covering consumer groups in particular. This includes a statement of the purpose of a voluntary consumer organization, an agenda for a meeting to organize, and the duties of some typical special committees, e.g., a business relations committee which works with local businesses to promote business-consumer relations, an education committee which develops guides for consumer education for use in schools. The pamphlet also includes 31 suggestions for programs and projects for consumer organizations and/or consumer committees of other organizations, a sample press release, and a bibliography of paperback books on consumer and organizational material.

156. U.S. Office of Consumer Affairs. **Guide to Federal Consumer Services.** 1971. 151 pp. Paper $1.

An excellent guide to information on consumer services provided by the federal government in 1971, it is now slightly outdated. The directory lists each agency concerned with such services and notes its main purposes, the principal laws it administers, major functions for consumers and how they are enforced, how to obtain service, and selected publications. The subject index is good, but cross-references would help.

157. Wasserman, Paul, and Jean Morgan, eds. **Consumer Sourcebook.** Gale, 1974. 593 pp. $35.

Wasserman and Morgan intended this as "a comprehensive compilation detailing the primary information sources, printed and otherwise, available to the American consumer . . . a one-stop source of supply for the consumer's needs." The section on government organizations consists, therefore, of a reprint of much of the (1971) annotated *Guide to Federal Consumer Services* ($1; *see* entry 156) and the nonannotated *Directory of State, County and City Government Consumer Offices* (1973 ed.; *see* entry 154). The editors never define or limit their subject; consequently, much of the material on private associations, centers, and institutes is extraneous. So, too, is the selected bibliography with annotations on farming information, the environment, food technology, and more. The bibliography is idiosyncratic and has too many outdated and/or out-of-print materials all lumped together by format without regard to content. The section on newspapers has been reprinted from a similar list in *Editor and Publisher*, with errors and misspellings unchanged. The largest section, "Companies and Trade Names," takes up an excessive amount of space to provide the name of a single person in each company to complain to. (The *Consumer Complaint Guide*, at $2.95 for the paperback, does just as well. *see* entry 54). A flawed book with a high price.

CONSUMER PROTECTION—HISTORY

158. Faber, Doris. **Enough! The Revolt of the American Consumer.** Farrar, Straus & Giroux, 1972. 184 pp. $4.50.

Faber presents an optimistic, popularized history of America's consumer movement beginning with its first consumer advocate, Dr. Harvey W. Wiley. In 1883, heading the chemistry division of the Department of Agriculture, Wiley lobbied for pure foods and drugs, labeling on packages, and other issues still unsettled. Faber traces the movement from passage of the Pure Food and Drug Act; founding of Consumers' Research and its offshoot, Consumers Union, Kallet and Schlink's *100,000,000 Guinea Pigs* (1933); the Food, Drug and Cosmetic Act of 1938, to its low point following World War II. She shows the impact of Vance Packard's *Hidden Persuaders* (1957), consumerism under Estes Kefauver, John Kennedy's Consumer Bill of Rights, Dr. Frances Kelsey's vigilance in averting a thalidomide tragedy, and the emergence of Ralph Nader and the current consumer movement. Faber notes the growing responsiveness and upgrading of Better Business Bureaus and "preventive enforcement" by regulatory agencies. The subject of consumer complaints—where they come from and how they are handled—is also covered. Faber concludes that there is much unfinished business—particularly the need to make regulatory agencies enforce laws stringently—but overall, she sees great progress and reason for hope.

159. Roberts, Eirlys. **Consumers.** International Publications Service, 1966. 220 pp. $3.75.

Eirlys Roberts, an editor of *Which?* (the British counterpart of *Consumer Reports* and *Consumers' Research*), writes on the history of the consumer movement from earliest times. She devotes two chapters to consumerism in the United States and shows how it affected consumer efforts in England and Europe. Other chapters deal specifically with developments in the European countries and with governmental as well as international activities. Published in 1966, the book necessarily is not up-to-date. It is, however, a fairly good condensation of the early struggles of twentieth-century consumer advocates and can be used by students and consumer groups studying the movement. A good complement to Faber's *Enough!* (*see* entry 158).

CONSUMER PROTECTION—LAWS AND LEGISLATION

For pertinent organizations see Part II, Private Organizations—Center for Study of Responsive Law; The Consumer Protection Center; Public Interest Research Group.

160. Consumer Class Action Legislation. (Legislative Analysis No. 23). American Enterprise Institute for Public Policy Research, 1972. 39 pp. Paper $2.

In this discussion of issues of consumer class actions by the conservative American Enterprise Institute the section entitled "Background" gives information on the pros and cons of such suits, class actions, and the courts (including federal rules under existing laws), bills in Congress as of August 1972, and proposals for new bills. "Key Issues" examines the effects of class actions on consumers, courts, and business. Since publication, little has been done to pass consumer action legislation, and courts have taken a narrow and restrictive view of them. The pamphlet presents arguments for and against in an unbiased manner, and as such, is a useful learning tool for anyone interested in the subject of consumer legislation.

161. Consumers League of New Jersey. **New Jersey Consumer Protection Laws.** 1971. 53 pp. Paper $2.

This guide to the major consumer protection laws and agencies that will handle consumer complaints in New Jersey is arranged by broad subject areas, e.g., public health laws; consumer credit: direct loans; consumer credit: time sales; marketing of agricultural products; and environmental protection. It lists the laws which the Consumers League of New Jersey feels are of greatest interest and concern to the citizens of the state and notes agencies to which questions and complaints are to be addressed. A chapter devoted to the State Division of Consumer Affairs, Office of the Attorney General, gives information on its enforcement powers. A very useful directory whose value would be enhanced by the inclusion of a subject index to the laws.

162. Morganstern, Stanley. **Legal Protection for the Consumer.** (Oceana Legal Almanac Series #52). Rev. ed. Oceana, 1972. 122 pp. $4.

Sketchy in detail and capricious in its choice of inclusions and exclusions, Morganstern's revision of the 1963 edition by Paul Crown deals mainly with selected state legislation covering deceptive trade practices and advertising. Only 16 states are covered, with several paragraphs devoted to a few other states. Morganstern has a good chapter on the pitfalls of franchise relationships, including a seven-point checklist to consider before entering into a franchise agreement. Another chapter deals with "intelligent buying," and the author gives advice, culled from pamphlets sent by a few state consumer agencies, on how to buy air conditioners and used cars, how to spot health and drug frauds and work-at-home gyps, and some material of use only to New York State residents. Appendices consist of Wisconsin franchise legislation and Ohio consumer legislation. Another drawback of the book is that it leaves consumers with an overly optimistic view of their rights in the marketplace. At best, it is acceptable only as supplementary material.

163. Nadel, Mark V. **The Politics of Consumer Protection.** Bobbs-Merrill, 1971. 257 pp. $8.50.

A detailed analysis of consumer legislation in Congress and an attempt to determine which factors influence the successful passage or failure of such legislation, Nadel's study is basically for the student of government—and only incidentally for consumers—but the material is of use to all. Tracing the history of consumer protection in the United States, Nadel shows that successful legislative passage is tied to arousing public opinion and public pressure; that the more dramatic and immediate the problem, e.g., drug safety and meat purity, the more likely the chances of legislative success. He also shows that consumer protection is a partisan issue, supported mainly by liberal Democrats, and that policy-making centers within government tend to respond to business interests rather than to consumers. Nadel sees the need for strong consumer agencies acting as advocates of the public interest before regulatory and other governmental bodies as well as the need for increasing the consumer constituency to broaden the base of public opinion.

164. Stigler, George J., and Manuel F. Cohen. **Can Regulatory Agencies Protect the Consumer?** American Enterprise Institute for Public Policy Research, 1971. 88 pp. $5.75.

The text of a debate between George J. Stigler (Chicago School of Economics) and Manuel F. Cohen (former chairman of the Securities and Exchange Commission) that was part of the American Enterprise Institute's Rational Debate Seminars. The arguments are given first in lectures by the two speakers and then in discussion moderated by Peter Lisagor. Stigler argues against public regulation and for consumer awareness and intelligence and competition in the marketplace. He feels regulatory agencies cannot control, and that they tend to become advocates of the industries they are supposed to regulate. Cohen, taking the opposite view, feels that regulatory agencies are necessary to protect the consumer and to ensure fair competition in the public interest. He cites regulation in the securities industry to show that it can be successful. Both men find that the tendency toward "bureaucratic ossification" is inherent in the regulatory commissions and a danger that must be constantly watched. In this debate, there is no summation and no conclusion; readers must form their own opinions. Since both men are highly respected in their field, this is a good guide to both sides of this consumer question.

165. †**There Is a Law Against It.** FilmFair Communications, 1972. Color. Sound. 16mm. 8 min. Sale $115. Rent $10.

Designed specifically for California residents, but of use to others, the film points up four consumer hazards and their remedies: unauthorized auto repair work (illegal under the California Auto Repair Act of 1971); garnishment of wages (an individual is entitled to a court hearing, and at most 50 percent of wages may be garnisheed); a payment demand for a paid debt (the remedy is Small Claims Court for items up to $500), and purchases bought from door-to-door salespersons and costing over $50 (such contracts may be revoked in a three-day-cooling-off period). The film makes the point that consumers must be aware of their rights in order to benefit from them. *There Is a Law Against It* was entered in the 1973 American Film Festival sponsored by the Educational Film Library Association (EFLA).

166. U.S. Office of Consumer Affairs. **State Consumer Action—Summary '72.** 1973. 239 pp. Paper $2.60.

A summary of state, county, and city activities reported to the Office of Consumer Affairs for 1972, it is arranged alphabetically by subject, from advertising, antitrust, and automobiles to trade and correspondence schools, utilities and warranties and guarantees. It lists all activities in each field on the three levels. These activities include the formation of consumer agencies, passage of new legislation, and the status of major cases in the courts. An index, arranged by state and subject, shows at a glance all governmental consumer actions in each state for the year. The directory combines items of major interest with those of marginal interest or import, but overall, if updated regularly, would be an excellent source of information for activities below the federal level.

CONTACT LENSES

See Eye Care

CREDIT

See also Debt. *For pertinent organizations see Part II, U.S. Federal Agencies*—Department of Agriculture, Extension Service; Department of Housing and Urban Development, Housing Production and Mortgage Credit—Federal Housing Administration; Federal Trade Commission; Veterans Administration; *Private Organizations*—American Association of Credit Counselors; Consumer Credit Counseling Service of Greater New York; Credit Union National Association, Inc.; National Consumer Finance Association.

167. Black, Hillel. **Buy Now, Pay Later.** Pocket Books, 1962. 240 pp. Paper 50¢.

Black's scrutiny of consumer debt and consumer credit practices is one of the pioneering efforts of the movement. His thesis, that the consumer who buys on credit is often "abused and deceived . . . and (sometimes) outrageously swindled," is well documented and well written. He recounts stories of auto dealers who will not sell cars for cash, finance and loan companies which encourage consumers to stay in debt and raise their debt limits, and credit gouging schemes, such as contracts with blank spaces, prepay swindles, and balloon notes. Some suggestions, such as forming state consumer councils and passing a Truth-in-Lending Law (Black calls it the Federal Consumer Credit Labeling Bill) have seen results. Other suggestions, such as urging consumers to start or join credit unions and to shop carefully for credit, can always stand reiteration.

168. Caplovitz, David. **The Poor Pay More; Consumer Practices of Low-Income Families.** Free Press, 1967. 225 pp. $6.95; paper $2.45.

Originally published in 1963 by the Bureau of Applied Social Research (Columbia University), Caplovitz's study of the consumer practices of low-income families is still relevant today. Not surprisingly, poor families were found to have more consumer problems than their middle-class counterparts. The residents of four low-income housing projects were interviewed about their shopping patterns, costs of credit and goods, lack of assets (and consequent debts), familial attributes that caused insolvency, and unfair selling practices to which they were subjected. The study concludes that in a consumer-oriented society, the poor will not stop purchasing beyond their means, and consequently, their exploitation will continue. Caplovitz believes that consumer education is needed to teach the poor how to buy better quality merchandise in better stores, to pay cash for purchases, and to become acquainted with helpful consumer organizations. He makes a case for more protective legislation, but concludes that reducing poverty is the best way to improve the lot of low-income consumers.

169. Cost of Personal Borrowing in the United States. Charles H. Gushee, ed. Annual. Financial Publishing. $12.50.

Good for anyone shopping for a loan who wants to understand what banks, credit unions, and other financial institutions are really charging. The book is designed to tell the borrower or lender both the dollar costs and the annual percentage rates for the maximum charges, based on monthly payments, of different loans in all 50 states. These include small loans, installment loans, auto loans, industrial loans, and insurance loans. It also explains how to compute interest rates—and how to learn the difference between the actuarial or annual percentage rate, the add-on method rate, the discount-per-year-method rate, and more.

170. Griffin, Al. **The Credit Jungle.** Regnery, 1971. 230 pp. $5.95.

A book aimed at exposing abuses of consumer credit, it highlights the greed of banks, loan and finance companies, and credit card firms. Griffin points out that such abuses can continue due to consumer naiveté and ignorance. He shows how credit card companies have glamorized spending, why banks would stop their credit card business if everyone paid their bills on time, why revolving credit is so good for lenders and so expensive for borrowers, and how overspending has caused an enormous increase in personal bankruptcy. Griffin details many illegal credit practices, particularly those swindles perpetrated on the poor. He notes that stores and banks, in conjunction with schools, have taught the young to value spending over thrift and have conditioned children to credit cards and borrowing at an early age. The chapter on invasion of privacy by credit bureaus is quite frightening. Not surprisingly, Griffin concludes that there is a great need for reform in the credit industry. Some of his suggestions are stopgap measures, but all his points are worth noting. His book should be read by all in an attempt to counter the effects of the procredit advertising in our lives.

171. Margolius, Sidney. **A Guide to Consumer Credit.** (Pamphlet No. 348A). Public Affairs, 1970. 24 pp. Paper 25¢. Quantity orders discounted.

Discussing the advantages and disadvantages of credit, Margolius, who has written on credit extensively, sums up much of his material in this short, but well-thought-out pamphlet. He warns against constant borrowing which causes an enormous drain on the income, but cites instances where reasonable borrowing is good (for example, if a family has a lot of laundry and borrows to buy a washing machine, it will save money in the long run). He compares credit costs from various sources, e.g., credit unions, which charge from 9 to 12 percent annually; department stores, which usually charge 18 percent. Margolius shows why the longer the payments, the higher the costs, and why prepayment of loans will not save much. He covers debt overload, including repossessions and garnishments, and credit standings in relation to the ability to get loans and pay them back.

172. Meyer, Martin J., and Mark Hunter. **How to Turn Plastic into Gold: A Revolutionary New Way to Make Money and Save Money Every Time You Buy Anything—with Credit Cards.** 2nd ed., rev. Farnsworth, 1974. 214 pp. $6.95.

Published in 1971 as *Credit-Cardsmanship*, this slightly updated version is still a somewhat misleading and unethical description of profitable as well as dangerous credit card practices. Meyer shows how to get two months' free credit on charges by using four free bank credit cards, and four months' credit using travel and entertainment cards. He suggests putting the still-available money into day-of-deposit to day-of-withdrawal accounts to earn 5¼ percent interest or into saving certificates to earn over 7 percent. (In respect to the latter, he fails to point out that the money could no longer be used to pay bills.) He is against traveler's checks, even free ones, as they tie up money that could be in savings banks earning interest. He believes in always using credit, unless merchants can be convinced to offer a 2½–3½ percent discount for the use of an "Uncredit Card"—money. (Since credit card companies charge 5–7 percent for the use of their cards, buyers and sellers alike would profit.) Meyer warns users that credit card companies cheat by listing incorrect charges and by rebilling for paid items. To guard against theft, he suggest carrying very few cards, keeping the others under lock and key, and using only cards insured by the issuers. After promoting credit cards as sources of savings, he states that credit card use has led to inflation, crime, and debt addiction, and forsees the time when one credit card will invade our privacy, do away with checks and money, and cause the loss of individuality. One of the most serious flaws is his arguments that saving money is the same as making it, e.g., if an item is bought on sale, in spite of interest charges, the result is profits. He also show how to cheat the system (incurring debts which the borrower knows cannot be paid) under the guise of warning against it. Recommended with heavy reservations.

173. **Money Management: It's Your Credit—Manage It Wisely.** Illus. Money Management Institute, Household Finance Corp., 1970. 42 pp. Paper 50¢. Quantity orders discounted.

An excellent, comprehensive guide to understanding and managing credit. In spite of its being published by Household Finance Corporation, the pamphlet presents its material in an objective and straightforward fashion. Pros and cons of borrowing are covered intelligently and succinctly: credit worthiness (character, capital, and capacity—or earning power); credit costs and sources (a very good chart spells it out at a glance); consumer credit agreements; establishing credit and handling financial difficulties (defaults, bankruptcies, credit counseling), etc. Concludes with a glossary of credit terms and an excellent appendix, "Methods for Quoting and Computing Consumer Credit Charges" (add-on, discount, charge on the declining balance, annual percentage rate, etc.). Highly recommended.

174. †Read before You Write. FilmFair Communications, 1972. Color. Sound. 16mm. 6¼ min. Sale $100. Rent $10.

To demonstrate the importance of knowing what is in a contract before it is signed, particularly, its total costs, the film shows a couple shopping for a television set. They are confronted by a salesman who makes them a "bargain" offer which they "must" accept immediately. Luckily, the TV set is tuned to a consumer education program in which the teacher is explaining that before signing a contract, the buyer must check cash price, unpaid balance, finance charges, and deferred payment price. She also makes the point that it is best to shop for credit. The couple heed her advice, and walk out with the promise that they will buy the TV, but finance it elsewhere.

175. †Your Credit Is Good . . . A Film about Paying Later. Journal Films, 1972. Color. Sound. 16mm. 15 min. Sale $175. Rent from University of Illinois at Champaign, $7.90.

A film on credit and contracts which makes its simple points well, it focuses on two young people making major purchases: a young man who needs a car to get to work and a young woman who wants to join a health club program. It shows how the "friendly and helpful" used car salesman and health club saleswoman steer all conversation away from information on cost and length of loan, real interest rates, etc. Both teenagers sign contracts and find that they must pay for shoddy goods because contracts are legal documents. The film points up the need to shop for credit and to put down as much money as possible and pay off quickly to minimize the loan.

DAY CARE

176. Guidelines for Day Care Service. Child Welfare League of America, 1972. 32 pp. Paper $1.

The Child Welfare League has been setting standards for day care facilities in the United States and Canada for many years. This material is abstracted from *Child Welfare League of America Standards for Day Care Service* (rev. ed. 1969). It describes the essentials of good service so that parents, community welfare officials, and the general public can measure the effectiveness of such facilities in their communities and can upgrade those that fall below the standards. *Guidelines* explains how an agency should be run, service elements to children and parents, and how a program should operate in family and group day care homes as well as in day care centers. It describes the physical plant, including furnishings and equipment. A glossary and a short bibliography conclude. The stress here is on day care centers, although guidelines for family and group homes supervised by a day care agency are included.

DEBT

See also Bankruptcy; Credit. *For pertinent organizations see Part II, U.S. Federal Agencies*—Department of Agriculture, Extension Service; *Private Organizations*—American Association of Credit Counselors; Consumer Credit

Counseling Service of Greater New York; Credit Union National Association, Inc.; National Consumer Finance Association.

177. Blaustein, B. J., and Robert Gorman. **How to Have More Money to Spend.** Julian Messner, 1962. 219 pp. $4.95.

On the advantages of responsible debt management and staying in debt, Blaustein and Gorman's book should be read with caution. Blaustein, a credit banker, and Gorman, a writer, have put together a book that sums up the working philosophy of the former: the best way out of debt is a bank loan twice as large as necessary. This will ease the burden of paying off the loan since half will be extra money. Only peripherally does he asknowledge that this will also cost extra. Listing several "acceptable" reasons for borrowing, since banks will not lend money indiscriminently, Blaustein points out that it is often advantageous to borrow: to establish a good personal or business credit rating, when the need is pressing (as in a medical emergency), or when there is such a good sale that, even with interest charges added in, the merchandise is still a bargain. He touts open-end loans as a means to stay perpetually in debt and only pay interest charges. (Readers must remember that Blaustein is in the business of lending money.) He does warn consumers to shop for loans, to be wary of various credit and loan agencies, and to compute true interest and credit charges. But basically, he is selling debt "to have more money to spend" and includes examples of loan uses that verge on the illegal. The advantages of declaring bankruptcy are never mentioned.

178. Burton, Rulon T. **How to Get Out of Debt . . . and Stay Out.** 2nd ed. Brigham Street House, 1971. 217 pp. Paper $3.50.

Getting out of debt, dealing with creditors, and learning money management techniques. Written by a lawyer and finance counsellor, it is the only book that offers four ways out of debt: lump-sum compromise settlement (for those on the verge of bankruptcy who can get a loan); voluntary settlement (for those who can pay); Chapter 13—the Wage Earner Plan (for those who want to avoid bankruptcy), and bankruptcy (for those who want to avoid payment of of their bills). All four plans are described plainly and succinctly. Burton is not in favor of bankruptcy, but neither is he adamantly against it. He points out that one advantage of Chapter 13 is that it can be used by those who have filed for bankruptcy and are within the six-year waiting period before another filing is allowed. The author lists nine places to find inexpensive (even free), qualified negotiators who can help solve debt problems and provides guidelines for getting a good, but not overly expensive lawyer. The section on creditors explains what to do when served with a summons, when taken to court, when threatened by repossession, etc., and gives useful information on debtors' rights. The last 100 pages, "Money Management Secrets," give rather standard advice featuring Burton's "Master Budget" as well as ways to save on expenses. One good way is to do without his *SBS* (*Save Before You Spend*) *Master Budget* forms costing $3.50.

179. Dowd, Merle. **How to Get Out of Debt and Stay Out of Debt.** Regnery, 1971. 280 pp. $5.95.

According to Dowd, 1970 U.S. consumer debts totaled $120 billion, and on the average, each person owed about $485, a family of four $1,940. He enumerates many of the personal and financial problems of people who owe money and outlines a plan for getting out of debt. The advice often sounds simplistic, but he offers many constructive ideas for cutting down "controllable" expenses on food, clothing, recreation, transportation, and personal care. Examples include taking a second job, returning expensive items (if possible), moving to cheaper quarters, and altering old clothes. Other suggestions, such as saving coupons and going from store to store to buy specials as often as possible, may not be worth the effort in time and money. He also provides some sensible information on whether to consolidate debts or to declare bankruptcy.

180. Grey, Jonathan. **How to Get Out of Debt and Stay Out.** Adams, 1967. 114 pp. Paper $3.50.

Not recommended. The language is stilted and with a pseudoreligious flavor. The author's views on health foods, exercise and simple diet mingle with his thoughts on the place of money in a materialistic society, the need for budgets noting every penny, and the value of positive thinking and faith in God to improve one's financial condition.

181. Groupe, Leonard M. **Going Broke and How to Avoid It.** Thomas Y. Crowell, 1972. 213 pp. $5.95.

Groupe, an attorney specializing in credit law, is the consumer interest editor of the *Chicago Daily News.* His book describes how one (fictional) family with a decent income became submerged in debt due to unscrupulous business practices and their constant abuse of credit. While the couple—followed from their engagement and wedding to parenthood and debt—seem too naive to be believed, the book shows how very easy it is to get into debt and how difficult it is to get out. Groupe points out that the laws favor creditors rather than borrowers and suggests areas of legislation to remedy the situation. He notes that Truth-in-Lending and other laws, hailed by consumer groups, have done little to stem the tide of indebtedness. Groupe feels that the most important aid to debtors is his specialty: a combination of legal and budget counseling. His "miracle budget," spelled out in laborious detail, is a penny-pinching plan for pulling debtors out from under their bills. He also explains Chapter 13—the Wage Earner Plan.

182. Kaplan, Melvin James. **Out of Debt through Chapter 13.** Simon and Schuster, 1972. 129 pp. Paper $3.95.

A simple, but adequate description of the value of Chapter 13—the Wage Earner Plan, written by a lawyer specializing in consumer bankruptcy and Chapter 13 cases. Its drawback is that it first presents a fictionalized account of a bungled case of straight (personal) bankruptcy and hints that this is typical; that for many people filing bankruptcy will not alleviate their problems. For those who do not wish to file bankruptcy, and whose principle source of income is derived from salary or commissions, the book sets forth, in as much detail as any lay person will need, the advantages of Chapter 13 and procedures for filing—

and does so in only 59 pages of text. The rest of the book consists of the appendices. The largest of these is devoted to examples of the author's nonstandardized forms (which are variations of the standard forms used across the country, most purchasable in stationary stores). The other appendices list federal court referees hearing Chapter 13 cases (and their locations), names and addresses of trustees administering the plan, and a chart showing the percentage of Chapter 13 proceedings in relation to other nonbusiness bankruptcies. A short glossary completes the book.

183. Margolius, Sidney. **How to Make the Most of Your Money.** 2nd rev. ed. Hawthorn, 1972. 240 pp. Paper $3.95.

For the moderate-income family in debt, this is one of the most realistic books written on the subject. The author discusses emotional factors leading to money problems and the need for learning personal financial management. He lists the most common money leaks: constant finance charge payments; overspending on food, housing, home maintenance, automobiles, insurance, commercial recreation, toiletries, cosmetics, drugs, and income taxes; not taking advantage of sales, and the unwise use of savings. Crash budgets to get out of debt quickly and helpful community sources, such as credit unions and family service agencies, are listed. Margolius explains Chapter 13—the Wage Earner Plan and points out that it is not available in all states. Practical information on how to stop overspending and hold down costs is spelled out nicely. "Teaching Children the Value of Money," "Newlyweds—For Richer, For Poorer," and "Improving Your Earnings" are unusual and useful additions.

184. †**Your Right to a Hearing.** FilmFair Communications, 1972. Color. Sound. 16 mm. 9½ min. Sale $130. Rent $10.

Geared for teenagers who do not yet have credit problems, the film focuses on a debtor's right to a court hearing before repossession or garnishment is allowed. An 18-year-old youth buys an expensive electric guitar, falls behind on his payments, and receives a court summons. Members of his band convince him to get legal help. A legal aid lawyer goes with him to court and explains the boy's predicament. The judge gets the store owner to let the boy pay under a refinanced contract, then points out how smart the boy was to answer the summons, since his credit rating was at stake as well as his guitar. The judge also notes that being 18 years of age means being responsible for one's debts. The film presents its message well with believable people in a believable situation.

DENTAL CARE

See also Medical Care; Professional Services

185. Denenberg, Herbert S. **A Shopper's Guide to Dentistry.** Consumer News, 1973. 23 pp. Paper $1. Free to Pennsylvania residents, from Pennsylvania Department of Insurance.

These "Thirty-two Rules for Selecting a Dentist and for Obtaining Good Dental Care" can benefit anyone needing the services of a dentist. Pointing out a general lack of standards for dentists, Denenberg offers advice ranging from where to get names of good dentists to spotting poor ones, e.g., those not participating in Blue Shield, who are extraction oriented, who do not give emergency care, state their fees or teach preventive methods, etc. In addition, he suggests using the clinic of a dental school for low-cost treatment and explains different types of dental specialties. The pamphlet concludes with a 1970 survey of dental fees in Pennsylvania for 84 different services: from diagnostic x-rays and preventive fluoride treatment to fillings and orthodontics. The pamphlet is now available as part of *The Shopper's Guidebook to Life Insurance, Health Insurance, . . .* (*see* entry 69).

186. Revere, Paul. **Dentistry and Its Victims.** St. Martin's Press, 1970. 305 pp. $8.50.

A pseudonymous dentist's unique "self-defense handbook . . . to protect your teeth and your pocketbook." The author shows why poor dentistry is the rule rather than the exception (placing much of the blame on the American Dental Society for promoting dental income rather than good work) and offers suggestions for change. He spells out procedures one should expect during various dental services and shows why differences between Dr. Poorwork and Dr. Goodwork turn out to favor the former. For example, discussing the eight steps necessary to produce an ordinary silver filling, he emphasizes that these steps take time and may well produce pain and soreness (due to complete removal of decay, how close one gets to sensitive areas, etc.). The poor dentist who does not take the time to do the procedures properly may well produce a painless filling and will surely do it in less time. Revere adds that the poor filling will have to be removed later (if it doesn't fall out), and the patient may easily end up losing the tooth. He reminds readers to avoid all dentists who suggest extraction without first trying to save a tooth. Revere is against unit fees as they produce fast and shoddy work, and argues in favor of fees based on time, experience, and knowledge. He is also in favor of group dental practice. "How to Avoid Dr. Poorwork" summarizes much of what is stated in detail in the rest of the book.

DIETS

187. Berland, Theodore, and the editors of Consumer Guide. **Rating the Diets.** Publications International, 1974. 386 pp. Paper $1.95.

Diets—ranging from grapefruit to ice cream, Dr. Atkins to Dr. Stillman, Mayo Clinic to Weight Watchers—are described, analyzed, and evaluated. The safety and dangers of each diet are noted by quoting its boosters and detractors. Not surprisingly, the best—four-star—diets are found to be rational, balanced, low-calorie "adaptations and modifications of Dr. Norman Jolliffe's 'Prudent Diet.' " These include the "New York City Department of Health Diet," "Weight Watchers Diet," and *Redbook*'s "Wise Woman's Diet." Diets which rate no stars and are considered unhealthy include the "Drinking Man's Diet," "Dr. Atkin's 'Diet Revolution,' " Dr. Stillman's "Inches-Off Diet," and one-food diets stressing candy, ice cream, rice, bananas-and-milk, grapefruit, or Zen macrobiotics. Berland discusses the hazards of starvation, the uselessness of resorts and spas, and the benefits of exercise in losing weight. Calorie charts and sample low-calorie menus round out the book.

DOCTORS

See Medical Care; Professional Services

DRUGS

See also Medical Care. *For pertinent organizations see Part II, U.S. Federal Agencies*—Department of Health, Education and Welfare, Food and Drug Administration—Public Health Service; *Private Organizations*—Center for Science in the Public Interest.

188. Consumer Reports. **The Medicine Show.** Rev. ed. Consumers Union of United States, Inc., 1972. 272 pp. Paper $2.

First published in 1955, *The Medicine Show* provides "plain truths about popular products for common ailments," lists of medical supplies for the home and car, and guides for choosing good hospitals and reliable doctors. (On the last, CU recommends internists or general practitioners on the staff of accredited teaching hospitals.) The bulk of the report covers uses and abuses of aspirins; cold and cough medications; gargles; antacids; laxatives; sleeping pills; eye washes; arthritis remedies; multiple vitamin supplements; reducing drugs and devices; skin medications, such as those for acne and eczema; first aid medicines for burns and wounds; medicines for poison ivy, foot troubles, and skin aging; preparations for mouth odors, perspiration, dandruff, and excess hair; and dyes, rinses, and bleaches for the hair. In addition, it discusses hazards from drugs during pregnancy and points up possible dangers of antibiotics, hormones, and psychoactive drugs. *The Medicine Show* will not only help save money, it will also aid in maintaining good health. A 1974 revised edition, with 384 pages and priced at $3.50, has just been published. It has not been reviewed.

189. Di Cyan, Erwin, and Lawrence Hessman. **Without Prescription: A Guide to the Selection and Use of Medicines You Can Get Over-the-Counter without Prescription, for Safe Self-Medication.** Simon and Schuster, 1972. 321 pp. $7.95.

Pharmacologist Di Cyan and internist Hessman look at the good and bad properties of over-the-counter drugs for "safe self-medication." While the authors do a good job of describing the preparations, they do not go far enough in warning to avoid many of them. For example, they state that the use of feminine hygiene sprays is probably not harmful, a fact which is contrary to much recent information on the subject. Covered in their study are the common cold; stomach and abdominal discomforts; eye, ear, nose, throat, and mouth irritations; insomnia and fatigue; allergy and skin eruptions; feminine hygiene; headache, arthritis, rheumatism, and muscle pain; and drugs for children. Under each ailment, readers can match a list of good and bad ingredients with brand name products and their contents. A potentially helpful, but too short chapter is devoted to the side effects of drugs; other chapters concern fever, bed rest, and biochemistry and the mental state. Appendix A is a list of synonyms for the chemical or established names of drugs, and Appendix B notes the side effects of certain ingredients.

190. Gulick, William. **Consumers' Guide to Prescription Prices.** Consumer Age, 1973. 320 pp. Paper $3.95.

The first—and only—guide to prescription prices, this excellent book lists thousands of drugs and their average retail price (in 1973). Gulick explains how to decode prescriptions, how to convert prescribed dosages to comply with his charts when they do not match, and how to determine the proper price to pay for each drug. He includes many generic drugs along with brand-name prescriptions. In addition, the author suggests questioning doctors about the price and quality of the drugs prescribed. He points out that since many drugs are equally safe and effective to treat most illnesses, it is worthwhile to use the cheapest of them. He also suggests learning about the reputation of each pharmaceutical manufacturer. Gulick stresses the need to comparison shop for price before purchasing a drug and to be prepared to walk out of the store if it is overcharging. If all consumers followed this advice, it is obvious that both manufacturers and pharmacists would have to lower prices.

191. Mintz, Morton. **By Prescription Only.** Beacon, 1967. 2nd ed., rev. 446 pp. Paper $3.95.

Essentially the same as the 1965 edition published as *The Therapeutic Nightmare,* it is still relevant today, almost ten years later. Mintz has emended the text and added a preface and epilogue to the book and an afterword to each chapter. He examines the interaction of an unscrupulous pharmaceutical industry with a weak government and an ignorant and apathetic American Medical Association and highlights the difficulties of those few public servants who report cases of "nonfeasance and misfeasance." Mintz exposes the weakness of FDA drug-testing procedures, citing FDA's approval of oral contraceptives and thalidomide. He holds doctors to account for their nonchalant overprescription of tranquilizers, antidepressants, antibiotics, and other drugs; universities for lack of concern; manufacturers and the FDA for poor testing and monitoring; and Congress for failure to act and regulate. He concludes with a plea for better testing and for the use of "rational caution and critical evaluation."

ELECTRICITY

See Environment; Household Equipment and Furnishings

ENVIRONMENT

See also Food—Adulteration and Protection; Product Safety. *For pertinent organizations see Part II, U.S. Federal Agencies*—Department of Commerce, National Bureau of Standards; Department of Health, Education and Welfare, Food and Drug Administration—Public Health Service; Environmental Protection Agency; *Private Organizations*—Center for Science in the Public Interest; Center for Study of Responsive Law; Concern; Public Interest Research Group.

192. **Citizen Action Guide to Energy Conservation.** Citizens' Advisory Committee on Environmental Quality, 1973. 64 pp. Paper $1.75; $1.31 ea., for 100 or more copies.

The thrust here is on ways citizens can save energy and the nation (government, industry, and individuals) can mobilize and prepare new plans for conservation. The book has many energy-saving suggestions for the home, the office, and the automobile. The editors note that the average American family in mid-1973 spent $743.46 for energy, or the equivalent of 3,231 gallons of gasoline. They show that car pooling can save $220 a year, a compact car, $132, using public transportation or bicycles, even more. Charts show savings in home heating through weatherstripping, adding storm doors and windows, turning down the thermostat, and insulating the ceilings, walls, and floors. Home appliances can be used sparingly and bought with an eye to economy, e.g., the difference between a 12-cubic-foot-refrigerator and a 17-cubic-foot, frost-free refrigerator-freezer is 1,520 kilowatt hours and $36 a year. Another chart shows energy consumption and costs of appliances and lighting fixtures. Checklists are provided at the end of each chapter for individual use.

193. Grozier, Mary, and Richard Roberts. **New York's City Streets.** Illus. Council on the Environment of New York City, 1973. 85 pp. Paper. Single copy free.

Crammed with information on "making your block more lively and more livable" it is designed for New Yorkers, but applicable to people in many other cities, too. The booklet itself is well structured and well written, with practical advice on ways to improve streets, e.g., by adding playgrounds, gardens, trees, and lights; cleaning up vacant lots, garbage, and other eyesores; upgrading city services, and improving individual and group morale. The authors suggest ways to supply all the improvements, give methods of raising small and large sums of money, and include a questionnaire (designed for duplication) that takes the pulse of any block. An excellently illustrated listing of the city and private organizations providing these services is included. Subjects range from where to get permits for bicycle racks and for scaffolding to the telephone number of the agency that removes abandoned cars. All New Yorkers concerned with their inner and outer environment should get a copy; persons in other cities should obtain it and produce similar booklets.

194. Rodale, J. I. and staff. **Our Poisoned Earth and Sky.** Rodale Books, 1964. 735 pp. $9.95.

Rodale (one of the earliest of the health food proponents) and his staff wrote this massive and frightening indictment of the current environment. Over 300 pages are devoted to pesticides, additives, and other contaminants of food alone. The authors are against most drugs and cosmetics, and they present an effective case against fluorides, the "intentional" water pollutants, as well as against industrial and chemical wastes. Appendices list artificial flavoring ingredients, food preservatives, conditioning and enrichment additives, and animal feed additives. While the book is over ten years old, most of the evils documented then are still around today. Many people will not agree with the philosophy behind the book (or some of its "facts"), but the case is presented well, with more evidence to back it up than is assumed.

195. Schroeder, Henry A. **The Poisons around Us: Toxic Metals in Food, Air, and Water.** Indiana University Press, 1974. 144 pp. $6.95.

Schroeder (professor emeritus of physiology at Dartmouth Medical School and an authority on trace elements) delineates metals dangerous to our health. He notes the benefits of many of these trace elements and the diseases caused by their absence, as well as their dangerous, often deadly effects if concentrated. One table lists elements essential for life or health and includes "Human Disease from Excess." Another table lists the toxicity of important elements and divides the list into three categories: the five elements which are toxic to living things (lead, antimony, beryllium, cadmium, and mercury), the nine which are slightly toxic, and the eight which are probably inert. A fascinating chapter deals with the hysteria surrounding mercury in fish. Schroeder feels that banning the fish was unnecessary, since he thinks the mercury is not harmful. On the other hand, elements which cause cancer and heart disease, such as arsenic and antimony, are still allowed to pollute the environment and reach our bodies in large quantity. This book is filled with charts and tables and the language is often technical. It is not easy reading; nevertheless, it is a useful guide for people who want to know which products to stay away from and which to use.

196. Swatek, Paul. **The User's Guide to the Protection of the Environment.** Friends of the Earth (Ballantine, dist.), 1970. 312 pp. Paper $1.25.

Designed to make people users rather than consumers of the environment, the book presents Swatek's arguments against waste, pollution, overpopulation and destruction of ecosystems and offers constructive alternatives to much of our present lifestyle. Swatek discusses efficient land and water use and ways to save energy and costs by proper home maintenance and the use of energy-efficient appliances. Gardening methods safe for ecosystems include natural pesticides, e.g., ladybugs, praying mantises, and pest-repellent herbs. Swatek covers health hazards from noise, pesticides, preservatives, and additives as well as from microwave ovens, color TVs, and dangerous chemicals in the home. He urges consumers to avoid most creams, cosmetics, and soaps (as they serve no useful purpose) and to boycott them if they endanger wildlife (e.g., cosmetics using turtle or whale products). He suggests bicycling and walking as healthful alternatives to the wasteful automobile, and gardening, hiking, walking, and camping as alternatives to recreation that misuses the environment. A good bibliography completes the book.

197. Weathersbee, Christopher, and Bonnie Weathersbee. **The Intelligent Consumer: How to Buy Food, Clothes, Cars, Vacations, Houses, Appliances at the Least Cost to Yourself and the Environment.** Dutton, 1973. 366 pp. $10.95; paper $5.95.

The Weathersbees are more concerned with saving the environment than in saving money, but since the basic principle of ecological consciousness—to limit one's intake of resources—will automatically cut down on spending, both can be accomplished. Some of their earth-saving, money-saving advice: cut down on meat (an uneconomical form of protein), do dishes by hand (save fuel and water), use small cars and/or car pools, or walk. They are against cosmetics, lots of clothes, and keeping pets (as cats, and particularly dogs, live on meat from wild animals, pollute the environment, and take food that could be better spent feeding humans). The authors suggest forming combines with neighbors to buy and share occasionally used tools and equipment and urge the formation of consumer groups to lobby for legislation prohibiting waste and pollution. All very earnest and ecologically sound. Consumers can pick up many good tips.

EYE CARE

198. . . . About Sunglasses. American Optometric Association, 1967. 10 pp. Free (send stamped self-addressed envelope).

The booklet discusses sunglass lens types (natural, colored, polarizing, and reflecting), how to buy quality glasses with the proper fit, and why it is dangerous to wear sunglasses indoors.

199. Baker, Jeffrey. **The Truth about Contact Lenses.** Putnam, 1970. 248 pp. $5.95.

The only book devoted exclusively to contact lenses, this is a distillation in popular terms of the available scientific knowledge. Several chapters of particular interest to potential buyers cover the relative merits of contact lenses and eyeglasses, where to buy lenses, and "Tips for Lens-Wearing Success" with information on cleaning and storing the lenses. Baker stresses the need for good professional fittings and frequent eye examinations. He points up the greater costs of contacts over traditional eyeglasses and discusses the risks involved in wearing them, as well as their physical and psychological benefits.

200. Contact Lenses . . . A Vital Role in Vision Care. American Optometric Association, 1972. 12 pp. Free (send self-addressed stamped envelope).

It explains the differences between scleral and corneal contact lenses, how to choose between them, adaptation to and dangers of lenses, and the advantages and disadvantages of contact lenses and eyeglasses. A very short history of the development of lenses is also included.

201. What to Expect in Vision Car. American Optometric Association, 1972. 12 pp. Free (send stamped self-addressed envelope).

A handy checklist for anyone going for an optometric examination, it lists ten "important guides to good optometric service." These include what types of procedure to expect, how glasses and contact lenses are fitted, and how to spot the poor practitioner.

FINANCE, PERSONAL

See Money Management

FISHING EQUIPMENT

202. Consumer Guide. **Fishing Equipment Test Reports.** Annual. Publications International. Paper $1.95. Also distributed by Pocket Books.

Issued annually in February, the guide covers all types of fishing equipment, from reels, rods, lures, and lines for every type of fresh and salt water fish to tackle boxes, electronic fishing gear, bass boats, and accessories, such as fishing knives, waders, boots, and ice augers. It rates the products, selects best buys, notes other recommended items, and lists discount prices when they are available. In addition, considerable space is devoted to explaining how to fish for northerns, muskies, salmon, walleyes, trout, and "lunkers." A state guide to fishing is appended, with license information, regulations, and prime fishing areas.

FOOD (FRUITS, HERBS, MEATS, NUTS, VEGETABLES)

See also Stores and Services. *For pertinent organizations see Part II, U.S. Federal Agencies*—Department of Agriculture; Department of Agriculture, Extension Service.

203. **The Buying Guide for Fresh Fruits, Vegetables, Herbs and Nuts.** 5th rev. ed. Illus. Blue Goose, 1974. 136 pp. Paper $2.; 50 or more, $1.70 ea.

Despite some promotional backslapping for the Blue Goose Company (it is a national marketing service organization for food producers and processors), this buying guide is the most attractive and reasonably priced book of its kind available to consumers. For each fruit, vegetable, herb, and nut, information is given on its history and nutritional value (often including caloric content), along with tips on how to judge ripeness and quality and how to store and use the food. For example, bananas should be stored in a refrigerator after they are ripe (their skin will darken, but that will not affect quality); raw strawberries are an excellent help to dental health; herbs should be dried in a dark, well-ventilated area (dried, they are 3–4 times stronger than when fresh), etc. Excellent color photographs help consumers recognize unfamiliar foods at their prime. A valuable "Guide to Average Monthly Availability of Fresh Fruits & Vegetables" lists 66 foods from 128 regions, enabling consumers to determine the best time to buy for quality and price. Extensive charts show the composition of all foods listed in the book in their raw and cooked form.

204. Carcione, Joe, and Bob Lucas. **The Greengrocer: The Consumer's Guide to Fruits and Vegetables.** Chronicle Books, 1972. 242 pp. $6.95.

Joe Carcione has been a produce worker for 40 years, writes "The Greengrocer" column for the *San Francisco Chronicle*, and has a daily radio commentary on KCBS called "Man on the Produce Market." Bob Lucas is a dentist, a Fellow of the American Public Health Association, and a lecturer at the University of California at Berkeley. Together, they have produced a fascinating book on fruits and vegetables. Information on each includes history, varieties, growing seasons, marketing practices, how to buy, nutritional content and calories, and uses as food. Marketing practice teaches that apricots can often be picked privately at farms, cabbages are graded for size as well as quality, and peaches are graded for their amount of pink or red, not for sweetness. The section on food uses frequently includes unusual recipes. Average notations run to three pages, but some fruits and vegetables, e.g., pineapples, apples, and tomatoes get more space. The only drawback to the book is its lack of pictures. Even though one line drawing of each fruit and vegetable is included, it is not enough of a help for picking best buys in a store.

205. Evans, Travers Moncure, and David Greene. **The Meat Book: A Consumer's Guide to Selecting, Buying, Cutting, Storing, Freezing and Carving the Various Cuts.** Illus. by Dana Greene. Scribners, 1973. 310 pp. $8.95.

An extensive source of information on meat, heavily illustrated and well written. Greene, a meatcutter, wholesale meat distributer, and lecturer, coauthored this book with Evans, a writer and consumer advocate. It covers just about every meat imaginable; the authors devote seven chapters to beef alone. Veal, lamb, pork, ham, variety meats, and sausages are also dealt with in depth. A glossary of sausage terms is invaluable: it indicates which sausages must be cooked, how long they can be kept, etc. "Consumer Power" covers meat in the supermarket, freezer sales, and buying in quantity. The authors make clear that the best buys will be found in the supermarket (purchase sale items, freeze at home and save). Freezer plans cost money and deal in inferior meats. Buying in quantity (sides of beef) is tricky. If not cut, the sides will not freeze properly in a home freezer and must be stored commercially. Aside from paying for waste (fat and bones), most people do not like many of the cuts of meat they end up with. Appendices cover meat cookery terms, basic roasting and broiling methods, an illustrated glossary of retail cuts and the best ways to cook them, a meat calorie counter, and a short bibliography.

206. McClure, John A. **Meat Eaters Are Threatened.** Pyramid, 1973. 159 pp. Paper $1.25.

Stressing abuses in supermarket meat departments, McClure, a meat cutter since 1961, shows how the lack of safety and hygiene is costly to employees and customers. He says that accidents are common and meat gets contaminated (when meat falls on the floor it is picked up and packaged). Further, new procedures can be dangerous, e.g., chickens are now cut by high speed power saws that rip through bones and leave jagged pieces throughout. While retail outlets need stiffer inspection, wholesale meat packaging and processing firms generally conform to health and safety standards. An eye-opening chapter shows methods of shortweighing that get by inspectors and consumers, e.g., scales are changed on Saturday when inspectors are off duty; chickens are weighed with lead weights in them, then the weights are noiselessly dropped onto sawdust. Several suggestions for consumers include buying by grade and cutting and tenderizing meat at home. McClure says that delicatessen should be bought packaged for health reasons, but offers a supermarket checklist: slicing machines, floors, and counters must be clean; employees healthy; food covered, etc. Ways to save money include buying at federally inspected processing plants and avoiding bulk freezer plans. McClure also makes a case against the use of pesticides and additives. A good bibliography is appended.

207. Miller, Erston V., and James I. Munger. **Good Fruits and How to Buy Them.** Boxwood, 1967. 123 pp. $3.50; paper $2.50.

Written by two science teachers, and aimed at gardeners and horticulturists as well as shoppers, it concentrates on the many varieties of more than two dozen fruits: how to judge maturity and/or ripeness, when to buy, and how to store them. Unfortunately, the book has only one color photograph and just a few black-and-white ones to help consumers recognize the fruits.

208. Pucci, P. G. **The Housewife's Handy Guide to Meat Shopping.** Dorrance, 1973. 63 pp. $2.95.

Written by an ex-butcher who undoubtedly knows his subject, this vanity press book suffers from a number of serious defects, not the least of which is a convoluted writing style. It has neither table of contents nor index, and its only illustration is on the dust jacket. Little here not found in more general food-buying books. Not recommended.

209. **Where to Pick-Your-Own Fruits and Vegetables in New Jersey.** Rutgers University, Cooperative Extension Service, 1973. 6 pp. Paper. Free.

Apples, blueberries, grapes, peaches, pears, raspberries, strawberries, eggplants, lima beans, peppers, snap beans, sweet corn, tomatoes, and flowers are the commodities listed in this pamphlet. The harvest dates of each item, names, addresses, and telephone numbers of growers, and a map of the state pinpointing each farm are included. Good for anyone interested in saving on food costs while having a healthy and enjoyable experience at the same time.

FOOD–ADULTERATION AND PROTECTION

See also Environment. *For pertinent organizations see Part II, U.S. Federal Agencies*–Department of Agriculture, Agricultural Research Service–Conservation, Research and Education; Department of Agriculture, Animal and Plant Health Inspection Service–Marketing and Consumer Services; Department of Health, Education and Welfare, Food and Drug Administration–Public Health Service; *Private Organizations*–Center for Science in the Public Interest; Center for Study of Responsive Law; Concern; *Canadian Agencies–National Agencies*–Department of Consumer and Corporate Affairs.

210. †**A Chemical Feast.** Benchmark Films, 1972. Color. 11 min. Sale $165. Rent $20.

In this excerpt from two segments of National Educational Television's *The American Dream Machine* comedian Marshall Ephron makes a funny, but pointed argument against chemicals and additives in foods. In the first segment, Ephron is a chef making a "lemon" pie using the artificial ingredients and chemicals listed on the label of a Morton's pie. In the second segment, he reads the labels of Froot Loops, Whip'N Chill, Potato Krisps and Kool-Aid, pointing out that they consist only of imitation flavorings, chemical additives, and/or unnourishing foods whose costs per pound are exorbitant. The film makes you laugh, but the message is damning. Highly recommended.

211. Harmer, Ruth Mulvey. **Unfit for Human Consumption.** Prentice-Hall, 1971. 374 pp. $6.95.

On the dangers of pesticides and household chemicals, Harmer's well-researched book shows how pesticides have made foods "unfit for human consumption" and how various household chemicals threaten life and health. (She also shows how they upset the balance of nature, kill birds and fish, and choke lakes.) Harmer makes a convincing, often frightening case against indiscriminate use of pesticides, particularly dangers from insects immune to all known pesticides and drugs. For example, she tells of insects fed DDT every day of their lives with enough in each dose to kill many humans. Ecologically safe "living pesticides," e.g., ladybugs, beetles, and wasps, and sterilization of unwanted animals, flies, etc., are offered as alternative methods of pest control. In conclusion, the author pleads for the removal of many pesticides from the marketplace, the labeling as dangerous those that are left, sense in the fight against germs, insects, and animals, and respect for all life on the planet.

212. Hunter, Beatrice Trum. **Consumer Beware! Your Food and What's Been Done to It.** Simon and Schuster, 1971. 442 pp. $8.95; paper $3.95. Bantam. Paper $1.95.

Hunter covers the decline of food quality and nutrition and the grave health hazards from additives, hormones, and preservatives. "Primer for the Consumer" is an overview of the food industry: its insidious use of advertising, skyrocketing food costs, emasculation of the Truth-in-Packaging bill, and the "unholy alliance" of the food industry, research centers, and regulatory agencies, e.g., Harvard Department of Nutrition, New York State College of Agriculture, and National Academy of Sciences—National Research Council. Hunter examines our diet and finds it poor in nutritional value and high in preservatives, additives, saturated fats, MSG, salt, synthetic vitamins, etc. The section on basic foods shows how meats, poultry, eggs, fish, shelled nuts, peanut butter, fats and oils, milk and dairy products, vegetables, breads and cereals have been adulterated or allowed on the market riddled with disease and pesticides. Harmful ingredients in baby foods and sweeteners are also covered. In conclusion, the author suggests that consumers eat high-quality proteins and other good foods, and band together for consumer action, e.g., improving the FDA, reappraising food labeling procedures, passing stricter food safety laws.

213. Hunter, Beatrice Trum. **Fact/Book on Food Additives and Your Health.** Keats, 1972. 116 pp. Paper 95¢.

A convenient guide with a low price almost entirely devoted to a description of food additives, it also offers some information on how to avoid them. The book is arranged by categories: additives commonly listed on food labels, those not listed, and types of additives and their functions. Hunter is against additives. In case after case, she cites their harmfulness in tests done on animals and reprimands the FDA for allowing those known or suspected of being dangerous on the market. Consumers are advised to shun convenience foods which are high in chemicals and to choose foods close to their natural states. Foods to avoid include baked goods, candies, ice cream and sherberts, soft drinks, breakfast cereals, luncheon meats, frankfurters, sausages, and snack foods. Foods to eat include fresh fruits and vegetables, nuts, grains, cheese, butter, crude vegetable oils, meats, fish, and poultry.

214. Jacobson, Michael F. **Eater's Digest: The Consumer's Factbook of Food Additives.** Doubleday, 1972. 260 pp. $5.95; paper $1.95.

Microbiologist Jacobson, founder and codirector of The Center for Science in the Public Interest (a Nader offshoot) on food additives. The first half of his book is a reasoned and informative overview of the subject. In it, Jacobson explains why additives were put into foods in the first place and methods for testing them. The second half is a close-up look at the most frequently used additives. It is sufficiently detailed to enable consumers to evaluate their safety or potential hazards. Arranged alphabetically, additives are defined, their uses are explained, and their possible effects are noted. References to both technical and nontechnical information are appended. An eye-opening section lists ingredients in such common foods as ice cream, sherbert, and margarine. Appendixes include a partial list of the GRAS (Generally Recognized as Safe) additives, their chemical formulas and a glossary. Dr. Jean Mayer, professor of nutrition at Harvard University, contributed the Introduction.

215. Longgood, William. **The Poisons in Your Food.** Rev. ed. Pyramid Books, 1969. 223 pp. Paper $1.25.

"The poisons in your food" are additives and preservatives. The author makes a connection between them and our ever-increasing incidence of cancer and a longevity rate much lower than in many other countries. One chapter deals with carcinogenic dyes found in foods ranging from ice cream, frankfurters, and sweet potatoes to packaged cereals, candies, and frozen desserts. Other chapters cover untested emulsifiers and their indiscriminate use, "test-tube" meats filled with everything from pesticides to tranquilizers, and overrefined sugars. Longgood feels we had better food protection in the 1930s because the government no longer enforces parts of the law. His advice includes staying away from meat fats (which concentrate pesticides), growing or buying fresh fruits and vegetables (and peeling their skins to avoid pesticides), and shopping in health food stores. He points out that if consumers would not buy heavily processed and adulterated foods, manufacturers would stop producing them. A bibliography on nutrition and health is included.

216. Marine, Gene, and Judith Van Allen. **Food Pollution: The Violation of Our Inner Ecology.** Holt, Rinehart & Winston, 1972. 385 pp. $8.95.

Sometimes chatty, but it is nonetheless a very serious and detailed account of additives, pesticide residues, and other contaminants in foods. The authors are conservationists worried about the earth. Thus, they are outraged by U.S. health policy (on additives and pesticides) and U.S. foreign policy (on the use of defoliants and other herbicides in southeast Asia). Marine and Van Allen expose the overly close relationship between regulatory agencies and the food industry and detail the sorry stories of mercury in the water and organic phosphates in the field. They feel that all use of additives and pesticides must be stopped. Another solution is the "Consie (conservation) Conspiracy," an ecological plan to organize and grow food organically, buy through cooperatives and at health food stores (albeit skeptically), bring pressure on local supermarkets to get dangerous foods off the shelves, and push for environmental reform. The book is somewhat difficult to read, although many of the chapters retell stories that have already made headlines. A disturbing book, well researched, with many suggestions well worth following.

217. Null, Gary. **Body Pollution.** Arco, 1973. 214 pp. $5.95.

A biased view of additive, drug, and cosmetic perils by the owner of a health food store and publisher of *Natural Life* magazine, its chapters cover carcinogens, synthetic and substitute foods, and cosmetic and drug pollution. Null cautions against eating overprocessed and additive-rich foods and thinks it best to avoid all unnatural substances. Suggestions include joining consumer groups to protest the selling of these foods in supermarkets, boycotting products and promoting consumer suits and actions. As a health food proponent, Null suggests cleansing the body by fasting and/or juice diets and offers an everyday health-food-oriented regime. A good chapter, "Know What You Are Buying: Handbook of Additives," details the hazards of additives and notes which foods contain which ones.

218. Wellford, Harrison. **Sowing the Wind: A Report from Ralph Nader's Center for Study of Responsive Law on Food Safety and the Chemical Harvest.** Grossman, 1972. 384 pp. $7.95. Bantam. Paper $1.95.

Wellford's heavily researched study on the dangers from chemical technology in the food industry covers hormones, antibiotics, nitrates, and other additives (particularly in meat and poultry) as well as insecticides and herbicides. He discusses shortcomings of U.S. regulatory agencies, difficulties of enforcement faced by federal meat inspectors, and hardships of farmers who must buy unwholesome and tainted feed and grain and sell their unhealthy products to the public. Wellford details several cases of well-known hazards, e.g., the cancer-producing hormone DES and the pesticide 2,4,5-T, noting the monetary gains to agribusiness from their use. He concludes by recommending consumer safeguards in agencies apart from the Department of Agriculture and the Food and Drug Administration; establishment of a consumer protection agency outside the Executive Department to advocate consumer interests in the courts; scientific agencies, such as research groups in universities, to check on government policies; and professional societies that will protect the integrity and jobs of their members in conflict with agribusiness and government.

219. Winter, Ruth. **Beware of the Food You Eat.** New American Library, Signet, 1971. 280 pp. Paper $1.25.

It claims to be a revised, updated version of *Poisons in Your Food* (1969), and while there is some revision (new information on the hazards of DDT and the unwholesomeness of fried fish sticks, a chapter on cracking food freshness codes, and deletion of three appendices), the books are basically the same. Winter discusses common food problems causing diseases or death: salmonella, ptomaine, sodium nitrate, contaminated water, natural food poisons, and food-borne diseases. She notes restaurant and supermarket violations of health and sanitary codes, tells how to spot them, and lists foods never to be ordered out, e.g., chicken salad (which is too often prepared from leftovers). The author sees a need for nutritional research, tough government regulations and inspections, and a reevaluation of many pesticides and chemicals. For consumers, she offers suggestions for home safety and sanitation, such as the proper use of refrigerators and freezers to preserve and maintain foods. One appendix on the hazards of papain as a meat tenderizer and another listing state agencies administering food protection activities are included in both books.

FOOD–COOPERATIVES

For pertinent organizations see Part II, Private Organizations–The Cooperative League of the USA.

220. Stern, Gloria. **How to Start Your Own Food Co-Op.** Walker & Co., 1974. 214 pp. $7.95; paper $4.95.

How to organize and run a food cooperative; how to buy wholesale; case histories of different types of co-ops, and the names and addresses of cooperatives and wholesale food suppliers in the United States and Canada are all included. Stern explains differences between small buying clubs, large clubs, co-op stores and storefronts, cooperative supermarkets, cooperative warehouses and federations, direct-charge cooperatives, and low-income co-ops. She includes actual samples of assignment sheets; explains why membership in small co-ops is desirable in multiples of 12 (things are cheaper by the dozen); discusses different types of equipment and space, e.g., station wagons, trucks, warehouses; quotes co-op workers and managers on tips for staying solvent and living harmoniously; points out possible savings, and explains how to get quality in food supplies. Stern's book is extremely practical and highly recommended for any individual or group considering the formation of such an organization.

FOOD–INDUSTRY AND TRADE

For pertinent organizations see Part II, U.S. Federal Agencies–Department of Agriculture; Department of Agriculture, Agricultural Research Service–Conservation, Research and Education; Department of Commerce, National Bureau of Standards; *Private Organizations*–The Cooperative League of the USA; National Consumers Congress; Women United for Action.

221. Cameron, Allan G. **Food–Facts and Fallacies.** Faber and Faber (Transatlantic Arts, dist.), 1971. 168 pp. $6.95.

Cameron, the head of the Department of Applied Science and Food Technology at Birmingham College, England, presents a British view of food, eating habits, health, and disease. He discusses the values of wholewheat versus white bread, effects of sweets and fluoridation on tooth decay, uses and abuses of vitamins, synthetic sweeteners (cyclamates and saccharin), and processed, preserved, and packaged "instant" convenience foods, filled with chemicals and additives. Cameron's material is aimed at those who know little about food and calories; for example, he explains why no foods by themselves are slimming. He also manages to reduce many of these controversial topics to their proper perspective, and he does so in a terse and readable style.

222. **†Consumer Education: Buying in a Supermarket.** AIMS Instructional Media Services, 1973. Color. Sound. 16mm. 15 min. Sale $205. Rent $20.

Buying in a Supermarket is a heavy-handed attempt to give shopping tips in a "fun" manner. Stanley, a supermarket cart, talks to shoppers and to other carts. Foods sing out operatically, "I'm the best, buy me!" Stanley explains the obvious: avoid overpriced imports; make sure something is really on special; buy day-old bread if absolute freshness is not a requirement. He also shows how to check weight and cost of items. The film is designed for the junior high through adult level, but most of its intended audience will find it trite at best.

223. Cross, Jennifer. **The Supermarket Trap: The Consumer and the Food Industry.** Indiana University Press, 1970. 258 pp. $6.95.

In her detailed analysis of the food industry and its relationship to the consumer, Cross recounts the rise of the food giants, shows how prices are set, and how advertising (in specials, trading stamps, games, contests, and other promotional events) adds to costs. She notes the odds against winning a prize and the real cost of food bought with trading stamps. She also shows how supermarket proliferation leads to fewer customers per store and drives up prices even higher. A chapter on shopping problems of the poor points out that those who can least afford it pay the most for their food. Looking ahead to the year 2000, Cross sees a worsening of consumer problems. Appendixes give facts behind price increases and charts detailing the rise of the top 20 food chains and manufacturers, chain store expenses, and state inspection laws. An excellent shopping supplement explains meat nomenclature and grades of foods. There is also a good bibliography for further reading. Some material is outdated, such as the chapter on packaging which was written before the Truth-in-Packaging Act and the introduction of unit pricing in some cities, but most of the book is as timely today as it was when first published.

224. Goldbeck, Nikki, and David Goldbeck. **The Supermarket Handbook: Access to Whole Foods.** Harper & Row, 1973. 413 pp. $7.95. New American Library. Paper $3.95.

The Goldbecks are against eating anything with additives and preservatives and for appetizing foods rich in vitamins and minerals and other nutritive values. Their book consists of noting which foods and brands to buy and which to avoid as well as recipes for using the unadulterated foods. Chapters on choosing fruits, vegetables, juices, salad dressings, oil, vinegar, and leavening agents are excellent. A word of caution: the authors are adamantly against all chemicals. This leads them to favor butter over margarine, for example, even for people with cholesterol problems.

225. Kemp, Judy Lynn. **The Supermarket Survival Manual.** Bantam, 1973. 134 pp. Paper $1.25.

Written in a style best described as breezy, by a housewife who calls herself "a food shrewdie, a cost-cutting cutie," it tries to show how to shop for food amid a "you and I don't really believe that pennies saved turn into dollars saved" attitude. Chapter headings range from "Your Honor Is at Steak" to "The Java Jive" and "The Toast of the Town." Innumerable Kemp supermarket rules of one sort or another are interspersed with anecdotes of her previous bad shopping habits and her good new ones. Confusion abounds: mixed in with material on cereals is information on coupons and refunding. Rather than a "supermarket survival manual," this is really one woman's account of her shopping habits. Not recommended.

226. Kramer, Amihud. **Food and the Consumer.** Avi, 1973. 256 pp. Paper $6.50.

The text covers food history, technology, nutrition and aesthetics, current and future foods, and consumer protection. Kramer (professor, Food Science Program, University of Maryland) is satisfied with the food industry as it is, government as protector of the consumer, and quality and safety of foods. His book is useful in itself and for the exposition of its currently rather unpopular views. Kramer admits that some foods and flavors have changed for the poorer, but stresses the technological benefits, e.g., fish and soy flours which can provide enough protein for the world's population. The chapter on consumer protection argues against zero tolerances of pollutants for many products, such as wheat and fruit, and warns that such overzealousness will lead to high costs for few gains. On convenience foods, Kramer notes that quality can range from poor to excellent, that some are quite valuable (e.g., imitation milks for people who cannot tolerate milk), and that additives add to shelf life as well as to aesthetics. Waste disposal and foods of the future wrap the text up.

227. Kratz, Carole, and Albert Lee. **The Coupon Way to Lower Food Prices.** Workman, 1973. 156 pp. Paper $1.95.

According to these authors, saving coupons for refunds is a wide-spread, challenging, enjoyable, and profitable pastime. Kratz, who publishes a newsletter, *Gold'n Refunds*, which has a circulation of almost 10,000, has been a "professional refunder" since 1965. The authors claim that by following their advice, following manufacturers' promotions, saving coupons, and trading off blanks, forms, and coupons with other refunders, consumers will save 10–25 percent or more each week at the supermarket. They also point out that refunding is tedious: it takes up a great deal of time and space and needs a lot of organization. It can also be costly: overeager refunders have ended up with unusable and/or expensive products. One very good idea is for groups to pool efforts and enter such plans as the General Mills Betty Crocker club program in which Betty Crocker coupons are redeemed for such items as a school bus or a kidney machine. While the authors do not clarify exactly how all the savings are accomplished, they do tell how to go about it—up to and including instructions on which labels to save and how to get them off the package.

228. **†Magical Disappearing Money.** FilmFair Communications, 1972. Color. Sound. 16mm. 11 min. Sale $145. Rent $15.

A food expert "witch," so distrubed by the poor buying choices she sees being made in a supermarket, stops shoppers and gives them a lesson in cost consciousness. Summoning foods from the shelves and making them return, wrinkling her nose in disgust, and looking in her oversized bag, she somehow finds time to show that convenience foods, such as sugar-coated cereals, instant pudding, and frozen breaded zucchini, are overpriced, and that it is much cheaper to buy noninstant foods. The entire lesson concerns price; there is no tie-in with quality or nutrition. The film is much too cute for adults, although some young students may find it to their liking.

229. Margolius, Sidney. **The Great American Food Hoax.** Walker & Co., 1971. 216 pp. $5.95. Dell. Paper $1.25.

Consumer expert Margolius tells how the food industry (processors, distributors, and supermarket owners)—with government acquiescence—have combined to raise prices and lower nutrition. Margolius states that the convenience of overprocessed, ready-to-eat foods has not been worth the costs in dollars or health. He shows how prices are assigned on the basis of looks (apples by their redness, prunes by their size) and packaging (individual packets of cereal can cost twice as much as a large-size package); how government supports not only keep prices high but cause waste (much of the butter stored in warehouses turns rancid). Margolius also explains how to shop for value and how to shop wisely in a supermarket. Private labels are almost always cheaper than brand-name counterparts; medium- or large-size containers average 18 percent savings, extra-large, often 10 percent more; lower grades (of fruits and eggs) differ from the higher grades only in looks. The appendix includes standards for canned and processed meats and poultry and for fish products as well as a short bibliography on nutrition and cooking.

230. Margolius, Sidney. **Health Foods: Facts and Fakes.** Walker & Co., 1973. 293 pp. $6.95.

While *The Great American Food Hoax* (*see* entry 229) deals with the commercial food industry, this volume deals with the specialized health food industry and its products. Margolius finds most health food claims untrue and cites authorities to debunk overinflated claims for honey, blackstrap molasses, yoghurt, and "organically" grown foods. However, he sides with environmentalists in cautioning against the use of DES, food colorings, and nitrates. Margolius presents charts to show costs per serving of certain foods, e.g., dry milk products, and comparative nutrients of others, e.g., yoghurt, cow's milk, and goat's milk. He concludes that both the commercial and health food industries are guilty of deceptions, exaggerations, and part truths; that consumers need complete disclosure of all ingredients on all products, and that vigilant supervision is needed to maintain honest advertising. Footnotes, a glossary, and six appendices complete the book. The appendices include "Vitamins and Minerals: What They Are, What They Do for You," "Why They Use Additives," "Nutrients in Health and Various Common Foods," and "Government Food and Environmental Offices." The Public Affairs Committee has excerpted portions of the book, particularly those sections debunking the fallacious claims of health food advocates, and published them in a pamphlet featuring the same title, *Health Foods: Facts and Fakes* (Public Affairs Pamphlet No. 498, 28 pp., paper 35¢).

231. **Money Management: Your Food Dollar.** Illus. Money Management Institute, Household Finance Corp., 1972. 32 pp. Paper 25¢. Quantity orders discounted.

Noting that a food spending plan must be tailored to a particular family or person, it covers nutrition, general shopping hints, and buying, storing, and preparing foods. Most of the information is standard, but presentation is good. Some material is of particular merit, e.g., pros and cons of convenience foods, product information on labels, freezing foods economically. Thirteen rules to increase shopping skill include the following: take advantage of unit pricing, make price comparisons based on costs per serving, buy seasonally, buy in the most convenient form, handle the merchandise carefully (breakage and spoilage costs are passed on to consumers), check cash registers and scales, avoid impulse buying.

232. Moolman, Valerie. **How to Buy Food.** Cornerstone (Simon and Schuster, dist.), 1970. 160 pp. Paper $1.

Moolman has taken 13 U.S. Department of Agriculture pamphlets on food, several chapters from *Food for Us All* (*see* entry 238), and a pamphlet from the New York State College of Agriculture and Home Economics, organized the material, and presented it in a short, conveniently arranged guide costing less than the total of the pamphlets themselves. Information on how to judge, buy, store, and use different grades of beef, seafood, poultry, eggs, milk, butter, margarine, cheese, fresh fruits, and fresh, canned, and frozen vegetables is included, along with information on how to cut food costs and get the best value for the dollar. This is basic information (as one would expect from government pamphlets) that is ideally suited for people just learning about food values and a convenient reminder for other consumers.

233. **†Nutritional Quackery.** AIMS Instructional Media Services, 1967. Color. Sound. 16mm. 20 min. Sale $270. Rent $25.

A heavy-handed approach, designed to destroy health food myths and to polish the reputation of the Food and Drug Administration, the film shows a health food "quack" expounding his views over radio. He states that foods grown in depleted soil are deficient in vitamins and minerals, that chemical additives and pesticides are unsafe, and that technological advances in harvesting and processing rob food of nutrition. Besides debunking these claims, viewers see the FDA testing harvested food for "safe" insecticide levels and are shown how modern technology causes less waste and healthier food. For example, the film notes the usefulness of many additives, such as antioxidants, which prevent oil rancidity, and anticaking ingredients, which keep salt free-running. Much of the film was photographed at the FDA laboratories in Los Angeles.

234. Omohundro, Delight Dixon. **How to Win the Grocery Game: A Proven Strategy for Beating Inflation.** Drake, 1973. 258 pp. Paper $3.95.

Omohundro proves that a family of four could (in 1973) eat deliciously and nutritiously on $100 a month by doing a lot of home cooking and by following the DOLODOL plan. DOLODOL involves planning two *d*ouble-meat meals, three *o*ne-meat meals, and two *l*eftover-meat meals each week (the leftovers are from double-meat menus). Omohundro provides sample menus: 13 breakfasts, 25 dinners, and several lunches, as well as a complete "Cost-of-Living Cookbook." She has valuable shopping advice, even for people not interested in such great economy: buy only lower-price foods (less tender meat cuts, seasonal vegetables); do not buy unnecessary items (everything except staples); know what things should cost; buy them when they are most abundant; shop at several supermarkets; cut and cook it yourself; substitute low-price ingredients; plan menus around plentiful foods. "Target Prices" notes regular (1973) prices, e.g., most canned fruits and vegetables, starches and condiments cost one cent an ounce. Knowing target prices gives shoppers a tremendous head start in evaluating sales and bargains. A good section points up common supermarket frauds, such as mislabeled meats and missing sales prices. Omohundro compares convenience food costs with additive- and preservative-free foods made at home and suggests cheap substitutes for products that waste money, e.g., vinegar and water instead of prepared window cleaner. Overall, here are unusual, but practical ideas for getting good value for the dollar.

235. Rainey, Jean. **How to Shop for Food.** Barnes & Noble, 1972. 177 pp. Paper 95¢.

Prepared in cooperation with the National Association of Food Chains, the book suffers from this bias. It shows how to shop for the best food values in meat (including veal, lamb, variety, and sausage meats); poultry, milk, and dairy products (ice cream and frozen desserts, butter, margarine, and cheese), fruits and vegetables; breads and cereals; beans, rice, and pastas; shortenings, oils, and salad dressings; and beverages. For each category, the author discusses nutritional values as well as costs per serving. Prices are for 1972 and are no longer useful. She has a relatively good chapter on convenience foods that stresses their positive effects: year-round availability through freezing, actual price reduction in some cases, e.g., frozen orange juice. On additives, Rainey takes the side of those who see them as flavor enhancers and spoilage preventers, going so far as to say that if they were not safe, the government would not allow their use. A chart of preservatives and the foods they are found in follows. A short chapter praises the government for protecting our foods. Various appendices include cupboard, refrigerator, and freezer storage charts; a daily food guide, and yields and equivalents of common foods.

236. Robbins, William. **The American Food Scandal: Why You Can't Eat Well on What You Earn.** Morrow, 1974. 280 pp. $6.95.

This is the first book since *The Supermarket Trap* (*see* entry 223) to deal exclusively with the problems caused by the food conglomerates (agribusinesses) which control the nation's food supply. Robbins, *New York Times* specialist on agriculture, shows how the giant businesses have driven out small farmers, taken over the growing, harvesting, processing, and distributing of products, and imposed standards on foods that have resulted in steadily decreasing quality, safety, nutrition, and taste while increasing price and sometimes even scarcity. Robbins documents how corporations have gone into agribusiness: ITT producing Smithfield hams, Boeing and Tenneco growing fruits and vegetables, and many others. These corporations have received subsidies from the government, set prices, and been protected by lobbyists and contacts in Washington. (The stories of the milk industry campaign contributions and the grain deals are recounted.) The book is heavily researched and documented, with material taken from other exposés, such as *Consumer Beware!, Sowing the Wind,* and *The Great American Food Hoax* (*see* entries 212, 218, and 229) as well as from news and Congressional reports, Senate investigations, magazine articles, and personal interviews.

237. Shell, Adeline Garner. **Supermarket Counter Power.** Warner Paperback, 1973. 209 pp. Paper $1.25.

Shell gives staunch support to nutrition and wise buying and heavy criticism to convenience and junk foods, additives, and preservatives. Information on nutrition, buying tips, and recipes with "home-made" nourishment are mixed indiscriminately. The book has no table of contents, index, or even chapter headings, and the information is therefore difficult to find and equally difficult to relocate. "Costly Food Shopping Mistakes" has some practical advice, e.g., check "specials" to make sure they are not higher priced than regular items; don't buy newly introduced foods (they are usually worthless); don't make rigid lists (real bargains may be missed). For the last Shell suggests such lists as "Buy 4 meat meals, 1 fish meal, 1 cheese meal," etc. She notes nutritionless ingredients in many common snacks and prepared foods plus their costs in winter 1972. The book concludes with a listing, prepared by the U.S. Office of Consumer Affairs, of voluntary consumer organizations and the March 1973 *Directory of State, County and City Government Consumer Offices* (*see* entry 154).

238. U.S. Department of Agriculture. **Food for Us All: The Yearbook of Agriculture, 1969.** U.S. Department of Agriculture, 1969. 360 pp. $3.50.

The 1969 *Yearbook* deals with the economics of food from farm to supermarket; buying, cooking and using meat, poultry, dairy products, fruits, vegetables, spices, and herbs, and nutrition, meal planning, and stretching the food dollar. Similar in format to other Department of Agriculture yearbooks, this one consists of many short and simple articles. The second section (using foods) is the most valuable for consumers, although there is little here that cannot be found in fuller and richer sources. Runaway inflation and product scarcity has invalidated the section on food economics. (Even in 1969, it was overly optimistic in its outlook, predicting that the food revolution would soon provide enough to feed all the peoples of the world.) It also has little or no criticisms of food packaging, labeling, supermarket prices, etc. The section on ways to stretch the food dollar is good, but not unusual. Much better material is available from other sources, including many Department of Agriculture pamphlets.

Coverage is broad and price is low, however, so the volume is recommended with reservations.

239. Wright, Carlton E. **Food Buying.** Macmillan, 1962. 410 pp. $8.95.

This volume remains a pertinent one on its subject, but an updated edition would be better. Written by Carlton Wright (associate professor of food information and extension economist in marketing at Cornell University), the material is designed to prepare students to shop wisely in the supermarket. Charts and graphs are interspersed throughout the text which covers consumers in the food marketing chain, shoppers and food dollars, costs of marketing, food supply, how food reaches supermarkets and independent stores, and how consumers buy. One chapter is devoted to the changing eating habits of the American family and highlights current food and health crises resulting from an overconsumption of meat and dairy products. Practical material on buying foods in season, getting good buys, cost comparisons, stretching the food budget, and buying home freezers and frozen foods is still good. "Food Still a Bargain" and the appendix, a detailed guide to 1961 costs per serving of many basic foods, are outdated.

240. Wurlitzer, Rudolph, and Will Corey. **How to Get the Most for Your Food Dollar.** Award, 1970. 252 pp. Paper 95¢.

Wurlitzer and Corey's book consists of 17 chapters from the U.S. Department of Agriculture 1969 yearbook *Food for Us All* (*see* entry 238)—i.e., those chapters that are most useful for consumers. Twelve are from the yearbook's 14-chapter second section, "Buying and Cooking Food," and five are from its 14-chapter third section, "Food and Your Life." They rightly considered the first section unnecessary, "Food from Farm to You." At 95¢ their book is an economical buy. But the publisher might have specified their source, rather than merely stating on the front cover: "The Invaluable U.S. Government Family Food Guide."

FOOD—LABELING

For pertinent organizations see Part II, U.S. Federal Agencies—Department of Agriculture, Animal and Plant Health Inspection Service—Marketing and Consumer Services; Department of Commerce, National Bureau of Standards; Department of Health, Education and Welfare, Food and Drug Administration—Public Health Service; *Private Organizations*—Center for Science in the Public Interest; National Consumers Congress.

241. †**Brand Names and Labeling Games.** Benchmark Films, 1972. Color. Sound. 16mm. 9 min. Sale $145. Rent $20.

The film is excerpted from two segments of National Educational Television's *The American Dream Machine.* In the first segment comedian Marshall Ephron humorously looks at a leading brand of aspirin, a flavor enhancer, and a bleach and compares their ingredients and prices to nonstandard brands. In each case, ingredients are exactly the same and prices for the famous brands are much higher than for the others. The second segment points up the need for changes in Department of Agriculture labels and grades. Ephron presents seven cans of olives, variously called large, mammoth, giant, jumbo, super colossal, etc., asks the viewer to grade them in ascending order of size, and proves that it can't be done. A very funny film which makes its points well. Highly recommended.

242. †**Food Labeling: Understanding What You Eat.** Journal Films, 1973. Color. Sound. 16mm. 11 min. Sale $145. Rent from University of Illinois at Champaign, $6.50.

The film tries to explain the emotional, cultural, and nutritional needs satisfied by food purchases, as well as to teach how to read food labels. It discusses food standards, vitamins, additives, preservatives, coloring, etc., and shows where to find information about foods on the label. Unfortunately, it is extraordinarily dull and didactic, and somehow looks as if it were filmed years ago. Not recommended.

243. †**Label Logic.** AIMS Instructional Media Services, 1968. Color. Sound. 16mm. 18 min. Sale $245. Rent $25.

About the Federal Drug Administration safeguarding consumers by insuring label accuracy and intended for school use, this film is better than *Food Labeling* (*see* entry 242), but is slow moving and heavy handed. It also begs the question whether the standards set by the FDA are safe in the first place. The FDA is shown testing foods to make sure they maintain standards of identity, quality, fill of container, safety, and sanitation. On drugs and other dangerous substances, e.g., household cleaners and aerosol cans, the narrator explains the necessity to read warnings, cautions, and directions. Labels should tell consumers the entire content of packages as well as enabling them to make weight/price evaluations. The film makes the point that even relatively well-educated persons all too often make unwise buying decisions and are involved in accidents because warnings are not heeded.

FRAUDS

See also Automobiles—Frauds; Consumer Protection; Medical Care—Frauds; Real Estate—Frauds. *For pertinent organizations see Part II, U.S. Federal Agencies*—Federal Trade Commission; United States Postal Service.

244. †**The Bunco Boys—And How to Beat Them!** William Brose, 1973. Color. Sound. 16mm. 21 min. Sale $295. Rent $60.

Potential victims are warned about the "3Gs": goodness, gullibility, and greed. Professionally acted and directed, the film makes its points quickly, intelligently, and effectively. Three episodes highlight the message. In the first, an elderly woman is saved from turning over her life savings to fraudulent "bank examiners," and actually takes part in their capture. The second sequence shows how an alert woman foils the "pigeon drop" scheme. Two women try to get her to hand over her savings as proof of trust before she can share in "found" money. Instead, she calls the police and the two women escape. The final sequence shows two con men working the "charity switch." They substitute paper for a priest's church money and disappear. A second priest who is approached recognizes the scheme and calls the police. With the aid of the first priest, the criminals are captured. The film makes the point that vigilance is always necessary, and that alert consumers can indeed prevent crime. A Leader's Guide pamphlet (information for groups, banks, and police) comes with the film. In 15 pages it gives a history of bunco through the ages and discusses other common cons not in the film. It also goes into precautions for bank employees and investigating officers and the psychological aspects of the crime.

245. Ducovny, Amram M. **The Billion $ Swindle: Frauds against the Elderly.** Fleet, 1969. 252 pp. $5.95.

A shocking exposé of the frauds and swindles that are practiced daily on the elderly, this book is an attempt to alert the public and end the rackets. Ducovny lists 36 items under health quackery, ranging from air purifiers and alcoholism treatments to hormones, psoriasis treatments and wrinkle removers. He devotes separate chapters to the worst offenders: arthritis cures and reliefs, cancer cures, hearing aids, and mail order eyeglasses. Photographs of many of the devices and drugs should help consumers recognize them. Unlicensed and understaffed nursing homes, cheap and often worthless health insurance, funeral swindles, et al., are also detailed. Chapters on recognizing con games in various guises—e.g., get-rich-quick through part-time employment; home "repairs" as well as Social Security Administration imposters—are very useful, as the author outlines each scheme and tells what to watch for. Ducovny sees a real need for government to educate as well as protect the elderly, pointing out that by the year 2000, there will be 28 million senior citizens. Appendices give a list of the changes in the Social Security Law of 1967 and a partial list of state consumer protection offices. Since the elderly are not the only victims of such frauds, this book can be read profitably by anyone.

246. **†Foot in the Door.** FilmFair Communications, 1972. Color. Sound. 16mm. 9¼ min. Sale $140. Rent $15.

The film re-creates an actual fraud enacted by the woman who spotted the criminal and the Pasadena police who apprehended him. Living in a low-income project, the woman had previously been victimized by an identical con. This time, a man was purportedly selling color TVs for as little as $12 down. The film shows how the woman ingeniously trapped him by checking his credentials and calling the police. Another segment shows a woman who sells baby-picture contracts expalining that while such contracts are legal, they trap the customer into buying much more than he or she would want. A police narrator makes the point that it is necessary to check any salesman's credentials, and to beware of fraudulent sales tactics, such as bait and switch (very common on hearing aids, sewing machines, vacuum cleaners, hi-fi equipment, add-a-room, and baby pictures). Particularly effective in the first sequence, it is overacted in the second by the actress "selling" baby pictures. All in all, though, a good film, especially useful for adult education classes.

247. Rosefsky, Robert S. **Frauds, Swindles, and Rackets: A Red Alert for Today's Consumers.** Follett, 1973. 338 pp. $6.95.

Rosefsky alerts consumers to the enormous range of frauds, swindles, and rackets they are likely to run into: from land deal hustles and home improvement and mail order cons to "E-Z credit" deals, contract hustles, and health club rackets. A lawyer and financial adviser, who writes a syndicated column "Speaking Dollar-wise," he is familiar with all these schemes and, in anecdotal form, spells them out for the reader. His villain, Snake Oil Sam, often seems too obvious to succeed, but each year billions of dollars are lost to thieves like him. Rosefsky concludes that *caveat emptor*—let the buyer beware—must remain the byword in the marketplace. He suggests learning about products, guarantees, manufacturers, and retailers before making a commitment; doing comparison shopping; determining realistically the ability to finance a purchase; understanding the financing arrangements and being prepared to fulfill obligations on a contract; and taking prompt action when product or service is misrepresented. Most importantly, he stresses the need to seek qualified help before undertaking any transaction that involves warranties, contracts, or other documents that are unclear. The last section of the book deals briefly with organizations that aid consumers, including state agencies handling consumer complaints.

248. Springer, John L. **Consumer Swindlers and How to Avoid Them.** Regnery, 1970. 246 pp. $5.95. Award. Paper. 95¢.

Cases of frauds, gyps, and assorted swindles, some information on how to avoid them, and background on why they continue are offered here. Springer discusses the most common frauds, such as appliance and auto repairs, home improvements, investments, land buying, medical "cures," "bargain" sales, credit and installment contracts, mail and telephone schemes. He notes that part of the problem is that even reputable manufacturers no longer produce quality merchandise, that repairmen who have too much business hire unskilled and unscrupulous help, that the temptation to "get rich quick" hooks many, and that ignorance is prevalent even among those who should know better. Since there is often no legal redress for the unwary, the author stresses the need to be on guard: to read and understand all contracts, to make no oral agreements, to deal only with reputable merchants and repairmen, and to avoid solicitation by phone, mail, and particularly, door-to-door salesmen. Nothing new, but useful.

249. †**This Is Fraud.** FilmFair Communications, 1972. Color. Sound. 16mm. 8¼ min. Sale $115. Rent $10.

Narrated by Herschel Elkins, head of the Consumer Protection Division of the State Attorney General's Office, State of California, the film points out various fraudulent schemes and violations of the law, such as bait and switch, hand on the scale, and shoddy home improvements. Elkins lists ten phrases that are clues to probable fraud: "You have won a free . . . ,"; "I'm not a salesman"; "This is your last chance"; "This item isn't for you, you want better," etc. This film is made up of bits and pieces of other films by FilmFair, e.g., *Foot in the Door* (*see* entry 246) and *Your Right to a Hearing* (*see* entry 184). It is a useful summation of consumer protection information aimed primarily at adults.

250. 20 Ways Not to Be "Gypped." Illus. Channing L. Bete, 1969. 16 pp. Paper 25¢. Quantity orders discounted.

Twenty of the more than 800 known consumer gyps and five warning signs of probable fraud are listed and illustrated. The gyps include bait and switch when buying unclaimed or repossessed merchandise, balloon note financing, and having to buy products to enter a "contest" or pay the "debts" of a recently deceased spouse. The simplicity of the writing and illustrations have made this pamphlet one of the most popular giveaway items by consumer organizations throughout the country. Frequently, the last page has information concerning the organization, e.g., its name, address, telephone number, and some material about it. Imprinting of such information costs a minimum of $15 for the first 999 copies.

FURNISHINGS

See Household Equipment and Furnishings

GARAGE SALES

251. Ullman, James Michael. **How to Hold a Garage Sale.** Scribners, 1973. 99 pp. $5.95; paper $1.95.

Ullman looks at the garage sale from a psychological as well as practical point of view. He leads prospective sellers step-by-step from preparation through actual sales. Since a good pricing policy is the keystone to success, the author suggests going to other sales to learn market values (as well as to see what they are really like). He shows how to organize, advertise, and pace the sale; display, price, and tag the merchandise; get friends to help sell and protect the merchandise from physical harm and theft, and "what to expect" while the sale is in progress—and afterwards. Appendix A, "House and Garage Sale Checklist," is a handy summary of the book. Two other appendices show typical newspaper advertisements and methods of record keeping. The paperback edition is recommended.

252. Wicka, Sunny. **Garage Sale Shopper: A Complete Illustrated Guide for Buyers and Sellers.** Dafran House, 1973. 160 pp. Paper $2.95.

Written by a confirmed addict who haunts the sales and sells at them too, it is chatty in execution, laden with reminiscences and family anecdotes, but filled with a good deal of sensible advice. Wicka not only shows how to shop the sales, but how to set them up, advertise, and manage throughout the sale day and beyond. She has many interesting ideas for using the "treasures" and provides photographs of garage sale items in their new settings (usually polished, refinished, and/or repainted). Her guidelines for pricing common items are undoubtedly the most practical aspect of the book (although she warns that what is the going rate in one neighborhood may be out of line in another). She gives average prices for items ranging from air conditioners to yard tools (in excellent to poor condition). The book will help buyers spot bargains and assure sellers of fair prices.

253. Young, Jean, and Jim Young. **The Garage Sale Manual: A Guide to Alternative Economics—Buying, Selling & Trading.** Illus. by Michael Young. Praeger, 1973. 224 pp. $6.95.

Despite its title, only a small portion of this book is devoted to the mechanics of a successful garage sale. Intended primarily for the counterculture audience, it also tries to show how to make money from country real estate, auctions, flea markets, restaurants, and the used book, clothing, and art fields. Too much of the material is too general to be of help to anyone seriously considering these as businesses. The charming and useful illustrations are the high spots of the book. It is only for those who are into scouring the local dump for recycled treasure or who want an overview of these topics.

GUNS AND HUNTING EQUIPMENT

254. Consumer Guide. **Guns & Hunting Equipment Test Reports.** Annual. Publications International. Paper $1.95.

An annual, available each July in time for the hunting season, the 1974 edition rates the latest model rifles, shotguns, handguns, black powder guns, pellet guns, and even hunting knives. In addition, it evaluates scopes, explains bullet performance, and discusses the chances of getting a bargain when buying a used piece of equipment. Consumer Guide points out that the best time to trade in an old gun for a new one would be in August or September; the worst time to shop is right before the opening of the hunting season. Within each category, CG offers recommendations and best buys by brand name and lists the suggested retail price of the items. A glossary and a manufacturers directory are also included.

HEALTH CARE

See Dental Care; Eye Care; Insurance, Health; Medical Care; Nursing Homes

HEALTH FOODS

See Food—Industry and Trade

HEALTH INSURANCE

See Insurance, Health

HOME OWNERSHIP AND MAINTENANCE

See also Houses—Buying. *For pertinent organizations see Part II, U.S. Federal Agencies*—Department of Agriculture, Agricultural Research Service—Conservation, Research and Education; Department of Agriculture, Extension Service; Department of Housing and Urban Development; Veterans Administration.

255. Dowd, Merle E. **How to Get More for Your Money in Running Your Home.** Parker Publishing, 1968. 263 pp. $5.95.

Somewhat dated by current events (the energy crisis and high mortgage rates), it still has much to offer both homeowners and apartment dwellers. Dowd's main thesis is simple—the more you do yourself, the cheaper it is. The pitfalls of do-it-yourself, however, are not spelled out, so the unwary may end up losing time and money by following some of his suggestions. Topics of interest to home owners: buying a house, remodeling, selling, home maintenance services, home insurance, and laws pertaining to home ownership. Material on reducing heating and cooling costs, on buying furniture, equipment, and appliances, and on decorating are of use to all consumers. On the whole, the book is a generally good overview of the subject, with simple and often helpful suggestions for overcoming many problems.

256. Garrett, Pauline G. **Consumer Housing.** Illus. by Abe Whitworth. Charles A. Bennett, 1972. 264 pp. $5.28; paper $3.96.

Designed for high school and adult education classes, this text covers the planning and choosing of livable space: buying, renting, selling, and moving; financing the home and home improvement; decorating; buying furnishings and appliances; planning for safety and health; landscaping and maintenance; housing for the aged and physically handicapped; and housing needs across the country. Garrett (program officer, Vocational and Technical Education Section, Office of Education, U.S. Department of Health, Education and Welfare) is knowledgeable about the subject and presents it in a style well suited for a basic consumer education course. The section on financing is good; particularly that part explaining the formula for determining the net amount of money received from a loan. Information on housing for the aged and the infirm is interesting—and not usually found in material of this sort. America's current and future housing needs are covered, with Garrett noting that those needs are not likely to be met. The language level of the text is quite low, and the accompanying illustrations have a comic book quality. Each chapter concludes with a review of terms and study questions and/or activities.

257. Johnson, Thomas A. **A Place to Live.** (The Consumer Education Series). Pendulum, 1973. 88 pp. Paper $1.25.

Presenting fairly simple information on apartment renting as well as single-family-home ownership, as part of a nine-set series for high school students, the booklet concentrates on basics—yet includes material on moving, furnishing a dwelling, home operating costs, maintenance and repairs, and getting mortgages and insurance. The stress is on costs and the need for careful purchasing. Student activities suggested in each chapter are occasionally thoughtful, e.g., sending for information on modular homes and for material on planned communities, such as Columbia, Maryland. In addition, the booklet stresses many sources of additional material that can broaden one's background.

258. Money Management: Your Housing Dollar. Illus. Money Management Institute, Household Finance Corp., 1971. 42 pp. Paper 30¢. Quantity orders discounted.

A well-thought-out pamphlet, it covers housing needs and preference; costs of buying versus renting; buying choices: new and old houses, modular and mobile homes, cooperatives, condominiums, and townhouses; building choices and specialists; home equipment: cooling, insulation, heating, wiring, sound, air conditioning; the sales contract; financing: sources and costs of home mortgage loans in the United States and Canada, other costs, such as title searches, insurance, and moving. One unusual checklist judges apartments; another houses. A good buy for the money.

259. Watkins, Art. **The Homeowner's Survival Kit: How to Beat the High Cost of Owning and Operating Your Home.** Hawthorn, 1971. 242 pp. $6.95.

Watkins, a consultant in the home buying field, shows how to save money on almost all household expenses. Tips include ways to reduce charges for utilities (gas, electric, and water), telephone calls, air conditioning installation and costs, home and personal property insurance, and even property taxes. He explains what to check for before calling in someone to repair a nonworking appliance and notes that bringing an appliance to a repair shop will reduce the bill. Watkins also lists (1971) costs for home improvements and loans, shows how to avoid home improvement rackets and protect against theft, and gives pointers on the art of selling a house for the highest possible price. "Homeowner's Checklist" is a review and summary of all his major tax- and money-saving tips. A well-written and sensible book, it is suitable for home owners and apartment dwellers.

HOUSEHOLD EQUIPMENT AND FURNISHINGS

See also Carpets; Stores and Services. *For pertinent organizations see Part II, U.S. Federal Agencies*—Consumer Product Safety Commission; Department of Commerce, National Bureau of Standards; *Private Organizations*—GET Consumer Protection, Inc.; *Canadian Agencies—National Agencies*—Department of Consumer and Corporate Affairs.

260. Brown, Jan. **Buy It Right: A Shopper's Guide to Home Furnishings.** 2nd ed. Career Institute, 1973. 172 pp. Paper $3.45.

Brown, an interior designer, discusses values in bedding, carpeting, wood furniture (including upholstery and fabrics), drapery, lighting and accessories, and plastic, glass, and metal furniture. She says that value is a combination of quality, price, service, function, and aesthetic appeal. Before walking into a store, she suggests determining the use of an item, its relationship to others in the room, its style, fabric pattern, and (affordable) price range. Checklists for use in a store summarize the main points of each chapter. Practical advice abounds: don't buy fabrics that can be torn by pets; buy allergy-free materials if necessary; get swatches of material to compare with the delivered item; buy extra carpeting for stairs for reversing treads and risers. She differentiates between loss leaders (good value) and bait and switch (fraud), explains fraudulent discounting and the value of shopping in reputable stores with good service. The author also offers a few guidelines for determining how much money can safely be spent on furnishing a first home and what percentage of it should be used in each room. Home decorating tips, fabric guides, and the names of a few consumer and home furnishings associations are also included.

261. Cannel, Elaine. **How to Invest in Beautiful Things without Being a Millionaire: How the Clever Consumer Can Outthink the Tastemakers.** McKay, 1971. 244 pp. $6.95.

"Investing" as used in this book has a twofold meaning: making a profit when reselling an item and deriving aesthetic pleasure while keeping it. Cannel explains why certain types of items lose value and how to pick those that will increase in worth: silver, paintings, prints, sculpture, furniture, china, glass, pottery, floorings, rugs, marble, linen, jewelry, watches, and clocks. Cannel also discusses the influence of decorators, designers, and the lighting industry and ways in which manipulated consumers can protect themselves. Author of the syndicated column "The Good Life," Cannel is knowledgeable and witty. Good browsing material as well as an accurate guide to the investment world of beautiful things.

262. Difloe, Donna. **How to Buy Furniture.** Macmillan, 1972. 142 pp. $6.95; paper $2.95.

A very basic primer for novice buyers on judging quality in furniture, its emphasis is on wood, but the author also covers plastic, chrome, wrought iron, and aluminium. Difloe explains the need to buy with an overall plan in mind; to make specific purchases fit specific needs, and to buy items that will last for years if not a lifetime. She cautions against refinishing cheap pieces or buying do-it-yourself kits (many are much too complicated for amateurs); insists that low-priced or unpainted furniture offers few, if any bargains, and suggests purchasing in the middle- to upper-price range if possible. Difloe covers wood values: how grain, color tones, and finish produce "warmth"; different uses of veneers and solid woods, and good furniture construction. Furniture for each room is discussed piece by piece as are special items, e.g., dual-purpose (hide-a-beds, jackknife sofas, studio couches) and outdoor furniture. Rooms for infants, children, and teenagers are noted separately. Shopping in stores and at home, with decorators and without, and at auctions, are briefly covered.

263. Habeeb, Virginia. **MACAP's Handbook for the Informed Consumer.** Major Appliance Consumer Action Panel, 1973. 63 pp. Paper 50¢.

MACAP (Major Appliance Consumer Action Panel) produced this booklet dealing with the purchase, use, and care of major appliances. This supposedly independent organization is sponsored by the Association of Home Appliance Manufacturers, the Gas Appliance Manufacturers Association, and the National Retail Merchants Association. In spite of some very good advice in the first section—e.g., checking *Consumer Reports* and *Consumers' Research*—material on individual appliances is poor, since it does not distinguish between good and useless "extras": features such as scrubbing attachments in dishwashers, which never do the job well. Not recommended.

264. Harris, Gertrude. **Pots & Pans Etc.** Illus. by Roy Killeen. 101 Productions, 1971. 96 pp. Paper $1.95.

To be revised in 1975 and cost $2.95, it is as yet the only guide to buying and caring for kitchen utensils. Harris discusses advantages and disadvantages of different types of materials and how to care for them: silver, copper, brass, tin, iron, steel, glass, porcelain enamelware, clay, aluminum, and nonstick coating. She notes that a cook should never store a sauce in copper or put copper over high heat; that it is better to cook with a dull rather than a shiny surface, since the latter reflects rather than transfers heat. Harris also describes and discusses the *batterie de cuisine* (kitchen equipment): utensils for surface and oven cookery, and tools and implements for preparing foods. These include pots and pans, spoons, knives, collanders, scales, and exotica, such as woks and fish steamers. Each item should be bought for a particular purpose, with efficiency and durability the prime factors. She notes that lids, handles, and spouts are often the best clues to quality in kitchenware, and she shows how to test for worth. In addition, a list of basic cookware for a small kitchen serving two–three persons is included, along with the results of a questionnaire filled out by 39 cookery experts. Questions range from favorite cookware to warnings against various pots and pans. An excellent buy.

265. Klamkin, Charles. **How to Buy Major Appliances.** Regnery, 1973. 186 pp. $6.95.

This rather expensive book is similar in content to articles on major appliances found in *Consumer Reports, Consumers' Research Magazine* and *Canadian Consumer,* although the magazines rate many different brands and report back on all tests whereas Klamkin does not. He lists an overall best appliance and a best value in each category, but does not say how he tested the appliances, which brands were tested, or how he arrived at his conclusions. Yet he gives a lot of useful information that should make buying appliances a more rational task. All major appliances are covered: refrigerators, freezers, clothes washers, dishwashers, ranges, television sets, compact stereo sets, trash compactors and garbage disposers, air conditioners and dehumidifiers. Chapter-end summaries provide an instantly accessible buyer's checklist of Klamkin's discussion, warnings, and suggestions. He also has good sections on general purchasing hints: how to find a good store and dealer, how to get service and parts, how to avoid being switched to an inferior brand or higher-priced items, and how to buy at the lowest possible price.

266. Klamkin, Charles. **If It Doesn't Work, Read the Instructions: The Electrical Appliance Jungle.** Stein and Day, 1970. 191 pp. $4.95.

This exposé of the electrical appliance "jungle" encompasses the manufacturing, distribution, selling, and servicing of refrigerators, washers, dryers, air conditioners, microwave ovens, TVs, radios, and stereo sets. The author stresses the need for comparison shopping to get the best warranty, lowest price, and best financing. He cautions against buying new electrical appliance models or products, since they are frequently put on the market without proper testing. Klamkin notes that the Gas Appliance Manufacturers Association is safety conscious and consumer oriented, that all its new products or devices are tested, and if found to conform to standards of safety and reliability, carry the GAMA seal of approval. Gimmicks involved in the distribution of appliances from manufacturer to wholesaler to store are discussed in detail and by brand name.

Taken as a whole, the book should make consumers more wary about buying appliances, no matter how reputable the manufacturer or the store.

267. **Money Management: Your Equipment Dollar.** Illus. Money Management Institute, Household Finance Corp., 1973. 40 pp. Paper 25¢. Quantity orders discounted.

The booklet emphasizes the importance of a home appliances spending plan based on present and future needs and on facilities in the home (space, electrical wiring, gas, and water). Safety requirements are also spelled out, and safety seals are illustrated and explained. Shopping tips and a buying guide for equipment comprise the bulk of the pamphlet. Ranges, refrigerators, freezers, dishwashers, food waste disposers, trash compactors, water softeners and heaters, clothes washers and dryers, vacuum cleaners and floor polishers are covered. A general checklist for portable electric appliances, ten hints for using household equipment properly and efficiently, and safety tips and service advice conclude.

268. **Money Management: Your Home Furnishings Dollar.** Illus. Money Management Institute, Household Finance Corp., 1973. 40 pp. Paper 25¢. Quantity orders discounted.

Half the pamphlet concerns decorating tips, the other half managing home furnishing dollars. The latter covers hints for judging furniture: upholstered pieces, case goods (desks, chests, tables, etc.), sleeping equipment, dual-purpose furniture, floor coverings, wall treatments (paint, wall coverings, paneling), and window treatments (shades, blinds, shutters, curtains, and draperies). It also explains basics of the spending plan based on present furnishings and future purchases and services. Two blank charts let consumers make their own individual room and spending plans for home furnishings.

269. **Shedding "Light" on Electricity . . . What You Need to Know and Have Never Been Told.** GET Consumer Protection, 1974. 45 pp. Paper $2.50. Quantity orders discounted.

Most material on electrical appliances gives average usage in kilowatts per year. This excellent pamphlet, covering almost every imaginable piece of equipment running on electricity, notes kilowatt usage per hour. Cartoons illustrate definitions of terms. An entire chapter is devoted to lights. Other chapters cover major appliances (refrigerators, freezers, dishwashers), everyday tools (saws, drills, soldering guns), and "extras" (scissors, musical instruments). Information covers wattage, volts, amps, and kilowatt use per hour, how to shop for energy-saving appliances, and how to cut down on usage. Alternatives are also included, e.g., doing dishes by hand (faster as well as cheaper), hanging clothes out to dry (better for clothes), using hand sanders, drills, etc. Practical and highly recommended.

270. Wilson, Patricia. **Consumer Guide to Used and Surplus Home Appliances and Furnishings.** Houghton Mifflin, 1973. 182 pp. Paper $3.95.

Wilson's useful and unique guide to evaluating and buying used (as well as new) appliances and furnishings starts with an overview of the surplus market, noting where to find secondhand goods. A checklist to determine need, storage, and utility of appliances points up the importance of being able to get repairs and parts. A life-expectancy table of appliances is invaluable. Wilson feels that secondhand refrigerators and freezers are excellent buys, ranges and dryers offer average to above-average buys, dishwashers and clothes washers are difficult to obtain, and water heaters should not be bought secondhand. Portable appliances, e.g., irons, coffeemakers, toasters, frypans, and toaster-ovens, as well as vacuum cleaners, floor polishers, scrubbers, rug shampooers, and sewing machines are discussed in detail. Two good chapters deal with proper appliance and home furnishing repairs and maintenance, but the one on buying used furnishings is too general to be of help. The final chapter covers budgeting to buy the merchandise.

HOUSES—BUYING

See also Condominiums; Real Estate. *For pertinent organizations see Part II, U.S. Federal Agencies*—Department of Housing and Urban Development, Housing Production and Mortgage Credit—Federal Housing Administration; Veterans Administration.

271. Cassiday, Bruce. **The Best House for the Money.** Belmont/Tower, 1972. 174 pp. Paper $1.25.

Would be a useful, albeit conventional guide to choosing a house, were it not for poor editing and consequent errors (no pagination listed in the table of contents, no index, an incorrectly printed chart for determining how much to pay for a house, "terrain" is "rain," and more). The author presents a very good method for checking out a house from cellar to roof to determine its soundness, as well as a good way to determine remodeling costs. For the latter, he notes percentages of costs in relation to the total house, e.g., exterior walls cost about 10 percent of the price, floors and roof 10 percent each. The best chapter deals with garages and outbuildings, as this material is fairly unusual. Cassiday discusses good and bad features of a garage (windows on one side, an entrance to the house, a fire wall are good); carport (only for mild climates); utility room (should be near the fuse box, with attachments to the sewer connection); workshop (must have adequate power supply, lighting, and heat, convenient sockets, concrete floor, etc.). He also cites features to look for in porches, patios, terraces, driveways, turnarounds, greenhouses, and decks. *How to Buy the Right House at the Right Price* (*see* entry 279) is better, but this is acceptable at its low price.

272. Cassiday, Bruce. **How to Choose Your Vacation House.** Illus. Dodd, Mead, 1974. 312 pp. $7.95.

Cassiday has written a book designed to acquaint would-be buyers with different types of vacation house construction (together with some rough cost estimates). If the house is chosen for round-the-year living, such factors as access to it, heat, and space must also be considered. Much of the book contains photographs, illustrations, and floor plans (some for vacation use only). Cassiday lists builders and manufacturers, and although he does not specifically do so, he is endorsing them. Whether they deserve such recommendation is unclear.

Houses are discussed by type of construction and/or by material: plywood, precut, interlock, prefabricated, mobile, modular, and custom built. Cassiday explains why site differences should affect vacation home choices. He also discusses painting, heating, installation, utilities, sanitation, landscaping, and winterizing. Building tips are included for the do-it-yourselfers. An appendix lists manufacturers of vacation homes and vacation house plans.

273. Cobb, Betsy, and Hubbard H. Cobb. **Vacation Houses: What You Should Know before You Buy or Build.** Illus. Dial, 1973. 261 pp. $7.95.

A good book for anyone planning to buy a second house, it offers sound, up-to-date advice on the modern market. The Cobbs discuss land prices, actual costs of buying and financing, carrying costs, and ways to reduce the bills, e.g., renting the house part time. They are in favor of using lawyers for the purchase and offer many money saving ideas for building and/or remodeling. Good chapters, with interesting photographs and floor plans, compare styles and designs of vacation homes: prefabs, precut, shells, stock-built, modular, domes, stock plan, mobile homes, vacation communities, etc. Island living is talked about: building in such places costs much more because everything must be shipped in. The Cobbs list price ranges for all the houses and advantages and disadvantages of each style, and they point out where do-it-yourselfers can cut costs. Several chapters are devoted to accessories, i.e., fireplaces, stoves, decks. They also discuss ways of protecting the house from weather, animals, and vandals, of insuring it, and of closing it for the season.

274. Griffin, Al. **So You Want to Buy a House.** Illus. by Peggy Griffin. Regnery, 1970. 244 pp. $5.95.

The good solid information is mixed with an overly cute glossary of real estate terms and chapter headings, such as "Brushing up on Your Paints" and "Stow It, Lady." Griffin covers old versus new homes, financing, good house construction, neighborhoods and blockbusting, schools and taxes, the community in general, advantages and disadvantages of using real estate brokers. He warns against buying a house on the basis of a model. Even if the model is well constructed, others may be built with inferior materials or never put up at all (leaving the prospective homeowner minus a down payment). A good section deals with safety features for the house and gives examples of shoddy workmanship and accident-causing construction—e.g., nonsafety-type architictural glass doors in patios; bathtub grab bars that pull loose. A short chapter deals with townhouse, cooperative, and condominium living; the concluding chapter, with moving. Tables cover mortgage payments, points, home loan rates for new and old houses in different cities, after-tax costs of paid interest, and the percentage increase in building costs from 1961 to 1969.

275. Higson, James D. **The Higson Home Buyer's Guide.** Illus. by Peggy Lynch. Nash, 1973. 229 pp. $7.95.

In his up-to-date primer on buying a house, designer and home builder Higson discusses the different aspects of home buying in cities, suburbs, and country. He suggests avoiding the odd house, i.e., the one modern in a sea of traditional, or the good, but expensive home surrounded by moderate priced houses. Excellent chapters cover what to look for in judging a house and include helpful illustrations of good and bad layouts. Another valuable section deals with remodeling costs. Higson also points out that older homes often come with many extras and built-ins not found in new houses. Material on price bargaining includes a chart with the asking prices and first low offers on houses in a buyer's and seller's market. (Price differences are in the thousands.) Information on financing and moving is adequate. A good suggestion is to include the cost of cleaning the older house in the written contract. (As Higson says, it is very depressing to be confronted with a filthy house.) One appendix contains the value of remodeling restrictions in California's Linda Isle development; a second has mortgage payments on 25-year loans.

276. Hoffman, George C. **The Comstock Western Home Buyer's Guide: A Manual for House Inspection.** (Comstock Editions). Balantine, 1973. 84 pp. Paper $1.50.

One long chapter on how to inspect a house before purchase by a man who does this for a living. Sadly, Hoffman does not note prices, so reading this book will not teach the consumer how much any house will cost to repair. He also offers some dangerous advice: how to buy without a lawyer, or even an agent–and how to get title and escrow companies to provide the necessary papers. Not recommended.

277. Margolius, Sidney. **How to Finance Your Home.** Rev. ed. (Pamphlet No. 360A). Public Affairs, 1971. 20 pp. Paper 35¢. Quantity orders discounted.

Margolius's text is more inclusive and broader in coverage than the title suggests. He concentrates on financing a home, but also discusses how to determine how much to spend on the house–i.e., how location, lot, the house itself (its soundness), and the housing market determine its value. VA and FHA loans, points and other fees, closing costs, second mortgages (very expensive), "open end" clauses and prepayment privileges (good values) are all covered. Margolius also explains loan provisions under Section 235 of the 1968 Housing Act and the 1970 Housing Opportunity Allowance program and tells how to get money for remodeling or expanding a house.

278. Moger, Byron, and Martin Burke, with Omar V. Garrison. **How to Buy a House.** Lyle Stuart, 1969. 204 pp. $4.95.

A basic primer on home buying, it is concerned mainly with judging a house: exterior and interior (by layout and function) and basic quality and construction. Design and quality are discussed together, e.g., a straight roof line makes a house look larger than it is; a hard-burned clay tile roof can be considered a permanent, almost trouble-free investment. A good section covers upkeep and recurrent expenses. For example, houses need repainting and lawns need replanting about once every four years, roofs and drains need repairing, and plumbing and fixtures need replacing about once every five years. The authors deal intelligently with selling and buying a house at a fair price. A good suggestion is for a buyer to make a low first offer, get a counteroffer, and not go above the price originally thought a good value. Shopping for mortgages is also handled well. The authors point out that while one institution may turn down a loan, another may grant it. A useful chart explains the basic difference between standard FHA loans and those for veterans. Appendices list monthly mortgage payments, FHA mortgage terms, a land measurement table, and an adequate glossary of building, banking, and legal terms.

279. Murray, Robert W., Jr. **How to Buy the Right House at the Right Price.** Collier, Macmillan, 1965. 220 pp. Paper $1.25.

This is a very practical guide, particularly in the area of financing the home (although introductory data need revision). Murray (formerly deputy director, Public Affairs, U.S. Department of Housing and Urban Development) writes knowledgeably and well. Material on regular mortgages, low-cost loans, and special mortgages for middle-income and low-income families is quite good, as is information explaining characteristics of good and bad floor plans and housing styles. Murray displays good and bad floor plans and tells what to expect from different types of houses. He notes neighborhood features to look at, from general community to specific street. He offers a ten-point checklist to differentiate a good builder from a poor one: check the builder's credit rating and the quality of workers and materials; look at the builder's previously constructed houses. A glossary of building and legal terms and a consumer's checklist for judging three houses are appended.

280. Perl, Lila. **The House You Want: How to Find It, How to Buy It.** Funk & Wagnalls, 1965. 210 pp. Paper $1.50.

This generally good though slightly dated book suffers from archness in the first chapter. There, the author details the story of the Blunders and their tract home bought on a VA mortgage in the early 1950s. Perl follows them into their second home (a split-level), detailing how they compounded their errors. Once over this, she devotes herself to explaining good and bad styles of architecture, and good and bad floor plans—with diagrams. These chapters are detailed and helpful. She points out that a Colonial home, with its two stories, may not be good for families with young children or for the infirm; on the other hand, its broad center hall ventilates the house as breezes flow through. Twelve tests for a "fool-proof" floor plan include the obvious adequate kitchen and closet space as well as a broom closet and a pantry, a basement accessible from the outside (with wide doors on the inside to allow for moving bulky materials), and adequate room for expansion. Never buy from a model, Perl says, but look at a new house during several stages of construction. Short chapters cover judging the community, using brokers and lawyers, bidding on a house, going to contract, and getting mortgages.

281. Reiner, Laurence E. **Buy or Build? The Best House for You.** Illus. Prentice-Hall, 1973. 240 pp. $6.95.

Reiner's emphasis is on buying the house; relatively little is devoted to building it. On the whole, the book is a workmanlike job of explaining how to go about finding a neighborhood and buying a house; determining the right type and price, and financing. Reiner also covers landscaping and maintaining a house and protecting it, e.g., with fire and burglar alarms. A very cursory chapter discusses real estate law. Separate sections deal with development houses, "speculative" houses put up by local builders, older houses (when and how to remodel them), and vacation houses. Reiner explains features found in well-designed rooms, and how to plan or remodel rooms. A good chapter on architectureal styles points out useless features of many homes (grafts from other styles) and unsuitable land sites e.g., split-levels belong on a hill (if not, there is no point to them). Almost all chapters summarize the pertinent checkpoints and list advantages and disadvantages of each type of house. Diagrams, floor plans, and other illustrations are exceptionally easy to read.

282. U.S. Department of Housing and Urban Development. **Wise Home Buying.** 1972. 36 pp. Paper. Free.

A very simple pamphlet explaining the basics of home buying to first-time purchasers, it tells how to shop for a house and determine how much to pay; how to find a real estate agent; how to inspect the property and house; how to finance and purchase, and what to do if mortgage payments cannot be met. A short glossary of housing and loan terms and a list of the addresses of all HUD regional offices are included. The publication is useful for adult education classes, and particularly good for people without knowledge of how to get mortgages and loans.

283. Watkins, Art. **Building or Buying the High-Quality House at the Lowest Cost.** Doubleday, 1962. 269 pp. Paper $1.95.

Part of this book has been revised in *How to Judge a House* (1972; *see* entry 285). Generally standard fare on building or buying a customized, development, or prefabricated home, the best chapter covers the five greatest areas of home upkeep: heating, insulation, and vapor barriers; wiring, termites, and wood rot, and water heaters. Interesting material is provided in "What's Wrong with America's Houses," which discusses the problems of exploding demand, poor design, low-quality construction, high costs, out-of-date construction methods, and the benefits of prefabrication, mass production, and interchangeable parts. Watkins has good words about Levitt homes, which are mass produced and which offer excellent space and utilities at (relatively) low costs. House design and floor plan layout are covered better in *How to Avoid the Ten Biggest Home-Buying Traps* (*see* entry 284). Material on financing is outdated. The concluding chapter is a checklist for buying or building a home and is similar to the author's checklists in his other books that are noted here.

284. Watkins, Art. **How to Avoid the Ten Biggest Home-Buying Traps.** Rev. ed. Hawthorn, 1972. 180 pp. Paper $2.95.

While the title is eye-catching, the book is basically a straightforward primer on house buying. Watkins discusses the importance of knowing the right price to pay for a house, how to compute expenses in buying and maintaining a home, how to get a mortgage in a tight money market, how to judge layout, style, and construction of a house, and how to buy for quality. "The Vanishing Builder" offers several guidelines by which to judge the integrity of builders and their work, e.g.: Are their names used in the firm names? Have the businesses been established for a long time? What are their reputations? A chapter on the "gimmick" house points out how unwary buyers have been blinded to obvious flaws in houses. While certain gimmicks do add value—e.g., dining room pass-through walls, wall ovens, and recessed lighting—they are only as good as the construction and layout of the rest of the house. A summary checklist concludes.

285. Watkins, Art. **How to Judge a House.** Hawthorn, 1972. 86 pp. Paper $1.50.

Update of Watkins's 1962 *Building or Buying the High-Quality House at the Lowest Cost* (*see* entry 283), minus the home-building information. Also very similar to *How to Avoid the Ten Biggest Home-Buying Traps* (*see* entry 284) in that a large portion of it deals with judging the house: its construction, floor plan, and location. The checklist is almost word-for-word. While the information on financing a home and money for mortgages is newer in this book, there is little of value in it. Of all Watkins's books, this one is the slightest.

HOUSES—BUYING AND RENOVATING

For pertinent organizations see Part II, U.S. Federal Agencies—Department of Housing and Urban Development.

286. Cobb, Hubbard H. **How to Buy and Remodel the Older House.** Illus. Collier, Macmillan, 1972. 519 pp. Paper $3.95.

Originally published in 1970 as *The Dream House Encyclopedia* (Wyden), this very practical book explains how to buy and remodel houses ranging from farms, barns, and vacation cottages to brownstones and mansions. Cobb (former editor-in-chief of *The American Home Magazine*) defines many real estate and housing terms and shows how to determine necessary renovations, how to buy and finance a house, and how to plan a renovation and carry it out to completion. A good checklist summarizes information on inspecting a house and covers some areas of interest only to a land owner, e.g., driveway and/or road, garage and/or outbuildings, as well as items of interest to everyone, e.g., water supply and pipes, number and condition of bathrooms. The "Cost Finder" is a checklist indicating rough prices of 34 major renovation items as of 1970, with space for estimated costs. The "Space Planner" includes standard specifications for house interiors, notes minimum space that can be allotted per room, and shows how to make floor plans. A large portion of the book is devoted to renovations, with many "do-it-yourself-and-save" tips. The last 150 pages consist of photographs, floor plans, and text about 20 remodeled homes. A glossary of building terms is appended. At the $3.95 price, this is an excellent buy.

287. McKenna, H. Dickson. **A House in the City: A Guide to Buying and Renovating Old Row Houses.** Illus. Van Nostrand Reinhold, 1971. 159 pp. $12.95.

McKenna (a remodeler of row houses as well as the executive director, New York State Association of Architects) aims his first-rate guide at prospective brownstone owners. A checklist for determining necessary renovations is extensive. Starting on the outside, and looking at size and orientation, it takes a buyer from the basement to the roof and discusses ceilings and walls, moldings and plasterwork, plumbing, heating, electricity, windows, staircases, floors, fireplaces, and front and back yards. McKenna talks about neighborhoods and price, advertising terms (such as "move in," "needs renovation," and "shell") and explains which renovations can be made by owners and which require professionals. He stresses the need for legal advice, discusses the legalities and complexities of three-unit houses (they are multiple dwellings), contracts, mortgages, and more. One chapter deals with four families who remodeled, two with ease and two with great hardship. An appendix lists the sequence of 14 procedures for a typical renovation, prices of surfacing materials in 1971, and recommended books. A history of row houses and row neighborhoods (almost all in New York) completes the text. Enhanced by black-and-white photographs and drawings, the book is beautiful as well as practical.

288. ***The Old-House Journal.** Clem Labine, ed. Old-House Journal Co., 1973– . Illus. Monthly. $12.

For city dwellers living in old houses, this monthly magazine is filled with practical information on restoring, renovating, maintaining, and decorating. The stress is on practical and inexpensive ways to accomplish it all without detracting from the character of the old homes. Articles are taken from other magazines, from booklets, and from knowledgeable individuals who live and work with old-house problems. Articles generally range from a half page to four pages in length in each 12-page issue. Recent issues included a short history of mansard roofs, a four-part series on working with plaster, the story of a renovation in New Haven (with photographs), information on how to replace a register with an outlet, and lists of publications for the novice, e.g., ceramic tile catalogs and products for the old-house owner. The journal is illustrated in a lively and intelligent manner; the articles are practical and easy to follow.

289. Stanforth, Deirdre, and Martha Stamm, **Buying and Renovating a House in the City: A Practical Guide.** Knopf, 1972. 400 pp. Paper $4.95.

This step-by-step guide to finding, financing, purchasing, and renovating a city house was written by two New York City women who went through the entire process. They have included an extremely interesting chapter on renovation neighborhoods in 19 cities across the country. The authors give an insightful picture of what it takes to live in a renovation neighborhood and in a partially renovated house. In chapters entitled "Basic Elements of a Renovation," "Drawing the Plan," "How the Work Will Be Done" and "The Renovation" they offer practical and explicit details on each subject. A listing of organizations devoted to historic preservation, restoration, and renovation in 12 of the major renovation cities is appended.

290. Wilkes, Joy, and Paul Wilkes. **You Don't Have to Be Rich to Own a Brownstone.** Illus. Quadrangle, 1973. 139 pp. $6.95.

While the book's emphasis is on self-renovating (in New York City), even those who will use professionals can read it with profit. The Wilkeses, who renovated their own brownstone (in partnership with another couple), tell how to check out the house and neighborhood, how to decipher ads and deal with real estate agents, and how to finance and renovate the building. The section on checking the structure also provides a cost breakdown on some items: e.g., crumbling brownstone costs over $6,000 to replace, flat roofs between $300 and $700. The section on getting financing has a valuable list of New York City banks that grant brownstone mortgages. Estimating costs is skimpy, while legal, tax, and insurance information and information dealing with New York City's building code and city inspectors is quite good. Since the Wilkeses lived on the site during renovation, they offer their own steps for logical progression. Interestingly, the list is slightly different from that in *A House in the City* (*see* entry 287). Renovation stories, appendices of historical districts, 27 New York City brownstone areas (plus Hoboken, New Jersey), places to buy hard-to-find items, and a bibliography which concentrates on how-to books are included. The information on New York City's brownstone areas is particularly useful, providing approximate costs, availability of housing, neighborhood characteristics, and persons to contact for further information.

HOUSES–BUYING AND SELLING

291. Beasley, M. Robert. **Fell's Guide to Buying, Building and Financing a Home.** Fell, 1963. 143 pp. $4.95.

If updated, *Fell's Guide* would be a very practical volume for anyone interested in building a home. Now it stands dated in many cost estimates and breakdowns, and its usefulness is limited. A still relevant chapter shows how much money should be spent building each part of the house, as Beasley uses percentages as well as actual costs. He also shows how to buy a lot (checking out lot shape, grading, soil, easements, rights-of-way, condemnation, etc.); how to plan a house properly for climate and light; how and when to hire a contractor and/or architect, and he offers many money-saving tips on how to build a house. One of the best of these tips is to use free services, such as heating, wiring and insulation advice from electric companies. Beasley explains how to check out an older house for defects and suggests various methods of disposing of a current home, ranging from a trade-in agreement with a builder to selling the house privately. He stresses the need for a written contract with the builder to make sure the new owner will not be responsible for settling, shrinkage, swelling, and other repairs on the new house. A brief final chapter highlights decorating with color.

292. Biddle, G. Vance. **To Buy or Not to Buy? That Is Only One of the Questions.** Vantage, 1972. 109 pp. $3.95.

The 109 pages of this vanity press publication have wide margins and many empty spaces. Written by a California land developer and former banker who specialized in commercial and real estate loans, the book is so short and information is so sketchy, that it cannot be used to buy a house intelligently. Not surprisingly, the best information covers financing. Here Biddle goes into some detail about various types of mortgages and how much money can be borrowed from different institutions for different types of loans. Much better material is available elsewhere. Not recommended.

293. deBenedictus, Daniel, J. **The Complete Real Estate Adviser.** Trident, 1969. 355 pp. $6.95. Pocket Books, 1970. Paper $1.50.

Four books make up this volume: *The Family Real Estate Adviser* (1967), *Laws Every Homeowner and Tenant Should Know* (1968), *Practical Ways to Make Money in Real Estate* (1967), and *How to Become a Real Estate Broker and Turn Your License into Big Money* (1968). The first two are relevant to the consumer. *The Family Real Estate Adviser* has some very practical hints on buying and selling a home. DeBenedictus, a broker and consultant, spends several chapters explaining how to spot a poor agent and/or broker, what to expect from agents and brokers, and ways to sell a house without them. When dealing with them, check on the asking price the agent is quoting, check to see if the house is really advertised, and never give in to a demand for an "exclusive" listing. A home buyer's checklist for neighborhood and house and a homeowner's list for determining affordability complete this section. *Laws Every Homeowner and Tenant Should Know* covers legal rights and obligations of buyers and sellers, mortgage financing, tax and insurance laws, contract laws for property owners, tenant and landlord law, rights to deposits, and property and personal rights and obligations. Some of it repeats information in the first book, e.g., rights of sellers and brokers. Some parts are too superficial, e.g., definitions of "condominium" and "cooperative." Some material is useful, e.g., definitions of "riparian rights," "easements," "encroachments," and "restrictions," (including legal restrictions), how to complain of discrimination, the importance of lawyers, etc. A revised, paperback edition of *The Family Real Estate Adviser* was published by Cornerstone Library in 1973 and is available at $1.50. The updating consists solely of a few price changes and does not warrent purchase on that basis.

294. Fowler, Glenn. **How to Buy a Home, How to Sell a Home.** Benjamin Co., 1969. 144 pp. Paper $1.45 (100 copies minimum).

A giveaway item for businesses, this guide to home buying and selling was written by the *New York Times* real estate editor. It is a very practical book, stressing the need to consider costs of houses plus upkeep when looking for a home. Fowler discusses the most sensible ways to find the right neighborhood and house, how to judge the quality of a house, how to make the transaction, how to finance it, and how to close the deal. He is in favor of using brokers and/or realtors, both for buying and selling a house, and notes the possibilities for listing with a national computer listing service. The section on selling points up the need to fix up a home by painting and cleaning and warns against making most major improvements as they will not return the investment. Examples include leaving the worn wall-to-wall carpeting and the unfinished basement and/or attic. (Most new owners would want to make these changes.) Fowler is very good at explaining how to make a deal for a home when buying and how to accept a good offer when selling. A glossary of construction and financing terms completes the book. An abridged pocket-sized edition put out by Benjamin Co. sells for 50 cents (minimum 100 copies). Useful for groups wanting to give away this type of consumer information.

295. Laas, William. **Lawyers Title Home Buying Guide.** 2nd ed. Popular Library, 1973. 160 pp. Paper $1.25.

Glib and without depth, most of the information is so sketchy that it qualifies as refresher material at best. Not surprisingly, the best section deals with insurance, specifically, title insurance. Here the author makes what amounts to an advertisement for the Lawyers Title Insurance Corporation, which holds copyright to this book. Not recommended.

296. Monefeldt, Jess. **How to Buy or Sell a Home.** Branden Press, 1970. 32 pp. Paper $1.

A poorly executed pamphlet by a real estate agent, it gives less than a bare outline of the procedures for buying or selling a home. Not recommended.

297. Nielsen, Jens, and Jackie Nielsen. **How to Save or Make Thousands When You Buy or Sell Your House.** Doubleday, 1971. 175 pp. Paper $3.95.

Despite a sensational title, this is actually an earnest and straightforward description of the procedures for selling and buying a house. The section on selling notes listings, real estate brokerage fees, attorney's fees, and special assessments. The Nielsens explain when brokers must be paid and the broker's obligations to sellers. To set a fair market value on a house, they suggest a professional appraisal, a look at tax records, a check of the selling price of similar properties in the area, and an accurate reflection of all home improvements. They also urge sellers to fix up their property before showing it. The Nielsens show different ways the same property can be advertised to appeal to different buyers. The section on buying a house has an excellent checklist for the neighborhood and the house. It explains how to determine the correct price of a house and notes a broker's duties to buyers. Information on purchasing in joint tenancy, on deed and title to the property, and on legal and financial aspects of the transaction are covered rather well. Worksheets for determining costs are appended at the end of each section. Land contract financing, property owner's rights, and real estate taxes and savings are also covered. The 20 forms that can be used in real estate transactions are defined and noted in the appendix.

298. U.S. News and World Report. **How to Buy Real Estate: Profits and Pitfalls.** Collier, Macmillan, 1970. 221 pp. Paper $2.95.

Only the second half of this book discusses the buying and selling of a private house; the first half is devoted to buying real estate for profit. In a rather once-over-lightly approach, the editors manage to point up several factors rarely recognized: "square footage" of a house can include carport or patio, if measured from the outside, wall thickness will reduce living space; the amount of needed space can be determined by looking at present quarters and noting the difference; a high-priced item bought on the installment plan shortly before a credit check (and not paid off) will adversely affect chances for a loan. When selling a home without a broker, it is best to set a time limit and stick to it. If the house isn't sold by then, get a broker. Other ways to judge whether or not to sell privately are to find out if others in the neighborhood did, if the house is desirable, if mortgage money is available, if homes in the neighborhood are in demand, if it is spring or early fall (the "good" buying seasons), if a "For Sale" sign can be seen by a driver. When selling, it helps to fix up the house, prepare a fact sheet, and advertise with price and all features listed. Vacation homes—for fun and profit—are discussed briefly. A glossary is appended.

299. Wren, Jack. **Home Buyer's Guide.** (Everyday Handbook No. 213). Barnes & Noble, 1970. 259 pp. Paper $2.50.

In one of the best guides to buying, financing, and selling a house Wren discusses different types and styles of houses (including vacation and mobile homes); gives check points for judging homes; and explains how location will determine environment (a house in a conventional grid plan and one in cluster housing will have different traffic patterns, noise, etc.). He covers special features, such as costs and importance of home protection (fire extinguishers and alarms, burglar alarms, vacation precautions), and pros and cons of home improvements (including pitfalls of dealing with fraudulent termite inspectors and tree surgeons). On financing, Wren has an excellent rundown on mortgages, e.g., VA, FHA, and conventional mortgage loans, how to take over existing mortgages, etc. Legal expenses (such as the binder, contract of sale, title insurance, deeds, closing costs, liens and foreclosures), moving costs; painting, decorating and landscaping costs; and recurrent expenses involving mortgage payments, taxes, insurance, utilities, commuting, and maintenance are all considered. When selling a house, Wren advises using a broker. He explains the trade-in, and shows that although easy, it is a costly method of home disposal. A home buyer's checklist, a seller's checklist, a home buyer's financial checklist, and glossaries of building and legal terms are appended.

HOUSING

See Condominiums; Home Ownership and Maintenance; Houses—Buying; Mobile Homes; Real Estate

HUNTING EQUIPMENT

See Guns and Hunting Equipment

INSURANCE

For pertinent organizations see Part II, U.S. Federal Agencies—Department of Housing and Urban Development, Housing Production and Mortgage Credit—Federal Housing Administration; *Private Organizations*—The Cooperative League of the USA; Insurance Consumers Union—Policy Holders Protective Association, Inc.

300. Baldyga, Daniel G. **How to Settle Your Own Insurance Claim.** Macmillan, 1968. 159 pp. Paper $4.95.

A claims manager for an insurance company, Baldyga has prepared a readable guide to saving lawyer's contingency fees. He admits that only those with legitimate claims in simple cases—*where the liability of the second party is absolutely clear*—should attempt this. For those willing to take the risk, this book is a step-by-step guide on how a claim is prepared. The focus is on automobile accident claims, and an entire section is devoted to the mechanics of building a file on the accident, e.g., how to find missing witnesses, locate the police report of the accident, get weather reports, and file death claims. The author also discusses other accidents: slip and fall, sidewalk, snow and ice, stairways, waxed floors, tenancy, and animals. The second part of the book deals with injuries, e.g., whiplash, fractures, and prenatal harm. It explains how to get records from physicians and hospitals and how to file for medical payments. The third section discusses disability in relation to damages: how to evaluate a claim, compute the price, and how and when to settle. Last is general commentary on various types of liability insurance, accident statistics, a definition of negligence, a glossary of insurance and legal terms, and charts of automobile stopping distances. A master checklist for a car accident, and a worksheet to compute the amount of the claim complete the book.

301. Chernik, Valdimir P. **The Claims Game.** Sherbourne Press, 1969. 208 pp. $5.95.

Chernik, a professional claims adjuster and manager, gives good advice to persons involved in accidents and unsure if they should sue for injury. He feels they should (but only with the help of an attorney). He points out that most people are ignorant of their rights and, in almost all cases, could not sue by themselves. Chernik tells how to retain a lawyer and doctor (for the injuries), how to decide when to settle (if the claim seems fair), and why honesty in the claim is the best policy. He has an interesting chapter on how to deal with the claims adjuster and another on those factors which influence insurance companies: nationality, age, profession, injury, etc. One appendix deals with "Length of Disability and Permanent Residuals" and another with "Values of Severe Injuries in Workmen's Compensation." A glossary of insurance terms completes the book. *The Claims Game* paints an accurate picture of accident claims from the insurance company view.

302. Chernik, Vladimir P. **The Consumer's Guide to Insurance Buying.** Sherbourne Press, 1970. 288 pp. $6.50; paper $4.50.

Here Chernik advises on how to avoid overinsurance. His basic premise is that the *only* good reason to buy insurance is for protection. Therefore, a family should get term life insurance (from a savings bank, if possible), since it is the cheapest and the best. He also suggests insuring only the breadwinner (which may be questionable advice). Health, disability, automobile, and property insurance, as well as insurance against lawsuits are also covered. Chernik's general tips on reducing all insurance costs include buying coverage with high deductibles (the higher the deductible, the lower the cost) and paying premiums by the year or longer (and saving the interest). Implicit in this book is the theory that most, if not all, insurance is not nearly as good as is claimed, and that a family must familiarize itself with the noncoverage features of its insurance and prepare accordingly.

303. Denenberg, Herbert S. **Shopper's Guide to Insurance: A Series of Tips on How to Shop and Save on Insurance.** Consumer News, 1973. 16 pp. Paper $1. Free to Pennsylvania residents, from Pennsylvania Department of Insurance.

As a ready-reference guide to insurance, this pamphlet cannot be beat for value. Denenberg prepared information covering automobile, health, personal liability, and life insurance when he was commissioner of Pennsylvania's Department of Insurance. He explains how to select an agent, and provides two tables for rating them: one for property liability agents and the other for life insurance agents. Material on when and how to complain (specifically aimed at Pennsylvania residents), how to shop for insurance, rules for planning a comprehensive insurance program, and information on special problems, such as how to collect on claims and the problems of small business people, is also included. When buying coverage, he stresses the need to shop around (costs can vary from 60 percent to 324 percent on life, health, auto, and homeowner's policies). Group coverage is cheaper and is often also better, and he urges consumers to get such policies if possible. Denenberg also suggests screening agents carefully and updating insurance yearly. For example, when property values go up and when family changes occur, as with a divorce or a birth, coverage should change accordingly.

304. Goodwin, Dave. **Stop Wasting Your Insurance Dollars.** (Essandess Special Edition). Simon and Schuster, 1969. 153 pp. Paper $1.50.

While parts of this book, written by a general agent for a life insurance company, are almost useless, coverage of property and business insurance as well as material on agents and settling claims are good. Goodwin is not out to denounce or expose the industry, but instead points up values of adequate protection and ways of getting it without becoming insurance poor. Rather than go into detailed descriptions of different kinds of policies, he conveys insurance principles. On the whole, he is too kind to insurance agents, even though much of this book warns that through their ignorance, self-interest and/or neglect most people end up spending their insurance dollars on inadequate and wasteful coverage. A good section notes differences between property and life insurance agents, and offers an 18-point checklist on rating them. Goodwin's suggestions for the future include a reform of auto insurance and fair labeling on insurance forms.

305. Hamilton, Richard T. **The Great Confidence Games: Game 1—The Insurance Game.** Exposition, 1971. 114 pp. $4.50.

An attempt to expose abuses in the insurance industry, it is written in an elliptical, confused manner, replete with coarse language. A pity, because there is merit to what Hamilton says. However, others say the same thing and in a more rational manner. Not recommended.

306. Mehr, Robert I. **Programmed Learning Aid for Principles of Insurance.** (Irwin Programmed Learning Aid Series). Learning Systems, 1973. 147 pp. Paper $3.50.

PLAID, a *p*rogrammed *l*earning *aid* for college-level students, is intended as an adjunct to course study or for self-review. Each topic is broken down into small sections called frames. After each frame, a short series of true-false questions reviews the material. If the student gets the material wrong, he or she is to reread the frame. The PLAID concludes with examination questions for each chapter. Answers follow. A combined index and glossary completes the book. This material has been prepared by Robert I. Mehr, professor of finance at the University of Illinois at Urbana-Champaign. Since it is designed for insurance students, it points up the benefits of various types of insurance, but does not bother much with their deficiencies. It is a rather thorough overview, covering insurance dealing with business and contracts, health and disability, liability, life, automobiles, oceans and inland water, fire, crime, social insurance, and pensions. In addition, chapters cover loss adjustment, pricing, underwriting, and insurance and the law. It is fairly up-to-date, giving pros and cons of no-fault auto insurance, for example. The chapter on health insurance is particularly bland and could stand improvement. Useful as an overview, but consumers will have to use other sources for more direct help.

INSURANCE, AUTOMOBILE

307. Denenberg, Herbert S. **Shopper's Guide To Pennsylvania Automobile Insurance.** Pennsylvania Department of Insurance, 1972. 26 pp. Paper $1. Free to Pennsylvania residents.

A guide to the annual premiums of the 12 largest automobile insurance writers in Pennsylvania, it covers six different insurance territories, and within each territory, three rating examples: adult operator, youthful male operator, and youthful female operator, with specific cars and accident histories. As each factor, such as age, marital status, usage of car, type of driving, etc. will affect insurance rates, this pamphlet can only be used as a general guide to the companies' insurance rates. However, there is enough spread between policies to make such comparison shopping worthwhile, particularly for residents of Pennsylvania.

308. Gillespie, Paul, and Miriam Klipper. **No Fault: What You Save, Gain, and Lose with the New Auto Insurance.** Praeger, 1972. 164 pp. $5.95.

Gillespie, a lawyer specializing in personal injury cases (formerly with a major insurance company's claims division), and Klipper, an editor in the field of business and economics, wrote this at a time when only Massachusetts had passed a no-fault act. The authors have few kind words for the new system; they describe its passage in Massachusetts as a disaster, view it as a bonanza for insurance companies (which will no longer have to compete for customers), and consider it inequitable for persons involved in accidents. The authors contend that had not Massachusetts lowered auto insurance rates, the law would not have passed. Hindsight, of course, tells consumers that after being in existence for a year, rates were further cut. The authors also feel that some way must be worked out to determine "optimum combination of cost to the consumer and equity to the victim." They also discuss various federal proposals for no-fault, including one version recommended by the Department of Transportation and another by Senators Hart and Magnuson. The latter allows options that would give accident victims the same right to compensation they have without no-fault. The authors seem to overlook the tremendous difficulties consumers have in settling claims and the financial burdens they must carry until they do settle without no-fault.

INSURANCE, HEALTH

See also Medical Care; Social Security and Medicare. *For pertinent organizations see Part II, Private Organizations*—The Cooperative League of the USA; Insurance Consumers Union—Policyholders Protective Association, Inc.

309. Denenberg, Herbert S. **A Shopper's Guide to Health Insurance.** Consumer News, 1973. 16 pp. Paper $1. Free to residents of Pennsylvania, from the Pennsylvania Department of Insurance.

Denenberg defines different types of health insurance, lists rules for determining good policies and companies, shows how and from whom to get the best coverage, and discusses special needs of those covered by Medicare and Medicaid. "What You Want in a Health Insurance Policy and in the Company You Buy It From" lists the following: get coverage which pays for a broad range of services with few exclusions and which pays the full amount or a very large percentage (not one that pays a flat fee); shop for a policy in order to pay the least and get the most back. (A chart showing the 25 largest commercial health insurance companies and Blue Cross plans in Pennsylvania ranks them by their loss ratios—the percentage of premiums companies pay back in claims.) Other rules: avoid companies with waiting periods and exclusions, such as preexisting conditions and few maternity benefits; make sure renewal terms are liberal; use a financially strong company without a history of fighting claims; take advantage of group policies whenever possible; consider Blue Cross first when shopping for an individual plan; avoid mail-order insurance; try to use a health maintenance organization, e.g., HIP, Kaiser (even though their premiums are high, coverage is good and they practice preventive medicine). "15 Questions to Ask about Your Insurance Policy" summarize the material. The pamphlet is included in *The Shopper's Guidebook to Life Insurance, Health Insurance*, . . . (*see* entry 69).

310. Gregg, John E. **The Health Insurance Racket and How to Beat It.** Regnery, 1973. 225 pp. $6.96.

The only full-length consumer guide to health insurance, it is also very good. Gregg, a former FBI agent and health insurance salesman, is now a lawyer and director of the Policyholders Protective Association International, a consumer group working for reform of the U.S. health care system. He exposes the health insurance field as one committed to deception and unconcerned with the interests of its clients. Chapters cover deceptive merchandising techniques, e.g., special policies for "union members in good standing" or for veterans; discrimination due to race and/or previous sickness and fraudulent alterations of applications (Gregg warns buyers to photostat applications since so many are changed to lay the basis for denying future claims). He suggests methods to cut the red tape of payments and ways to bring pressure when all else fails. Since the main point of health insurance is to cover long and/or catastrophic illness, major medical coverage should be bought first. If possible, it helps to become part of a group health insurance plan (costs are lower, coverage is better, claims are processed faster, renewal is automatic, etc.); when buying disability insurance, insure only those whose incomes are necessary for the functioning of the household; avoid mail order insurance; use a doctor whose nurse is familiar with claims procedures (an improperly filed claim loses benefits). Useful appendices include samples of typical health insurance applications and claimants' statements, a comparison of five national health insurance proposals, and the names and addresses of state insurance departments. "Guide to Buying Health Insurance" summarizes much of the very good advice.

311. Hoyt, Edwin P. **Your Health Insurance: A Story of Failure.** John Day, 1970. 158 pp. $4.95.

Hoyt presents a convincing case for better health insurance and health care; for community health centers and cooperative medicine, and for a federal government responsible for health quality and cost controls. He points up the poor coverage of most health plans, including Blue Cross and Blue Shield and the poor quality of health care, and he offers necessary steps to remedy the situation. He shows that health services for members of the armed forces and their dependents are excellent, that coverage of some private health plans, such as the Kaiser Plan and the United Mine Workers plan is very good, and that health coverage and health care afforded to the poor, particularly Eskimos, Aleuts, and Indians, is dreadful. The author attacks the callousness of many hospitals and doctors for their outrageous (mal)practices and exorbitant fees. He suggests a health care program similar to Canada's: one that provides adequate hospitalization for all and examination and control of hospital costs by outsiders.

INSURANCE, LIFE

For pertinent organizations see Part II, U.S. Federal Agencies—Veterans Administration; *Private Organizations*—Insurance Consumers Union—Policyholders Protective Association, Inc.

312. Belth, Joseph M. **Life Insurance: A Consumer's Handbook.** Indiana University Press, 1973. 248 pp. $6.95.

Some of the information provided by Belth, professor of insurance, School of Business, Indiana University, is similar to that in the shorter, less technical, and less expensive *Consumers Union Report on Life Insurance* (*see* entry 313), but there is still enough here to make the book worth reading. Belth feels that "when carefully purchased," life insurance in savings-type policies can be good. Charts show how to determine an adequate amount of life insurance. The author explains how to find and buy the right policy and riders; which companies to buy from; how to buy from other sources (e.g., banks, the government, industrial and fraternal benefit societies); how to decide whether or not to use an agent—and how to select one. Belth analyzes an insurance contract, lists payment schedules, gives examples of eight different family situations calling for eight different insurance decisions, and discusses why public ignorance and apathy, coupled with the complexity of the subject, produces consumer exploitation. He suggests buying from insurance companies recommended by *Best's Life Insurance Reports* (127 companies are listed in the 1971 edition). He also shows prices and premiums on various policies of regular insurance companies and on nonagency organizations, such as banks and annuity associations. Addresses of state insurance commissioners are also appended.

313. Consumer Reports. **The Consumers Union Report on Life Insurance: A Guide to Planning and Buying the Protection You Need.** Rev. ed. Grossman, 1973. 135 pp. $4.95.

A revision of the series "How to Buy Life Insurance" in the January, February, March, and June 1967 *Consumer Reports*, with a section on Social Security expanded and worksheets for individual insurance protection appended, this edition is only slightly altered: the statistics are based primarily on the 1967 articles. One object of this report is to show consumers how to judge the amount of life insurance needed—and to see the importance of buying that amount and no more. The second purpose is to point up the relative merits of term insurance over all other types. It has been Consumers Union's position since 1937 that the only life insurance worth buying is term insurance; that cash-value insurance such as ordinary life or 20-year endowment are not wise investments. Today, that view is shared by almost all consumer advocates in the field, and CU's advice is worth noting. The guide has chapters on determining whom to protect and to insure; how much coverage to buy; the difficulty of determining costs of different policies, and some comparative premiums and prices of five-year term policies. The editors point up the wisdom of "reading the fine print" before purchase, list pros and cons of insurance as forced savings, and discuss Social Security as a form of life insurance. The "Life Insurance Planning Worksheets" are designed for present and future computations of a family's insurance needs, as CU stresses the need for periodic insurance reviews.

314. Dacey, Norman F. **What's Wrong with Your Life Insurance.** Macmillan, 1963. 445 pp. $6.95; paper $1.50.

This is an early exposé of insurance industry abuses—mammoth profits raked in by companies and small returns given out to policyholders. Dacey feels that a major problem is the use of outdated mortality tables. Anticipating changed tables in 1966, he insists they are neither up-to-date nor fair to the consumer. The author says that both mutual and stock insurance companies make excessive profits from lapsed policies, spend enormous sums on commissions and expenses, and give little to policyholders in death claims or other benefits (particularly savings life insurance or tax shelter savings). Dacey describes a large group of policies and finds fault (even fraud) with almost all but term and group insurance. He warns consumers not to buy educational endowments or retirement income policies tied to insurance policies, discusses the effects of inflation on insurance, explains why extras, such as disability and double indemnity clauses, are good for insurance companies and poor choices for buyers and why insurance dividends are neither bargains nor savings (but returns on premiums that were set too high). Dacey's suggestions include buying term insurance and leaving it in a trust tailored to each family's needs. He makes a convincing case for regulation of the insurance industry as a whole and sales practices in particular. Reading the book now proves that nothing has been done to correct these abuses in all this time.

315. Denenberg, Herbert S. **Shopper's Guide to Straight Life Insurance.** 2nd ed. Consumer News, 1973. 34 pp. Paper $1. Free to Pennsylvania residents, from the Pennsylvania Department of Insurance.

Denenberg provides cost information on $10,000 and $25,000 straight life policies collected from 330 life insurance companies and from the 25 largest of the 100 fraternals licensed in Pannsylvania. (Since the largest firms operate all over the country much of this information is pertinent to everyone.) Charts rank the $10,000 and $25,000 policies (participating and nonparticipating) for the largest companies and the lowest and highest cost $10,000 participating and nonparticipating policies of all companies. The data are broken down further by age: 20, 35, and 50 years, respectively. The charts are clearly explained, so a prospective buyer can judge almost immediately which policies to look into. In addition, the guide offers eight rules for buying and determining how much of what type of life insurance is needed for each family. The rules include shopping for the best buys (saving thousands of dollars over the years), paying premiums annually (saving up to 6 percent on costs), getting an affordable policy, buying and holding onto as few plans as possible, and getting a good agent and company. The pamphlet is included in *The Shopper's Guidebook to Life Insurance, Health Insurance, . . .* (*see* entry 69).

316. Denenberg, Herbert S. **A Shopper's Guide to Term Life Insurance.** Consumer News, 1972. 19 pp. Paper $1. Free to residents of Pennsylvania, from the Pennsylvania Department of Insurance.

The Pennsylvania Department of Insurance collected data from all 380 life insurance companies licensed in the state and from 25 of the 100 fraternals licensed there and found that the cost of term life insurance varied by as much as 140 percent. This guide defines term insurance and explains why premiums are lower than on other types of life insurance. It also covers participating and five-year renewable-convertible policies, when to switch or keep policies, when to add riders, and how to get the best buys. Charts show the lowest and highest costing five-year term policies, and the costs of the five-year term policies on all the largest companies doing business in Pennsylvania. Since many of these firms are national, consumers all over the country can use the information. Included in *The Shopper's Guidebook to Life Insurance, Health Insurance, . . .* (*see* entry 69).

317. Fogiel, Max. **How to Pay Lots Less for Life Insurance . . . and Be Covered for as Much and as Long as You Want.** Research and Education Association, 1971. 208 pp. $5.95.

Particularly recommended for people unfamiliar with insurance and its jargon, the guide is written by a licensed life insurance agent and registered life insurance consultant. Fogiel discusses term, whole life, and endowment policies and explains why term is the best. He explains why only those with dependents should be insured, how to compute the amount of insurance needed, why and how to save as an adjunct to life insurance, how to determine whether to change policies and make the change if necessary, how and when to get insured, how to select an agent and a company, various ways to collect on policies (e.g., lump sums, annuities), and special types of insurance (e.g., group, credit, business, and partnership life). The author recaps most of this material in two checklists: the first, 15 points to consider before buying life insurance: the second, 11 points to consider before changing a current policy. A glossary concludes.

318. Geier, Arnold. **Life Insurance: How to Get Your Money's Worth.** Collier, 1965. 192 pp. Paper 95¢.

Writing from the standpoint of a dealer in insurance who is seeking commissions, Geier, director of National Insurance Consultants, stresses the positive aspects of insurance coverage. He minimizes the need to shop for an agent or a company, plays down term insurance, and plumps for buying whole life. (He even states that the latter's popularity is proof of its usefulness.) Geier is also in favor of insuring the young and adding riders to basic policies. Since all his suggestions are misleading, the book is not recommended.

319. Gollin, James. **Pay Now, Die Later: What's Wrong with Life Insurance: A Report on Our Biggest and Most Wasteful Industry.** Random House, 1966. 267 pp. $5.95.

A report on the industry by a former salesman and underwriter, *Pay Now, Die Later* indicts management, not the system. Gollin feels that the problems are conservative business practices and old-fashioned control rather than a lack of social orientation. Yet he admits discrimination, based on race, sex, age, and health, and callousness to undertrained salespeople who are not expected to remain long in the business. One of Gollin's major theses is that these untrained agents underinsure and/or provide insurance not tailored to most people's needs. He also feels it is unnecessary to shop for insurance companies, stating that there is little difference in rates between companies, and that for most families, whole life is better than term insurance (views not shared by consumer advocates). Gollin is in favor of insuring some working women and divorced women with children, and he feels that as beneficiaries, wives should know exactly what their benefits would be in the event their husbands die. Overall, readers not well versed in this subject should read with caution. Gollin attacks side effects and symptoms and some advice is questionable.

320. *Maloney, Richard F., ed. "Life Insurance from the Buyer's Point of View," **Economic Education Bulletin**, vol. 13, no. 7 (1973): 1–27. Paper $1 for issue.

Maloney provides detailed analyses of various types of life insurance (including group and industrial insurance); a discussion of insurance settlement options, premiums, dividends, and cash values; a method to compute the net costs of policies, and a way to determine the best insurance company. The last includes checking a company's regular expenses, mortality expenses, and investment yields. In addition, insurance companies and policies (mainly in Massachusetts and New York) have been rated, and suggestions are given for dealing with insurance agents, medical examiners, etc. The pamphlet packs a great deal of substantial information into very little space—and is also a good source for determining the right type of policy to buy and the least costly company to buy it from.

321. Will, Charles, A. **Does It Make Sense?** National Underwriter Co., 1973. 79 pp. Paper $3.

Underwriter Will's thesis is that life insurance cannot be issued if financial need is greatly out of proportion to death benefits, or if it "does not mesh with logic." In other words, if salespeople oversell insurance, the underwriters will not accept the policies if they are out of line. For example, a 55-year-old man, who never had a life insurance policy, will either not be issued one or will get one that pays out little and costs a lot. Will also exposes many pointless and prejudicial restrictions that abound in the industry. These restrictions often work against honest people to make them buy insurance at inflated rates (if they can get it at all). This list includes persons who are divorced, separated, promiscuous, hippies, homosexuals, in show business, bankrupts, and crooks. For those interested in knowing why they must be investigated, why they must have physicals, and why they must pay higher rates than their neighbors, this book suggests the answers. It can also be used as a primer to determine for oneself why one should be insured, and for how much money. Cases cover both business and familial beneficiaries.

INSURANCE, MOBILE HOMES

For pertinent organizations see Part II, U.S. Federal Agencies—Department of Housing and Urban Development, Housing Production and Mortgage Credit—Federal Housing Administration.

322. Denenberg, Herbert S. **A Shopper's Guide to Insurance on Mobile Homes (Pennsylvania).** Consumer News, 1973. 7 pp. Paper 50¢. Free to Pennsylvania residents, from Pennsylvania Department of Insurance.

Prepared specifically for Pennsylvania's flood victims buying mobile homes, it explains 12 basic rules for buying insurance. The best buy is the package policy, which is the mobile homeowner policy and covers property and liability. It also suggests buying comprehensive coverage rather than named perils coverage; getting a special collision policy if the home is to be moved, and making sure that there is enough liability, flood, and property coverage on the home and its contents. General insurance buying rules also apply here: the need to shop for the best buy, to cut premiums by getting high deductibles, and to buy on a longer than annual basis (for lower premiums). Nine companies and their premiums, deductibles, and flood coverage (if any) are charted. The chart is for companies doing business in Pennsylvania, but many of them are national firms.

KITCHEN UTENSILS

See Household Equipment and Furnishings

LANDLORDS AND TENANTS

323. Goodman, Emily Jane. **The Tenant Survival Book.** Bobbs-Merrill, 1972. 215 pp. $8.50; paper $3.95.

Highlighting the rights of landlords and the powerlessness of tenants, it is also a "how-to" for tenants wanting to organize for boycotts, strikes, fund raisings, court appearances, collective bargaining, squatting, calling the media, and hiring lawyers. Goodman points up the similarity of problems facing renters in luxury buildings and those in tenements, stressing the need for both groups to act in concert for change. A lawyer, she provides a much needed clarification of the lease by translating clauses from various standard leases. The book emphasizes the weakness of tenant positions and the legal advantages of landlords (particularly in the courts). Goodman writes clearly and makes both the laws and the procedures for change easy to understand.

324. Ranney, George, Jr., Edmond Parker, and Richard Groll. **Landlord and Tenant.** (Justice in America Series). Houghton Mifflin, 1974. 86 pp. Paper $2.28.

An excellent text for junior and senior high school students, it concentrates on problems between landlords and tenants, particularly rental law. Subjects include duties of landlords and tenants, basic rental contracts, parts of the lease, breaches of contract by either party, and injuries, i.e., negligence, contributory negligence, and lead poisoning. A concluding chapter deals with pitfalls of buying a house: how much money to spend, how to get proper title and a good mortgage, dangers of installment contracts, and the layout of a good home. Each section of the text cites actual cases that state and local courts have ruled on and an explanation of the decisions. Exercises for students cover things to do and review questions.

325. Striker, John M., and Andrew O. Shapiro. **Super Tenant: New York City Tenant Handbook: Your Legal Rights and How to Use Them.** Brownstone Publishers, 1973. 268 pp. Paper $2.95.

Designed for New York City tenants in particular, the book can be of value to others as well. Contrary to Goodman (*The Tenant Survival Book*; *see* entry 323), these authors state that tenants have rights and that they should exercise them. The book is divided into several sections: know your rights, information on rent control and rent stabilization, maintenance and repairs (including when to withold rent, go on a rent strike, and sue a landlord); and the eviction process. Appendices include lists of New York City tenant organizations, free legal service and rent-impairing violations, New York's Maximum Base Rent (MBR) Order, MBR Protest Form and Rent-Stabilized Tenant's Complaint Form, legal rent increases for new services under rent control, and some information on how to sue in small claims courts. Much of what the authors say is substantiated with citations to recent decisions in New York City courts. The only criticism is that the book is too optimistic and does not concern itself with evicted tenants. For its positive tone and useful suggestions it is highly recommended.

LAWYERS

See Legal Services; Professional Services

LEGAL SERVICES

See also Professional Services

326. Bianchi, Carl F. **How to File a Suit in the New Jersey Small Claims Division.** New Jersey Department of Community Affairs, Office of Legal Services, 1970. 28 pp. Paper. Free to New Jersey residents.

Adapted from a similar pamphlet prepared by New York City's Consumers' Advisory Council as a guide for indigent consumers who wish to use the New Jersey small claims courts, the pamphlet is extremely easy to understand. It spells out the entire process: defines legal terms ("defendant," "plaintiff"), explains who can sue whom, types of damages that can be asked, costs, preparation for trial, how to choose between a trial by judge and a trial by jury, the trial itself, and collecting damages. An appendix carries addresses of county district courts where suits may be filed and the 14 legal services projects offices of the Office of Economic Opportunity available to those who need aid and cannot afford to pay.

327. Coulson, Robert. **How to Stay Out of Court.** Crown, 1968. 224 pp. $5.95.

Coulson, executive vice-president of the American Arbitration Association, has written a guide for those who have legal disputes which can be handled out of court. While primarily directed to business people, there is much here for persons with other problems. "Settling the Most Common Disputes" includes family dissension (divorce, alimony, child support, tuition expenses, allowances), personal injury claims, professional fee disputes, home improvement and construction costs, and debt collection. Coulson points up the high costs of lawyers' fees and court litigation and the value of using arbitration as an alternate. (It can settle problems amicably and save time and money as well.) He explains professional techniques for settling disputes as well as methods used by labor unions (grievance procedures and collective bargaining). Coulson feels that these techniques can be used by many other groups (farmers and buyers, landlords and tenants, franchise holders and franchise corporation) as well as by individuals and groups wanting to organize for social change and bargaining power on the local neighborhood level. As such, the book can be a useful tool for many people who want to make their voices heard without going to court.

328. Denenberg, Herbert S. **A Shopper's Guide to Lawyers.** Consumer News, 1973. 20 pp. Paper $1. Single copy free to residents of Pennsylvania, from the Pennsylvania Department of Insurance.

Choosing, using, and, sometimes, firing a lawyer are discussed. Contrary to most sources, Denenberg says that it is best to avoid using the *Martindale-Hubbel Law Directory* or lawyer's referral systems. He suggests asking company lawyers, satisfied friends, and other professionals and shopping around. In the interview, prospective clients must find out how much work the lawyer will do, if he or she will appeal a case (if necessary), the lawyer's specialty, etc. The section on fees lists different ways lawyers are paid: retainers, hourly rates, contingency fees, bonus fees, minimum fees, and costs and expenses. Eight Bar Association guidelines help to determine if the fee is reasonable: lawyer's time and labor, difficulty of the case, results, lawyer's experience and reputation, fees for similar service in a particular region of the country, whether it is a fixed or contingent fee. Denenberg adds 20 tips for a good lawyer-client relationship, e.g., itemized bills, no free advice, complete understanding of the fee arrangement. If not satisfied, Denenberg suggests complaining, firing the attorney, going to the Bar Association, or filing a malpractice suit and telling friends and the local newspaper.

329. Matthews, Douglas. **Sue the B*st*rds: The Victim's Handbook.** Arbor House, 1973. 228 pp. $6.95; paper $2.95.

Written for those who have been cheated out of basic goods and services and are unfamiliar with the workings of the small claims courts. In a very chatty colloquial manner, Matthews explains who can sue whom and for how much, how to file and bring suit, dos and don'ts of courtroom behavior, claim settlements and how to collect. An excellent chapter discusses tenant civil rights, e.g., getting a security deposit back or collecting for negligence. An activist lawyer, Matthews has a section on small claims court reform. Appendix A is a state-by-state small claims court compendium that includes type of court, claim limit, age limit, filing fees, service of process, venue (where to sue), normal waiting time, arbitration system, lawyers (if allowed in court), corporations (if they may sue), transfer of the case to regular court, appeal, statute of limitations, and a miscellany of additional information. Appendix B is a series of typical forms and documents: Defendant Summons, Court Order for Appearance of Judgment, Order to Show Cause, and Counterclaim of Defendant. An extremely useful book for groups as well as individuals.

330. Wehringer, Cameron K. **When and How to Choose an Attorney.** (Legal Almanac Series No. 63). Oceana, 1970. 120 pp. $3.

Wehringer, a practicing attorney in two states, describes the ways one can locate an attorney, what services the client can expect from him or her, fees, methods of getting more efficient legal service, and the lawyers' Code of Professional Responsibility. Wehringer breaks down the choice of attorney by need and place, i.e., casually, for civil law purposes; with a sense of urgency, for civil law purposes; for specific purposes, such as wills and inventions; for criminal prosecution; in small towns; in large cities. He describes different methods of locating lawyers: directories, other lawyers, banks, bar referrals, etc., and stresses the need for finding an attorney with whom one has rapport. (Competence is a given at this point.) The author spells out the attorney's obligations to the client and vice versa. Fees for different types of work are also discussed, and time-cost factors are explained.

LIFE INSURANCE

See Insurance, Life

LOANS

See Credit

MEDICAL CARE

See also Dental Care; Drugs; Eye Care; Insurance, Health; Nursing Homes; Professional Services. *For pertinent organizations see Part II, U.S. Federal Agencies*—Department of Agriculture, Extension Service; *Private Organizations*—The Cooperative League of the USA.

331. Blum, Richard H. **A Commonsense Guide to Doctors, Hospitals and Medical Care.** Macmillan, 1964. 333 pp. $5.95.

Similar in many ways to the slightly newer *Guide to Modern Medical Care* (*see* entry 341), Blum's book deals with the whys and hows of choosing doctors, hospitals, and health insurance. He discusses various types of nonmedical help, e.g., osteopaths and faith healers, and urges the use of trained physicians for most ills. His guidelines for choosing doctors are spelled out in detail, and while some seem naive—e.g., asking doctors if they would recommend specialists if it seemed necessary—much of what he says is useful. He also suggests using only accredited hospitals with good reputations (although it may not be possible in an emergency). Blum notes that patients are often hospitalized without real cause, and he cautions against allowing that to happen. He discusses health insurance programs and finds great gaps in financial coverage. The author explains what to expect from doctors, hospitals, and treatments and how to handle illness physically, emotionally, and financially. Awkwardly written, this book will acquaint readers with what they can realistically expect from medical care—and how to try to get the best.

332. Citizens Board of Inquiry into Health Services for Americans. **Heal Your Self.** 2nd ed. rev. American Public Health Association, 1972. 177 pp. Paper $2.95.

This account of the state of health care in America is highly researched and documented. The Citizens Board of Inquiry, composed of members of various medical professions, labor unions, national, state, and local government officials, welfare rights leaders, and interested citizens, finds all health care deficient. Even for the well-to-do, who can participate in health insurance plans or prepaid plans, service is either costly, inefficient, or too impersonal. For the poor, it is sometimes nonexistent and almost always humiliating and second-rate. The board found people paying more for medicines, hospitals, and doctors through Medicare than before. They found the best service was with prepaid plans, such as Kaiser (California) and HIP (Health Insurance Plan, New York), but even these have drawbacks. The board urges all citizens to work for the enactment of legislation that would put health care policies into the hands of the consumers; to support or initiate action for consumer representation on boards of health; to support the development of new types of health services; and to join together to get the power to enact these reforms.

333. Denenberg, Herbert S. **Shopper's Guide to Surgery: Fourteen Rules on How to Avoid Unnecessary Surgery.** Consumer News, n.d. 6 pp. Paper $1. Free to residents of Pennsylvania, from the Pennsylvania Department of Insurance.

Denenberg provides 14 rules for determining whether to undergo surgery. First and foremost is the need to go to an internist or general practictioner for an opinion and then to have a second doctor verify the decision. This is particularly necessary if the surgery is of a type notoriously overperformed, e.g., hysterectomies, hemorrhoidectomies and tonsillectomies. Other rules: don't insist on surgery—some doctor will always oblige; have the physician and surgeon explain alternatives to surgery as well as its benefits and complications; use only board-certified Fellows of the American College of Surgeons; have the operation performed in an accredited hospital; know the fees and costs beforehand. The guide packs a great deal of information into very little space at low cost; an excellent buy. It is included in *The Shopper's Guidebook to Life Insurance, Health Insurance, . . .* (*see* entry 69).

334. Dickens, Doris Lee. **You and Your Doctor.** Exposition, 1973. 80 pp. $5.

Dickens is a practicing psychiatrist, and her book is slanted toward the emotionally ill as well as those needing physical care. Much of it is obvious and weighed down in platitudes; other material is extraneous to a book of this type, i.e., advice on keeping a sound and healthy mind and body. Material on choosing a doctor leaves much to be desired: she suggests family recommendations and information from medical societies. The basic points of a good doctor-patient relationship are better: she discusses what patients can expect from doctors in the way of time, physical examinations, advice, information, and drugs. Stressing the need for a good relationship, she suggests changing doctors when not satisfied, even if the doctor is competent. In addition to its other faults, the book is highly overpriced. Not recommended.

335. Doyle, Patrick J. **Save Your Health & Your Money.** Acropolis, 1971. 240 pp. $6.95; paper $3.95. Arco. Paper $1.50.

Doyle, a physician who once practiced privately and taught at the medical school level, has provided material on ways to choose a doctor and a hospital, reduce drug bills, take medical deductions (on income tax) and use Medicare benefits and health insurance. At times Doyle seems to be reflexively defending the medical establishment, but most of his advice is sound. Discussing malpractice suits, he points out that consumers lose in the long run, since insurance rates and laboratory fees rise in response to the suits. (One gets the impression that the doctor is against these suits.) Several chapters cover illnesses and special problems—e.g., old age, quackery, over-the-counter drugs—and includes cost ranges for some medical procedures, e.g., abortions, vasectomies, plastic surgery, and some dental services. In addition, Doyle offers advice on preventing illness, ranging from avoiding pollutants such as noise (don't buy appliances if they are noisy) to notes on proper diet, exercise, and more. The thrust of the book is positive; Doyle feels the U.S. medical system is the best in the world, even if the poor do have trouble using it. A good list of paperbacks and free or inexpensive pamphlet material for the home library is unfortunately mostly out of print. Appendices also list voluntary and government health organizations, a medical history checklist, and the contents of an adequate family medicine chest. Most of the book is in question-and-answer form, but a good index makes it all readily available.

336. Edwards, Marvin H. **Hazardous to Your Health.** Arlington House, 1972. 318 pp. $9.95.

This is a conservative reaction to such books as *The American Health Empire* (*see* entry 338), *Don't Get Sick in America* (*see* entry 347) and *The Gerber Report,* by Edwards, editor of *Private Practice,* a magazine for doctors, who feels that there is no health crisis. According to him, there is no doctor shortage; U.S. infant and mortality rates compare favorably with Sweden's, Holland's and those of other European countries (when the statistics are looked at properly); there is no shortage of medical school graduates, no problem of access to physicians, and no real increase in medical costs. He further states that most medical increases have come about due to Medicare and Medicaid, and that the tax burden will be enormous if a national health plan goes through. Edwards warns of impersonalized rote medicine practiced by unskilled and unqualified physicians coupled with a spiraling of costs. He urges consumers to work to defeat the passage of any laws permitting a national health plan.

337. Frank, Arthur, and Stuart Frank. **The People's Handbook of Medical Care.** Vintage, Random House, 1972. 494 pp. Paper $2.95.

The authors, socially conscious doctors, provide a medical guide for the student activist, counter-culturist, and the like. They have included material on handling medical emergencies in sit-ins, demonstrations, police stations, and so on. They explain free clinics, abortion laws (outdated since the Supreme Court decision), and medical standards and deferments of the armed forces (presently unnecessary since the abolition of the draft). They also suggest various ways of selecting a doctor, hospital, or free community clinic and some guidelines by which to judge each. The bulk of the book describes common and uncommon ailments and medical emergencies, with procedures for dealing with each. The chapter on medical rights and privileges explains limits and responsibilities of doctors and hospitals, e.g., they do not have to treat you, but if they do, they must continue treatment competently or face malpractice suits; they are legally responsible for reporting certain diseases, e.g., venereal disease, and certain problems, e.g., gunshot wounds; they must have parental authorization to treat minors, etc. This chapter also discusses the (lack of) rights of the mentally disturbed, persons in jail, the poor, and so on. While some material can and should be read by all, many people will be put off by the authors' bias toward the activist young, and may even be distressed by their levity in discussing the essentially serious business of health.

338. Health Policy Advisory Committee. **The American Health Empire: Power, Profits and Politics.** By Barbara and John Ehrenreich. Random House, 1970. 279 pp. $7.95.

This challenge to the current American medical health care system points up some of the struggles of activists to change the system. The report discusses the Student Health Organization, a group of students in various health profession disciplines which worked for community control of local hospitals and to make teaching hospitals "safe for the community." One section discusses an unsuccessful attempt at worker takeover of a health service. Lincoln Hospital Mental Health Service in New York City had recruited nonprofessionals from the local indigent population. It promised a career ladder that would result in professionally fulfilling work. The promise was broken; the nonprofessionals were not advanced. Another attempt at community involvement in the Gouverneur Health Center in New York's Lower East Side also met with frustration and failure on the part of the community. The report concludes that unless citizens become truly concerned and involved, such situations will continue. Health services will stay unresponsive to needs, and adequate health care will be denied to all.

339. Kennedy, Edward M. **In Critical Condition: The Crisis in America's Health Care.** Pocket Books, 1972. 196 pp. Paper $1.50.

Senator Kennedy's book on "the five crises in America's health care" is little different from many of the others on the same subject. It is interspersed with Senate testimony by victims and critics of the system, depicting the callousness of the medical profession, lack of care for the poor, hospital facilities padlocked because personnel were not hired to staff them, people whose health insurance coverage is so bad they are thousands of dollars in debt, and people who cannot get health insurance coverage. He compares our system with that in various European countries and in Israel. Kennedy proposes his Health Security Plan, a federal "group insurance plan" that would cover everyone equally, would be paid for in proportion to earnings, would benefit everyone without exclusions, and would provide preventive medical care as well. For those who wish to see legislation of this sort passed, reading this book and determining its merits would be a constructive first step.

340. Kime, Robert E. **Health: A Consumer's Dilemma.** (Basic Concepts in Health Science). Wadsworth, 1970. 68 pp. Paper $1.50.

Part of a series for beginning students of health science, it makes for good reading in or out of the classroom. Kime covers the basic ignorance of Americans about health concepts and preventive medicine, the waste in lives and money through medical quackery, and the powers and limitations of the Food and Drug Administration, Federal Trade Commission, United States Post Office, American Medical Association and its magazine *Today's Health,* Consumers Union's *Consumer Reports,* The Better Business Bureau's Food, Drug and Cosmetic Division, and other state and local agencies in protecting consumers from false and misleading information. Kime also describes various types of medical specialists and gives pointers for finding a good doctor and dentist. An interesting discussion concerns the right time to use medical help—and when to rely on home remedies and simple bed rest. The author compares America's medical care to that in other countries and describes both voluntary and public medical insurance plans. He concludes that Americans need national governmental control to pay for medical costs and have a long way to go to catch up with other nations in getting these benefits.

341. Klotz, S. D. **Guide to Modern Medical Care.** Scribners, 1967. 365 pp. $7.95.

Dr. Klotz's book is intended to make the individual aware of the various health professions and services, i.e., medical specialists, assistants, nurses, paraprofessionals, dentists and their assistants, and others, such as osteopaths, chiropodists, and optometrists. In addition, Klotz offers advice on choosing a physician and a hospital and on devising a plan for emergencies. He covers the responsibilities of doctors and hospitals, medical and clinical services and costs, and health plans and coverages. Klotz briefly suggests ways of choosing a good dentist (asking your doctor is one way), of choosing a good pharmacist, and of getting drugs prescribed at the lowest price. He also discusses health care for the aging, mental health, death and dying (in which he tells how to leave one's body to medical science and the scientific value of an autopsy), and tips on medical care when traveling. Appendices list doctors' specialty boards, health and medical organizations, voluntary health organizations, and laboratory charges at a community hospital in 1967. Klotz has also annotated a short bibliography of medical directories, books, and pamphlets, and appended a glossary of medical terms. His book is for those wanting basic information about the health professions, and as such, can also be used by students interested in career guidance in the field. Consumers should note that it plays down faults and highlights good points.

342. Kunnes, Richard. **Your Money or Your Life: Rx for the Medical Market Place.** Dodd, Mead, 1971. 205 pp. $5.95.

Psychiatrist Kunnes (University of Michigan at Ann Arbor, and spokesman and cofounder of the Medical Liberation Front) has very little to say in support of the medical community. His book is a sweeping denunciation of the training, dehumanizing and cynicism of doctors; of the greed and callousness of what he calls the medical-industrial complex (which includes hospitals, research facilities, and pharmaceutical companies); and at the profiteering at the expense of all, particularly the poor, the nonwhite, and women. Kunnes charges hospitals with using the poor for research and training purposes, for total unresponsiveness to the community, and for standing in the way of progressive medical care. He urges citizens to band together to demand true community control of hospitals, and he states that unless the proposed national health insurance programs remove physician control and replace it with citizen control, the basic health morass will only get worse. Undoubtedly one of the most biting attacks on the medical establishment available to the general reader.

343. *McGarrah, Rob. "It's Time Consumers Knew More about Their Doctors," **Medical Economics,** March 4, 1974. Reprint. 5 pp. **Supplement to Medical Economics Reprint on A Consumer's Directory of Prince George's County Doctors.** Health Research Group, 1974. 19 pp. n.p.

The Health Research Group, a Nader organization, produced *A Consumer's Directory of Prince George's County Doctors* in 1973. McGarrah's article is the introduction to the *Directory* in condensed form. The *Directory* is available from the Health Research Group for $1.50, or 50¢ for Medicare and Medicaid patients. The *Supplement* is provided for all consumer groups that wish to duplicate these efforts. It explains the survey (including why it had to be done by telephone and why each question was chosen), reproduces a representative listing, has information on advertising laws, and provides the questionnaire. The 22 questions range from type of practice (solo or group), office hours, after-hours coverage (vacations, evenings, and weekends) to average waiting time for a regular appointment, average time spent on each patient, whether the doctor takes Medicare and Medicaid patients, average fees for first and routine office visits, and whether the doctor can handle non-English-speaking patients. The letter sent by the Prince George's County (Maryland) Medical Society enjoining its physicians from participating in the survey is also reproduced. As the first attempt at a qualitative comparison of doctors in the country, the survey deserves a wide audience.

344. McTaggart, Aubrey C. (Howard L. Slusher, consulting ed.). **The Health Care Dilemma.** (Foundations of Health Education Series). Holbrook Press, 1970. 233 pp. Paper $3.95.

This excellent compendium of information gathered from other sources outlines the problems confronting anyone wanting decent medical care. The editors present information on the study and practice of medicine, dentistry, and other health practices, e.g., osteopathy, chiropractic, podiatry, Christian Science. Quoting from *A Commonsense Guide to Doctors, Hospitals, and Medical Care* (1964; *see* entry 331) McTaggart describes the best way to get a competent physician: pick one who teaches at a respected medical school and/or who has full staff privileges at reputable hospital(s). The author points out that doctors usually choose specialists to treat them, and the public should do likewise. Determining the worth of a hospital and choosing among the good ones is also described. The chapter on drugs points out that doctors often rely on pharmaceutical companies for their information; also that doctors who own pharmacies usually end up with conflicts of interest. The material on clinical laboratories underscores their shortcomings and urges that with important tests, split samples should be sent to two labs so results can be compared. Not only are Medicare and Medicaid explained, but also why abuses occur, e.g., doctors often charge more now than before the programs were instituted in order to collect more from the government. "Group Practice" describes three comprehensive services: Health Insurance Plan (HIP) of New York, Kaiser in California, and Group Health Cooperative of Puget Sound. The book lists all the advantages of group service—including doctor-peer surveillance, 24-hour medical care, prepaid bills, and efficiency—as well as the disadvantages, not least among them physician hostility. The concluding chapter stresses the need for health rather than sickness services and for more efficient use of the health practitioners and hospitals. Highly recommended.

345. **Money Management: Your Health and Recreation Dollar.** Rev. ed. Illus. Money Management Institute, Household Finance Corp., 1968. 36 pp. Paper 25¢. Quantity orders discounted.

An overview of health services and facilities, health insurance and costs, recreational needs, vacation planning and expenses, the pamphlet suggests ways to find a good doctor, nurse, hospital, nursing home, and dentist. It covers different types of health protection in the United States and Canada. Information on vacation planning is very general, but some costs and methods of payment are enumerated, e.g., prepaid vacation trips, pay-as-you go.

346. Placere, Morris N., and Charles S. Marwick. **How You Can Get Better Medical Care for Less Money.** Walker & Co., 1973. 192 pp. $7.95.

Placere, a pseudonymous practicing surgeon in a metropolitan area, has harsh words for many doctors and particularly for surgeons. His thesis is that the poor in America are neglected and the middle and upper classes overmedicated and overdrugged—often by inferior doctors, hospitals, services, and pharmaceuticals. Placere says surgeons are too quick to operate and often practice their specialty without qualification. He offers sensible guidelines for finding a competent doctor (is the physician easily reached on the phone? are fees, specialty, and personality acceptable?), a good druggist, and low-cost drugs. He feels that many suburban hospitals are dangerous and suggests using large medical centers when at all possible. He cautions against accepting hospital bills without minute examinations and encourages fighting them if they are unreasonably high. He explains that such services as Blue Cross now cover less and cost more because they are representative of hospitals not patients, and urges consumers to get health insurance covering most expenses. Placere is in favor of government health insurance and stresses the need for more peer review of doctors (as health care foundations are now doing). The book is a warning against accepting medical advice per se, and a plea for greater controls and more adequate services for all. Enlightening and dismaying.

347. Schorr, Daniel. **Don't Get Sick in America.** Aurora, 1970. 224 pp. $5.95.

The result of a CBS two-part series "Health in America" aired in 1970, it makes the usual indictments against the system: inadequate health services for the poor; unrealistic, expensive, and incomplete health insurance coverage for the middle class; inefficiencies and price escalation due to Medicare and Medicaid; inadequate and overly expensive hospitals; lack of surveillance and supervision of private practitioners. It also covers the advantages of group practice; some discussion of health care programs in Sweden, Germany, Great Britain, Canada, France, and Russia; and a discussion of the drive for a national health insurance, with several different proposals explained. An American Medical Association rebuttal to the program, an angry letter from a viewer to Schorr, and the recommendations of the Task Force on Medicaid and Related Programs complete the book. No surprises, but simple and direct.

348. Williams, Lawrence P. **How to Avoid Unnecessary Surgery.** Nash, 1971. 221 pp. $6.95. Warner Paperback, $1.25.

Lawrence P. Williams (a pseudonym) is a surgical specialist and Fellow of the American College of Surgeons. His persuasive and enlightening book is designed to prevent the 20–80 percent of unnecessary operations performed here each year, to save patients "time, pain, inconvenience, money, and life itself," and to acquaint them with enough facts so that needed surgery becomes understandable. Williams feels that surgeon selection is the most important factor in safe and necessary surgery. Unethical surgeons perform operations for money, to have full schedules, and often because of faulty knowledge. He advises consultation with other surgeons and other specialists to make sure the problem cannot be treated in another way; provides checklists to determine surgeon qualifications and the need for consultation; tells how to judge hospitals and why their policing of operations is poor; lists mortality rates for different operations, and stresses the importance of knowing what complications can occur. He also lists average fees for various surgical procedures, fee splitting, and ghost surgery (wherein one doctor takes over from another after the patient is anesthetized). Williams also covers major illnesses which are often treated by surgery: their symptoms, surgical advisability, possible complications, and suggestions for nonsurgical treatment. Operations range from the common, mainly unneeded tonsillectomies and hysterectomies to removal of breast masses, eyes, gall bladders and ulcers, and radical cancer surgery.

349. Winter, Ruth. **How to Reduce Your Medical Bills.** Fawcett, 1970. 246 pp. Paper 95¢.

Winter explains in clear, easy-to-follow language how to save money on all types of medical expenses. Her advice is extremely practical. Each chapter gives a number of hints on saving time and/or money as well as ways to get the best available service. For example, she suggests checking into a hospital on Tuesday, Wednesday or Thursday, since tests are not done on weekends and holidays except in emergencies, and since on Mondays the facilities are overcrowded with the weekend check-ins. Another suggestion is to get vaccinated at a local public health station instead of at a doctor's office. Buying drugs at discount drugstores and buying private label over-the-counter medicines will reduce bills considerably. Winter also covers nursing homes and extended care, mental health therapy, and health insurance. She discusses currently available health plans as well as proposed plans, e.g., the Javits, Kennedy, and Eilers plans. She points out the money-saving benefits of a healthy society and deals with the problems of preventive medicine. An extremely interesting chapter covers medical tax deductions. The book is well researched, and references to sources are cited throughout.

MEDICAL CARE—FRAUDS

See also Frauds. *For pertinent organizations see Part II, U.S. Federal Agencies*—Department of Health, Education and Welfare, Food and Drug Administration—Public Health Service.

350. Seaver, Jacqueline. **Fads, Myths, Quacks—and Your Health.** (Pamphlet No. 415). Public Affairs, 1968. 28 pp. Paper 35¢. Quantity orders discounted.

Consumer ignorance, gullibility, hope, and/or faith account for most of the reasons Americans are swindled out of $2 billion annually in the health field alone. Seaver, a writer who specializes in health, has unkind words for chiropractors, health cultists, and users of X-ray machines and other apparatus. The author warns of the dangers involved in mole removals, face lifts, and other beautifying procedures by anyone other than a doctor, and in the unsupervised use of reducing pills and diet plans. She discusses major sources of health quackery: "cures" for arthritis, cancer, diabetes and epilepsy; hair "restorers"; "invigorators"; mail order dental plates, etc. She says fraud is usually involved if special or secret machines are used, if the invention is written up in a sensational magazine or promoted by faith healing groups, and if it is said that the medical profession is trying to "suppress" the invention or that conventional methods are harmful. Seaver concludes by noting various organizations active in the fight against health rackets.

351. Tuck, Miriam L., and Arlene B. Grodner, **Consumer Health.** (Contemporary Topics in Health Science Series). New ed. William C. Brown, 1972. 54 pp. Paper 95¢.

A well-written text on medical quackery for the high school student, it can also be used by others first learning about health services and abuses. The authors document the toll in human lives as well as in excessive costs, show advertisements of specific products that have been banned from the American market, and provide information on quackery dealing with cancer, arthritis, and weight loss. In addition, they cover charlatanism often associated with sensitivity training, food fads, and advertising. A short discussion of consumer protection agencies that may protect the public from the unscrupulous is included. A glossary completes the book.

MEDICARE

See Social Security and Medicare

MINIBIKES

See Motorcycles and Minibikes

MOBILE HOMES

See also Insurance, Mobile Homes; Recreational Vehicles. *For pertinent organizations see Part II, U.S. Federal Agencies*—Department of Housing and Urban Development, Housing Production and Mortgage Credit—Federal Housing Administration.

352. Engel, Lyle Kenyon. **The Complete Book of Mobile Home Living.** Arco, 1973. 143 pp. $5.95.

Similar in intent to *So You Want to Buy a Mobile Home* (*see* entry 353), this book deals with information on choosing and buying a mobile home and park space. Engel places far too much importance on living with one's peers, and he seems to think his reading audience consists only of persons who can afford the expensive five-star parks. His guidelines are sprinkled throughout the text—useful but inconvenient. Information on mobile home construction is virtually meaningless, but his suggestion to visit a manufacturing plant is a good one, as is his stress on buying a home that meets the highest construction codes and standards. Engel points out that the Consumer Action Bureau set up by the Mobile Home Manufacturers Association in 1972 is intended to help owners resolve problems with manufacturers, even those that are not members of the association. Engel's material on financing a home is overly simple, but his material on buying used homes is good. He concludes the book with a 15-point buyer's checklist.

353. Griffin, Al. **So You Want to Buy a Mobile Home.** Illus. Regnery, 1970. 182 pp. $5.95. Pocket Books. Paper $1.50.

A practical book for mobile home buyers, it points out advantages and disadvantages to that style of living and to the homes themselves. Griffin starts by noting that the popularity of the mobile home is due to its economy in purchase, but also goes on to warn about hard-to-get financing and excessive depreciation (since outmoded laws treat the homes like cars). He explains how to spot good quality, construction, and layout and offers guidelines for convenience, quality, and safety. Griffin takes the industry to task for failing to revamp mobile home styles; i.e., while no longer really meant to be mobile, they are still built as if they were and are often not anchored to foundations. The danger here is that thousands are overturned during hurricanes. Old-fashioned 12-foot-wide models are compared to expandable, homelike, and convenient newer ones. He believes in buying only from companies belonging to the Mobile Home Manufacturers Association which promulgated a building code of performance. He points out that in this field, brand names and company names are useless: one company can manufacture an excellent mobile home in one plant, and in another its product will be second-rate. Also, many companies have similar brand names. When considering a secondhand model, the author feels it should be checked out for safety, termites, and wood rot by an engineer. In addition, Griffin covers buying accessories for the mobile home and appends a list of manufacturers and a series of well-designed floor plans of various sizes by different companies.

354. Nulsen, Robert H. **Mobile Home Manual.** Illus. (Book No. 6A, vol. 1), Trail-R-Club, 1972. 372 pp. $4.50.

Nulsen provides guidelines on buying new and used mobile homes and trailers, information on how to pull them, how to find parks and live in them, and how to buy and operate certain apparatus. The section on buying homes and trailers is very good. Nulsen first gives many good reasons for purchase, and then follows up with what to look for before buying. He stresses the commonsense need for caution and urges buyers to take a long time before making any decision. He lists all mobile home manufacturers and advises buying only from dealers who will honor a reputable manufacturer's warranty. The checklist for new mobile home buyers has 20 items, including price, warranties, insurance and finance arrangements, and specific considerations for interior furnishings, construction, and insulation. Similar guides are devoted to buying new and used travel trailers. For those who buy trailers, the author discusses towing: what type of car to buy, how to pull the trailer, effects on the car, etc. The section on living in mobile home parks is similar to that found in *All about Parks for Mobile Homes and Recreation Vehicles* (*see* entry 356), although the latter goes into much greater detail.

355. Scherer, John L. **All about Mobile Homes.** Illus. Fawcett, 1972. 160 pp. Paper 95¢.

Written by a one-time editor for *Mobile Home Journal* who is now a resident of a mobile home park, the book is heavy on praise for this type of living. Scherer concentrates on parks from the medium to luxury range, emphasizing the advantages of living in the luxury park. Much of it is too general to be of much use, but several chapters are good. The best one deals with add-ons to the mobile home, e.g., built-in tie-down anchors that should be attached to any home, but most particularly to homes in high-wind and hurricane areas, colored brick skirting rather than aluminum for a more homelike, finished appearance, concrete carports, utility rooms, steps, etc. Another good chapter points out the very high cost of moving such a home from one site to another. A mobile home with concrete carport, bricks, without wheels or trailer hitch can cost more than $1,000 to move. Scherer points out that it is cheaper to sell and buy a new home. He cautions against buying any home before finding a location for it; parks often make tenants buy a complete package and will not let an old home in. Chapters on judging the house suggest buying only a home which meets safety standards. Two chapters cover the amenities of luxury parks. An appendix listing a few magazines, newspapers, and associations completes the book.

MOBILE HOMES—PARKS

356. Nulsen, David. **All about Parks for Mobile Homes and Recreation Vehicles.** Illus. (Book No. 27). Trail-R-Club, 1973. 264 pp. Paper $4.50.

Overfilled with photographs and sketches of established and proposed mobile home models and parks submitted by manufacturers and owners, the written material has a lot to offer the would-be mobile home dweller. "Selecting a Park" lists 50 guidelines, ranging from the important to the picayune. For example, Nulsen stresses the need to find out about the availability of electric power, since a particular home may need more amperes than the park can supply. He also suggests checking appearance, roads, lighting, restrictions, rent, lot size, upkeep, inhabitants, and recreational facilities. On this last point alone, he suggests 26 sports, hobbies, and other pasttimes that could be available. In addition, Nulsen advises the park dweller to use Woodall's annual directory (*see* entry 357) for its one- to five-star ratings of mobile home and recreational vehicle parks. A good chapter deals with parks that sell lots. The list is extracted from Woodall's 1972 *Mobile Home and Parks Directory.* To consider costs in these parks, 12 points are to be considered, among them costs of land, landscaping, and maintenance; special assessments; escrow charges, and tax rates. Possible restrictions and a sample lot deed are included. Similar material is given for co-op parks. "How to Live in a Mobile Home Park" includes sample rules and regulation of various established parks. In spite of its title, the author deals very generally with parks for recreational vehicles. He also tends to gloss over the negative aspects of mobile home living. While the book is flawed, it has much practical information.

357. Woodall's Mobile Home & Parks Directory. Illus. Annual. Woodall. Paper $5.95.

The 1974 edition of the directory lists approximately 13,000 of the 24,000 mobile home parks in the United States. Inclusion in the directory means that a park meets minimum requirements of cleanliness and facilities. A rating system of one to five stars further differentiates the parks. Size, facilities, and sanitation determine the ratings. In addition, information about each park includes its address, location in relation to a downtown business section or city limit, number of sites, facilities (e.g., laundry, community hall), and special policies (e.g., pets, children). This edition includes an issue of *Mobile/Modular Living* magazine. It lists the names and addresses of dealers and park owners that rent mobile homes as well as 1974 prices and descriptions of new homes in luxury, medium, and moderate price ranges. The directory also includes valuable lists of transport companies that move mobile homes intra- and interstate, state laws and regulations on moving, and the names, addresses, and purposes of local and state mobile home associations. The most important part of the directory, the parks ratings, must be used with some caution, as the publisher accepts advertising, and it seems the larger the park and the higher the rating, the more likely one is to find an advertisement.

MONEY MANAGEMENT

For pertinent organizations see Part II, U.S. Federal Agencies—Department of Agriculture, Extension Service; *Private Organizations*—American Association of Credit Counselors; Consumer Credit Counseling Service of Greater New York; Credit Union National Association, Inc.; National Consumer Finance Association; *Canadian Agencies—National Agencies*—Department of Consumer and Corporate Affairs.

358. Banker, John C. **Personal Finances for Ministers.** Rev. ed. Westminster, 1973. 127 pp. Paper $1.65.

This guide to money management geared to the minister shows him how to make a budget and spending plan, how to deal with debts and borrowing, savings, banking, life, health and property insurance, investments, and retirement. The special advantages are enumerated, e.g., free housing or a nontaxable housing allowance, special income tax deductions, a tax-sheltered annuity plan for the clergy, etc. Conversely, the author notes the minister's image and responsibilities: the need to stay fiscally sound, the suggestion that it is unwise to invest in real estate or speculate in the stock market, the likelihood of a relatively small income. For investments, the author suggests mutual funds. The section on spending includes pros and cons of tithing. The book concludes with charts of eight money management records: year-end review; year-end inventory (net worth); family document finder; life insurance record; other insurance records; savings and checking accounts; investment record; spending record for one month.

359. Blair, Lorraine. **Answers to Your Everyday Money Questions.** Regnery, 1968. 200 pp. $4.95; paper $1.95.

Blair, head of an investment counseling firm and founder and executive director of the Finance Forum of America, has produced a question-and-answer book on money management. A pioneer in the mutual fund investment movement, she is still a strong advocate of mutual fund investing. She stresses the need for competent handling of money: preparing and collecting personal papers, knowing one's monetary worth, and figuring out a rational savings plan. Shopping tips are practical, e.g., before going out of the way to find a bargain, make sure that car depreciation and gas and time used do not outweigh savings. Before using credit, borrowers should ask: Is it essential? Are there long-term benefits? Does the convenience offset the cost? Is it good for tax purposes? Is it a method of forced savings? Family problems, e.g., who will handle the money and make money decisions, how to teach financial responsibility to children, and how to agree on where the money goes, are covered. Blair approves of double indemnity and disability riders to life insurance policies if costs are low. To overcome inflation, she advises readers to invest in real estate, common stocks, mutual funds, commodities, antiques, and diamonds and points out that the money used as down payment on a house could be invested in other things where the return is greater. Twenty rules for successful investing are included.

360. Blodgett, Richard E. **The New York Times Book of Money.** Illus. Quadrangle, 1971. 223 pp. $7.95.

A book for the personal financial management novice. Each topic is broken down into sections; most paragraphs are set apart and noted by descriptive headings; on each page there are sections entitled "Wiseguides" (set off by red lines and a graduation cap) that are tips or summaries of the material covered, and the entire book is heavily illustrated for further clarity. Blodgett covers all the usual topics of money management: budgeting, saving, borrowing, and banking; buying homes and getting mortgages; insurance on life and health, automobiles, medical care, and education; investments in stocks and mutual funds; retirement; wills, and taxation. One chapter deals with women and money: sources of discrimination in obtaining loans and keeping credit standings and possible remedies (some of which have been acted on in the interim). Blodgett concludes with situations involving money and the law: when to get a lawyer (and how to find one), lawsuits, installment purchases, installment "contracts," forgery, usury, bankruptcy, etc. Addresses of some federal, state, and professional organizations offering aid and information to consumers conclude the book. A very basic guide giving sound, if not original, advice, it is one of the easiest to use.

361. Bowman, George M. **How to Succeed with Your Money.** Rev. ed. Moody, 1974. 192 pp. Paper $1.25.

A religiously oriented book whose author says that trust in the Lord is the first step in qualifying for financial success. He discusses Christ and the profit motive, revivals in the home, the necessity of tithing, and more. The "10-70-20" plan refers to 10 percent for savings and investment, 70 percent for living expenses, and 20 percent for debts and a buffer fund. (The tithe and taxes are not included in net income.) The plan is mechanical and straitjacketing. The stress is on fundamentalist Christian thinking. Not for the general public. Not recommended.

362. Brake, John R., ed. **Farm and Personal Finance.** Interstate, 1968. 132 pp. Paper $2.95.

Intended for use by junior and senior high school students and graduates, *Farm and Personal Finance* is aimed primarily at those whose business interests will be geared to agriculture. As Brake points out, farming is just one form of business, so the book could serve as a text for others. Its drawbacks include outdated statistics and examples that will simply not appeal to city students. This is a pity, because the book does not talk down to its audience, and it makes its points clearly and concisely. It covers introductory finance and budgeting, where and how to get capital and credit for business and private uses, figuring the costs of borrowing, differentiating between business and consumer types of credit, and farm and family insurance. As an example of the applicability of this book for other students, the section on insurance for the farm deals with fire, liability, and Workman's Compensation, the farmowner's policy which is akin to the homeowner's policy, and crop-hail insurance. Each chapter concludes with exercises for the students. A very good book if updated.

363. Britton, Virginia. **Personal Finance.** Text ed. Van Nostrand Reinhold, 1968. 406 pp. Paper $5.50.

A college-level text written by a former teacher at the University of Maryland, *Personal Finance* deals with finance, expenditures, investments and protection, all revolving around the family unit. Britton covers the expected material (budgets, income, consumer prices, credit, taxes, expenditures for food, clothing, shelter, cars, medical care, savings, Social Security, life insurance, retirement, annuities, investments, and wills) in a no-frill and somewhat scholarly manner, yet manages to include information not usually covered. For example, in discussing the need for different budgets during different parts of the family cycle, she includes material on divorced and remarried couples. She also devotes some space to special occasions: births, coming of age, marriage, and death, and questions the need for large expenditures, suggesting better ways to channel money and/or gifts at those times. Unfortunately, the book is also filled with statistics —many of which have only historic interest at this time and some of which were questionable even in 1968. For example, discussing household furnishings and equipment, Britton states that 5 percent of consumer income goes for those items, and 4 percent for household operations, e.g., telephone and telegraph, postage, cleaning and laundry products, etc. In spite of this drawback, this is one of the better college texts, complete with questions following each chapter and suggestions for further reading.

364. Burns, Scott. **Squeeze It till the Eagle Grins: How to Spend, Save and Enjoy Your Money.** Doubleday, 1972. 237 pp. $6.95.

Burns provides no solutions to money management problems in this book. Instead, he shows how we are overspending our own resources and that of the planet, how and why the majority cannot hope to invest/save/compound money for an even reasonable retirement, and why current economic and production theory is leading to an ever-worsening situation. The author has few answers; along the way he points up ways to decrease the outflow of cash and (possibly) increase savings. Theoretical rather than practical, this book will appeal to sophisticated consumers who are interested in the why of our economic distress and who can accept the lack of easy answers.

365. Cohen, Jerome B., assisted by Harry H. Bingham. **Programmed Learning Aid for Personal Finance.** (Irwin Programmed Learning Aid Series). Learning Systems, 1972. 184 pp. Paper $3.50.

The PLAID review is a *p*rogrammed *l*earning *aid* for college-level students intended as a supplement to course study or for self-review. Each topic is broken down into small sections called frames. After each frame, a short series of true-false questions reviews the material. If the student gets the material wrong, he or she is to reread the frame. The PLAID concludes with examination questions for each chapter. Answers follow. A combined glossary and index completes the book. This material has been prepared by Jerome B. Cohen, professor of finance and dean (emeritus) of Baruch College of the City University of New York. The topics and material are standard: income and occupation, expenditures, budgeting, taxes, charge accounts, credit cards, loans, bank services, savings, insurance, Social Security, annuities and pensions, home buying, investments, securities, mutual funds, and estate planning. The PLAID itself is open to doubt: the questions follow so closely on the heels of the information that a student may think there is knowledge and comprehension where none is involved. But the basic flaw is content: the material covered is much too basic and uncomplicated to be considered a review of a personal finance course at the college level. It covers basic principles, often not distinguishing between good and bad, in insurance, investments, etc. It can be recommended for high school, rather than college students.

366. Coleman, B. D. **Money: How to Save It, Spend It and Make It.** Pergamon, 1969. $5.50; paper $4.

A British book that is confusing for an American: the terms and monies are British, the examples are suitable to Britain, not to the United States. Not recommended.

367. de Camp, Catherine Crook. **The Money Tree: A New Guide to Successful Personal Finance.** New American Library, 1972. 352 pp. Paper $1.50.

A very-well-thought-out and well-written book on money management by an economist and teacher, it starts with the premise that overuse of credit is one of the basic problems of our society (contributing to inflation, worry, and constant debt). De Camp proceeds to a discussion of the credit revolution and how to live with it. She shows how to determine one's assets and set up a spending plan "for survival." An excellent chapter on the home office shows how and what to keep in temporary and permanent files. Temporary records for a year are all bills (paid and unpaid), earning vouchers, Social Security payments, etc. These are for tax purposes. Current warrantees should be kept in case products break down. Permanent records include bank statements and cancelled checks, installment contracts, real estate records and stockbrokers' statements. A nice section shows how to balance the checkbook. Credit; buying homes, cars, and insurance; saving, investing, and estate planning; and wise shopping, all are well covered. De Camp has 13 rules to avoid con games, frauds, and quacks. She says not to change bills in a dark place (they may be counterfeit), not to accept C.O.D. parcels for a neighbor, not to trust or buy from a flatterer. The bibliography, though short, is excellent. Appended, too, are personal record forms and work sheets for income tax preparation.

368. Donaldson, Elvin F., and John K. Pfahl. **Personal Finance.** 5th ed. Ronald, 1971. 802 pp. $10.50.

This standard college text on money management is republished on the average of once every five years, and in spite of the statement in its preface, guaranteeing total revision, it is revised only to a very limited extent. Since the material did not need extensive revision and is somewhat updated, the authors would have done better with honesty concerning revised editions. Donaldson and Pfahl are professors of finance in the College of Commerce and Administration at Ohio State University, and their text is devoted to teaching their students how to plan, spend, save, and invest their money. Most of the material is very useful, e.g., the chapter on borrowing money has charts that compare costs of borrowing and maximum loans in each state and from various lending sources, ranging from credit unions to commercial banks to usurers. Another good section deals with banking services, e.g., check cashing, transfering money, paying bills, using safe deposit boxes. Other sections deal with money and personal goals, financial planning and budgeting, insurance, home ownership, federal taxes, Social Security and Medicare (good, but no longer up-to-date), retirement and estate planning, wills, and trusts. Several chapters relate to investing: learning sources of information, buying stocks and mutual funds, investing savings. Questions and case problems review each chapter. If the authors continue on their schedule, a 1976 edition should be published, which will bring this information up to date.

369. Dorries, W. L., Arthur A. Smith, and James R. Young. **Personal Finance: Consuming, Saving and Investing.** Merrill, 1974. 562 pp. $11.95.

Up-to-date, practical, and easy to understand college text written by three teachers at East Texas State University, it covers all personal finance topics and relates them to business management and economics. The authors point out that consumer choices influence business practices as well as supply and demand. If consumers would boycott shoddy merchandise and demand quality, the market would respond. Material on consumerism makes many points in favor of business. The authors warn that prohibitive restrictions can price a company or product out of the market. For example, safety regulations imposed by the government, such as automobile shoulder harnesses, are not used by most people, yet add to the cost of cars. The best material covers family spending, e.g., food, clothing, homes, appliances, autos and insurance. The authors note that merchandise bought at a sale is no bargain unless the shopper had intended to buy it and had really needed it in the first place; also, that certain convenience foods can be useful (small sizes are good for individuals; single packages are useful at picnics). *Personal Finance* has the best material on working women, job discrimination and the women's movement of any book on this subject. It is also fair and objective in presenting both the business and consumer points of view. Generally very good discussion questions follow each chapter.

370. Halcomb, Ruth. **Money & the Working Ms.** Books for Better Living, 1974. 191 pp. Paper $1.25.

A personal finance book for women on their own (and likely to remain so), it is a blend of practical advice mixed with anecdotes (many of them stereotypical) of women in financial difficulties. The advice ranges from the necessity for keeping a budget and the practicalities of changing jobs (from a dead-end job to one that offers advancement) to information on saving, investments, and retirement and on how to cut expenses on cars, food, housing, and vacations. Halcomb suggests keeping old clothes and breaking the habit of being "fashionable," making do with inexpensive furniture, and learning to be self-sufficient. She also discusses the problems of living with roommates of both sexes and raising children by oneself. Her ideas are good, although not novel, but style and presentation are poor. The book also suffers from a useless table of contents and the lack of an index. Secondary material at best.

371. Hastings, Paul, and Norbert Nietus. **Personal Finance.** Text ed. McGraw-Hill, 1972. 472 pp. $10.95.

One of the best texts, suitable for high school as well as college students, it can be recommended for independent readers as well. The authors, both professors of management, take a business approach to their subject. "The Acquisition of Property" includes some useful material on owning one's own business. "The Enjoyment of Property" has an excellent explanation of what money is and what it buys, how to reconcile a bank statement, different bank services available to the public (including financial counseling), and buying for cash versus buying for credit. "Increasing the Value of Property" covers saving, borrowing, and investing (the surplus money) in stocks, bonds, securities, and investment plans. Life, health, property and liability insurance, as well as income taxes, are discussed under "The Conservation and Protection of Property." "Comfortable Retirement and the Disposition of Property after Death" includes retirement and estate planning. Hastings and Nietus have the facility to write concisely and easily; there is a lot of information in relatively little space. Readers get medical advice in a section entitled "Have a Heart," and see examples of endorsements on checks, over-the-counter treasury bond quotations, simple formal wills, a declaration of trust, etc. Questions for discussion, problems, projects, and bibliographies follow each chapter. All are good.

372. Janeway, Eliot. **What Shall I Do with My Money?** McKay, 1970. 209 pp. $5.95.

Eliot Janeway, the noted economist and newspaper columnist, collected the questions sent to him over the years by his readers and divided these into chapters dealing with personal finance, cash, property, mutual funds, stocks and bonds, and the uses of financial advisers. Janeway says that the tight money situation and credit squeeze were brought on by the government's fiscal policies of the last forty years, and he feels that the current money crisis will not change until the stock and bond markets can get back on an even keel. His rules include keeping within a 25 percent limit of net income for shelter (preferably a home), keeping 10 percent of gross income in a savings reserve, and owning straight life insurance equal to five years' gross income plus five years of mortgage and/or short-term debts. The book fails as a guide to explaining money management principles to the average person; it is too heavily geared to answering specific questions. In general, theory must be extrapolated from the answers. The book can be considered supplementary reading for anyone interested in this subject.

373. Janeway, Eliot. **You and Your Money: A Survival Guide to the Controlled Economy.** McKay, 1972. 284 pp. $5.95.

Taking up where *What Shall I Do with My Money?* (*see* entry 372) left off, this book deals specifically with extending and broadening the "investment insurance policy" of the earlier volume. Again, the author uses questions from his readers to offer his theories and advice, but in this book, he uses the questions as concrete examples to develop further the theme of each chapter. Janeway takes the government to task for the fiscal crisis of the 1970s, shows its causes, and proceeds to explain how to deal with it. Since the rising cost of services outstrips the falling cost of goods, he notes that "do-it-yourself," ranging from sewing clothes to camping out, can ease the financial burden and even let a family get ahead. He says that in an era of "stagflation" (stagnation of earnings and inflation of costs) cash is at a premium and will buy more in assets and earning power than before. He feels that homeowning is economical and moneymaking, providing his rules for mortgages and debts (as set forth in the previous volume) are adhered to. He also suggests buying mutual funds that invest in property. Other topics covered are stocks, bonds, and financial advisers.

374. Johnson, Thomas A. **Dollar Power.** (Consumer Education Series). Pendulum, 1973. 80 pp. Paper $1.25.

Aimed at "young consumers just entering the marketplace," it deals with wise decision making, budgeting, savings, banking services, credit, investing in stocks and real estate, and owning a business. Each chapter is followed by a review that includes thought and value judgment questions as well as outside activities relating to the subject. Even though chapters only run from 6 to 10 pages, a good deal of information is provided; sometimes even too much. The major criticisms are that it glosses over the pitfalls of improper money management, i.e., overspending, unwise investments, and overly expensive homes, and is so condensed that the information must be extracted with the aid of the teacher.

375. Kirk, John. **How to Manage Your Money.** Benjamin Co., 1966. 144 pp. Paper $1.50 (100 copies minimum). Essandess Special Editions. Paper $1.

Useful when it first appeared in 1966, this guide to money management is now out of date, since much of its material is based on the economy of the 1960s. One glaring example is a description of bank credit cards as a "new kind of shopping convenience" with a description of their uses and possible abuses. Information on the need for family planning is good, as is an explanation of a credit rating and suggestions of ways to borrow money, e.g., from a credit union or on a savings account. A very good feature of this book is the 32-page workbook that includes space for monthly records of payments, monthly records of charges (to grocer, drug store, department stores, etc.), records of bank accounts and stocks, location of important papers, contents of the safe deposit box, and a record of insurance policies. Another good chapter deals with choosing and using banks, and a too-short one deals with investing in stocks and mutual funds. A condensed 1968 edition for 50¢ (100 copies minimum) is also available without the worksheets. The book is very general and written on a level suitable for high school or adult education classes, but the material must be updated.

376. J. K. Lasser Tax Institute. **J. K. Lasser's Managing Your Family Finances.** Rev. ed. Doubleday, 1973. 274 pp. $7.95.

Originally published in 1968, it is the J. K. Lasser Tax Institute's manual on financial planning for the family. Poorly written, it is a bland setting out of facts and figures for the unsophisticated, one of the most elementary texts in print. Chapters deal with planning a financial program (through family cooperation), cutting costs, increasing the family income, buying on credit, buying and financing a home, saving and investing, buying life and health insurance, Social Security, and estate and retirement planning. All the material is presented in so brief a fashion that the writers have been forced to leave out much relevant information, e.g., the shortcomings of certain savings and investing programs. This book will add little or nothing to the information of those who know the basics of money management.

377. Leibenderfer, John E. **Planning Your Financial Independence.** University of Oklahoma Press, 1954. 294 pp. $8.95.

Twenty years out of date, the book suffers from unusable statistics and examples that have no relevance to today's living. It could be updated; but as it now stands, it is not recommended. (Reviewed due to its university press imprint.)

378. McKay, Quinn G., and William A. Tilleman. **Money Matters in Your Marriage.** Deseret, 1971. 259 pp. $5.50.

As stated in its foreword, this book is designed specifically for Latter-Day Saint families. The philosophy of the church is evident on every page; people not sharing these beliefs may well disagree with them. For example, while the authors say that the best way to manage money is for both parents to be responsible for records and bills, if only one is to assume that responsibility, the husband should be that one, so that he can exert his leadership role. Discussions on family matters with children should be directed by the father. Women should not work outside the home unless there is dire neccessity (e.g., widowhood, divorce), but even then, they should try to avoid it. Women who feel the need to work should do volunteer work. Tithing is discussed as a matter of necessity rather than of choice. Not for the general public.

379. Margolius, Sidney. **Family Money Problems.** (Pamphlet No. 412). Public Affairs, 1967. 20 pp. Paper 35¢. Quantity orders discounted.

Consumer expert Margolius notes and discusses various family money problems. He points up emotional causes of these problems and shows how frequently money is used by one spouse to punish the other, e.g., by withholding funds, by overspending on luxuries. (A frequent problem is a husband's overspending on recreational goods.) Unrealistic expectations of newlyweds, overindebtedness, and keeping up with the Joneses are common problems. Realistic reasons for money problems include low income, high housing expenses, medical expenses, support of aged parents, and college expenses. To solve money problems, families must communicate and agree on long-range goals, have a sense of vocational purpose, learn how to handle money wisely, and initiate a spending plan. Margolius lists sources of financial counseling, including credit unions, family agencies, and extension services run by the state or federal governments. A very short bibliography on money management is also included.

380. Margolius, Sidney. **How to S-t-r-e-t-c-h Your M-o-n-e-y.** (Pamphlet No. 302A). Public Affairs, 1970. 24 pp. Paper 35¢. Quantity orders discounted.

The basic rule for money management, according to consumer expert Margolius, is to make a personalized money plan that takes into consideration the individual family's special needs. He tells families to estimate monthly take-home income and to estimate basic (rather than fixed) expenses and test the data with a spending record that will show where the money actually went. Charts are provided for one hypothetical family's needs and another for the reader's spending plan. Costs-of-living for various parts of the country and "moderate" monthly budgets for families of different ages and sizes are given. Margolius also suggests ways to plug spending "leaks" in food, insurance, and household expenses, to name just a few areas. For example, he points up how expensive convenience foods are, how much cheaper it is to pay insurance premiums annually, how much a family can save on fuel bills by weather stripping, caulking, and insulating. A short section on borrowing completes the pamphlet.

381. Markstein, David L. **Manage Your Money and Live Better: Get the Most from Your Dwindling Dollars.** McGraw-Hill, 1971. 252 pp. $6.50.

Anecdotal in style and filled with a cast of characters named George, Sophie, Edith, Ethelred, Frederica, Ernest Electrix, Lemuel D. Plainfellow, et al., it covers the usual topics: food, clothing, the home, cars, insurance, education, recreation, credit, and savings. The book begins with a short and overly simplified explanation of economics, and concludes by stating that caveat emptor has been replaced by "buyer's rights." In between, Markstein suggests ways of saving money that range from the practical to the whimsical, e.g., buying magazines by subscription and newspapers at a news stand, using cologne instead of perfume, taking advantage of all possible government benefits, planting a vegetable garden and/or buying at farmers' markets. Each chapter is filled with information collected from government sources and is followed by a summary that highlights the tips in each field, plus a list of suggested readings—often by Markstein himself. The appeal is primarily for those who want their money management pill sugar coated.

382. *Money. Time, Inc. 1972– . Illus. Monthly. $15.

Money is designed to explain the current financial situation and suggest ways for consumers to cope with it. The magazine accepts advertising, and this may slant certain articles and keep others from being published. Regular features include: "The Angry Consumer/Early Warning," which notes frauds and devious business practices; "Washington Memo," which discusses government action (or inaction); "Shopping Center," which deals with a variety of topics, e.g., new or updated products and other items of consumer interest. Major articles are signed and run the gamut from practical to offbeat to luxury interests. Recent topics covered costs of living in cities around the world, cheap vacations in the Caribbean, the cost of medical checkups, how to hire and keep cleaning help, a warning against franchises as a way to make money, and brokers who do not know their business. *Money* is aimed primarily at upper-middle-income consumers interested in material on investments, savings, and recreation.

383. Money Management: Reaching Your Financial Goals. Illus. Money Management Institute, Household Finance Corp., 1971. 32 pp. Paper 30¢. Quantity orders discounted.

Entirely devoted to helping consumers set up a personalized money management plan, it stresses the importance of such a plan and shows step-by-step how to make one, i.e., how to determine net spending power by finding fixed and flexible expenses (whatever is left over can be spent). Any person or family can work out an individual plan using the pamphlet: blank charts are included for recording income, expenses, trial plan, master record of spending and saving, savings goal record, a net worth statement, etc. At the price, this is a good buy.

384. †The Money Tree. AIMS Instructional Media Services, 1973. Color. Sound. 16mm. 20 min. Sale $280. Rent $25.

Financial difficulties in general and the abuse of credit in particular are shown as major factors in breaking up a marriage. While there is a somewhat unreal quality to the film, the problems are real. Young Jerry and Ann Brooks rush out to furnish their apartment and buy a new car and clothes without thinking of the consequences. They sign credit contracts without reading them or understanding the costs involved. Parenthood and the loss of Jerry's job add to the stress. The film ends with a credit report on the Brookses: the car, TV, and all furniture are repossessed, hospital and other bills "skips" (unpaid), Ann suing for divorce and Jerry's whereabouts unknown. Geared for the high school and college consumer education class.

385. Mumey, Glen A. **Personal Economic Planning.** Holt, Rinehart & Winston, 1972. 312 pp. $6.95.

A very theoretical approach to money management, its emphasis is on the development of an overall personal economic plan and on methods of decision making. Mumey, who teaches at the University of Alberta (Canada), stresses business techniques. Chapters are entitled "Accounting as a Planning Tool," "Income Taxes and Their Effect on Planning," "Capital and Its Use," "Compound Interest and the Effect of Time on Plans," etc. He covers budget making, the necessity for deferred spending and consumption to allow for appreciation of savings, insurance, "involuntary benefit programs" (Social Security, Medicare, pensions, unemployment insurance, and the like), housing, taxes, annuities, and personal borrowing. While not a complete college text for consumer education, money management or investment courses, it can be used as an adjunct to more basic books on those subjects. Each chapter concludes with summaries, questions, and problems.

386. Neal, Charles. **Sense with Dollars.** Doubleday, 1967. Rev., enlarged ed. 393 pp. $5.95; paper $1.95.

Conventional advice at best, it is conservative and extremely sexist. Neal gives advice on how wives can help husbands and has a special section on the "young man on the way up." "Managing Your Income" includes material on a home office, ways to increase income, working wives, and being one's own boss. "Managing Your Spending" offers standard information on where it all goes. Much better material is available. Not recommended.

387. Nelson, Roger H. **Personal Money Management: An Objectives and Systems Approach.** Addison-Wesley, 1973. 766 pp. $11.95.

The author teaches at the College of Business, University of Utah, and his book is aimed at business students. Consequently, this is a money management text that stresses the need for "individual responsibility coupled with individual knowledge and clear personal objectives" in handling one's affairs. It is divided into sections concerned with earning and allocating money, saving and borrowing, getting the most for the money, and safeguarding income and property. Each chapter is followed by "feedback" in the form of "action programs" aimed at making students understand life situations and focus their goals. Discussion questions, case problems, and suggested readings also follow. In spite of the stress on individual responsibility, the section on consumer protection services is good: it deals in depth with government's role as well as with laws, labeling, advertising, the history of consumerism, and not surprisingly, the protective services of business and professional groups. Basically, Nelson's advice is sound, if conservative. One of the better college texts on the subject, it is somewhat marred by a few sexist cartoons.

388. Niss, James F. **Consumer Economics.** Prentice-Hall, 1974. 193 pp. Paper $4.95.

Niss, who teaches economics at Western Illinois University, fuses a course in economics with one in consumer education, to provide college students with the information on how to become good consumers who can see the relationship and ramifications of fiscal policies, antitrust policies, wage-price guidelines, etc. He manages to pack a great deal of information into relatively little space. "The Economics of Housing" discusses the price of homes in relation to supply and demand, mobile homes, economics of apartment buildings, renting, rights and responsibilities of landlords and tenants, methods of financing a home, and costs of home ownership in retirement (when the mortgage is paid off). The author does as well with other standard topics: insurance, investment, occupation and income, buying goods and services, credit, budgeting, and consumer choices and manipulation. In most chapters, he shows how supply and demand determine cost and how to compute implicit and explicit costs of goods. For example, explicit costs of a home freezer would include depreciation, maintenance, and electric bills. The implicit cost is the lost interest on the price of the freezer. Each chapter has questions for thought and review and a good bibliography of suggested readings.

389. Nuccio, Sal. **The New York Times Guide to Personal Finance.** Harper & Row, 1967. 240 pp. $4.95.

This basic guide to personal money management is based in part on Nuccio's "Personal Finance" column in the *New York Times.* The *Time's* business, financial, and real estate experts, as well as persons in the banking, insurance, and business communities were used to produce this practical book. Although lacking an index, the contents are sufficiently detailed to make finding a subject relatively easy. The usual topics are included: planning a family financial program, loans and credit, housing, life insurance, retirement plans, medical expenses and insurance, home insurance, savings, investing, taxes, and estate planning. Nuccio deals with budgets, salaries, and costs from the early 1960s, so that statistics are dated but his advice and analyses remain as valid today as they were then.

390. O'Toole, Edward T., **How to Gain Financial Independence.** Benjamin Co., 1969. 142 pp. Paper (100 copies minimum). Essandess Special Editions. Paper $1.

This book on money management is highly sexist and offensive: the chapter on the single person deals only with the single man; education deals with the need to send a boy to college; the references to earnings of college graduates, noncollege graduates, and those with postgraduate degrees pertain only to the lifetime earnings of men. Otherwise, the book is a standard amalgam of why one needs to budget and plan ahead, save and invest, how to buy a house, plan for retirement, teach children the value of money, etc. It offers nothing of special interest and is not recommended. Neither is the pocket-sized 1972 edition, *Family Guide to Financial Security,* selling for 50¢ in minimum orders of 100 copies. Groups wishing to give away material on money management can find better material elsewhere.

391. Phillips, E. Bryant, and Sylvia Lane. **Personal Finance.** 3rd ed. Wiley, 1974. 525 pp. $11.95.

Designed for use in a one-term college course in money management, *Personal Finance* deals with income and budgeting, credit, saving and investment, major personal expenditures (housing, transportation, medical care, government services, insurance), retirement, and estate planning. Phillips is professor emeritus of economics at the University of Southern California. Lane is professor of agricultural economics at the University of California at Davis. Their book, now in its third edition, relies heavily on theories of economics to explain financial situations. For example, they note that high-income groups oversave and low-income groups overspend. The lack of spending on the part of the high-income group diverts the circular flow of funds. This combined with overinvestment in industry and underconsumption of consumer goods and services leads to business failures and recessions. The section on housing discusses the government's role in the housing industry and the interrelationship of interest rates, mortgages, and housing starts. This section also deals with the pros and cons of renting or owning and building or buying and concludes with information on deeds and titles. The authors handle the material very well; it is clear and simple to understand, and the typography makes it very easy to read.

392. Rabell, Paquita. **More Dollars for Your Cents.** Trend Publications, 1971. 102 pp. $5.95; paper $3.95.

It is unfortunate that money management books for women are so poor. This one is on the most simplistic of levels, written by an importer-exporter who has been a member of many civic and trade boards and associations. She intends the book for other businesswomen; it could only be used by those older women (who through divorce or widowhood) have been pushed out into the real world for the first time. Rabell discusses earning opportunities for women over 40 without an awareness that age discrimination is illegal. Her advice is predicated on the assumption that women who have not worked in the past are not equipped for anything but the simplest jobs. Rabell suggests school and offers a list of "good" jobs for women—all with a sexist bias. Some advice is wrong, e.g., endowment policies are good ways to save; all brokerage firm members are competent. The rest of what she has to say is obvious and elementary. Not recommended.

393. Reader's Digest Editors. **How to Live on Your Income.** Reader's Digest, 1970. 639 pp. $8.95.

An excerpted, condensed collection of dozens of books, pamphlets, and magazine articles, it is arranged in broad subject areas dealing with income and budgeting; housing, home maintenance, and home furnishing; food, clothing, and car buying; college expenses; vacations; life, health, and disability insurance; credit, saving, retirement, and tax law changes (as of 1969). The material is taken from magazines, such as *Changing Times* (*see* entry 59), *McCall's,* and *Good Housekeeping*; books such as *J. K. Lasser's Managing Your Family Finances* (1968 ed.; *see* entry 376), *$$$ and Sense* (*see* entry 75), *How to Get More for Your Money in Running Your Home* (*see* entry 255), and *Help Your Family Make a Better Move* (1968 ed.; *see* entry 416), and pamphlets put out by the National Canners Association, J. C. Penney Company, and the American Automobile Association. The format of the book is similar to an issue of *Reader's Digest*: heavy type and headings setting off new paragraphs, tips set off from the rest of the page by different type and printer's marks, big, clear charts, definitions of words used in the articles, etc. Although some of the material is outdated (it is all from the 1960s, with some material from early 1969), most of it is still useful, e.g., the list "What Records to Change at Marriage," includes the note to change insurance and wills as well as advice that some women will no longer follow (to change credit cards and driver's license to the husband's name). All in all, *How to Live on Your Income* is good, practical (although often obvious) material brought together in an easily read and assimilated package.

394. Reddin, W. J. **The Money Book.** Scribners, 1972. 288 pp. $8.95.

Reddin starts with the interesting premise that people do not need more money–they just need to know how much money they will have in order to budget resources and plan for the future. Originally published in Canada, Reddin's book is written very simply and offers little that is new. Budgeting, short- and long-term savings, life insurance, investing (including an extensive explanation of mutual funds), housing, real estate investment, credit and loans, buying cars, wills and estate taxes are covered. Unusual in a book of this type, the concluding chapter is devoted to consumer frauds and schemes. Reddin writes for the uninformed reader, carefully explaining everything as he goes along. Not a bad book, but the price is high.

395. Rodda, William H., and Edward A. Nelson. **Managing Personal Finances.** Prentice-Hall, 1965. 383 pp. $10.50.

This is a workmanlike but rather dull approach to the subject of money management, with questions following each chapter. The authors feel that the text is suitable for all readers, and while this may be true, there is other, much better material, presented in a much more engaging manner, with newer information, statistics, and viewpoint, that the general reader could use. The book itself is quite comprehensive, covering all fields of financial planning. Its major flaw is that it glosses over inadequacies or fails to point up hazards in many areas. For example, Rodda and Nelson leave the reader with the impression that Blue Cross coverage is adequate for the needs and expenses of the middle-income family; that choosing the proper life insurance is easy and will fulfill a family's needs, etc. While not completely outdated, *Managing Personal Finances* could use substantial revision, and is therefore not recommended.

396. Rogers, Donald I. **How to Beat Inflation by Using It.** Arlington House, 1970. 211 pp. $6.95.

The title is misleading–very little space is devoted to beating inflation and a great deal is given to Rogers's extremely conservative views on government spending and the once-proposed guaranteed annual income. Rogers feels that government spending since 1932 has been the main cause of inflation, and he explains that since spending continues to rise at an ever-increasing rate, so, too, will inflation. His advice on cutting costs on food, clothing, automobiles, home furnishings, and home maintenance is run-of-the mill and definitely directed to the solid middle-class family. His method of beating inflation is to invest in inflation-proof common stocks and real estate, e.g., paper companies, home builders, food companies, banks, and finance companies. He also suggests buying a house, cooperative or condominium (on waterfront property, free from pollution) as another hedge against inflation. Much of Rogers's advice is sound, but his long diatribe on the government and his antifeminist views will make it impossible for many people to read through the book.

397. Scaduto, Anthony. **Handling Your Money.** McKay, 1970. 236 pp. $6.95. Warner Paperback. Paper 95¢.

Like its predecessor *Getting the Most for Your Money* (*see* entry 95), this book concentrates on money management. The language is clear, the instructions are simple, and the advice is generally sound. Wages and other sources of income are discussed as well as ways to keep as much of one's income as possible. Scaduto points up the value of pensions, profit sharing, and stock options; self-employment and franchising; and the possible contributions of working wives. He covers budgets and credit, credit sources (including pawnshops), investments, tax planning, and tax information. Material on estate and retirement planning is also included. There are four chapters on housing: pros and cons of buying a house, cooperative, or condominium versus renting; how to finance the home, and how to sell it profitably. Although a great deal of information dates back to 1968 and suffers somewhat from time lag, there is still much to be gained from it.

398. Smith, Carlton, and Richard Putnam Pratt. **The Time-Life Book of Family Finance.** Illus. Time-Life, 1969. 415 pp. $11.95.

A lively and easy to understand guide, it is written by the coauthors of a personal finance column. It is also heavily illustrated with graphs, charts, and line drawings that simplify and/or amplify the text. Smith and Pratt discusss general money management and budgeting; how to use credit; the cost of buying, owning, and running an auto; life insurance; homes; vacations; stocks, bonds, and other investments; planning and leaving an estate, and retirement. Information on children ranges from teaching money principles and giving allowances to paying for college and providing trust funds. A chapter on second incomes is well though out and quite up-to-date: it deals in reasonable and practical ways with working wives' income (pointing out that it doesn't all go to taxes even if there isn't much of it) and the second job held by the husband (which should be more convenient to get to than the full-time job). Material on savings covers not only the essentials, such as various interest rates and how they are computed, but also how to obtain brokered certificates of deposit (which pay more than the bank's allowed interest) and the real interest rates on accounts that nominally give the same interest. The authors also show the value of investing in real estate (as opposed to speculating in land) and offer many arguments for investing in common stocks. A chapter on vacations offers fascinating glimpses into the American leisure mode as well as suggestions for good buys and good trips at various price levels. The only drawback to this book is its steep price, but consumers will find it more enjoyable reading than the average book of its type and thus worth the money.

399. Springer, John L. **Financial Self-Defense.** McGraw-Hill, 1969. 201 pp. $5.95.

This is an oversimplified approach to personal financial security for those with money to spare. Investing in real estate, art, convertible debentures, oil wells, etc., as a hedge against inflation is not advice for the average family. Ways to reduce taxes, get and use credit wisely, buy insurance, and plan an estate are also discussed. When investing during inflationary times, Springer suggests companies that benefit from inflation or are necessary to consumers: oil, gas, lumber, metal, and mineral firms; oil refineries; tobacco and food producers; and companies with high leverage. A chapter on how to protect oneself from gyps and frauds is interesting in this context. Much of the material here is designed for the well-to-do; their financial counselors and advisers should be able to do more for them than Springer.

400. Stillman, Richard J. **Guide to Personal Finance: A Lifetime Program of Money Management.** Illus. Prentice-Hall, 1972. 356 pp. $7.50; paper $4.95.

A serious, sophisticated guide to personal financial planning, it is jarringly interspersed with personal examples and fictional anecdotes. Stillman (professor of management, Louisiana State University) uses a managerial concept and systems approach to his subject. The book is divided into six parts: financial health, housing, insurance, diversified investments, other potential investments, and income taxes and estate planning. Appendices include a list of financial literature: magazines, services, books, pamphlets, and articles, as well as a glossary of financial, life insurance, and commodity trading terms. The text is filled with charts, tables, and graphs to illustrate its material. Particularly useful are the in-depth chapters on investments with sections on stocks, bonds, investment companies, commodities, and real estate. The section on estate planning, wills, and trusts is also superior.

401. Sullivan, George. **The Dollar Squeeze and How to Beat It.** Macmillan, 1970. 213 pp. $5.95.

A discussion of personal finance with the stress on credit, borrowing, debt, and bankruptcy, much of it is obvious and covered better in other books. It also has information on family budget planning, wise buying, investing and saving, and second incomes. The last is very superficial and will probably not be of great value to many people. Sullivan discusses the second job (moonlighting) and the second income (the wife's job), and his suggestions for the wife are outmoded and often misleading. There is also some incorrect information on car buying; either Sullivan does not know the difference between automatic transmissions and power steering or his editor does not. The book stresses Sullivan's specialty: debt and bankruptcy. In this volume, he paints a better picture of bankruptcy than he did in *The Boom In Going Bust* (*see* entry 36), although he still feels that consolidating debts and paying off under Chapter 13—The Wage Earner Plan of the Bankruptcy Act is preferable. This volume is recommended only for those wanting a book that emphasizes the dangers of improper spending.

402. Thal, Helen M., with Melinda Holcombe. **Your Family and Its Money.** Rev. ed. Houghton Mifflin, 1973. 294 pp. $7.20.

A text for junior and senior high school students, its authors place family money management in the context of the national economy as well as stress family decision making and family goals. They point out that every family member has individual needs and the unit as a whole must decide on plans to arrive at their goals. Two very different budgets for families with similar incomes illustrate the differences well. The authors also distinguish nicely between different types of income: gross, net, real. They point out that many decisions may not turn out for the best even if well thought out, but that without foresight, the outcome is worse. Thal, who is director of the education division of the New York Institute of Life Insurance, devotes considerable space to the positive aspects of insurance (protecting a family's property, health, automobile, and life). She also discusses Social Security as a form of insurance. Drawbacks are not mentioned. Other chapters cover the wise use of credit, savings, and thrift; checking accounts, record keeping, and taxes. Questions and summaries are good. The multimedia bibliographies, for students and teachers alike, are excellent.

403. Unger, Maurice A., and Harold A. Wolf. **Personal Finance.** 3rd ed. Allyn & Bacon, 1972. 735 pp. $10.95.

Written by professors of real estate and finance, respectively, this text is designed for college and adult education courses. Comprehensive in coverage, there is little evaluation of the material. Also sad to note is that although the book was revised in 1972, an extraordinary sexist bias runs through it—from cartoons depicting women as foolish and stupid to the dismissal, in a few short paragraphs, of the subject of working wives and their incomes. The book itself is built around the personal budget to show how money goes in and out of the family unit, how to protect it, and how to build on it. Personal income and budgeting (including consumer protection information); insurance, Social Security, annuities, pensions, and retirement investments; and taxes, assets, and estate planning are covered. Questions and cases conclude each section. It would be a very good text if corrected; as it now stands, it is not recommended.

404. †**Using Money Wisely.** Journal Films, 1971. Color. Sound. 16 mm. 18 min. Sale $240. Rent from University of Illinois at Champaign, $6.35.

Narrated by professional money management counselor Ron Webster, the film tries to show how three families in three different economic brackets are helped by professional counselors. Unfortunately, the film suffers from a variety of problems, not the least of which is that it is dull. It also does not show how the counselors work: we simply see the families in trouble going to them, and having their problems solved in a minute or two. Not recommended.

405. Watkins, Art. **Dollars and Sense: A Guide to Mastering Your Money.** Quadrangle, 1973. 284 pp. $7.95.

While a great deal of this material can be found in several of Watkins's earlier books, e.g. *How to Avoid the Ten Biggest Home-Buying Traps* (*see* entry

284), *The Homeowner's Survival Kit* (*see* entry 259), *Making Money in Mutual Funds,* and *Building or Buying the High Quality House at the Lowest Cost* (*see* entry 283), it does not negate the essential quality of the material, although it does make the other books somewhat superfluous. Watkins has a good writing style, he concentrates on the important facts, and he summarizes each chapter or gives checkpoints and tips as he goes along so that all his material is easily available. He shares a common fault with such authors as Dowd (*How to Live Better and Spend 20% Less, see* entry 70) by labeling chapters "Save 20 to 50 Percent on Postage and Mailing Costs," inasmuch as such savings can be attained only if the consumer was very wasteful in the first place. The newest material is better than average and very up-to-date; e.g., information on the Type A personality in the chapter on saving on medical bills. (Watkins suggests reducing tension and stress, even if that means seeing a psychiatrist.) A very good chapter shows how to get the most from a checking account, warning not to buy fancy pictured checks with name, address, and phone number and not to postdate checks or cash them if not covered by sufficient cash in the bank (computers are very fast today). "How to Get the Most for Your Savings" effectively rebuts the advice in *Don't Bank On It!* (*see* entry 489). Watkins says banks will throw out an account if they catch on to the scheme. Information on insurance, savings, investing, and tax savings are all very worthwhile. Readers would do well to use this book in lieu of his previous ones.

406. West, David A., and Glenn L. Wood. **Personal Financial Management.** Houghton Mifflin, 1972. 705 pp. $10.95.

Mostly standard material for college students on personal money management, which emphasizes problems pertaining to or of particular interest to that age group. The authors, both university teachers, have provided a great deal of information on career planning, education, owning a business, learning to invest, and the importance of taxes, as well as on managing cash income, budgeting, home ownership, insurance, retirement income, and estate planning. The material is not overly up-to-date; some statistics are from the 1960s. The information is presented in straightforward fashion. It is too often lacking in illustration, but some attempt at humor is evident in the "Case Problems" which follow each chapter, most notably, in the chapter on investing. The bibliographies provided at the end of each section are generally of excellent quality; also helpful are the short summaries following each chapter. There is no material per se on the mechanics of wise buying, although the authors cover many of these topics.

407. Wilder, Rex. **The Macmillan Guide to Family Finance.** Macmillan, 1967. 235 pp. $6.95.

Published in 1967, with statistics that never go beyond early 1966, this remains one of the more lucid and practical books on money management. The author is a family financial adviser and consultant with extensive experience in his field. Food, clothing, appliances, homes, automobiles, insurance (life, health, property, and auto), credit, savings, investment, tax information, and budget planning are covered, with a great deal of unusual material throughout. For example, in the chapter on cars, Wilder reproduces an actual Hartford Insurance Group auto insurance policy in order to explain how to read a policy and show what to look for in it. He adds 16 "cautionary notes" on how *not* to void one's auto protection through ignorance. "Uncle Sam's Share" is a long and detailed explanation of income taxes. He explains instructions on a 1040 form and proceeds, step-by-step, to help fill it out. "Protection against Inflation" advises nonprofessionals to avoid real estate investment and to concentrate on stocks. Each chapter is followed by sources of further reading—a checklist of the best books and pamphlets available at the time *The Macmillan Guide* was published. Since many of the books are continually revised, the list is still valuable.

MONEY MANAGEMENT—BY CHILDREN

408. Duncan, Rodger Dean. **Teaching Your Child the Fiscal Facts of Life.** Abbey Press, 1973. 103 pp. Paper 95¢.

A book devoted more to teaching good life values in general than financial management in particular, it has a warm and humane approach to child rearing. Duncan stresses the need for parents to give and show love, the values of close-knit familial ties, the need for realistic attention to a child's capabilities. Since children unconsciously learn by example, they will pick up their parents' views and habits on money—whether the parents are tightfisted or spendthrift, rational or not. He is in favor of explaining to a small child such apparent contradictions as the need to spend a large some of money on a necessity and not being able to spend a small sum on a luxury. Allowances should be given regularly: from every one to three days for preschoolers to once a month for older teens. Occasional unwise spending should be allowed so a child can learn from the mistake. Since children learn by example, Duncan offers wise money management tips for the family that are economical and environmentally sound: save on water bills by taking a shower instead of a bath; take at-home vacations and rediscover bicycling or canoeing; cut gasoline bills by driving slower. He also deals with showing children how to distinguish faulty or illogical (TV) claims, how to develop good reading habits, and more.

409. Gruenberg, Sidonie Matsner. **Your Child and Money.** (Pamphlet No. 370). Public Affairs, 1965. 28 pp. Paper 35¢. Quantity orders discounted.

A pamphlet that deals realistically with the problems of children and money, it shows that learning to deal with money is one aspect of a child's character development. Gruenberg points out that children will pick up the prevailing attitudes of their parents and sometimes overreact to them, e.g., spendthrift parents may end up with overcautious and tightfisted children. She says that allowances are rights that cannot be withheld. Children should learn to use allowances wisely: with age and increasing responsibilities, allowances should increase, too. While saving is not possible for young children, teens should be encouraged to put part of their money aside for future needs, be it clothes, travel or education. In situations where families need income from their working children, family discussions should bring out the necessity and the fairness of the need. Uses and abuses of credit by teenagers and borrowing on allowances are also discussed.

410. Lee, Mary Price. **Money & Kids: How to Earn It, Save It and Spend It.** Westminster, 1973. 137 pp. $4.75; paper $2.75.

Lee says this book is for preteens, and many of her examples are related to them; however, it is so good, it would be a pity if young teens did not read it. More than a third of the book is devoted to earning money, much of it in novel and interesting ways. Lee divides jobs into quickie-organized, one-time projects; longer-term, individual projects; cooperative or group efforts; and "big business." The first category includes operating a rental service, car washing, seashell decorating, and street sweeping. The second group includes running a hobby show, photography contest, or repair shop and peddling flowers door-to-door. Cooperative ventures include staging athletic events and running a birthday party service or a backyard library. The last group consists of home projects, such as household services, yard work, and being a mother's helper. Lee explains each project and shows how to profit from it and to set it up. The section on saving includes information on savings and checking accounts, savings certificates, government bonds, and stocks. The one on allowances discusses the "step-up allowance" that increases with age and added responsibilities. Budget making, wise buying, cost comparisons, recognizing fraudulent and/or excessive advertising, and generally learning the value of bargains and prices are also covered. The last chapter, "Money in Your Future," relates current interests to possible future occupations. Lee's book is helpful, imaginative, well-arranged, and nonsexist. Highly recommended.

411. **Money Management: Children's Spending.** Illus. Money Management Institute, Household Finance Corp., 1968. 36 pp. Paper 25¢. Quantity orders discounted.

Intended for parents, teachers, or group leaders, it can easily be read by children: the print, larger than usual, and the illustrations seem geared to them. The pamphlet differentiates between children at various age levels: preschoolers, six- through 12-year-olds, and early teenagers. It explains responsibilities and types of spending money: allowances, handouts, gifts, and earnings. "A Child's Spending Plan" offers suggestions for using money: buying clothing, stocks, grocery items; putting it into savings, etc. A very helpful chapter covers special problems: what to do when a child loses money, hoards it, goes on a spending spree, damages property, steals. The pamphlet concludes with a checklist for adults, to see how well they rate in helping children manage money wisely.

MORTGAGES

See Credit; Houses—Buying

MOTORBOATS

For pertinent organizations see Part II, U.S. Federal Agencies—Department of Transportation, U.S. Coast Guard.

412. Griffin, Al. **So You Want to Buy a Motorboat: A Handbook for Prospective Owners, Describing and Evaluating Current Makes and Models.** Regnery, 1971. 162 pp. $7.95.

Covered are safety, performance, and comfort of different categories of motorboats: Class A, Classes 1–4, deck, and houseboats and specialized boats, such as power canoes, inflatables, collapsibles, novelties, and do-it-yourselfs. Griffin explains construction: materials, safety features, hulls, motors, and engines. Discussing materials, he points out the pros and cons of woods, fiber glass, metals, inflatables, and ferrocement. He shows how hull design determines performance (i.e., stability and speed) and discusses each type's advantages and disadvantages. Griffin stresses the need to buy motors to fit boats and provides charts at the end of each chapter listing their specifications and costs. Sections covering different types of boats follow a similar format: the author discusses each type of boat and what it can be expected to do and gives examples of specific models with their good and bad features. He does not compare brands. A practical way to cut costs is to determine the markup, to bargain, and to arrange financing before going out to look for a boat. Griffin points out that boats are easily (and often) repossessed. Disenchantment, lack of real need, and the inability to keep up payments, all contribute. He lists necessary and optional accessories and equipment and shows how costly they are. Addresses of major manufacturers and a glossary complete the book.

MOTORCYCLES AND MINIBIKES

413. Edmonds, I. G. **Minibikes and Minicycles for Beginners.** Macrae Smith, 1973. 153 pp. $4.95.

Designed for young people, the book's language is simple and its style is direct. Basically, this is an explanation of how minibikes and minicycles work and how to maintain them, but the author also includes a rather good general chapter with tips on buying the bikes. While he does not specifically rate particular models, Edmonds does mention some good bikes by name. He also stresses the necessity for test riding to make sure the bike fits the rider. Edmonds offers rather detailed instructions for buying a used bike, plus the name of one manufacturer who puts out kits for the build-your-own trade. For specific brand-name discussion, buyers should consult magazines devoted to the sport, e.g., *Minibike Guide* magazine. As a general overview, this book is a good beginning.

414. Griffin, Al. **Motorcycles: A Buyer's and Rider's Guide.** Regnery, 1972. 271 pp. $7.95.

Motorcycles, scooters, minibikes, and accessories for the bike and rider are discussed and evaluated. The evaluations point up the good and bad features of each model and let consumers make the ultimate buying decision based on specific need. Griffin rates bikes for horsepower, speed, weight, suspension, brakes, comfort, appearance, and price, although the criteria differ slightly from class to class of motorcycles. The usefulness of accessories for riders (jackets, pants, helmets, face shields, goggles) and for motorcycles (windshields, semifairings, full fairings, mufflers, ammeters, lights, fuel gauges, luggage racks, locking chains) are set forth. Safety rules are noted. Griffin includes a history of motorcycling in America, with a brief look at clubs and associations. "Economics" deals with theft and liability and lists companies specializing in motorcycle insurance. Buying from dealers is compared to buying from stores and mail order houses where service cannot be guaranteed. State laws are included in the appendix, as are lists of local motorcycle clubs, outlaw gangs, speed records, piston displacement equivalents, motorcycle publications, and U.S. distributers of foreign manufacturers. A revised 1974 edition of this book is now available. It has not been reviewed.

415. Richmond, Doug. **All about Minibikes.** H. P. Books, 1970. 89 pp. Paper $5.

The first chapter of this expensive paperback is devoted to guidelines for buying a minibike. The language is slangy; there seems to be an implicit assumption that if you want to buy a bike, you will talk that way. Since the book does not deal with brand names (although all bikes pictured in the book are approved by the author), there seems little point to buying it. Not recommended.

MOVING

For pertinent organizations see Part II, U.S. Federal Agencies—Interstate Commerce Commission.

416. Giammattei, Helen, and Katherine Slaughter. **Help Your Family Make a Better Move.** Rev. ed. Dolphin, 1970. 176 pp. Paper $1.45.

This guide is directed toward the woman who is wife and mother—whose husband has just had a job change. While the approach may put people off, particularly such advice as "forget your own concerns occasionally" and "smile when you complain," there is such a wealth of information here that it is worthwhile to overlook the few sore points. Giammattei and Slaughter go step-by-step through all types of moves: local, interstate, and overseas, and include military moves, apartment moves, small town moves, and mobile home moves. The emphasis is on the long-distance move from one house to another, and material on selling an old home and finding and buying a new one is included. All in all, a book well suited to its purpose of making the venture as emotionally positive and financially inexpensive as possible.

417. Gourlie, John. **How to Locate in the Country: Your Personal Guide.** Garden Way, 1973. 97 pp. Paper $3.00.

The book to read before considering a move to the country. The author explains advantages to country living and also points out some drawbacks. He suggests camping trips and weekends in the area; the need to develop self-sufficiency (particularly the need to know how to use tools). Getting a library of do-it-yourself and how-to-fix-it books is a first step. A good section shows how to determine whether any particular property or village is for you. The 21 points covered range from air purity, beauty of the area, quality of the local government, taxes and cost of living to culture and education, medical facilities, availability of help, recreational opportunities, and zoning. One point, the "Garden Way" suitability determines whether the house and land are adequate for economy, security, and contentment, i.e., whether it can grow enough to supply basic food needs and whether it can do so ecologically. Gourlie lists addresses of state economic development offices, promotion and advertising offices, and national weather bureaus to get information about specific localities. His 21-point checklist is reproduced at the back with room for personal ratings of different areas.

418. Hopkins, Robert. **I've Had It: A Practical Guide to Moving Abroad.** Holt, Rinehart & Winston, 1972. 318 pp. $7.95.

Hopkins's book is for people wishing to leave the United States and settle in a foreign country. It concentrates on the 16 countries to which most Americans have migrated in the last few years and deals more broadly with a second group of countries that they have gone to in lesser numbers. Hopkins explains how to apply for and get entry permits, visas, and work permits, and he discusses climate, schools, language, and taxes. He covers the hazards of emigration and pinpoints those problems of culture and distance that often make moves unsuccessful for all but the most committed. It is a practical guide for anyone contemplating such a step, particularly since it highlights the failures as well as the successes of such ventures.

419. Interstate Commerce Commission. **Summary of Information for Shippers of Household Goods.** Rev. ed. 1974. 33 pp. Paper 55¢.

All movers are required by law to submit this helpful pamphlet to their customers. It explains the difference between estimates and actual costs; how to determine costs and weight; how to read weight records, bills of lading, and vehicle-load manifests; how to pack and unpack; how to submit loss and damage claims. Money-saving tips are also included, e.g., reducing the weight of a shipment by sending such items as books, tools, and other heavy unbreakables by slower methods. A moving-day checklist and moving-in hints complete the pamphlet. A consumer questionnaire is appended, to be filled out by the customer after the move, and sent to the chairman of the ICC.

420. Rosefsky, Robert S. **The Ins and Outs of Moving: A Common Sense Guide to an Easy, Thrifty Move.** Follett, 1972. 218 pp. $5.95.

Rosefsky's practical guide starts off by dealing with the impact of leaving home, friends, and family, goes on to discuss the best time to move, how to do it, the physical move and its impact on the family, what to do on arrival at the new home, and settling in. He discusses finances between moves, costs of scouting for new living quarters and of showing the old house. He tells how to find a mover and determine moving costs and how to change specialists, services, and utilities (stockbrokers, lawyers, bankers, insurance agents, creditors, debtors, medical specialists, dentists, druggists, and appliance service people as well as telephones, schools, and newspapers). The author explains how to get rid of all items that should not be moved; he includes certain pets and plants in this category. Advice on packing and marking packages suggests leaving certain breakable items, e.g., dishes and glassware, for the movers to pack. Short chapters on military and international moves are also included, along with an appendix that explains government regulations for shippers of household goods. Some of this information repeats material in the text, but much of it is new, and it gives consumers definite information on the movers' responsibilities. Some tax considerations and a mortgage rate table are also in the appendix. Written simply and a bit lightheartedly, it should help most people.

421. Ruina, Edith. **Moving: A Common-Sense Guide to Relocating Your Family.** Funk & Wagnalls, 1970. 238 pp. $8.95.

Another book written with the premise that this is a family move with the wife responsible for the job. The chapter headings are overly cute, and the material is filled with anecdotes about the author's family that could have been edited, but the book remains an excellent guide to the subject. Ruina has moved her family often, and she has the job down to a science. She begins by suggesting that the family discard as much excess baggage as possible, contact movers, get information on the new area and its services, e.g., doctors, banks, schools, etc. She outlines tactics of packing and moving on a countdown basis through the day of the move and on to the move into the new home. She also discusses in some detail the mechanics of moving overseas, i.e., getting passports, immunization shots, methods of shipping, where and how to bank, finding servants and schools. A chapter on moving by oneself is too short and tells little. The author provides a small, but useful bibliography after each chapter. In many practical ways, this book is superior to *Help Your Family Make a Better Move* (*see* entry 416), but the cute chapter headings and family confidences may put some people off.

422. Sullivan, George. **Do-It-Yourself-Moving: All You Need to Know to Save Money by Moving Your Own Household Belongings.** Macmillan, 1973. 184 pp. $7.95; paper $3.95.

Presenting the mechanics of the do-it-yourself move, Sullivan points out hazards (of moving large and/or heavy pieces of furniture), shows how to pack, lift, and load, how to rent and drive a van and hitch and tow a U-Haul, and how to organize and move. Organizing includes disposing of unwanted items (by donations, garage sales, etc.), getting ready to move pets and valuables, changing insurance, brokerage accounts, and other services, and preparing the car (checking tires, batteries, etc.). Sullivan lists major expressways along with their respective speed limits and tolls. State laws on trailers and trucks and some tricks of safe truck driving are also included. Practical advice is interspersed throughout, e.g., listing the contents on each carton and checking cartons for weight specifications. Sullivan shows how to pack household items ranging from furniture and appliances to garden hoses and rugs, how to estimate load size, and how to determine which trailer or truck to rent. He includes advice on getting insurance covering all phases of the move and on renting moving accessories, such as furniture dollies and hand trucks. A brief overview covers professional movers, settling into the new home, and tax decuctible expenses related to the move. Appendices list pamphlets on moving, state sources on road conditions and restrictions, offices of the Interstate Commerce Commission, and an ICC consumer questionnaire rating mover or shipper. Although designed specifically for the long distance do-it-yourself mover, the book is so practical that even those intending to hire professionals would do well to consult it.

MUSIC

See Phonograph Recordings; Pianos; Stereo and Tape Equipment

NURSING HOMES

See also Medical Care. *For pertinent organizations see Part II, U.S. Federal Agencies*—Department of Health, Education and Welfare, Administration on Aging—Office of Human Development; *Private Organizations*—Public Interest Research Group.

423. Mendelson, Mary Adelaide. **Tender Loving Greed: How the Incredibly Lucrative Nursing Home "Industry" Is Exploiting America's Old People and Defrauding Us All.** Knopf, 1974. 256 pp. $6.95.

The result of ten years of work with the Federation for Community Planning in Cleveland, one of three voluntary groups in the United States dedicated to nursing home reform, Mendelson's account of conditions in nursing homes almost belies belief: patients overpowered by operators who keep them penniless, beat them, and starve them; unsanitary and unsafe conditions; the contributary negligence by government officials who do not act on consumer complaints; inspectors financially tied to nursing home operators. Mendelson concentrates her attack on the financial arrangements implicit in the scandals: how greed moves these people into the industry; how it is controlled by just a relatively few; how and why government does not force disclosure of excessive profits, and why more laws, regulations, and inspectors will not correct the situation. As the author points out, the laws are on the books, but how do you teach people not to be crooks or teach them to care? Despite her pessimism, Mendelson believes that if enough people band together and join in activist groups to pressure government, change may be effected. It is her only solution. That, and caring enough to make sure that one's loved ones do not end up in the inhumane institutions.

424. Routh, Thomas A. **Choosing a Nursing Home: The Problems and Their Solutions.** C. C. Thomas, 1970. 157 pp. $8.00.

Routh (planning, evaluation, and training specialist in the Division of Welfare, Hospital and Welfare Board, Tampa, Florida) has written a book that can be used by nursing home workers and those looking for nursing homes. His writing style is somewhat florid, but his intentions are the best. Chapters entitled "Nursing Homes—A General View," "Visitors," "Volunteer Services," "Realistic Recreation," "Religion," and "A Code of Ethics" can all be used by people interested in guidelines for judging a home. For example, "Volunteer Services" stresses careful screening of these persons, the types of work they should and should not do: volunteers should be expected to listen to and care about the patients, work in the library, do messenger work, physical therapy, or similar work. Volunteers should not concern themselves with a patient's financial situation or gossip about patients. Other guidelines to good nursing homes include access to all religious services, clean and neat living and recreational quarters, privacy with visitors, and safety standards. Not all recreation should be planned, but newspapers, color TVs, AM-FM radios, and magazines should be provided. Several chapters deal with the need for providing emotional as well as physical support for patients. Routh discusses counseling and therapy for senior citizens and points out reasons for the apathy and ill health of the elderly. The book does not deal overtly with abuses in nursing homes, but if consumers look for the type of home Routh suggests, a good one will be chosen.

425. Townsend, Claire, project director. **Old Age: The Last Segregation: Ralph Nader's Study Group Report on Nursing Homes.** Grossman, 1971. 229 pp. $6.95.

An indictment of the nursing home field, and one of many Nader reports reviewing the quality of services to Americans, the book offers no surprises: nursing homes in the United States are dominated by greed, insensitivity to their patients, lack of proper facilities, untrained staff, and more. Many of the recommendations are of concern to consumers only indirectly. The report stresses the need for greater supervision by the Department of Health, Education and Welfare, for a revamping of federal government organizations to provide a centralized concern for the elderly, and for state governments to take greater interest in their senior citizens (from transportation to nursing home personnel standards). A checklist for consumers has 45 "Questions to Ask when Visiting a Nursing Home." These include finding out if the home is licensed; if it is certified for Medicare and Medicaid; the type of care it provides; the size of the staff; its total costs; when the last federal inspection was made; its safety and sanitary facilities; its attractiveness; how satisfied its current patients are, and last, deciding whether one would want to leave a parent in that home. The checklist is extremely valuable and should be made available to everyone interested in looking at and finding a nursing home.

PENSIONS

See also Retirement. *For pertinent organizations see Part II, U.S. Federal Agencies*—Department of Health, Education and Welfare, Administration on Aging—Office of Human Development; Social Security Administration; Veterans Administration; *Private Organizations*—Public Interest Research Group.

426. Nader, Ralph, and Kate Blackwell. **You and Your Pension.** Grossman, 1973. 215 pp. Paper $5.95.

An exposé of the inequities and insufficiencies of the American pension system, it provides suggestions for improvements. In case after case, the authors document how easy it is to lose a pension: i.e., sometimes just by changing from one local (union) to another or retiring before a certain age. They emphasize the havoc caused by ignorance of pension rights and the importance of knowing pension qualifications: number of years of continuous service, minimum retirement age, what constitutes a break in service, how service credits are computed, how to apply for a pension (before retirement), how to check on the fund periodically. The last is to see whether there is a separate fund for pension contributions or if monies are (riskily) being paid out from employers' operating budgets. They also suggest learning how monies would be distributed were the plan terminated. "Your Turn to Play" brings together the 21 questions all prospective pensioners should ask. Appendix F is a listing of people to contact for information and complaints, such as the Internal Revenue Service, Secretary of Labor, and officials of the National Labor Relations Board. Both as a major indictment of the system and as a guide to determining the worth of a specific pension plan, the book will be helpful to all.

PERSONAL FINANCE

See Money Management

PHARMACEUTICALS

See Drugs

PHONOGRAPH RECORDINGS

427. Consumers Union's Music Consultant and the Editors of Consumer Reports. **Consumers Union Reviews Classical Recordings.** Bobbs-Merrill, 1973. 376 pp. $7.95; paper $3.95.

Each of the reviews included in this book originally appeared in the *Consumer Reports* feature "Record Reviews" between March 1959 and mid-1972. Only reviews of records still available (as listed in the April 1972 *Schwann Record and Tape Guide*) are included. The reviews are arranged by composer, and each provides the date of the original review, the artist or group performing the work, the record label and price, the original review, and an updated comment. If a record is also available on 8-track cartridge tape or on cassette, this information is noted, too. Generally, all records are in stereo. Also included is an important and extremely useful nine-page "Basic Discography of Classical Music" that lists preferred artists and labels. The anonymous CU music consultant is a respected authority in his field; his opinions on over 13 years' worth of recordings are worth noting and following.

428. Harris, Kenn. **Opera Recordings: A Critical Guide.** New ed. Drake, 1972. 328 pp. $5.95.

Lists all records available at time of publication for every opera mentioned in the book, plus evaluations of the most important recordings. Albums of particular merit are also noted. Harris chose to evaluate recordings which were either "generally distinguished or . . . important due to the presence of one or more major artists . . . ." Very poor records are not included. Articles range from less than two pages for minor operas to six or seven pages for the major ones. Harris's critiques are short, pointing out the best qualities of each album along with their drawbacks, thus making it quite easy for readers to decide whether to buy a particular album. He also points out that persons seriously interested in purchasing opera records should first listen to them and learn to make their own judgments. While following his instructions would appear to negate the need for this and similar books, most people appreciate a second opinion, particularly a reasonable and knowledgeable critic's opinion.

429. High Fidelity. **Records in Review.** Annual. Scribners. $9.95.

An annual collection of reviews of classical and semiclassical records from *High Fidelity* magazine (originally published as *High Fidelity Record Annual*), the eighteenth edition includes reviews from the 1973 monthly issues. Each record is judged on its individual merits: the music, artistic rendering, and quality of the record are considered, but not compared with others. Frequently, excellent critics do the reviewing, e.g., Henry Lang reviews early classical music; George Movshon and Peter G. Davis, opera, and Harris Goldsmith, piano music. Annuals back to 1969 are still in print and available for purchase.

430. McCarthy, Albert, et al. **Jazz on Record: The First 50 Years 1917–1967.** Hanover Books (Quick-Fox, dist.), 1969. 416 pp. $7.95; paper $4.95.

According to its four authors and twelve contributors, *Jazz on Records* is a guide to "the best, most significant, or occasionally simply the most typical recorded works" of the famous jazz and blues artists of 1917–1967. Biographical material is included, along with evaluations of the artists' total work and contributions, but the emphasis is on evaluation of each record. Only recordings available for purchase at the time of publication were considered. The publisher is a British firm and the focus of the book is British to some extent, although American and European labels are also included. While the label, country of origin, and number of each record are listed, some of the discs may no longer be available for purchase.

431. Rolling Stone Editors. **The Rolling Stone Record Review.** Vol. 2. Pocket Books, 1974. 599 pp. Paper $1.95.

The original *Record Review,* published in 1971, is unfortunately out-of-print. Volume 2 covers reviews that appeared in *Rolling Stone* magazine between 1970–1972. Some of the reviews are slightly abridged, but the flavor and feel are all here. Signed articles by such reviewers as Jack Shadoian, Jon Landau, and Bob Palmer cover contemporary music from rock and roll, soul, jazz, blues, country and western, with sections devoted to individual groups, e.g., the Beatles and their demise, and individual stars, e.g., Bob Dylan. Reviews average two–three pages, although some are longer. The index by album name and name of artist makes the information easily accessible. Prices for albums have been left off, but label numbers remain. A good collection for anyone wanting to buy the older albums, without having to dig through back copies of the magazine.

432. Russcol, Herbert. **Guide to Low-Priced Classical Records.** Hart, 1969. 832 pp. $10; paper $2.95.

This guide should be on the list of everyone interested in hearing and collecting fine classical recordings at low prices. Its author, a professional French horn player and music critic, brings to the book an excellent background and a good critical judgment. Russcol says that low-priced records are comparable to paperback books, i.e., they are often produced by major companies with quality as good if not better than the name label. Arranged alphabetically by composer (over 300 are listed), biographical material and critical evaluations of the oeuvre are followed by a rating of each record. Russcol uses a rating system of zero to four stars and compares various recordings available at time of publication by musician, orchestra, and label. He occasionally cites the opinions of major critics, such as Harold Schonberg on Chopin, Nathan Broder on Bach, and Arthur Cohn on modern music. Over 3,000 records are evaluated with a top price of $3. Record prices have risen since publication, but this book is still a good buy.

PHOTOGRAPHIC EQUIPMENT

433. *Consumer Guide. **Photographic Equipment Test Reports.** Publications International. Quarterly. Paper $1.50. Annual. Paper $2.50. Also distributed by Doubleday.

In the fall of 1973, *Photographic Equipment Test Reports* became a quarterly publication. The first cumulated annual was published in summer 1974; it updated and enlarged on the previous issues. The quarterlies concentrate on all the different types of equipment available to amateur and professional photographers. The fall 1974 issue rates various single-lens reflex cameras; rangefinder cameras; accessories, such as tripods, exposure meters, screens, lighting equipment, and close-up devices; video tape and Super 8 film systems; movie cameras and projectors, and new products: electronic flash units, pocket-size cameras, etc. In addition, a discount price guide is included which lists the suggested retail and discount prices on the various brand-name models. A regular feature of the quarterly is referral to firms that will sell at the low price.

434. Emanuel, W. D., and Leonard Gaunt. **How to Choose the Camera You Need.** Illus. American Photographic Book Publishing Co. 1963. 74 pp. Paper $1.25.

Provides a detailed explanation of how a camera works: outside and inside, including such refinements as linked exposure controls, built-in exposure meters, automatic exposure controls, preset and automatic irises, etc. Diagrams showing what various types of cameras do are also included. A very helpful chapter discusses the consumer in relation to the camera: the kinds of work a particular camera can do matched to one of 32 different photographer types. While price ranges for these cameras are no longer applicable, the booklet itself, written for the novice and the slightly more-advanced camera buff, is still of use.

PHYSICIANS

See Medical Care; Professional Services

PIANOS

435. Schmeckel, Carl D. **The Piano Owners Guide.** Apex Piano, 1971. 114 pp. $3.98; paper $2.95.

Primarily for prospective piano owners, it is concise and instructive. The author explains differences between types of pianos and shows how size, case, construction, and tone affect quality. He covers the piano warranty and manufacturer's service booklet and lists American manufacturers of top-quality pianos. Schmeckel feels that when shopping for a piano it is wise to consider only those instruments which are already properly tuned, to check all pedals and keys, and to look on the inside. When buying a quality used piano, he thinks a piano tuner/technician should examine and appraise it (although he offers guidelines for those wanting to appraise the instruments themselves). Material on player pianos, reproducing pianos, and new and used music rolls is included. Hints on piano care and service has a 1971 service fee guide to some basic costs, a typical piano service agreement, and information about the piano technicians' guild.

436. Stamm, Gustav W. **How to Buy a Piano.** Stamm Industries, 1967. 18 pp. Paper $1 (enclose 25¢ for postage and handling).

The booklet gives brief explanations of piano construction and the differences between types of pianos, i.e., spinets, consoles, and grand pianos. Stamm notes properties to look for in tone, sustaining ability, dynamic range, dropped actions, sounding board, pin-block, third pedal, and keys. He favors buying from a reputable dealer and having a pianist or teacher evaluate the instrument. A short discussion of old piano construction and a checklist of ten items to look for when buying a used instrument are also included. On some items, e.g., loose tuning pins or a cracked bridge, Stamm mentions the costs of fixing the defect as of 1967. Less complete than *The Piano Owners Guide* (*see* entry 435), it nevertheless contains good checklists and is recommended for purchase.

PRODUCT SAFETY

See also Consumer Protection *and specific subjects, e.g.*, Toys. *For pertinent organizations see Part II, U.S. Federal Agencies*—Consumer Product Safety Commission; Department of Health, Education and Welfare, Food and Drug Administration—Public Health Service; *Private Organizations*—Center for Science in the Public Interest; Consumer Federation of America; Consumers' Association of Canada; Consumers' Research, Inc.; Consumers Union of United States, Inc.; L'Institut de Promotion des Intérêts du Consommateur; *Canadian Agencies—National Agencies*—Department of Consumer and Corporate Affairs.

437. Bruce, Ronald, ed. **The Consumer's Guide to Product Safety.** Award, 1971. 252 pp. Paper $1.25.

This is an edited version of the *Final Report* of the National Commission on Product Safety authorized in March 1968 (National Commission on Product Safety. *Hearings and Final Reports*. 13 vols. Law-Arts, 1970. $300). Very similar to the report by the President's Committee on Consumer Interests, *Product Safety in Household Goods* (*see* entry 439), it, too, discusses the need for more rigid safety standards and the lack of industry concern. Certain hazards are covered in both books, but some are in this volume only, e.g., glass bottles, hi-rise bicycles, household chemicals, infant furniture, ladders, and protective headgear. The commission states that there is a great need for a centralized data bank on injuries (now in existence). It finds many manufacturers totally unconcerned about safety standards and hazards, e.g., shoe and infant furniture producers. The commission does not see consumer education as a productive method of reducing injuries. It proposes a Consumer Product Safety Commission (which has since been established), a Consumer Advocate, and the greater use of class actions, treble damage suits, and strict application of tort liability for consumers. It also favors strict certification of manufacturers by the Federal Trade Commission. (*See also* entry 441 *Beware*).

438. Bureau of National Affairs. **ABC's of the Consumer Product Safety Act: The Law in Brief, Commission Directory, Text of Act, Consumer Product List.** Bureau of National Affairs, 1973. 57 pp. Paper $2.

BNA's excellent booklet spells out the 1972 Consumer Product Safety Act, characterized by President Nixon as "the most significant consumer protection legislation" of the 92nd Congress. The law is explained in great detail: its purpose, products covered, how it affects manufacturers, private labelers, distributors, retailers, foreign trade, private consumers, states, courts, other federal agencies, and product standards. The booklet also includes the complete text of the law, a revised consumer product list, and the names of the members of the Consumer Product Safety Commission. Highly recommended.

439. Dickerson, F. Reed, ed. **Product Safety in Household Goods.** Bobbs-Merrill, 1968. 190 pp. $7.50.

Originally published in the *Indiana Law Journal* (vol. 43, no. 2) as "Report on Product Safety: Household Goods," this study was designed to produce a philosophy of consumer protection and guidelines for implementation of the formulated policies. It focuses on 13 household products that produced "significant threat(s) of physical injury": power lawn mowers, glass doors and panels, refrigerators (entrapment), wringer washing machines, gas-fired appliances, floor furnace grates, electrical appliances and wiring, televisions, aerosol containers (explosions), toys, products that are slipping hazards, power tools, and private swimming pools. Recommendations for a framework of legal liability and protections include the use of criminal sanctions, licensing, seizure of unsafe products, publicity, and the use of consumer suits, injunctions, and boycotts. The study notes the need for improving consumer information sources and for compensating the injured through damage suits and insurance. Information on federal and state statutes relating to household products safety and a bibliography complete the study. Produced for the President's Committee on Consumer Interests for the use of the National Commission on Product Safety, it is the basis for the commission report published in *The Consumer's Guide to Product Safety* (*see* entry 437).

440. Epstein, Samuel S., and Richard D. Grundy, eds. **Consumer Health and Product Hazards—Chemicals, Electronic Products, Radiation.** (The Legislation of Product Safety, vol. 1). MIT Press, 1974. 342 pp. $15.

The articles in this volume deal with the problems of developing a "protective response" to toxic materials in the environment: chemicals, electronic products, and radiation. Volume 2 (not published at time of review) deals with cosmetics, drugs, pesticides, and food additives. The books describe current regulations as well as the present state of knowledge about these substances. Articles in the first volume are by Richard Carpenter, Samuel Epstein, Hanno C. Weisbrod, and Richard Grundy. The first article deals with "legislative approaches to balancing risks and benefits" in chemical regulation. Two other chapters deal with hazards from chemicals and other toxic substances in various consumer products. The last two articles deal with radiation exposure from consumer products and services. The second volume has articles by Ralph Nader on the regulation of cosmetics, by Harrison Wellford on the Federal Trade Commission and its regulatory revival, by Roberta G. Marks on pesticides, and more. Not for the consumer in the marketplace, but for students and consumer groups concerned with the need for legislative action.

441. Nader, Ralph. **Beware.** Illus. Law-Arts, 1971. 93 pp. Paper $1.95.

Highlighting the findings of the National Commission on Product Safety held in 1969 and 1970 (*see also* entry 437, *The Consumer's Guide to Product Safety*), the pages are filled with statistics on injuries, maimings, and deaths from faulty products and with case histories of accidents and examples of industrial contempt and indifference to the safety of consumers and government failure to safeguard its citizens. Nader points out that product standards often do not include safety standards, that if consumers do not complain, regulations will not be passed or enforced, and that *Good Housekeeping* and *Parents' Magazine* seals of approval are totally unreliable from a consumer safety standpoint. Cited hazards range from hi-rise bicycle falls and electric clothes dryer fires to household cleaner poisonings and cuts from sliding glass doors. The 20 illustrations, while lacking visual appeal, spotlight some product hazards and point up steps for citizen action. A useful book that compresses a lot of information into relatively small space.

PROFESSIONAL SERVICES

See also Dental Care; Legal Services; Medical Care

442. Golde, Roger H. **Can You Be Sure of Your Experts?** Macmillan, 1969. 243 pp. $5.95.

The aim is admirable—to provide consumers with sufficient information to choose competent doctors, lawyers, and investment counselors. One chapter explains general principles of choosing experts and another deals with groups that can help: professional societies, foundations, universities, government agencies, and consumer organizations. The major drawback is that the book is, for the most part, unusable. Most people would not attempt to interview a doctor or lawyer to ask them questions about their background, habits, achievements or to ask "provocative general questions," e.g., "what things give [them] a real kick." The book has a lot to offer those who can follow Golde's suggestions. For everyone else, it still has value in that it points up where the professional's expertise will help—and where it won't.

REAL ESTATE

See also Houses—Buying. *For pertinent organizations see Part II, U.S. Federal Agencies*—Department of Housing and Urban Development, Office of Interstate Land Sales Registration; *Private Organizations*—The Consumer Protection Center.

443. Boudreau, Eugene. **Buying Country Land.** Macmillan, 1973. 105 pp. $4.95.

Mainly about completely undeveloped land, but it is filled with such practical information that it can be used profitably even by those looking at other kinds of real estate. The author, a geologist, states that the cardinal rule of buying land is to examine it in person. Boudreau discusses the value of topographic maps in checking properties and shows how to read them. He explains the procedures for judging land: finding out about a property, looking at it on a topographic map, visiting the site to do a title search, checking the zoning ordinances, assessing costs of bringing in utilities and an access road, getting an estimate of survey costs, checking on ground water potential and/or existing wells or springs, checking the building site for ground stability, making a percolation test, surveying the boundaries, and drilling a well. At each point, Boudreau suggests minimum requirements and possible costs. He shows good and bad layouts for homes and points out possible natural hazards, e.g., landslides, excessive wind, heaving ground. A good chapter deals with water rights in different states; two short ones, with buying campsite land in the U.S. and buying land in Canada. A short bibliography, a list of geological survey map sale offices, and the Sonoma County (California) percolation test procedure are appended.

444. Kinney, Jean, and Cle Kinney. **How to Find and Finance a Great Country Place.** Parker Publishing, 1974. 228 pp. $7.95.

The emphasis is on investment, but whether a country place is bought for that purpose, for retirement, or for everyday living, many of the procedures are the same. The Kinneys are in the real estate business and themselves buy property for appreciation in various parts of the country. Some of their advice must be taken with more than a grain of salt: (1) that buying without a broker is usually advantageous only to the seller; (2) that "great buys" can be found in national land catalogs. (To buy without seeing land is always dangerous.) They explain how to buy land from the government and note the differences between public and private land. They offer some interesting ways to reduce purchase prices on homes, e.g., giving seller and broker shares in the buying syndicate, making an offer in the form of a check (it is hard to turn down), and trading a mortgage for rent for a specified period of time. The Kinneys also suggest rather low-cost and offbeat housing possibilities, e.g., a railroad station that can be turned into a combination home and dance hall, a one-room schoolhouse that can be used by one person. Most of the book concerns ways to earn money from land and houses by appreciation, remodeling, and selling, but career possibilities outside the cities are also covered.

445. Moral, Herbert R. **Buying Country Property.** Rev. ed. Garden Way, 1973. 119 pp. Paper $3. Bantam. 167 pp. Paper $1.75.

Moral writes for the man in the family, but nevertheless has some fairly practical suggestions that anyone can use. He differentiates between various types of families who settle in the country: daily commuters, retirees, second-home owners, full-time farmers, the self-employed, or those who work in the country for others. He shows how their needs differ and the types of homes each should consider. Information for determining how much a family can afford for a home is rather difficult to follow, but the advice is sound. Moral explains how to determine acreage, where to site the house, how to determine the quality of the land and the amount of water on it. He suggests looking at a home under the worst conditions (a rainy day, during the winter) since he emphasizes country living for enjoyment rather than for speculation and profit. Moral feels that in high-interest periods, it is best to pay cash, but also explains where to go for the best loans. The concluding chapter is very good. It spells out in detail every item that the purchaser should have in writing before the sale, along with a step-by-step explanation of the sale itself—from binder and deposit to insurance, closing, and filing of the deed.

446. Price, Irving. **Buying Country Property: Pitfalls and Pleasures.** Harper & Row, 1972. 173 pp. $5.95. Pyramid. Paper $1.50.

A practical book concentrating on the monetary aspects of buying land and homes in the country, its author is a banker, real estate broker and builder, and his text is basically a discussion of many of the pitfalls involved in the transaction. Very good chapters cover buying a house: getting a survey, using a broker and country lawyer, finding a mortgage. Price notes that land bought for agricultural purposes entitles the owner to federal and state help and to mortgage money. He advises the use of surveyors (since a lot of country property has not been surveyed in decades) and a very close look at the zoning (or lack of it), in order to minimize costly errors. In checking the house and property, he suggests a survey to make sure of an adequate water supply and electricity. A pond or lake must be checked for cleanliness and quantity. Price cautions against buying land with other people and against buying large tracts with the intention of paying for them by subdividing and selling (regulations may prevent this). He notes that after a property is bought, taxes will go up (most land is not often appraised). Price feels that country village living is an excellent choice for the retired, but warns them not to buy into retirement villages until the buildings are up. All in all, a comprehensive book.

447. Scher, Les. **Finding and Buying Your Place in the Country.** Illus. by Carol Wilcox. Macmillan, 1974. 393 pp. $12.95. Collier, Macmillan. Paper $4.95.

Lawyer, teacher, and consumer advocate, Scher is eminently qualified to write this extremely comprehensive book on real estate. Emphasis is divided equally between buying the right land at the right price and making sure all legal matters are handled properly. He covers the best ways to find and check out land, bargain and finance the purchase, examine the contract, go through escrow, and find and use a lawyer. In addition, the book is replete with sources for further information: lists of land catalogs and other advertising sources; addresses of the Bureau of Land Management; pamphlets on homesteading and mining claims; lists of state lands, etc. In one section, Scher warns buyers to avoid subdivision properties, in another, he points out that real estate agents will sell anything and offer nothing. Scher suggests using his checkpoints to make sure lawyers perform all their required work, and he warns buyers not to use lawyers whose interests may be with local sellers or agents. Samples of legal forms include contracts, an owners agreement, a buyer's escrow instructions, a title insurance form. The book can be considered essential reading for anyone interested in buying land and houses.

448. Young, Jean, and Jim Young. **People's Guide to Country Real Estate.** Praeger, 1973. 192 pp. $6.95.

Nowhere as good or as exhaustive as *Finding and Buying Your Place in the Country* (*see* entry 447) the *People's Guide* is aimed at the counterculture audience and is heavy on personal anecdotes. The best chapter deals with living in "strange pads" and is an imaginative listing of alternative homes, e.g., outbuildings on estates; woodsheds; barges; lofts; factories; domes (the Youngs don't like these); churches; schools; vans; gas stations; train stations; cabooses, pullmans, and other railroad cars; barns; cabins, and chicken coops. They suggest buying used trailers and mobile homes rather than new ones, so as to lessen depreciation; they favor older homes, which they consider good bargains. The Youngs suggest that the services of an appraiser are unnecessary, but recommend a country lawyer for the legal transaction. Other chapters are skimpy on detail and should not be used to judge the house or the property, finance the home, etc. Chapters on remodeling a house are heavy on do-it-yourself advice. One chapter concerns women working as real estate agents, and a concluding chapter covers other ways for both men and women to earn a living in the country.

REAL ESTATE—FRAUDS

For pertinent organizations see Part II, U.S. Federal Agencies—Department of Housing and Urban Development, Office of Interstate Land Sales Registration; *Private Organizations*—The Consumer Protection Center.

449. Paulson, Morton C. **The Great Land Hustle.** Regnery, 1972. 240 pp. $7.95.

Paulson, business and financial editor of the *National Observer*, concentrates his investigation and exposé of the interstate land sales industry on companies that use the installment plan to sell unimproved lots ranging from small parcels of raw land (many under water) to those in developments that have few, if any, improvements other than unpaved access roads. He exposes political payoffs, manipulations, and illegal and unfair selling tactics, shows how consumers are sold land by misdirection and withholding of important information, and relates how they often end up paying as much as 20 times the original cost of the land, and if a payment is missed can end up with nothing at all. Paulson cites progress made in several states in the reform of land sale rules, and he urges all citizens to lobby for and support such laws. He also quotes investment counselors who warn that ordinary investors should never buy land for speculation. An appendix with a list of the principal regulatory agencies in the federal and state governments, as well as a few private organizations offering information on subdivided land, completes the book.

RECORDINGS

See Phonograph Recordings

RECREATION

See Airplanes; Bicycles; Camping Equipment; Fishing Equipment; Guns and Hunting Equipment; Mobile Homes; Motorboats; Motorcycles and Minibikes; Recreational Vehicles; Skiing Equipment; Stereo and Tape Equipment; Travel

RECREATIONAL VEHICLES

See also Airplanes; Bicycles; Camping Equipment; Mobile Homes; Motorboats; Motorcycles and Minibikes

450. Bauer, Erwin. **The Sportsman on Wheels.** Illus. (Outdoor Life Books). Popular Science (Dutton, dist.), 1969. 146 pp. $4.50.

The book's very general information is of limited value to users of recreational vehicles. Bauer takes notice of disadvantages to each class of vehicle, but most of the material reads like a puff piece. A chapter on snowmobiles says nothing about individual models and concentrates instead on optional equipment and safety rules. Two chapters could be of interest to buyers. The first deals with "dream outfits," individual collections of vehicles and gear put together by a variety of sportsmen (including the author). It is useful because it gives an overall view of what is needed for certain sports year round. The other good chapter describes proper procedures for handling trailers: how to install a hitch, pick a car for trailering, trailer maintenance, towing, parking, and boat launching. 1969 state regulations for RVs, e.g., towing speeds, width and height of vehicles, required safety devices, and overnight parking regulations at roadside, are included. Listings of U.S. campground guides and associations and of Canadian campsites completes the book.

451. Engel, Lyle Kenyon. **The Complete Book of Trailering.** Illus. Arco, 1973. 192 pp. $5.95; paper $2.95.

Supplies general information on buying tow cars and packages for new and old cars, trailers, appliances, and accessories and safety and driving tips. Engel points out that compact cars are more than adequate for hauling most boats, motorcycles, and small cargo trailers. Material on tow car and trailer tires, hitches and brakes, as well as on winterizing and winter storage is good. The author gives a few good rules for parking the coach, maintaining the body and parts, and preventing it from freezing. The section on accessories looks as if it came from a manufacturer's catalog. It is a haphazard grouping of photographs with one or two lines of text for each item. Camping trailers, mini, medium-size, and luxury trailers are covered simply by noting what each RV does and then listing a few models in each category (in effect, recommending them without explanation). Information on RV appliances lists pros and cons of each item: pressurized water system, water heater, space heater, refrigerator, range, oven, hookups, and fuel source. The book concludes with information on trade associations of the mobile home and recreational vehicle industry.

452. Gartner, John. **All about Pickup Campers, Van Conversions and Motor Homes.** Illus. (Book No. 16). Trail-R-Club, 1969. 224 pp. Paper $4.50.

While this purports to be about self-propelled recreational vehicles: pickup campers, converted vans and motor homes, overall, less than 50 pages are devoted to information of any type. A large part of the book consists of reasons for buying RVs: (women and children love them) and reasons not to buy them (lack of space and size). The rest is photographs of RV models. Information on manufacturers ranges from one–three lines. Gartner says that only products of reputable manufacturers are included, and he occasionally offers an opinion if he likes a brand. Not recommended.

453. Griffin, Al. **Recreational Vehicles: A Buyer's & User's Guide.** Illus. Regnery, 1973. 269 pp. $10.

Griffin's book is essential reading for any first-time buyer of a recreational vehicle. Griffin tested the most popular, unique, and/or notorious makes and models and also used the opinions (good and bad) of RV owners. When models were loaned by manufacturers or dealers, the information is so noted. Griffin divides the RV field into two basic sections: those that are driven and those that are towed. The first section provides material on self-powered pickup covers, slide-in campers, chassis mounts, van conversions, and motor homes. Camping, travel, aircraft-type, telescoping, and fifth-wheel trailers are tested in the second section. For each type of RV, the author suggests uses, advantages, and disadvantages; discusses individual models, and gives some information about the manufacturers. He also lists addresses of many companies whose models are not discussed. Each chapter concludes with ratings pertinent to that type of vehicle. Price as such is not a criterion; value is. For some types of RVs, Griffin subdivides by size and/or style, e.g., he tests tailgaters and hang-overs in the slide-in truck camper group and compact, intermediate, and full-sized travel trailers. One very good chapter points up advantages of renting (cost, use, need to try before purchase), and another one tells how to buy used RVs intelligently. The index makes access to all information exceptionally easy.

454. Hull, Clinton. **How to Choose, Buy and Enjoy a Motor Home, Van Camper, Tent-Top or Tent.** Illus. (Book No. 97). Trail-R-Club, 1970. 308 pp. Paper $4.95.

For those who can get past Hull's views on "coddled criminals," "criminal loving judges" and "thoughty" husbands who will take their wives out for dinner during a vacation, he offers some practical advice on buying trailers, tent tops, and motor homes. Hull cites their pros and cons, e.g., lower costs and always ready to move against lack of privacy and lack of space. Hull lists recommended equipment for camper bodies and guidelines for determining what to buy. Information covers the interiors and exteriors of vehicles. He also has some suggestions on appropriate accessories, noting brand names, but not models. A very large portion of the book is taken up by photographs and sketches of different vehicles. Additional material covers living suggestions, maintenance, and safety tips.

455. Kneass, Jack. **How to Buy Recreational Vehicles.** Illus. (Book No. 94). Trail-R-Club, 1969. 164 pp. Paper $2.95.

Kneass explains good recreational vehicle construction, but neither compares nor evaluates models. Instead, he often uses one model to explain a point simply because its manufacturer sent him promotional material. The information itself is good, but its arrangement is poor and confusing. First he covers luxury trailers (and accessories) and conventional trailers. The next 22 chapters deal with trailer construction—from undercarriage, tires, axles, and springs to sanitation systems, insulation, and floor coverings. A short chapter on one type of fiberglass camper follows. Kneass says that since basic construction is almost the same for trailers as for campers, there is no need for an exhaustive study of the latter. A concluding chapter has a practical list of important accessories. It is marred by the author's inclusion of another list of accessories produced by a manufacturer.

456. Kneass, Jack. **How to Select a Car or Truck for Trailer Towing.** (Book No. 93). Trail-R-Club, 1969. 144 pp. Paper $2.95.

Kneass, a former editor of the official magazine of the Travel Trailer Clubs of America, used to test and rate cars as trailer-towing vehicles. In this book, he states that listing specific models is self-defeating, i.e., they change too often and there are too many variables. Instead, he offers guidelines and information to allow readers to make their own decisions. Kneass discusses gear ratios and motors and explains how and what to expect in towing from small cars, sports cars, intermediate- and full-sized cars, luxury models, and trucks. He uses specific models, but refuses to be pinned down on recommendations. Summary chapters entitled "How to Select a Tow Car," "Addenda—Or Odds & Ends" and "Some Conclusions" review the entire book. The author emphasizes the need to buy a manufacturer's trailer package, to overequip when buying, to get a good equallizing hitch (the most important piece of equipment of all), to buy a car with a big motor with moderate gearing, etc. Consumers interested in towing should also read "How to Pull Trailers" in the *Mobile Home Manual*, volume 1 (*see* entry 354).

457. Nulsen, Robert H. **How to Buy Trailers, Mobile Homes, Travel Trailers, Campers.** Illus. (Book No. 31). Trail-R-Club, 1969. 118 pp. Paper $2.95.

An almost word-for-word duplication of the chapter "How to Buy Trailers and Mobile Homes" in Nulsen's *Mobile Home Manual* (*see* 354), only a few photographs and sketches are different. If consumers are only interested in buying a vehicle, they can look at this book; otherwise, the larger, more complete volume is recommended.

RECREATIONAL VEHICLES—CAMPGROUNDS

458. **Trailer Life's Recreational Vehicle Campground and Services Guide.** Illus. Annual. Trailer Life. Paper $5.45.

The 1974 edition lists 7,000 private parks and campgrounds in the United States, Canada, and Mexico; 5,000 public parks, and 10,000 businesses associated with campgrounds and parks, such as general stores. Trailer Life editors rate the parks on the basis of their facilities, on a 1–4 scale (from 1, minimum to 4, outstanding). Approximately 5,000 parks are rated. Other information includes name, address, directions to the site, its elevation, facilities, fees, and occasionally, a few personal observations. With advertisements, so caution must be exercised.

459. **Woodall's Trailering Parks and Campgrounds Directory.** Illus. Annual. Woodall (Simon and Schuster, dist.). Paper $6.95.

Over 19,000 parks and camps in the United States, Canada, and Mexico are listed in the 1974 edition. Private parks are inspected and rated; government facilities are listed without ratings. Based on a scale of 1 W to 5 W, the ratings are assigned by category; that is, within the groupings of campgrounds, recreational vehicle parks, recreational vehicle areas/mobile home parks, and overnight stops. Overnight stops in mobile home parks and primitive facilities are not rated. Good maintenance is the most important factor in the ratings, with the higher ratings dependent on number of facilities and sophistcation. Fees are not listed. The parks are arranged by state and listed according to nearest town or city. Name, address, and directions are also included. Woodall's accepts advertising and, frequently, the higher the rating, the more likely one is to see an advertisement for the place. In addition to the listings, each annual includes articles on various subjects. The 1974 edition has a guide to planning long trips, with checklists for recreational vehicles and personal items, and another article on camping for beginners.

RESTAURANTS

460. Christy, George. **The Los Angeles Underground Gourmet.** Simon and Schuster, 1970. 159 pp. Paper $1.95.

Christy lists 225 restaurants by name, address, telephone number, hours, liquor and wine service, credit cards, parking accommodations, price range, and rating. He awards four stars to no stars to each place, based on food, service, and atmosphere. Comments on each place are generally short, noting house specialties, ambiance, or anything else out of the ordinary. There are no lists by ethnic speciality, price range, or ratings. The author includes a short chapter on good California wines and another one entitled "How to Get First-Class Service." The latter chapter explains how and when to make a reservation, how to deal with the maître d'hôtel, how to send back food, etc. The book should be updated. Many restaurants have undoubtedly gone out of business, others have new managements, new ones have sprung up, and service has changed since this edition was published in 1970; it should be used with caution.

461. Collin, Richard H. **The Revised New Orleans Underground Gourmet.** (Fireside Book). Simon and Schuster, 1973. 248 pp. Paper $2.95.

Noting restaurants serving "great meals" for under $3.75, this revision of *The New Orleans Underground Gourmet* includes over 250 restaurants in the city, with material on Gulf coast country dining in Alabama, Mississippi, Louisiana, and Texas. The author is an associate professor of history and the writer of a weekly restaurant column in the *New Orleans States-Item*. He rates restaurants primarily on the basis of their specialties, i.e., a fish house must serve good fish, not good steak. Ratings are also given for elegance and atmosphere and for meals under $1.75, $2.95, and $3.95. Information on each restaurant includes name, address, telephone number, hours, and comments on the food and ambiance. Lists of restaurants from four stars to one for cuisine, and from three diamonds to one for elegance and atmosphere are included.

462. Glaser, Milton, and Jerome Snyder. **The Underground Gourmet.** Simon and Schuster, 1967. 224 pp. Paper $1.95.

The original underground gourmet, its use at this time is not recommended. However, as its popularity has not declined over the years, it can be noted that the authors have compiled a directory of 101 restaurants that in 1966 and 1967 prepared "great meals in New York for less than $2 and as little as 50¢. A new edition would be extremely useful. In the meantime, the authors continue to rate underground restaurants and their current ratings appear in *New York Magazine*.

463. Kahn, Joseph P., and E. J. Kahn, Jr. **The Boston Underground Gourmet.** (Fireside Book). Simon and Schuster, 1972. 112 pp. Paper $1.95.

The authors describe 45 restaurants in Boston and the surrounding areas of Cambridge, Medford, and Brookline which were serving good, complete meals for less than $4 at the time their guide was published. The restaurants are listed alphabetically, and the information on each notes name, address, telephone number, hours, drinks policy, and credit cards honored, with the authors' comments on each place averaging two–three pages. An index by food specialty and another by location are included.

464. Lewis, Roz. **The Little Restaurants of Los Angeles.** Camaro, 1973. 211 pp. Paper $1.95.
Lewis, Roz, and Joe Pierce. **The Little Restaurants of San Francisco.** Illus. by David Yeadon. Camaro, 1974. 218 pp. Paper $1.95.
Wagstaff, Lanny. **The Little Restaurants of San Diego.** Illus. by David Yeadon. Camaro, 1974. 126 pp. Paper $1.95.

The "little restaurants" of the series are not restricted to the city noted in the respective title, but include good places to eat in surrounding areas. In San Diego restaurants, prices for meals range from $1.50 to $4.50; in San Francisco, from $1.50 to $4.95, and in Los Angeles, from $1.50 to $3.95. Each guide lists approximately 100 restaurants according to the type of food served: e.g., American, health, Japanese. One restaurant is described on each page. Information includes descriptions of decor, service, and food. The facility's address, telephone number, hours, parking facilities, drinks policy, credit cards honored, and reservation policy are noted. In the San Diego and San Francisco guides David Yeadon has provided a sketch of the outside of each place on the page facing its listing. In all three guides, each restaurant is located on a city or country road map. The San Francisco and San Diego guides also list a few "splurge" restaurants, and the San Diego guide includes a description, by Karen Wagstaff, of speciality food shops in the area. The books are handy, fairly up-to-date, and manage to impart the flavor of each place.

465. The New York Times Guide to Dining Out in New York. Rev. ed. Atheneum, 1971. 351 pp. Paper $3.95.

It lists over 600 restaurants, all but 13 of them in Manhattan. Information on each place gives name, address, telephone number, drinks policy, days open, and credit cards honored. The restaurants are rated on a none to four stars scale, but the editors have omitted any explanation for the ratings. If their basis is that of the earlier editions, then food, service, and decor are rated in relation to price range. Comments on each restaurant stress ambiance, food quality, and price range as of 1971. Listings by ratings, geographic area, and food specialty complete the book. Craig Claiborne, former food editor of the *New York Times* and author of earlier editions of the guide, was not associated with this edition's publication.

466. Quinn, Jim. **Word of Mouth: A Completely New Kind of Guide to New York City Restaurants.** Mixed Media (Lippincott, dist.), 1972. 207 pp. Paper $2.95.

A very personal guide to New York City restaurants, its author seems to be a member of the counterculture. Quinn begins by explaining what is wrong with all the other New York City restaurant guides and why his is untrustworthy, too. He rates restaurants from A to F on the basis of food alone and he discusses ambiance, service, food, and prices in long, often funny texts. Name, address, telephone number, days open, credit cards honored, and price range are given. Inexpensive means under $5; moderate, between $5 and $10, and expensive, over $10. His rating is accompanied by the ratings from *The New York Times Guide* (*see* entry 465) and *Myra Waldo's Restaurant Guide* (*see* entry 474) so that the reader can compare the books as well as evaluate the restaurants. A special section is devoted to the $100 meal: ten of New York's most famous and expensive places to eat (nine are French, one is Spanish). Here, Quinn discusses service, treatment accorded him, food, patrons, and more. No doubt many people will be outraged by the book, but it is fun to read if nothing else.

467. Rader, Barbara. **The Long Island Underground Gourmet.** (Fireside Book). Simon and Schuster, 1973. 191 pp. Paper $2.95.

The author is food editor of the Long Island (New York) newspaper *Newsday* and her book is an updated collection of her weekly column's restaurant reviews. She lists each restaurant's name, address, telephone number, credit card policy, and price range and provides a general assessment of each as well as driving directions. Six price-range categories are listed: low cost (to 95¢), inexpensive (to $3), moderate ($4–$7), moderately expensive ($7–$10), expensive ($10–$14), and very expensive ($14 and up). The book is arranged by areas on Long Island. An index by food category is included.

468. Read, R. B. **The San Francisco Underground Gourmet.** Rev. ed. (Fireside Book). Simon and Schuster, 1971. 288 pp. Paper $2.95.

"An irreverent guide to dining in the Bay Area," this is a true underground gourmet—with top price (as of the fall of 1970) of $5 for a complete dinner. Undoubtedly, these prices have all disappeared, and restaurant quality may have changed as well. Read includes only those restaurants that offer "something special," and he notes that many restaurants are not included simply because he did not get to review them. Besides ethnic restaurants, the author also discusses seafood houses, organic, al fresco, soul food, coffeehouses, young spots and "something else"—those that have special service and/or ambiance. Seventeen gay restaurants are listed without annotations. Information on each restaurant includes name, address, hours, telephone number, reservation policy, and the author's comments. Classifications by price and by location are also given.

469. Rubin, Jerome, and Cynthia Rubin. **Boston Dining Out: A Guide to Dining in Boston.** Emporium, 1972. 128 pp. Paper $2.50.

The authors consider all of the 103 restaurants they list as good. In addition, they include the complete menus from 24 of the restaurants as well as recipes from many of them. Information is very brief: i.e., limited to name, address, telephone number, specialties, hours, and price range for a la carte meals. One useful feature of *Boston Dining Out* is its lists of places by categories, such as "Elegant Dining," "Intimate Dining," "Traditional Dining," and "Continental Dining," as well as by ethnic specialty. For more detailed notations, see the Rubins' *The Real Boston Underground Dining* (*see* entry 471), which includes many of these same restaurants.

470. Rubin, Jerome, and Cynthia Rubin. **Boston Lunching Out: A Guide to Lunching in Boston.** Emporium, 1972. 128 pp. Paper $2.50.

Similar in style and content (they include many of the same restaurants) to *Boston Dining Out* (*see* entry 469), this volume lists 160 restaurants rated for food, service, and decor. Food was judged for quality, presentation, preparation, and taste; service was judged for quality, efficiency, congeniality, polish, and direction; and decor was judged for physical appearance, appropriateness, comfort, and cleanliness. No comments are offered in the text, except for a note on house specialties. Other information lists name, address, telephone number, hours, a la carte prices, and credit cards honored. Luncheon menus from many of these restaurants and recipes from some of them are also included. For more detailed information on many of these places, see *The Real Boston Underground Dining* and *The Boston Underground Gourmet* (*see* entries 471 and 463, respectively).

471. Rubin, Jerome, and Cynthia Rubin. **The Real Boston Underground Dining.** Emporium, 1973. 157 pp. Paper $1.95.

Confining themselves to "small, interesting, hard-to-find and often inexpensive restaurant(s)," the authors tried to limit their list of 71 restaurants to those serving dinners for under $4, but found that the inflated economy made that limitation too restrictive. Information on each place lists name, address, telephone number, days and hours of operation, drinks (if any), credit cards honored, air conditioning (if any), train directions, house specialty, and ratings from fair to excellent on food, decor, and service. In addition, the Rubins offer their comments about the style, food, and prices of each place. About half these restaurants are also listed in *The Boston Underground Gourmet* (*see* entry 463). See also the Rubins' *Boston Dining Out* and *Boston Lunching Out* (*see* entries 469 and 470 respectively).

472. Tolf, Robert W. **Florida Trend's Guide to Florida Restaurants.** West Coast/Central Edition. Gold Coast/Keys Edition. Trend House, 1973. Paper $1.75 ea.

Information in these guides to Florida restaurants includes the restaurants' name, address, telephone number, hours, closing dates, and reservation policy. In addition, the author devotes from a third to a half page to a description of each establishment, discussing its ambiance, service, and house specialties. Tolf usually notes price range, i.e., inexpensive (lunch, under $2; dinner, under $3.50), moderate (lunch, $2–$3.50; dinner, $3.50–$5.50), and expensive (lunch, over $3.50; dinner, over $5.50). Prices do not include wines and liquor. Tolf tends to be lavish in his praise, so caution should be exercised. Each guide is arranged by area and each has an alphabetical index. In both guides, Tolf offers his particular version of the restaurant Grand Tour; these restaurants are generally in the expensive range.

473. Tolf, Robert W. **100 Best Restaurants of Florida.** Trend House, 1974. 24 pp. Paper 50¢.

A compilation of the best restaurants listed in Tolf's *Florida Trend's Guide to Florida Restaurants* (*see* entry 472) plus a few restaurants in north Florida. Unfortunately, the arrangement of this pamphlet makes access to its information extremely difficult. The material is arranged by region, e.g., central, west coast, north, but the towns and cities within each region are not listed alphabetically. Also, there is neither an alphabetical index nor a list by food type. Prices have been deleted, and it is impossible to know whether the restaurant is expensive or not. Not recommended.

474. Waldo, Myra. **Myra Waldo's Restaurant Guide to New York City and Vicinity.** Rev. ed. Macmillan, 1973. 437 pp. Paper $3.95.

Waldo lists more than 800 restaurants in the New York City metropolitan area but her basic concentration is on Manhattan. She rates the restaurants on the basis of from one to five crowns "in relation to the prices charged." Therefore, an inexpensive resturant is more likely to rate higher than an expensive place. In this edition, she does not give five crowns to any restaurant. Price ranges go from inexpensive ($6 or less), to moderate ($6–$11), to expensive ($12–$20), to very expensive (over $20), not including drinks, tax, or tips. There are listings by ratings (number of crowns), by geographic area, by food type, and by special service, i.e., serving Sunday brunch, Sunday dinner, after theater, "in a hurry," and special restaurants for children. The last list is particularly suspect. Information on each restaurant lists name, address, telephone number, days open, price range, credit cards honored, and rating. Comments range from the specific to the very vague.

475. Yeadon, Anne, and David Yeadon. **Hidden Restaurants: Northern California.** Illus. 1973. 218 pp. **Hidden Restaurants: Southern California.** Illus. 1972. 213 pp. Camaro. Paper $1.95 ea.

While Sacramento, Carmel, Monterey, and Reno (in the northern edition) and Palm Springs, Santa Barbara, and Malibu (in the southern edition) hardly constitute "surprising" or "out-of-the-way places," according to the Yeadons, the restaurants listed serve "good food at inflation-fighting prices." Restaurants that serve canned or frozen vegetables, have one-winery lists, and/or have rushed service are not included; those with homemade breads and soups, steaks cooked to order, spotless silver and china, and courteous service (all with reasonable prices) are included. The Yeadons describe restaurants in terms of service, ambiance, and menus; give examples of price; note hours, address, type of food, bar, credit cards honored, and reservation policy; and on the facing page, sketch the outside of the restaurant and spot it on a city or road map for extra clarity. "Splurge" restaurants in the Southern California guide are those with meals for over $6; the Northern California guide, while not explicit, seems to follow an even lower definition of "splurge." By and large, the places are small, family-run, and give individual attention; many are in unusual and attractive settings. The guides are pocket-sized and handy.

RETIREMENT

See also Annuities; Money Management; Nursing Homes; Social Security and Medicare. *For pertinent organizations see Part II, U.S. Federal Agencies*—Department of Health, Education and Welfare, Administration on Aging—Office of Human Development.

476. Buckley, Joseph C. **The Retirement Handbook.** Revised by Henry Schmidt. 4th rev., enlarged ed. Harper & Row, 1971. 357 pp. $7.95.

A standard in the field, *The Retirement Handbook* has information on all aspects of planning for retirement: finding a mild climate suitable to one's retirement needs, finding suitable housing, income planning, suggestions for starting and/or running a small business or farm, Social Security and Medicare. The book stresses the positive sides of retirement, but does not go into all the problems that make retirement difficult for so many. Bibliographies appended to all chapters can lead readers to more thoughtful material. Should be read with caution and in conjunction with such books as *How to Avoid the Retirement Trap* (*see* entry 478).

477. Collins, Thomas. **The Complete Guide to Retirement.** Prentice-Hall, 1970. 221 pp. Paper $2.95.

Syndicated author (*The Golden Years* and *The Senior Forum*) Collins's book is a blend of jocular humor, practical information, and sexist advice. He points out the need to determine one's retirement income at least a year ahead of time and to learn if any company benefits (e.g., buying at discount; health insurance) will continue. One good suggestion is to take a vacation about five to six weeks after retirement when depression usually sets in; another is to check out a possible retirement community by living there on a rental basis while renting one's own home. Probable higher costs of living, e.g., medical and auto services, should be taken into account in totaling expenses. The most popular retirement areas are discussed very briefly: Florida, California, North Carolina, the Gold Coast, Arkansas, the Rio Grande Valley, and Mexico. While cautioning against moving into retirement homes, the author does feel that they are usually well designed for the elderly, i.e., with ramps, low shelves, etc. Chapters dealing with a happy retirement are extremely sexist: husbands should not do housework neighbors can see; single women should look for husbands, but batchelors should not look for wives. Other chapters cover health, Medicare and Medicaid, legal affairs, and ways to use leisure and increase income. A short, outdated bibliography is included.

478. Cooley, Leland Frederick, and Lee Morrison Cooley. **How to Avoid the Retirement Trap.** Nash, 1972. 285 pp. $7.95; paper $1.50.

A disturbing view of retirement by the authors of *The Retirement Trap,* a great deal of space is given to enumerating traps, but relatively little to showing how to avoid them. The Cooleys stress the economic importance of saving and investing. They show that Medicare, Social Security, and private pension plans offer little real help to most people, particularly the sick. They point up the emotional, physical, and financial difficulties of settling in a "cheap" foreign country and the problems inherent in retiring to such a new and different lifestyle. For those interested in life-care facilities, such as retirement communities and retirement hotels and apartments, there is a lot here to read and ponder. The book also points up the lack of health care facilities for the elderly poor as well as the need to rethink the entire problem of age and retirement.

479. Ford, Norman D. **Where to Retire on a Small Income.** 18th rev., enlarged ed. Harian, 1973. 203 pp. Paper $2.50.

In his excellent, all-purpose retirement book Ford concentrates on locating "pleasant communities with rock-bottom living costs." He explains what to look for in retirement communities: climate, healthfulness, and medical facilities; scenery, altitude, and topography; opportunities for physical recreation, for cultural and intellectual activity, for religious and social activities, and the companionship of other retirees; cost of living, taxes, etc.; opportunities for hobbies, job, or business; and town or country living and accessibility. In addition, he points out advantages and disadvantages of mobile home and retirement community living and suggests that in the latter case, the best buy is renting. Ford notes that after age 75, when ill health and/or the death of a spouse make independent living impractical, many people must move from such facilities. Ford lists and explains his personal choice of the 24 "most liveable, worry-free towns" in the country. The main portion of the book is a section-by-section survey of each retirement area in the United States (including Puerto Rico and the Virgin Islands). He notes each area's recommended sections, and lists the facilities and opportunities in each of the recommended cities and towns. He also charts areas by health, e.g., those free from hay fever, those good for persons suffering from heart trouble, gout, pleurisy, etc. Highly recommended.

480. Gilmore, Forrest E. **How to Plan Now for Your Retirement.** Gulf Publishing, 1961. 108 pp. $3.95.

Written in 1961, some of Gilmore's chapters (e.g., on life expectancy) are outdated, but since the emphasis here is on planning for retirement, most of what the author has to say remains fairly pertinent. Unfortunately, the best ideas in the book are the most commonplace, e.g., the need to prepare for a good retirement by keeping healthy through diet, exercise, and good living; by developing lifelong hobbies; and by providing the funds for a secure future. The section on retirement areas shows that Americans have been moving to Florida and California for a long time. He points out that many other southern areas are good for the retiree, too. Gilmore has kind words for retirement residences, just beginning to come to the fore when he wrote this book, and he predicted a great expansion in their number. One good suggestion is to taper off from the job. Unfortunately, that is possible for very few people. Another good idea is to try to keep working at some type of job, or else to use one's hobbies creatively. A short chapter deals with fears and problems of retirement: loss of money, illness, loneliness. Overall, the book concentrates on the upbeat and the inspirational; it can be considered supplementary reading material on the subject.

481. Hayes, Richard L. **How to Live Like a Retired Millionaire on Less than $250 a Month.** (Book No. 15). Trail-R Club, 1968. 96 pp. Paper $2.50.

Even the publishers note that inflation has caused the title to be outdated. The book itself, written by a retiree living in a luxury mobile home park, is a paean of praise to such a life. He extols the people and the recreational facilities and suggests that such living facilities are available for $250 a month. The author is verbose and says nothing that cannot be found in more comprehensive and practical books on the subject. The worst fault is that he lists no disadvantages to mobile home living; the poor ones, he says, are things of the past. Not recommended.

482. J. K. Lasser Tax Institute and Sam Shulsky. **Investing for Your Future.** Annual. Simon and Schuster. Paper $3.95.

Directed primarily at the individual interested in investments, the book includes several chapters dealing specifically with the retiree. Even here, though, the stress is on financial security and reinvestment. Chapters are devoted to stretching ones portfolio when retiring; retiring successfully by avoiding or minimizing income taxes (e.g., investing in tax-exempt bonds or in companies whose operations are tax protected); benefits of joint ownership; advantages and disadvantages of home ownership (it is a nice luxury); insurance, annuities, Social Security, and pensions; and reinvestment in the retirement years. Each chapter concludes with questions from individuals about their particular problems that relate to the general topic under discussion. This book is not for persons nearing retirement, but for those who want to plan now for future financial security. It can be read by retirees as an adjunct to more general books on the subject.

483. Musson, Noverre. **The National Directory of Retirement Residences: Best Places to Live when You Retire.** Rev. ed. Fell, 1973. 214 pp. $9.95.

A misleading title. One part of the book is a directory, the other tells how to judge good and bad homes. The directory lists villages of single residences, apartment houses, and group residences which (generally) "have appropriate auxiliary services and facilities, and are designed and operated especially for older people." Nursing homes, trailer camps, and homes which limit applicants to particular communities, organizations, or religious faiths were excluded. So, too, were residences built before 1950 and not remodeled. What remains, however, is only a list of residences whose owners or managers filled out the author's questionnaire. There is no way of knowing which facilities are good, bad, or terrible. Information on each residence is listed by state, and within the state, by city. Name, address, telephone number, year built, sponsor, type of facility, entrance fees, monthly fees, nursing fees and medical care, food, waiting list, location (central city, suburban, rural), nearby facilities (shopping, churches) are noted. The first section discusses the advantages of these residences, finances and legal problems in retirement, selling the old home, and moving. The only worthwhile chapters list checkpoints to note when visiting the homes before signing up. Readers can do almost as well by referring to Townsend's *Old Age: The Last Segregation* (*see* entry 425).

484. Rogers, Donald I. **Save It, Invest It, and Retire.** Arlington House, 1973. 191 pp. $7.95.

Most of the book spells out a plan for saving money and investing regularly. According to the author, if followed, the plan should provide for retirement. The last section covers the actual retirement. Rogers, once financial editor of the New York *Herald Tribune*, notes that a successful and happy retirement depends on enough funds and a wide variety of interests. He makes one interesting point: many people could retire well before age 62 or 65 if they planned; some could do it now if they realized their current assets. Ideas for financing retirement are conventional. They include getting the cash from insurance policies and savings, adding in investments from house and stocks (plus monies from pension and/or Social Security if over 65). Investing during retirement must be done conservatively to produce a sound and safe return. Rogers feels that part-time work is beneficial to the psyche as well as to the pocketbook, although hobbies are good, too. A formula for independent retirement summarizes his information. A glossary of stock market terms concludes the book.

485. Wise, Sidney Thomas. **Invest and Retire in Mexico.** (Dolphin Books). Doubleday, 1973. 200 pp. Paper $3.95.

The author of this interesting and intelligent guide to investing and living in Mexico is the director of the Mexican Financial Advisory Service. He devotes the last chapters to retirement. On the question of cost of living, Wise points out that your lifestyle and place of residence will determine the answer. Mexico City, one of the most expensive places, averages about 80 percent of comparable costs of Washington, D.C. If money is not spent on imported food, costs are cheaper. Labor is cheap and household help costs little. Building a home runs about half as much as in the United States. Wise stresses that many

Americans cannot acclimate to the tempo of the country, to its sanitary conditions, medical facilities, language barrier, etc. He says it is no place for those who like organized activities, although there are many American fraternal organizations. He urges travel and vacation stays in several areas to test them out, and he notes that at those times, it is best to try to live like a resident rather than like a tourist. He briefly notes and characterizes the major retirement areas of the country. Other chapters deal with immigrant status and the need for income; how to bring a car into the country, etc. Very practical and well organized.

486. Woods, Eugene. **How to Retire in Mexico.** Illus. by J. R. Garrison. Knapp, 1965. 126 pp. Paper $1.95.

Since its 1965 publication, Wood's advice on how to live in Mexico on $2.47 a day has long since gone the way of inflation. Prices are completely out of date. Most of the book reads like a bad travel guide to the retirement communities of Mexico. There is little practical information. Not recommended.

RUGS

See Carpets

SAVINGS AND THRIFT

See also Money Management

487. Break the Banks!: A Shopper's Guide to Banking Services. San Francisco Consumer Action, 1973. 63 pp. Paper $1.50.

While directed at the California shopper in general, and the San Francisco Bay area resident in particular, there is much in this booklet that is of use to people everywhere. The San Francisco Consumer Action's "Shopper's Guide to Banking Services" not only provides statistics on the least expensive places to bank, get loans, and keep checking accounts, but also shows how to compile such information in other parts of the country, e.g., with charts of the SFCA's findings and blank charts to be filled in by other interested consumers. In addition, it explains how banks violate the Truth in Lending Law (by not fairly stating their costs for loans); how to compute interest charges; prices consumers pay for cash advance bank card loans; when it is more advisable to have special checking accounts rather than regular accounts; how to determine where to get different types of loans; where to save; when to put money in long term time deposits; and more. As a primer of banking costs and services, this booklet can be of help to everyone.

488. Jenney, George. **How to Rob a Bank without a Gun.** Goodnews, 1973. 192 pp. Paper $6.95.

Similar in concept to Meyer's *Don't Bank on It!* (*see* entry 489), this volume gives the same information and costs $6.95. For your money you get many pages with just one or two sentences on them, others with just a heading. Jenney, like Meyer, confuses spending with saving. One piece of advice urges the reader to start ten small bank accounts to get ten $5 bank gifts rather than one $50 gift, as "they are worth more" and concludes that the gifts, which he counts as worth their retail price, are equivalent to interest. There is much more along this vein. Not recommended.

489. Meyer, Martin J., and Joseph M. McDaniel, Jr. **Don't Bank on It!** Farnsworth Publishing, 1970. 219 pp. $8.95.

Designed to teach the consumer how to increase bank earnings, the book leaves it up to each individual to decide whether the bother of moving money from one account to the other is worth the results. Part I describes methods by which banks and savings and loan associations earn their high rates of returns (loans, credit card and check credit operations) and why government regulations preclude such returns for depositors. The authors point out that commercial banks can give depositors extra value for their money, e.g., offering interest-free loans and free credit. Part II gives step-by-step descriptions of various ways of increasing interest rates on savings, such as earning daily compound interest, juggling "interest to date of withdrawal" accounts with accounts giving grace or bonus days on "interest from day of deposit" accounts. The authors also suggest buying commercial paper for short-term deposits and show how to make money on uncollected funds (by using the principles of daily interest, grace days, and transfer drafts). Juggling billing dates of various credit cards and depositing the saved monies into daily interest accounts earns money on income already spent. Ways to defer taxes on interest, using the Keogh Plan for the self-employed and Deferred Income Bonds or Certificates for others, are explained. The conclusion is devoted to the United Security (Bank) Account which earns savings bank interest while functioning as a checking account. (See Watkins's *Dollars and Sense* (*see* entry 405) for a warning against using this banking system.)

490. Money Management: Your Savings and Investment Dollar. Money Management Institute, Household Finance Corp., 1973. 40 pp. Paper 25¢. Quantity orders discounted.

A good overview on how to set up a savings and investment program tailored to individual goals: those of young people; beginning, growing, and contracting families; single adults; retirees. Different types of savings are described: bank accounts, savings and loan association accounts, government bonds, credit union shares. Life insurance, annuities, Social Security (in the United States) and security plans (in Canada), pensions, and retirement plans are also covered. Material on investments includes not only the usual stocks, bonds, and real estate, but also education, durable goods (car, house, home furnishings, etc), and business ownership—called "investing in yourself." A chart to assess net worth concludes.

SHOPPING

See Food; Food—Industry and Trade; Stores and Services; Stores and Services—Discount and Secondhand

SKIING EQUIPMENT

491. Consumer Guide. **Ski Equipment Test Reports.** Annual. Publications International. Paper $1.95.

Issued annually in October, this evaluative report covers all types of ski equipment and accessories. Skis for the novice and for the expert, for downhill racing, giant slaloms, and cross-country competition are included. Four factors are analyzed to help consumers decide on equipment: where it will be used; what it is intended to do; the skier's own ability; and the general price the skier is willing to pay. Within these limits, skis, boots, poles, bindings, accessories (such as safety straps, goggles, boot straps, and bags), and clothing are discussed and rated for both alpine and Nordic skiing. Best buys are noted, along with suggested retail prices of the items. In addition, Consumer Guide explains how to buy different products, e.g., how to determine ski and boot size for children and adults. A directory of major manufacturers, a few skiing hints, and a glossary of ski terms are also included.

SMALL CLAIMS COURTS

See Legal Services

SOCIAL SECURITY AND MEDICARE

See also Insurance, Health; Medical Care; Retirement. *For pertinent organizations see Part II, U.S. Federal Agencies*—Department of Health, Education and Welfare, Social Security Administration.

492. Biossat, Bruce. **What You've Got Coming in Medicare & Social Security.** 4th rev. ed. Enterprise Publications, 1972. 96 pp. Paper $1.

A small booklet published in 1972 with an addenda and corrections through 1974, the first section is on Social Security: basic coverage, how to compute retirement pay, survivor and disability benefits, and Social Security taxes and 1973 changes in the law. In addition, one chapter explains what to do if a Social Security card or check is lost and how to appeal a Social Security decision. It notes which people are covered under the new laws. The second half of the booklet discusses 1973 features of Medicare: qualifications; applying for benefits; dropping out of the program; hospital, extended care, and home health benefits; and medical insurance. Although changes go through 1974, it must be stressed that this can only be used as a general guide. Anyone needing specific information should contact a Social Security office. A helpful feature of this booklet is its checklist of documents for Social Security purposes.

493. Boggers, Louise. **Your Social Security Benefits.** Funk & Wagnalls, 1968. 116 pp. $5.95.

Boggers's book cannot be recommended; there have been too many changes in the Social Security law. Should the material be updated, it would be good, as Boggers writes well, and her information is easy to understand.

494. J. K. Lasser Tax Institute. **Your Guide to Social Security and Medicare Benefits.** Cornerstone Library, 1973. 96 pp. Paper $1.50.

Since this publication is not an annual, and benefits are listed only through 1972, it is not recommended. Other booklets listed cover the same material and give more of the "up-to-the-minute" information that this one promises.

495. Schottland, Charles I. **The Social Security Program in the United States.** 2nd ed. Prentice-Hall, 1970. 210 pp. $7.95.

Originally published in 1963, this is basically a theoretical work written by a former commissioner of Social Security who served from 1954–1959. Schottland gives a historical account of the social welfare programs in the United States: need, passage, and programs. He covers basic Social Security, i.e., Old Age, Survivors, Disability, and Health Insurance (OASDHI), as well as unemployment insurance, Workmen's Compensation, the railroad workers' program, the federal employees' retirement system, veterans' benefits, public assistance under Social Security, and some voluntary programs. Although essentially a history, the text does explain types of coverage, eligibility, and benefits (as of 1970). Schottland's concluding chapter deals with the (probable) future expansion of social welfare programs, e.g., a Family Assistance Plan, expansion of Workmen's Compensation, and health insurance.

496. **Social Security and Medicare Explained–Including Medicaid.** Annual. Commerce Clearing House. Paper $5.

This annual volume covers yearly changes in the law concerning Social Security, Medicare, and Medicaid, as well as basic rules, regulations, and coverage. The 1974 edition notes benefit increases effective March 1974. This text is not designed for the average reader: it is filled with citations to laws, regulations, manuals, etc., and is specific to coverage, eligibility, and exclusions. It reviews the system and its financing, notes tax rates, withholding taxes, returns, payments, penalties, and refunds. Coverage for employers, employees, and the self-employed is cited, as well as benefits (including computation of monthly rate), disability, and family benefits, how to figure reduced benefits, and how to file claims. Medicare and Medicaid are covered in separate chapters. For each, the editors note qualifications, payments, and administration. For Medicare, they discuss deductibles, coinsurance, and reimbursement. Medicaid services and payments are explained in the concluding chapter. Separate topical indexes for Social Security, Medicare, and Medicaid make retrieval of any piece of information relatively simple. For further details on any topic, the editors suggest using the Commerce Clearing House loose-leaf *Reporters: Unemployment Insurance Reporter* (*with Social Security*) and the *Medicare and Medicaid Guide.*

497. U.S. News & World Report. **Social Security and Medicare Simplified.** Collier, Macmillan, 1970. 240 pp. $5.95; paper $2.95.

This book is not recommended for determining Social Security and Medicare benefits (it is outdated in those respects), but for its easy-to-understand explanation of the system itself. Coverage and retirement benefits, insurance for dependents and disability, collecting when living abroad, coverage for the self-employed, etc. all are discussed. The editors deal with the question whether the method of dispensing benefits (in 1970) was fair, and conclude that it was not. (Some changes have since been made.) Two chapters give a brief history of Social Security and Medicare, and a concluding chapter covers possible future developments. The editors offer suggestions ranging from increasing an employer's share of the payroll tax to allowing low-income families to use a part or all of their Social Security tax as a credit against their income tax. An appendix, "Planning for Your Later Years," provides space for readers to compute their current financial situation (total owned and owed) and to estimate monthly income and expenses at retirement.

STEREO AND TAPE EQUIPMENT

498. *Consumer Guide. **Stereo & Tape Equipment Test Reports.** Publications International. Quarterly. Paper $1.50 ea. Annual. Paper $1.95.

Stereo & Tape Equipment published its first annual cumulation in February 1975. Quarterly issues report on tests and evaluations in the ever-expanding field of stereo and tape equipment. The summer 1974 issue tested turntables, phono cartridges, tuners, amplifiers and receivers, speaker systems, open-reel tape machines, cassette tape machines, and indoor and outdoor antennas for FM. There is also information on how to arrange a room to hear stereo and four-channel sound at their best. A discount price guide lists both the suggested retail and low prices of all stereo and tape equipment mentioned in the text. Prices for other models and accessories are also included. Recommendations of best buys and editorial comments are given in each section.

STORES AND SERVICES

499. Dorst, Sally. **The New York Food Book.** Workman, 1973. 218 pp. Paper $3.95.

Dorst lists stores in Manhattan that have the best quality and/or prices on their products. She covers butcher and fish shops and stores selling breads, cakes, candies, dried fruits and nuts, coffees and teas, dairy and cheese products, fruits and vegetables, and even cooking utensils. Each chapter is preceded by information on how to buy the food, how to store it, and how to cook it. For example, the author notes that fish does not have to be federally inspected, and that it is therefore imperative to know how to spot the fresh item. It is best to leave if stores smell stale. The fish itself should look healthy, with firm skin, clear, bulging eyes and red gills. It should never be left at room temperature, but thawed in the refrigerator. Information on each shop notes name, address, telephone number, subway directions, and hours. Comments highlight ambiance, service, and specialties. Indexes by nationality and geography, and shopping maps of different areas are included. Some of the stores are listed in *The Passionate Shopper* (*see* entry 501), but this volume concentrates on foodstuffs, is newer, and has many stores not listed in the other book.

500. Scharlatt, Elisabeth Lohman, and the Editors of New York Magazine. **How to Get Things Done in New York.** Dutton, 1973. 184 pp. Paper $2.95.

These articles based on the *New York Magazine* feature "The Urban Strategist" were updated and revised as of 1973. The book tells New Yorkers where to get the best services for their money. Suggestions range from the obvious to the arcane, e.g., from adoption referrals, decorators, piano tuners and exterminators to airplanes for commuters, chimney sweeps, copper retinners, and plant sitters. The editors also give sources for block association information, New York City marriage requirements, and voter registration information. Basic data for each listing include name, address, telephone number and hours, plus the editors' opinion of why the listing is one of the best. A very useful appendix notes 24-hour and emergency services: from public and private ambulances to locksmiths, plumbers, and newsstands. A second appendix lists whom to complain to about 50 different services, e.g., abortions, potholes, air pollution, real estate brokers. The addresses of the New York State Supreme Courthouses in each borough complete the book.

501. Scharlatt, Elisabeth Lohman, and the Editors of New York Magazine. **The Passionate Shopper.** Dutton, 1972. 257 pp. Paper $2.95.

Updated and revised consumer articles from *New York Magazine's* "Passionate Shopper" column, it is a guide to "shopping [New York City] for price and quality." The listings are divided into two sections, "Living Well" and "Eating Well," and include stores with unusual items, excellent bargain-basement prices, and/or items of superior quality. "Living Well" covers stores that run the gamut from antiques and art supplies to bikinis, handmade cigars, lumberyards, custom-made shoes, wallpaper, and wicker. In addition, it includes descriptions of city auctions, museum memberships, and New York City guidebooks. "Eating Well" lists shops by type of food: from beans, beer, and bread to French pastries, fish, nuts, and wines. Each store's address, hours, telephone number, house specialities, and prices at time of publication are noted.

STORES AND SERVICES—DISCOUNT AND SECONDHAND

502. **Bargain Finder.** 2nd rev. ed. Consumers' Alliance, 1973. 384 pp. Paper $4.95.

A directory of 851 shops in New York City with discounts ranging from 20 percent to 70 percent on all merchandise. Only stores which offer high-quality goods at low prices are included and their approximate discounts noted. Thirty categories of goods are covered: appliances, bikes, motorbikes, clothing, musical instruments, office equipment, pets, stationary, art supplies, toys, games, hobbies, wines, liquors, cameras, and more. There is also some information about free or inexpensive entertainment (concerts, movies, plays, pubs, and restaurants) and inexpensive business and financial services, e.g., rubber stamp makers, printers, free personal checking accounts, insurance. Information on each store includes name, address, telephone number, hours, payment (checks, cash, and credit cards), exchange and refund policies and subway directions. In addition, the stores are pinpointed on shopping maps, making all-day shopping very convenient. There is very little overlap between this and the New York City edition of the *Factory Outlet Shopping Guide* (*see* entry 503). *Bargain Finder* is by far the more comprehensive, although it is not all-inclusive. It is very highly recommended.

503. Bird, Jean. **Factory Outlet Shopping Guide.** 5 annual regional editions: Eastern Pennsylvania; Maryland, Washington, D.C., Delaware, and Virginia; New England; New Jersey and Rockland County; New York City and Long Island. F.O.S.G. Paper $1.95 ea.

Begun in 1970, the *Factory Outlet Shopping Guide* has grown from three regional editions to five in just a short time—proof of the interest in discount shopping. All the guides explain how to shop the outlets. Buyers are advised to scout the stores to learn their cash and return policies and try-on facilities. Differences between manufacturer's, importer's, distributor's, and wholesaler's outlets are explained; markup, margin, sample, overcuts, seconds, etc., are defined. An alphabetical listing of stores makes up the bulk of each guide, providing each store's name, address, phone number, hours, check and credit card policies, and some descriptive material. The last may include prices, specialities, label policy (are labels left on?) and directions for getting there if the store is hard to reach. The guides cover clothes for children and adults, shoes, fabrics, home furnishings, accessories, china, and gifts. One index lists stores by type of merchandise and another by area. There is an occasional overlap among the editions, but persons living in border areas and those interested in traveling distances for bargains can consult more than one of them. Discounts on the books are available to buyers of three or more editions at the same time.

504. Bonnesen, Judith A., and Janet L. Burkley. **The Factory Outlet Bargain Book.** Belmont/Tower, 1972. 292 pp. Paper $1.50.

The title page calls this *The Factory Outlet Bargain Book*; the cover says it is *The Bargain Hunters Field Guide*. In any case, it is a very incomplete listing of over 700 discount stores and factory outlets in about 40 states. It is not clear whether such states as Alaska, Hawaii, North Dakota, and South Dakota were omitted due to the absence of such stores or oversight on the part of the authors. Information about each place includes name, address, hours, directions, and refund, check and credit card policies. A short paragraph filled with hyperbole and exclamation marks describes the merchandise and discounts. The stores are arranged by state and within the state by city. (There are no indexes either by store name or by merchandise.) A comparison of listings for New Jersey shows that this guide lists 40 stores, the *Factory Outlet Shopping Guide* (*see* entry 503) lists about 360, and 28 of the 40 stores in this guide are also listed in the other. A further comparison shows that the two-volume *Bargain Hunting in L.A.* (*see* entry 508) lists over 600 stores, only one of which is found in this book, but that *The Factory Outlet Bargain Book* has 17 listings not found in the other. All of which points up that, although this book is incomplete, it does provide information not found in other guides.

505. ***The Factory Outlet Newsletter.** F.O.S.G. Publications. 8 issues a yr. $3.

A four-page newsletter which is really a supplement to the *Factory Outlet Shopping Guide* editions (*see* entry 503), each issue has information on featured stores, as well as shorter listings of other new or newly discovered outlets. Store closings and other changes and a few listings of new types of stores are also included. The newsletter can be purchased separately, but it can only be recommended to persons who buy the *Guide* (*s*).

506. Goldstein, Sue, and Ann Light. **The Underground Shopper.** 6 regional guides: Dallas-Ft. Worth Area (2nd ed. 1973); Houston Area (1973); Minneapolis-St. Paul Area (1973); St. Louis Area (1973); Southeast Florida Area (1974), 48 pp., paper $1.95 ea. Greater Boston Area (1974). 64 pp. Paper $2.50. SusAnn Publications.

Publication of *The Underground Shopper* began in 1972 with the Dallas-Ft. Worth issue. The third edition of that booklet is expected shortly (at $2.50). Each guide tells shoppers where to buy "samples, seconds, overruns and unusual bargains" in shoes, clothing, fabrics, housewares, wallpaper, bed and bath furnishings, toys, and miscellaneous items (e.g., wigs, tuxedos). Some of the guides have an index by subject while others do not, a serious omission. Goldstein and Light have worked out a rating system ranging from zero to four stars, with a four-star rating going to a store with merchandise of excellent quality, selection and/or "fantastic" savings. Information on each shop includes name, address, telephone number, credit card and check policy, the rating, and a code letter for the main items sold in the store. In addition, each shop is described in a brief paragraph, ranging from the informative and serviceable to the overly cute, e.g., Filene's Basement (Boston) is described as a "pandemonious plethora of pulsating people pondering perennial piles at preposterously proportioned prices!!!"—and the paragraph continues similarly for another two sentences. The Boston edition also includes a glossary of terms useful to bargain hunters, e.g., "bankrupt stock," "factory outlet," and "schlock."

507. James, Judy, and Danny Goldman. **Nothing New: A Guide to the Fun of Second-Hand Shopping in Los Angeles and Surrounding Areas.** Tarcher, 1973. 145 pp. Paper $2.95.

Secondhand outlets include thrift stores, resale boutiques, flea markets, and swapmeets. Pawnshops are discussed, but not noted by name. The authors list over 400 sources for goods, ranging from adding machines to barrel staves, Coca-Cola memorabilia to X-ray equipment. A small sprinking of these places is listed in *Bargain Hunting in L.A.* (*see* entry 508), but the overlap is minimal. In addition to saving money and having fun, consumers are urged to recycle their own unwanted items, either by donating them to thrift shops (and getting tax deductions) or by trading them in. The authors offer a list of excellent places for beginning secondhand shoppers to train in: stores that are well organized, clean, and have straightforward presentations. Basic information on each store includes name, address, phone number, hours, parking situation, and purchase policy, i.e., cash, check, and/or credit cards. Descriptive material (the authors' opinions) is available on most stores. A nice section explains how the authors ran their own garage sale, including advertising, pricing, scheduling, and bookkeeping. Geographical, subject, and alphabetical listings complete the book and offer added convenience.

508. Patridge, Barbara. **Bargain Hunting in L.A. and Surrounding Areas.** Vol. I. Tarcher, 1972. 145 pp. Paper $2.95.

Patridge, Barbara, and Geri Cook. **Bargain Hunting in L.A.: Including 150 Listings in the San Fernando Valley and Orange County.** Vol. 2. Tarcher, 1973. 146 pp. Paper $2.95.

These bargain hunter's guides for the Los Angeles area cover more than 600 stores that offer at least 20 percent off retail prices (discounts go up to 70 percent off). Most of the shops have new merchandise or seconds; there is an excellent section devoted to secondhand and abandoned items. Patridge says that she has tried to include only outlets offering the best quality for the money, and to list only stores that have been around for while, on the theory that they will survive. Deletions and corrections prove this does not necessarily hold true. Basic information on a store includes name, address, phone number, hours, parking situation, and purchase policy, i.e., cash, check, and/or credit cards. Descriptive material is chatty and very much the authors' own opinions. All the usual types of merchandise are covered, from appliances to pet supplies to uniforms. Sources of bargains, such as end-of-the-month sales and entertainment, e.g., movie previews, are unusual, and very good. Under secondhand merchandise are noted rummage and charity sales, gift exchanges, salvage and wrecking companies, and more. Auctions are listed, but here buyers can get new items, e.g., government-confiscated goods. The geographic index makes for extra convenience.

509. S.O.S. Directory. S.O.S. Directory, Inc., 1974. Unpaged. Paper $4.95.

Another directory attempting to list the thousands of factory outlets across the United States and Canada, this one apparently relied on shoppers in different areas for its listings. There is very little overlap between it and the other directories listed in this section. Outlets are listed geographically—by cities within each state and province—and include only name, address, and telephone number. Most, but not all stores have a line or two noting the type of merchandise carried; for a few, the discount is also listed. Since the term "factory outlet" is not defined, stores are included that would not normally fall into this category. A case in point is the inclusion of S. Klein in New York City—without even a basic notation indicating that it is a department store. The most serious flaw is the lack of an index—which makes shopping for a particular type of merchandise extremely tiresome. S.O.S. also issues a quarterly newsletter, *Bargain Hunter*, for $4.95, which lists the "newest, unpublished information, maps, shopping vacation combinations." The newsletter has not been seen by this author.

510. Socolich, Sally, and Kathy Filaseta. **Bargain Hunting in the Bay Area: Including San Francisco, the East Bay, the Peninsula, San Jose and Surrounding Areas.** Tarcher, 1973. 118 pp. Paper $2.95.

Exactly the same format and information as the two-volume *Bargain Hunting in L.A.* (*see* entry 508).

511. **Some North Carolina Manufacturing Firms with Outlet Stores.** North Carolina Department of Natural and Economic Resources, 1974. 4 pp. Paper. Free.

Replacing a previously published booklet, this is a simple listing of 75 outlet stores arranged alphabetically by city. Information consists of name, address, and manufactured item. There are no annotations.

SURGERY

See Medical Care

TENANTS

See Landlords and Tenants

TOYS

See also Consumer Protection; Product Safety. *For pertinent organizations see Part II, U.S. Federal Agencies*—Consumer Product Safety Commission; Department of Health, Education and Welfare, Food and Drug Administration—Public Health Service.

512. Swartz, Edward M. **Toys that Don't Care.** Illus. Gambit, 1971. 289 pp. $6.95.

The title says it all: a book describing and listing dangerous toys manufactured and sold with total disregard for the health and safety of children. The first section cites major hazards and notes the absence of toy industry self-regulations and federal laws and safety programs. It also covers the harmful effects of advertising on children and the self-serving interests of major family magazines, e.g., *Parents' Magazine*, and stores, e.g., F.A.O. Schwartz, that promote and sell goods without regard for their customers. Swartz, a lawyer who specializes in accident cases, discusses the difficulties of winning suits against manufacturers (even when children are maimed for life). The second section is a highly recommended shopper's guide. It includes lists of safe and unsafe products by category and brand names. Toys; clothes, blankets, and other flammable articles; playground equipment and swimming pools; and children's jewelry and cosmetics are covered. Swartz also provides an excellent list of shopping guidelines: 24 don'ts and nine dos to consider before buying any toys.

TRAVEL

For pertinent organizations see Part II, Private Organizations—The Cooperative League of the USA.

Note: Literally hundreds, if not thousands of books on travel are in print. Many are devoted to tips on best places to visit, stay at, shop and/or eat in. Others discuss different ways to travel cheaply, but well. A small, but growing group of books concern health and medical information for tourists. J. A. Neal's *Reference Guide for Travellers* (1969) can be consulted for annotated reviews of all books in print on these subjects through October 1968. Many of the most useful of the guides are annuals, e.g., Mobil travel guides to the United States (now published by Rand McNally), or the Fodor and Nagel guides to foreign countries. Others, like the French-produced Michelin guides, are revised periodically, as are books devoted exclusively to budget travel, e.g., Tyarks and Robinson's *Europe on a Shoestring* (Harian) or Arthur Frommer's *Europe on Five and Ten Dollars a Day* (Essandess Special Editions). Some publishers, such as Harian, specialize in travel books; but most of these books are published by general trade publishers. The books reviewed below are those that attempt to show consumers how to save money and get the best travel values. They have all been published since 1969 and were not reviewed by Neal.

513. Planck, Charles, and Carolyn Planck. **How to Double Your Travel Funds.** Celestial Arts, 1973. 133 pp. Paper $3.95.

The Plancks are a retired couple who have taken up travel for enjoyment and business, i.e., they have previously written three other books on the subject. They claim to offer information that will double travel funds, but never spell out exactly how that is done in plain dollars and cents. Their basic pitch is to the retired couple (or to any others to whom time is of no importance). A lot of their advice is good, although little is new or different. They are best when offering suggestions for travel and accommodations, e.g., a sheep station in New Zealand, a farm in Great Britain. Most of the book is actually a brief guide to individual countries, including the United States, with food, travel, and accommodation prices that seem to date from 1972 or early 1973. The first few chapters are the most useful to the novice. The Plancks give information on buying transportation, covering airplane, ship, and freighter travel, as well as on buying new and used cars abroad. A good chapter, "Fixed Bases," discusses the advantages of renting homes abroad: live like a native, cut costs, make friends, etc. Charles and Carolyn Planck, ages 76 and 63, respectively, seem to be having at least as much fun as people half their age. While their advice may not double travel funds, it will stretch them. The book's major drawback is that many of its suggestions are very general, e.g., most countries in Western Europe are covered in a paragraph or two.

514. Rand, Abby. **How to Get to Europe and Have a Wonderful Time.** Rev. ed. Scribners, 1974. 275 pp. $7.95; paper $3.50.

A good book for travelers, no matter where they are going. Rand, travel editor of *Ski* magazine, has updated the very successful 1971 edition of her book, and has provided information on how to plan a vacation, get abroad, and enjoy the trip. She suggests ways to cut travel costs, find ethical and helpful travel agents, get passports, health cards, and shots, select and pack a wardrobe, medicines, and miscellany, even 28 things to do before leaving home and what to expect at the airport. The second half of the book deals with the pleasures of the trip. Rand suggests foods and drink, shopping strategy, nightlife and transportation (intracity and international). She has a very practical chapter, "Life Goes On—Chores and Duties," that covers laundry, dry cleaning, mail, cigarettes, religious services, beauty and barber shops, even public restrooms. Another excellent chapter tells travelers how to cope with lost passports, baggage, credit cards, and stolen traveler's checks, as well as with missed planes, illness, bad service, and legal difficulties. Appendices give an explanation of the metric system, weather charts of 15 European cities, a well-annotated list of guidebooks, and "Suggested Itineraries" for two–four week trips by air or car. The book is written in a lively, irreverent style and is loaded with practical and important information.

515. San Roman, Peter. **Travel at ½ the Price.** Drake, 1973. 217 pp. Paper $3.95.

San Roman's is another travel book that promises to cut costs in half, but does not bother to tell how to do it. The author explains how and why luxury-, first-, and second-class rates differ, describing the respective accommodations, and does the same for individual and group air fares, But that can hardly qualify as "travel at ½ the price." San Roman's book is also marred by typographical errors that result in mismarked charts and unintelligible advice. Prices for food, accommodations, and travel are for early 1973. A nice section tells what to take abroad plus some useful foreign phrases for countries where a traveler may have difficulty finding someone who speaks English. The author is in favor of renting cars, which is costly advice. He also covers tours, sightseeing and entertainment, photography (buying cameras, film, and processing), as well as shopping and tipping, mail and phone service, and employment opportunities. The last is almost totally misleading because many countries do not allow tourists to work. A concluding chapter is devoted to the countries of eastern Europe, with information on the amount of money allowed in, languages spoken, visas, where to shop, exchange rates, hotel rates, and car-rental information. The book is filled with anecdotes relating the experiences of the author and his friends; not all of which is interesting.

WINES

516. Bespaloff, Alexis. **Alexis Bespaloff's Guide to Inexpensive Wines.** Illus. by Paul Bacon. Simon and Schuster, 1973. 157 pp. $5.95.

Bespaloff evaluates inexpensive wines from all over the world. He describes close to 350 wines from France, Germany, Spain, Portugal, Italy, Yugoslavia, Austria, Hungary, Greece, Chile, and the United States and picks 120 good wines for under $3.50 a bottle (more than half are priced at under $2.50). He also lists a few French and German wines that reach $4.50 a bottle. All prices are from the summer of 1973 in New York City wine stores. An expert on the subject, Bespaloff devotes a large part of his book to explaining wines: vintages, prices, where to find good wine stores, how to read wine labels, and how to taste, store, and serve wines. He also discusses the inexpensive red, white, and rosé wines. Three appendices list "120 Inexpensive Red, White and Rosé Wines," "50 Wines in Gallons and Half-gallons," and "Comparative Price Ranges of Inexpensive Wines."

517. Massee, William E. **An Insider's Guide to Low-Priced Wines.** Dolphin, 1974. 230 pp. Paper $2.95.

Massee, a noted oenologist and author of several other books on wine, shows the novice "how to find, buy & serve wines costing under $5." Quality and price are the standards rather than famous names and vintages, and this book is filled with lists: good jug wines and regional wines, and wines listed by districts and townships around the world. Massee describes wines and winemakers, and where wine lists are extensive, he divides them by price groups: $3, $4, and $5 a bottle, respectively. He also covers good wines from shippers and importers, wines that can be sampled together in one wine tasting, and several price alternatives for stocking a wine cellar. He includes lists of some of the best French wines from the Bordeaux châteaux, from the country, and from the Midi, as well as some sweet wines. The extensive index includes all wines, labels, importers, dealers, and even stores mentioned in the text, making access to the information very simple. (*See also* entry 518.)

518. Massee, William E. **Massee's Guide to Wines of America.** Saturday Review Press (Dutton, dist.), 1974. 264 pp. Paper $3.95.

A revised, updated and expanded version of the 1970 *McCall's Guide to the Wines of America*, parts of this book are similar to Massee's *An Insider's Guide to Low-Priced Wines* (*see* entry 517). This volume, however, is devoted entirely to American wines, so the wines of New England, the Great Lakes region, and the Ozarks as well as the wineries of the Northwest are represented along with the well-known New York and California wineries. Massee discusses individual vintners, gives their history, and notes their good wines. Prices are not given. A few pages are devoted to Canadian, Mexican, and South American wines. Appendices explain how to taste wine; how to store it; how to stock a wine cellar. Names of wineries for tours and from which direct purchases may be made are also appended. Massee's two books do not name the same "best" wines from each winery. That is because the *Insider's Guide* concentrates on quality plus price, and this book uses the guildeline of quality alone.

519. Pratt, James Norwood, and Jacques de Caso. **The Wine Bibber's Bible.** Illus. by Sara Raffetto. 101 Productions, 1971. 192 pp. $6.95; paper $3.95.

Two chapters in *The Wine Bibber's Bible* are of particular interest to consumers: "Wine Buying: What Are You Looking For?" and "Wine Varieties: What Are We Drinking Anyhow?" The first deals with buying ordinary California wines and some not-so-ordinary ones. The authors offer their opinions on all of them. They suggest finding a good wine shop and dealers who have special wines at reasonable costs. They explain labels, when to buy wines in restaurants (very expensive wines are a waste of money unless cellar and handling are first-rate), and when to send wines back. The other chapter covers the better California wineries and their products. There, too, the authors pronounce on the good and the bad. Other chapters give information on wine history, winemaking, wine talk and tasting, and a glossary. The book also includes "An Essay on Wine" by Charles Baudelaire. The drawings by Sara Raffetto are beautiful.

II. ORGANIZATIONS

Arrangement is alphabetical for U.S. federal agencies and for American and Canadian private organizations. It is geographical by state for state, county, and city agencies (including Puerto Rico), and by province for Canadian agencies. Within each state, entries are alphabetical by county and by city. All cross-references in this section refer the reader to the numbered entries in Part I.

U.S. Federal Agencies

Civil Aeronautics Board. 1825 Connecticut Ave. N.W., Washington, D.C. 20428. Robert D. Timm, Chairman. (202) 393-3111. John A. Yohe, Director, Office of Consumer Affairs. (202) 382-7735.
Established: 1938.

Regulates the economics of air transport. Reviews passenger and freight rates and fares; works to protect consumers against unfair or deceptive practices in advertising, scheduling, bookings, and rates. Can suspend fares and rates if unlawful. The Office of Consumer Affairs handles complaints of travelers, shippers, and others not resolved by airlines. Pamphlets: *Civil Aeronautics Board—What It Is and What It Does; Air Travelers' Fly-Rights,* etc.

Consumer Product Safety Commission. 7315 Wisconsin Ave. N.W., Washington, D.C. 20016. Richard O. Simpson, Chairman. (301) 495-6327. Ron Eisenberg, Public Affairs Director. (301) 495-6361.
Established: May 14, 1973 (activated).

Enforces the Flammable Fabrics Act, Hazardous Substances Act, Poison Prevention Packaging Act, Refrigerator Door Safety Act. Develops and establishes uniform safety standards. In order to protect citizen from injuries it can ban hazardous products or seize them under court order. Enforces civil and criminal penalties with fines and jail sentences. Set up the National Electronic Injury Surveillance System (NEISS) to monitor injuries. Aids consumers in evaluating comparative safety of products; promotes research and investigations to reduce product-related deaths, illnesses, and injuries. Recently removed a trouble (mechanic's) light from market. Promulgated new standards for children's sleepware (effective May 1975), bicycle standards (January 1975), crib safety standards (February 1974). Periodicals: *NEISS News* (daily injury report). Pamphlets: *A Compilation of Laws Administered by the U.S. Product Safety Commission; U.S. Consumer Product Safety Commission; Your Voice Counts;* 20 fact sheets, e.g., *Power Lawn Mowers, Crib Safety, Toys* (last two available in Spanish).

Toll-free telephone numbers: (800) 638-2666 (except Alaska, Hawaii, Maryland); Maryland: (800) 492-2937.

Branch offices:

1330 West Peachtree St. N.W., *Atlanta*, Ga. 30309. (404) 526-2246.
408 Atlantic Ave., *Boston*, Mass. 02110. (617) 223-5576.
1 N. Wacker Dr., 5th fl., *Chicago*, Ill. 60606. (312) 353-8260.
DEB Annex, 21046 Brookpark Rd., *Cleveland*, Ohio 44135. (216) 522-3886.
P.O. Box 15035, 500 S. Ervay, Rm. 410C, *Dallas*, Tex. 75201. (214) 749-3871.
Suite 938, Guaranty Bank Bldg., 817 17 St., *Denver*, Colo. 80202. (303) 837-2904.
1125 Grand Ave., Suite 1500, *Kansas City*, Mo. 64196. (816) 374-2034.
3360 Wilshire Blvd., Suite 1100, *Los Angeles*, Calif. 90010. (213) 688-7272.
International Trade Mart, Suite 414, 2 Canal St., *New Orleans*, La. 70130. (504) 527-2102.
830 Third Ave., Bldg. 1, 8th fl., Bay 7, *New York* (*Brooklyn*), N.Y. 11232. (212) 965-5036.
Continental Bldg., 10th fl., 400 Market St., *Philadelphia*, Pa. 19106. (215) 597-9105.
160 Pine St., *San Francisco*, Calif. 94111. (415) 556-1816.
1131 Federal Bldg., 909 First Ave., *Seattle*, Wash. 98104. (206) 442-5276.
650 Federal Bldg., Fort Snelling, *Twin Cities*, Minn. 55111. (612) 725-3424.

Department of Agriculture. The Mall between 12 & 14 Sts. S.W., Washington, D.C. 20250. Earl L. Butz, Secretary. (202) 447-3631.
Established: May 15, 1862.

Agricultural Marketing Service—Marketing and Consumer Services. The Mall, 14 St. and Independence Ave. S.W., Washington, D.C. 20250. Erwin L. Peterson, Administrator. (202) 447-5115.

Protects competition in the marketplace on all foods; buys surplus foods for distribution through the Food and Nutrition Service; prepares educational materials on best food buys. Pamphlets: *Your Money's Worth in Foods* (50¢); *Food and Your Money;* How to Buy Series; e.g., *How to Buy a Christmas Tree* (25¢); *Keys to Quality*, etc.

Agricultural Research Service—Conservation, Research and Education. Administration Bldg., Jefferson Dr. between 12 & 14 Sts. S.W., Washington, D.C. 20250. T. W. Edminster, Administrator. (202) 447-3656.

Safeguards foods and fibers from disease and pests; conducts research on ways to improve the processing and storing of food, on nutrition, and on new uses for wool, cotton, and other fibers. Inspects facilities and licenses veterinary vaccines and serums; quarantines or prohibits unhealthy or diseased foreign imports; can seize interstate shipments. Prepares and disseminates a wide variety of consumer information materials, including materials on family budgeting and gardening. Pamphlets: *Food Is More than Just Something to Eat; Nutritive Value of Foods* (85¢); *Care of Purchased Frozen Foods; Budgeting for the Family* (25¢); *Food Safety*, etc.

Animal and Plant Health Inspection Service—Marketing and Consumer Services. 14 St. & Independence Ave. S.W., Washington, D.C. 20250. Francis J. Mulhern, Administrator. (202) 447-3668.

Inspects all meat and poultry products for safety and quality; responsible for all foods in plants doing business across state lines. Reviews state inspection programs and foreign inspection systems and packing plants exporting to the United States. Sets standards for the states engaged in interstate commerce. Approves all USDA labeling in federally inspected plants.

Extension Service. 14 St. & Independence Ave. S.W. Washington, D.C. 20250. Edwin L. Kirby, Administrator. Betty Fleming, Information Specialist. (202) 447-3377.

Part of a three-way cooperative effort by the Department of Agriculture, state land-grant universities, and county governments to provide information on a variety of consumer needs. Specialists in agriculture, home economics, marketing, community development, environmental affairs, and other related subjects provide information on family-related concerns, such as food and nutrition, housing, money, credit, clothing, health, safety. Prepares radio and television programs, newspaper articles, pamphlets and audiovisual materials. Extension Service Offices are found in post offices, courthouses, and other government buildings in each locality. Periodicals: *Extension Service Review* (monthly; $2.50). Pamphlets: *This Is Cooperative Extension; Extension Helps Today's Food Shoppers* (script of a slide presentation); *Used Sewing Machines—A Good Buy; 5 Years of Progress through EFNEP* (Expanded Food and Nutrition Program); *Helping Low-Income Families Improve Their Diet; Simple Home Repairs . . . Inside* (40¢), etc. Filmstrip/slides: *Shoppers Guides* (1967; 57 frames; filmstrip $6.50; slide set $14).

Office of Communication—Office of the Secretary. Administration Bldg. Jefferson Dr. between 12 & 14 Sts. S.W., Washington, D.C. 20250. Claude W. Gifford, Director. (202) 447-5247.

Provides educational materials to the public through Publications Division, Press Division, Special Reports Division, Radio and TV Division, Motion Picture Division, Photography Division. Puts out many publications researched by other agencies of the Department of Agriculture, e.g., *Yearbooks* of the Department of Agriculture (*see* entries 100, 101, 238). Periodicals: *Service: USDA's Report to Consumers* (monthly newsletter; *see* entry 97).

Department of Commerce. Commerce Bldg. 14th St. between Constitution Ave. & E St. N.W., Washington, D.C. 20230. Rogers C. B. Morton, Secretary. (202) 783-9200. Thomas E. Drumm, Jr., Office of Ombudsman. (202) 967-3178.
Established: March 4, 1913.

Promotes and aids the economic development and technological advancement of the nation by serving the interests of states, regions, local communities, industries, and individual businesses. The Office of Ombudsman for Business was established in 1971. It handles requests for information and service, complaints, criticisms and suggestions. It offers the Secretary suggestions to improve services. Helps states, local governments, industries, and trade associations establish similar offices.

National Bureau of Standards. Gaithersburg, Md. 20760. Richard W. Roberts, Director. (301) 921-1000. Mailing address: Washington, D.C. 20234.

Sets standards for some consumer goods and industrial materials; encourages the development of uniform weights and measures laws; works with industry to voluntarily reduce the number of sizes in packaged consumer goods. Produces consumer information of a generic nature (brand names are not mentioned). Established an Energy Conservation Labeling Program. Pamphlets: Consumer's Guide Series, e.g., *Fibers and Fabrics* (65¢); *Tires, Their Selection and Care* (65¢); *Product Standards on Melamine Dinnerware for Household Use* (10¢); *Energy Efficiency in Room Air Conditioners; Home Energy Saving Tips from NBS*, etc.

Department of Health, Education and Welfare. 330 Independence Ave. S.W., Washington, D.C. 20201. Caspar W. Weinberger, Secretary. (202) 245-6296. Established: 1953.

Administration on Aging—Office of Human Development. 330 C St. S.W., Washington, D.C. 20201. Arthur S. Fleming, Commissioner. (202) 245-0724.
Established: 1965.

Provides a central clearinghouse for all programs and materials relating to older people. Publishes and disseminates information of help to the elderly. Conducts research and demonstration projects. Concerned with the general problems of aging, health and health care services, retirement, etc. Pamphlets: *Are You Planning on Living the Rest of Your Life?* (30¢); *Consumer Guide for Older People* (5¢); *You, the Law, and Retirement* (60¢); *Nursing Home Care* (40¢); *Know Your Pension Plan; Community Services for Older Americans* (60¢), etc.

Food and Drug Administration—Public Health Service. 5600 Fishers Lane, Rockville, Md. 20852. Alexander M. Schmidt, Commissioner. John T. Walden, Acting Assistant Commissioner for Public Affairs (301) 443-3380. Established: 1953.

Functions date back to the Bureau of Chemistry, Department of Agriculture, 1907. The FDA safeguards consumers by enforcing food, drug, and cosmetic laws and regulations which prevent the distribution of adulterated or mislabeled foods, drugs, cosmetics, medical devices, or potentially hazardous consumer products. Tests, inspects, and sets standards of safety for additives, preservatives, pesticides and radioactive residues, etc. Sets and enforces standards of identity, quality, and fill-of-container for food products. Checks prescription drug advertising. Can seize or ban hazardous products. Handles consumer complaints. Conducts workshops for industry; provides an enormous variety of information to consumers on its services and products. Periodicals: *FDA Consumer* (ten times a year, $5.30). Pamphlets: *We Want You to Know about Today's FDA; We Want You to Know What We Know about the Laws Enforced by FDA; Aspirin; Brand vs. Generic Drugs; Myths about Vitamins; How the Consumer Can Report to the Food and Drug Administration; Quackery*, etc.

Office of Consumer Affairs—Office of the Secretary. 330 Independence Ave. S.W., Washington, D.C. 20201. Virginia H. Knauer, Director.

(202) 395-5024. Ed Riner, Director, Consumer Communications (202) 245-6877.

The functions of the Office of Consumer Affairs of the Office of the President were transferred to HEW-OCA by Executive Order 11702 on January 25, 1973. The office promotes, formulates, coordinates, and reviews all HEW consumer programs; conducts investigations; holds conferences; acts as a liaison between interested groups, such as business, professional, labor, consumer, and volunteer organizations; prepares and disseminates information on HEW programs; receives and handles consumer complaints. Periodicals: *OCA Consumer News* (*see* entry 140) (bimonthly; $4). Pamphlets: *See Part I*, entries 108, 113, 114, 154, 155, 156, 166.

Social Security Administration. 6401 Security Blvd., Baltimore, Md. 21235. John B. Cardwell, Commissioner (301) 594-1234.
Established: 1935, reorganized 1953.

Provides benefits to the aged, sick, disabled, dependent. Administers Social Security Act programs, such as Supplemental Security Income Program for the Aged, Blind and Disabled, Retirement and Survivors Insurance, Disability Insurance, and Medicare—the health insurance and care program. Conducts research; provides educational assistance to consumers. Its more than 800 offices located throughout the country provide the latest information on all Social Security and Medicare benefits. Pamphlets: *Your Social Security* (35¢); *Social Security Benefits* (35¢); *A Brief Explanation of Medicare* (25¢); *Your Medicare Handbook* (60¢), etc.

Department of Housing and Urban Development. HUD Bldg., 451 Seventh St. S. W., Washington, D.C. 20410. Carla A. Hills, Secretary. (202) 655-4000. Louise North, Director, Program Information Center (202) 655-5280. Established: 1965.

Administers all programs providing aid for public and private housing, the development of new communities, and the preservation of historic buildings and areas. Coordinates planning with states and localities.

Federal Insurance Administration. HUD Bldg., 451 Seventh St. S.W., Washington, D.C. 20410. George K. Bernstein, Administrator. (202) 755-6770.

Administers National Flood Insurance Program covering floods and mudslides, Riot Reinsurance Program, and Federal Crime Insurance Program. Conducts studies to prevent natural and other disasters.

Housing Production and Mortgage Credit—Federal Housing Administration. HUD Bldg., 451 Seventh St. S.W., Washington, D.C. 20410. Sheldon B. Lubar, Commissioner. (202) 755-5995.

Insures loans and mortgages, gives counseling and information on buying, building, remodeling single and multifamily houses; disseminates information through a variety of publications. Pamphlets: *Wise Home Buying* (*see* entry 282); *Buying and Financing a Mobile Home; Closing Costs; Home Heating* (40¢); *Questions and Answers on Condominiums; Buying Lots from Developers; Be an Energy Miser in Your Home*, etc.

Office of Interstate Land Sales Registration. HUD Bldg., 451 Seventh St. S.W., Washington, D.C. 20410. George K. Bernstein, Administrator. (202) 755-5860.

Regulates out-of-state land sales through registration and disclosure requirements. Also safeguards buyers through requirement of printed property reports before purchase. The office can bring civil proceedings and criminal prosecutions for violations. Has corrected some of the worst abuses in the interstate land sales industry. Pamphlets: *Get the Facts . . . Before Buying Land.*

Department of Transportation. 400 Seventh St. S.W., Washington, D.C. 20590. William T. Coleman, Secretary. Office of Public Affairs. (202) 426-4321. Charles R. Horner, Consumer Affairs Specialist, Office of Consumer Affairs. (202) 426-4520.
Established: April 1, 1967.

Serves a wide variety of functions relating to safety and administration of all transportation programs and facilities. The Office of Consumer Affairs conducts public hearings across the county and encourages citizen involvement in planning and rule making. It develops programs for consumer information and education. The Office of Public Affairs informs through media exposure of news releases, pamphlets, articles, and audiovisual materials and by providing speakers to interested groups. Periodicals: *Transportation Topics for Consumers* (quarterly). Pamphlets: *Transportation Consumer's Guide to Programs and Services of the United States Department of Transportation; U.S. Department of Transportation—Facts and Functions; Better Transportation for Our Senior Citizens*, etc.

Federal Aviation Administration. 800 Independence Ave. S.W., Washington, D.C. 20591. Administrator (vacant). (202) 426-3500.

Sets safety standards for air operations, ensures efficiency, works toward air and noise abatement to upgrade environmental standards, issues regulations, licences air personnel, holds hearings on violations, registers aircraft. Periodcals: *FAA Aviation News* (monthly, $3.50). Pamphlets: *FAA: What It is, What It Does; Federal Aviation Administration.*

Federal Highway Administration. 400 Seventh St. S.W., Washington, D.C. 20590. Norbert T. Tiemann, Administrator. (202) 426-0677.

Regulates interstate trucks, buses, and other carriers to ensure their safety and reliability; administers highway beautification (billboard removal, junkyard control); builds and maintains highways and roads; works for highway safety. Produces a wide variety of informational materials. Pamphlets: *Federal Assistance Available When Natural Disaster Damages Roads, Streets and Bridges* (10¢); *The New Look in Traffic Signs and Markings* (35¢); *Cost of Operating an Automobile* (25¢); *Are We Running Out of Gas?; Car Pool and Bus Pool—Matching Guides; The Effect of Speed on Automobile Gasoline Consumption Rates*, etc.

National Highway Traffic Safety Administration. 400 Seventh St. S.W., Washington, D.C. 20590. James B. Gregory, Administrator. (202) 426-1826.

Sets and enforces safety standards on automobiles, e.g., front and rear bumper standards. Establishing diagnostic inspection demonstration centers. Conducts consumer education programs, among them a plan to publish comparisons of average repair costs and "crashworthiness" of different cars. Establishes standards requiring true odometer readings. Sets standards for driver training, vehicle codes and laws, and other safety programs; conducts research on causes and prevention of accidents. Handles complaints through Office of Consumer Affairs and Public Information. Produces many publications relating to safety. Pamphlets: *What to Buy in Child Restraint Systems* (20¢); *Studded Tires—What Every Motorist Should Know; The Hazards of "Mixing" Tire Types; The Safety Belt Game* (75¢); *Consumer Protection under the New Anti-Tampering Odometer Law*, etc.

U.S. Coast Guard. 400 Seventh St. S.W., Washington, D.C. 20590. Owen W. Siler, Commandant. (202) 426-2158.

Enforces safety standards on ships, establishes minimum safety standards for recreational boats and equipment. Educates small boat operators on safety requirements and ensures compliance with the laws. Enforces antipollution laws, such as those pertaining to oil spills. Provides educational materials. Pamphlets: *U.S. Coast Guard Recreational Boating Guide* (60¢); *Federal Requirements for Recreational Boats; Emergency Repairs Afloat; Skipper's Course* (programmed learning course; $1.50), etc. Film: *Legal Requirements for Boatmen* (color; 16 mm; 17½ min; sale $66; also available for free loan).

Environmental Protection Agency. 401 M St. S.W., Washington, D.C. 20460. Ann L. Dore, Director of Public Affairs. (202) 755-0700. Established: December 2, 1970.

Protects the environment (and consumers) by setting and enforcing standards for the purity of air and water, solid waste management, noise, pesticide and radiation levels. Coordinates actions and research into the problems of pollution. Acts as a public advocate for the environment. The Office of the Assistant Administrator for Enforcement and General Counsel supplies legal support for control programs; provides directions; plans and coordinates enforcement conferences, hearings, and other legal protections. Pamphlets: *Clean Air and Your Car; The Environmental Protection Agency; Johnny Horizon '76 Children's Kit to Improve the Environment; How to Conduct a Clean-Up Campaign*, etc.

Federal Trade Commission. Pennsylvania Ave. at Sixth St. N.W., Washington, D.C. 20580. Lewis A. Engman, Chairman. J. Thomas Rosch, Director, Bureau of Consumer Protection (202) 962-2358. Established: 1915.

Promotes free and fair competition in the marketplace. Administers Federal Trade Commission Act, Clayton Act, Wool Products Labeling Act, Fur Products Labeling Act, Truth in Lending Act, Textile Fiber Products Identification Act, Fair Credit Reporting Act, Fair Packaging and Labeling Act, and Lanham Trade-Mark Act. Acts to prevent price fixing, monopolies, deceptive advertising, packaging, and labeling. Investigates individual complaints as well as inspects and monitors advertising media. Handles complaints. Can issue cease and desist orders. Conducts conferences and seminars; issues advisory opinions and guidelines. Provides consumer information and protection through field offices and consumer protection committees throughout the country. Produces news releases, discussion guides, pamphlets, and other consumer materials. Periodicals: *Consumer Alert* (monthly newsletter). Pamphlets: *Mail Order Insurance* (25¢); *Truth in Lending; Know Your Rights under the Fair Credit Reporting Act* (25¢), etc.

General Services Administration. GSA Bldg., 18th & F Sts. N.W., Washington, D.C. 20405. Arthur F. Sampson, Administrator. (202) 343-1100. Established: July 1949.

As the central purchasing agent of the United States Government, the GSA sets standards for a large variety of consumer goods. Business Service Centers aid and advise persons interested in doing business with the government (procurement or disposal). Federal Information Centers have recently been set up in 35 cities to act as clearinghouses for federal government information and to eliminate the maze of referrals (*see* listing, below). Foreign-language specialists can be found in many of the centers. The centers also sell government publications. Thirty-seven other cities are connected with 25 of the centers by toll-free telephone tielines (*see* listing, below). Pamphlets: *Index of Federal Specifications and Standards* ($9); *Facts about GSA; Doing Business with the Federal Government*, etc.

Federal Information Centers

Albuquerque, N. Mex. (505) 843-3091. Federal Bldg., U.S. Courthouse, 500 Gold Ave. S.W., 87101

Atlanta, Ga. (404) 526-6891. Federal Bldg., 275 Peachtree St. N.E. 30303

Baltimore, Md. (301) 962-4980. Federal Bldg., 31 Hopkins Plaza, 21201

Boston, Mass. (617) 223-7121. John F. Kennedy Federal Bldg., Government Center, 02203

Buffalo, N.Y. (716) 842-5770. Federal Bldg., 111 W. Huron St., 14202

Chicago, Ill. (312) 353-4242. Everett McKinley Dirkson Bldg., 219 S. Dearborn St. 60604

Cincinnati, Ohio (513) 684-2801. Federal Bldg., 550 Main St., 45202

Cleveland, Ohio (216) 522-4040. Federal Bldg., 1240 E. Ninth St., 44199

Denver, Colo. (303) 837-3602. Federal Bldg., U.S. Courthouse, 1961 Stout St., 80202

Detroit, Mich. (313) 226-7016. Federal Bldg., U.S. Courthouse, 231 W. Lafayette St., 48226

Fort Worth, Tex. (817) 334-3624. Fritz Garland Lanham Federal Bldg., 819 Taylor St., 76102

Honolulu, Hawaii (808) 546-8620. U.S. Post Office, Courthouse & Customhouse, 335 Merchant St., 96813

Houston, Tex. (713) 226-5711. Federal Bldg., U.S. Courthouse, 515 Rusk Ave. 77002

Indianapolis, Ind. (317) 633-8484. Federal Bldg., U.S. Courthouse, 46 E. Ohio St., 46204

Kansas City, Mo. (816) 374-2466. Federal Bldg., 601 E. 12 St., 64106
Los Angeles, Calif. (213) 688-3800. Federal Bldg., 300 N. Los Angeles St., 90012
Louisville, Ky. (502) 582-6261. Federal Bldg., 600 Federal Place, 40202
Memphis, Tenn. (901) 534-3285. Clifford Davis Federal Bldg., 167 N. Main St., 38103
Miami, Fla. (305) 350-4155. Federal Bldg., 51 S.W. First Ave., 33130
Minneapolis, Minn. (612) 725-2073. Federal Bldg., U.S. Courthouse, 110 S. Fourth St., 55401
New Orleans, La. (504) 527-6696. 1210 Federal Bldg., Loyola Ave., 70113
New York, N.Y. (212) 264-4464. Federal Office Bldg., U.S. Customs Court, 26 Federal Plaza, 10007
Newark, N.J. (201) 645-3600. Federal Bldg., 970 Broad St., 07102
Oklahoma City, Okla. (405) 231-4868. U.S. Post Office & Federal Office Bldg., 201 N.W. Third St., 73102
Omaha, Nebr. (402) 221-3353. Federal Bldg., U.S. Post Office & Courthouse, 215 N. 17 St., 68102
Philadelphia, Pa. (215) 597-7042. One E. Penn Square Bldg., 17 N. Juniper St., 19107
Phoenix, Ariz. (602) 261-3313. Federal Bldg., 230 N. First Ave., 85025
Pittsburgh, Pa. (412) 644-3456. Federal Bldg., 1000 Liberty Ave., 15222
Portland, Ore. (503) 221-2222. 208 U.S. Courthouse, 620 S.W. Main St., 97205
St. Louis, Mo. (314) 622-4106. Federal Bldg., 1520 Market St., 63103
St. Petersburg, Fla. (813) 893-3495. Wm. C. Cramer Federal Bldg., 144 First Ave., S. 33701
Salt Lake City, Utah (801) 524-5353. Federal Bldg., U.S. Post Office, Courthouse, 125 S. State St., 84111
San Diego, Calif. (714) 293-6030. 202 C St., 92101
San Francisco, Calif. (415) 556-6600. Federal Bldg., U.S. Courthouse, 450 Golden Gate Ave., 94102
Seattle, Wash. (206) 442-0570. Arcade Plaza, 1321 Second Ave., 98101

Telephone Tielines for Federal Information Centers

Akron, Ohio 375-5475 for Cleveland Center
Albany, N.Y. 463-4421 for New York City Center
Austin, Tex. 472-5494 for Houston Center
Birmingham, Ala. 322-8591 for Atlanta Center
Charlotte, N.C. 376-3600 for Atlanta Center
Chattanooga, Tenn. 265-8231 for Memphis Center
Colorado Springs, Colo. 471-9491 for Denver Center
Columbus, Ohio 221-1014 for Cincinnati Center
Dallas, Tex. 749-2131 for Fort Worth Center
Dayton, Ohio 223-7377 for Cincinnati Center
Des Moines, Iowa 282-9091 for Omaha Center
Fort Lauderdale, Fla. 522-8531 for Miami Center
Hartford, Conn. 527-2617 for New York City Center
Jacksonville, Fla. 354-4756 for St. Petersburg Center
Little Rock, Ark. 378-6177 for Memphis Center

Telephone Tielines (*cont.*)
Milwaukee, Wis. 271-2273 for Chicago Center
Mobile, Ala. 438-1421 for New Orleans Center
New Haven, Conn. 624-4720 for New York City Center
Ogden, Utah 399-1347 for Salt Lake City Center
Providence, R.I. 331-5565 for Boston Center
Pueblo, Colo. 544-9523 for Denver Center
Rochester, N.Y. 546-5075 for Buffalo Center
San Antonio, Tex. 224-4471 for Houston Center
San Jose, Calif. 275-7422 for San Francisco Center
Santa Fe, N.Mex. 983-7743 for Albuquerque Center
Scranton, Pa. 346-7081 for Philadelphia Center
St. Joseph, Mo. 233-8206 for Kansas City Center
Syracuse, N.Y. 476-8545 for Buffalo Center
Tacoma, Wash. 383-5230 for Seattle Center
Tampa, Fla. 229-7911 for St. Petersburg Center
Toledo, Ohio 244-8625 for Cleveland Center
Topeka, Kans. 232-7229 for Kansas City Center
Trenton, N.J. 396-4400 for Newark Center
Tucson, Ariz. 622-1511 for Phoenix Center
Tulsa, Okla. 584-4193 for Oklahoma City Center
W. Palm Beach, Fla. 833-7566 for Miami Center
Wichita, Kans. 263-6931 for Kansas City Center

Consumer Information Center—GSA. David F. Peterson, Executive Director. Mary M. Arsenoff, Educational Coordinator. (202) 343-6171.
Established: October 26, 1970.

Formerly known as the Consumer Product Information Center. Shares product information with the public. The center works with all federal agencies to develop and release relevant consumer materials. It helps by translating technical information and giving editorial assistance. Publishes educational materials; prepares radio and television releases entitled *Federal Consumer Focus*. Periodicals: *New for Consumers; Highlights of New Federal Consumer Publications* (weekly); *Consumer Information* (quarterly, *see* entry 64); available in Spanish as *Información para el Consumidor*.

Government Printing Office. North Capitol & H Sts. N.W., Washington, D.C. 20401. Thomas F. McCormick, Public Printer. Wellington H. Lewis, Superintendent of Documents. (202) 541-3000.
Established: 1860.

The largest printer in the world, the GPO produces and sells publications of Congress and all other federal agencies at a low cost to consumers. Prepares and issues free price lists. *Selected U.S. Government Publications* is a free biweekly list of new materials. The *Monthly Catalog of U.S. Government Publications* costs $12.50 per year. The GPO maintains six bookstores in the District of Columbia and one each in Atlanta and in Birmingham (Ala.); Boston; Canton and Cleveland (Ohio); Chicago; Dallas; Detroit; Kansas City (Mo.); Los Angeles; New York, Philadelphia; San Francisco, and at the Pueblo (Colo.) sales outlet. In many other cities, publications are available in field offices of other departments, e.g., Federal Information Centers (*see* list under General Services Administration), National Park service stores. The GPO administers the library depository program which makes many publications available to the public in libraries across the country. Mail orders for publications should be addressed to the Superindendent of Documents, U.S. Government Printing Office, Washington, D.C. 20402.

Interstate Commerce Commission. 12 St. & Constitution Ave. N.W., Washington, D.C. 20423. George M. Stafford. Chairman. (202) 343-1100. Warner L. Baylor, Public Information Officer, Office of Public and Consumer Information. (202) 343-4761.
Established: 1887.

Regulates interstate moving companies, trucks, trains, buses, oil pipelines, barges, domestic shipping, freight forwarders, and express companies. Sets rates and handles complaints. Recently opened consumer affairs offices in Los Angeles, Miami, and Indianapolis. Provides information and assistance on moving. Pamphlets: *Summary of Information for Shippers of Household Goods* (55¢; *see* entry 419) *Interstate Commerce Commission Public Advisory Leaflets* (on consumer topics); *Interstate Commerce Commission (What the ICC Is and What It Does); Information on Moving Your Household Goods* (40¢); *Moving: Protect Your Household Goods*, etc.

Office of Consumer Affairs—Executive Office of the President. 330 Independence Ave. S.W., Washington, D.C. 20201. Virginia H. Knauer, Special Assistant to the President for Consumer Affairs. (202) 962-2246.

Established by Executive Order 11583 February 24, 1971, to advise the President on all matters relating to consumer interests. Executive Order 11702 of January 25, 1973, transferred this function to the Department of Health, Education and Welfare—Office of Consumer Affairs (*see* HEW listings in this section). The Special Assistant also functions as Director of HEW-OCA. Before being transferred, the office produced a wide variety of consumer materials. *See Part I*, entries 108, 113, 114, 154, 155, 156, 166, for annotations of some pamphlets.

United States Postal Service. 475 L'Enfant Plaza S.W., Washington, D.C. 20260. Benjamin F. Bailar, Postmaster General. (202) 245-4000. Thomas Chadwick, Consumer Advocate. (202) 245-4514.
Established: July 1, 1971, as independent agency of the Executive Branch (Postal Reorganization Act).

Provides postal service and insurance for the 90 billion pieces of mail yearly; sells U.S. Saving Bonds and money orders; protects against mail fraud, pornography, contraband, and dangerous articles. The Postal Service polices the mail and collects evidence of fraud; refers criminal violations to the General Counsel of the Postal Service or to U.S. attorneys; arrests postal offenders. Established the position of postal ombudsman in the Consumer Advocate. The advocate represents the interests of individual consumers by solving their problems and bringing their complaints and suggestions to the postal management. Pamphlets:

Consumers Guide to Postal Services and Products; Mail Fraud; Mailing Permits; How to Pack and Wrap Parcels; Prohibiting Delivery of Offensive Mail, etc.

Veterans Administration. Vermont Ave. between H & I Sts. N.W., Washington, D.C. 20420. Richard L. Roudebush, Administrator. (202) 393-4120. Established: 1930.

Provides a wide range of benefits and services to qualified veterans of the United States Armed Forces, their dependents, and their survivors. Services include hospitalization, medical and dental care, and prosthetic devices; monthly compensation or pensions for service-connected disabilities; educational assistance; loan guarantees (GI loans) for purchases of homes, farms, and/or businesses; burial allowances, and the administration and supervision of Servicemen's Group Life Insurance Program, Veterans Mortgage Life Insurance Program, and other life insurance programs. Pamphlets: *Medical, Dental, and Hospital Benefits for Veterans with Service Since January 31, 1955; Questions and Answers on Guaranteed and Direct Loans for Veterans; Federal Benefits for Veterans and Dependents* (60¢); *Home Buying Veteran*, etc.

Private Organizations

American Association of Credit Counselors. 1803 Washington St., Waukegan, Ill. 60085. James L. Gibson, Jr., President. H. Don Morris, Executive Secretary. (312) 623-6650.
Established: 1955.

Membership is restricted to established credit counseling firms subscribing to AACC Code and subject to approval of the trustees. Dues are based on number of employees and full-time officers. Counselors work with families heavily in debt who need assistance in developing a workable repayment plan and need training in money management. Advice is free. Service costs are based on length of family debt management program. Costs average $12 per $100 of debts; program averages 22 months. Pamphlets: *Seven Facts You Should Know about Family Debt Management.*

American Council on Consumer Interests. 238 Stanley Hall, University of Missouri, Columbia, Mo. 65201. Edward J. Metzen, Executive Director. (314) 882-3817.
Established: 1953.

Primarily an organization for professionals in consumer affairs and education, but membership is open to all. The dues, $10, include subscriptions to all three publications listed below. ACCI conducts research into consumer problems; counsels consumers on money management, debt, shopping, etc.; produces books, visual aids, and magazines to aid professionals teaching consumer education. The council also holds workshops, meetings, conferences, and courses designed for teachers and keeps teachers informed on legislation, government activities, and consumer groups. Periodicals: *ACCI Newsletter* (9 issues per year; September–May); *Consumer Education Forum* (3 issues per year); *The Journal of Consumer Affairs* (2 issues per year). (*See* entry 116.) Also publishes proceedings of the conferences.

American Home Economics Association. 2010 Massachusetts Ave. N.W., Washington, D.C. 20036. Doris E. Hanson, Executive Director. (202) 833-3100. Established: 1909.

Membership is open to persons with bachelor's or advanced degrees in the home economics field and living in the United States or Canada. Membership currently stands at 52,000. AHEA provides education and research to improve the quality and standard of life. Home economists teach in elementary and high schools, colleges and adult education programs; provide further education through extension services; conduct product testing; communicate the needs of businesses and consumers to each other. Recently AHEA established the Center for the Family, which is devoted to education, information, and research, and which acts as a clearinghouse for information and programs related to family concerns. Periodicals: *Journal of Home Economics* (bimonthly; $1.50 per issue); *Home Economics Research Journal* (quarterly; $10); *AHEA Action* (bimonthly newspaper). Pamphlets: *HELPs* ($2 ea., *see* entry 111); *A Guide for Evaluating Consumer Education Programs and Materials* ($1.25, *see* entry 110); *Answers to Questions Consumers Ask about Meat and Poultry* (75¢); *Consumer and Homemaking Education—Opportunity and Challenge* ($2.50), etc.

Automobile Protection Association/L'Association de Protection Automobile. 292 St. Joseph Blvd. W., Box 117, Sta. E, Montreal, Que. H2V 2N7. L. P. Edmonston, President. (514) 273-5318; 273-2477.
Established: June 1968.

Membership open to anyone but automobile industry or company personnel. Yearly $10 dues are optional. Current membership is 4,200. A nonprofit, public-interest consumer corporation that helps motorists victimized by fraud or mechanic's incompetency. Handles consumers' complaints through a mechanic committee for verification, a publicity committee, and a legal committee. Where fraud exists in a franchised gas station or incompetency in a well-known new car dealership, and dealers ignore legitimate complaints, the APA organizes boycotts, press conferences, pickets or brings legal actions. Provides members with a list of honest and crooked garages, legal assistance support in settling claims, free automobile repair inspections, mechanic consulting, new and used car purchase consulting, insurance consulting, honest and competent repairs at reasonable rates, and the *APA Monthly.* Has prosecuted hundreds of auto dealers, recovered thousands of dollars for cheated customers, successfully campaigned for annual auto inspections in Quebec, and pressed for stronger consumer protection laws. Has five branches. Periodicals: *APA Monthly.* Books: *Justice for the Exploited Motorist!* (*Automobilistes Defendez-Vous!*) by L. P. Edmonston (paper $1.50); *Roulez Sans Vous Faire Rouler* (*Driving without Being Taken*) by L. P. Edmonston (paper $3.95).

Center for Law and Social Policy. 1751 N St. N.W., Washington, D.C. 20036. Joseph Onek, Director. (202) 872-0670.
Established: August 1969.

The center is a public-interest law firm providing representation to consumer groups on such issues as drug effectiveness, import quotas, product safety, etc. There is no charge. Does not publish educational materials, but provides clinical education for law students. A Nader-sponsored organization, it has sued the Department of Transportation (for not enforcing automobile safety standards) and the Federal Trade Commission (to adopt more rigorous advertising standards).

Center for Science in the Public Interest. 1779 Church St. N.W., Washington, D.C. 20036. Albert J. Fritsch, James B. Sullivan, Michael F. Jacobson, Co-Directors. (202) 332-6000.
Established: 1971.

Membership open to all. Subscription to the newsletter included for $5 dues. The center investigates and exposes hazards in household chemicals and other products used in the home, in food, in automobiles, and in the general environment. It releases reports to the news media and distributes and sells materials. Takes legal actions, such as petitions to regulatory agencies and lawsuits. Organizes citizen actions. Provides further services through the Professional in the Public Interest. Recently exposed dangers of aerosol sprays and asbestos products; helped get the Environmental Protection Agency to initiate a lead phase-out schedule; helped bring about content labeling on food products and beverages. Periodicals: *Center for Science in the Public Interest Newsletter* (quarterly, $5); *Public Interest Letter* (monthly; $7.50); *Nutrition Action* (monthly; $5) Pamphlets: *How Aerosol Sprays Can Affect Your Safety and Health* ($2); *Nutrition Scoreboard* ($2.50); *Chemical Additives in Booze* ($1); *How Sodium Nitrite Can Affect Your Health* ($2); *Foodmakers* (50¢), etc.

Center for Study of Responsive Law. Box 19367, Washington, D.C. 20036. Theodore J. Jacobs, Executive Director. (202) 833-3400.
Established: 1969.

No members. Center referred to as Nader "think tank." Publishes reports and studies of consumer, governmental and environmental issues. Undertakes litigation, e.g., Freedom of Information Project. Published *Working on the System: A Comprehensive Manual for Citizen Access to Federal Agencies* (Basic Books, 1974; $14.95).

Chamber of Commerce of the United States. 1615 H St. N.W., Washington, D.C. 20006. Charles H. Smith, Jr., Chairman of the Board. Arch N. Booth, President. Nancy Nord, Director of Consumer Affairs. (202) 659-6126.
Established: 1912.

Over 5 million members consisting of businesses, trade associations, and manufacturers. Dues vary. Works to coordinate and improve relationships between business and consumers. Sponsors consumer programs in local, state, and national trade and professional associations. Pamphlets: *Association Leadership in Consumer Affairs* ($1); *Business and the Consumer—A Program for the Seventies* ($1); *Chambers of Commerce and the New Consumer* ($1.50); *Fulfilling Consumer Rights—Company Leadership in Consumer Affairs* ($2); *Association Consumer Affairs Activities* ($4), etc.

Concern, Inc. 2233 Wisconsin Ave. N.W., Washington, D.C. 20007. Mrs. Paul Ignatius, Chairman. Mrs. Paul Mickey, President. (202) 965-0066.
Established: March 1970.

Open to anyone interested in safeguarding the environment. No dues; 100,000 members. Publishes environmental education guides; with Audubon Naturalist Society cosponsors The Living Garden Calendar (gardening without chemical pesticides). Work done by volunteers with help from government agencies, independent scientists, academic institutions, and industry. Pamphlets: *Eco-Tips on Energy* (three published in 1974; $1); Concern Calendar ($3): Eco-Tips Series, e.g., *Pesticides; Drinking Water Alert; Additives.* Film: *Drinking Water Alert* (color; sound; 16mm; 29 min.; sale $245; rent $45).

Consumer Credit Counseling Service of Greater New York. 919 Third Ave., New York, N.Y. 10022. Arthur S. Joice, President. (212) 421-3221. Established: May 1973.

Open, without restrictions, to anyone in need of credit counseling. Provides debt repayment programs and money management counseling. Since January 1974 when operations began, through July 1974, over 700 persons were helped. Pamphlets: *Consumer Credit Counseling Service of Greater New York; Over Your Head in Debt?*

Consumer Federation of America. 1012 14 St. N.W., Washington, D.C. 20005. Carol Tucker Foreman, Executive Director. (202) 737-3732. Established: 1968.

Membership open to national, state, and local consumer groups. Individuals may become Friends of CFA. Total membership is over 30 million. Represents consumer interests before federal and state legislative bodies; acts as a clearinghouse for national, state, and local consumer groups and problems. Testifies before committees; mobilizes grassroots support for consumer legislation. Has been lobbying for creation of U.S. Consumer Protection Agency and other consumer bills. Conducts studies, e.g., auto repairs, natural gas, life insurance. Periodicals: *CFA News* (monthly; $15); *CFA Information Service* (legislative memos, press releases, newsletter subscription, $50). Pamphlets: *Prescription Drug Pricing* ($1); *The Natural Gas Explosion* (25¢); *The Auto Repair Mess* (50¢); *Directory of State and Local Government and Non-Government Consumer Groups* ($2; *see* entry 150), etc.

The Consumer Protection Center. 2000 H St. N.W., Rm. 100, Washington, D.C. 20006. Donald P. Rothschild, Director. (202) 676-7585. Established: May 1970.

A clinical law project of the George Washington University Law School, the CPC has no members as such. Projects are run by law students and community volunteers under the direction of a law student director. Provides self-help, nonlegal information to Washington, D.C., area consumers. Also handles consumer complaints from all over the country by mail. Since May 1970, received almost 27,000 complaints, successfully resolving approximately 90 percent of them. Produces TV and radio consumer documentaries for use on local Washington stations. Publishes *Consumer Protection Reporting Service* (loose-leaf) for use by attorneys and paraprofessionals in the field. Consulting work led to the creation of a local consumer protection agency in Arlington County, Virginia; opening of a senior citizen's storefront complaint center (Operation P-E-P);

drafting of a list of dos and don'ts for land buying that has been adopted by the U.S. Department of Housing and Urban Development. Periodical: *Consumer Protection Reporting Service* ($55). Pamphlets: *Help!; Lot Buyer's List of Do's and Don'ts* (in conjunction with WTTG-TV).

Consumers' Association of Canada. 251 Laurier Ave. W., Rm. 801, Ottawa, Ont. K1P 5Z7. Maryon Brechin, President. Robert C. Cross, Executive Director. (613) 238-4840.
Established: September 1947.

Membership open to all through subscription to *Canadian Consumer* at $5 a year. Over 70,000 current members. Nonprofit organization which studies consumer problems and makes recommendations for their solutions; acts as a voice for consumers to governmental, trade, and industrial groups; provides a channel from those groups to consumers; produces consumer information and counsel through tests of goods and services; unites consumers to improve the Canadian standard of living. Helped draft and pass 1974 Packaging and Labelling Act, Hazardous Products Act and Textile Labelling Act. Influential in creating the Canadian Department of Consumer and Corporate Affairs. Helped to set standards for children's garments, for labeling fiber contents of textiles, and for a cooling-off period on installment purchases. Periodical: *Canadian Consumer (Le Consommateur Canadien;* six times a year; $5; *see* entry 58). Pamphlets: *CAC . . . And What It Can Do for You!;* Buying Guide Series: *Don't Make a Move; Tent Trailers; Baby's Needs; Tires; Buying a Bike*, etc. (25¢ ea.); *How to Cut Dental Costs; Carpets and Rugs; Water Skiis*, etc. (All pamphlets available in French.)

Consumers Education and Protective Association. 6048 Ogontz Ave., Philadelphia, Pa. 19141. Max Weiner, Executive Director. (215) 424-1441.
Established: February 1966.

Open to all consumers. Fees are $3 to join and $2 dues per month. Organized as a local consumer organization, it is still basically intended to help residents in the Philadelphia area. Educates and organizes consumers to protect their individual and group long-term and immediate interests against fraudulent and exploitative business practices. Organizes consumer actions, e.g., pickets, media exposure; conducts negotiations with individual businesses. Responsible for innumerable refunds and settlements to consumers. Organized the Pennsylvania Consumer Party which ran candidates in the 1974 elections. Periodical: *Consumers Voice* (ten times a year; $3).

Consumers' Research, Inc. Washington, N.J. 07882. F. J. Schlink, Director. (201) 689-3300.
Established: 1927.

Membership open to anyone subscribing to *Consumers' Research Magazine*. Currently between 130,000 and 140,000 members. The oldest nonprofit, noncommercial consumer organization in the country. Tests and reports on products and services used by consumers. CR's own staff conduct the Consumers' Research laboratories, although in certain specialized fields, the services of outside experts and consultants are used. Also produces slides and books. Lobbies for consumer safety. Has received innumerable awards, e.g., National Safety Council Public Interest Award (1958 and 1963), Association of Home Appliance Manufacturers Award, for information on home appliances, 1971. Periodical: *Consumers' Research Magazine* (monthly; $9 a year, *see* entry 68; its October issue is the *Handbook of Buying Issue; see* entry 77). Pamphlets: reprints of CR articles, e.g., *Food and Nutrition* (50¢); *Consumer in the Market Place* (40¢); *Labels and Seals–What They Mean to the Consumer* (15¢); *Travel Guidelines* (20¢); *Baby Food in Jars* (45¢); etc. Slides (color; sale $30 ea. set; rent $5 ea. set): *Testing at Consumers' Research* (34 slides); *Deceptive Packaging* (24 slides); *Food Additives* (28 slides); *Safety in the Home* (34 slides); *Bicycle Safety* (33 slides).

Consumers Union of United States, Inc. 256 Washington St., Mount Vernon, N.Y. 10550. Colston E. Warne, President. Rhoda H. Karpatkin, Executive Director. (914) 664-6400.
Established: 1936.

Membership open to subscribers of *Consumer Reports.* A nonprofit, noncommercial consumer advisory organization with approximately 375,000 members. Tests and rates products to provide consumers with information and counseling on consumer goods and services and all other matters relating to the expenditure of family income; initiates and cooperates with individual and group efforts to create and maintain decent living standards. CU puts out a monthly magazine and many special publications as well as audiovisual materials. Operates a Washington office which monitors government activity, files petitions, and enters into litigation on behalf of consumer issues. The Education Division cooperates with consumer educators and provides consumer education materials. The Communication Division works with and encourages the news media to cover consumer news. In June 1974, CU started producing one- and two-minute news program inserts for TV. By August 1974 the twice-weekly features were syndicated in 52 markets. Also edits many books (see annotations in Part I of this *Guide*). Periodical: *Consumer Reports* (monthly; $8; includes *Buying Guide* issue, December; *see* entry 65). Pamphlets: Reprints of many *Consumer Reports* articles, e.g., *Soft Contact Lenses* (25¢); *Hearing Aids* (25¢); *How to Buy a Used Car* (25¢); *Drug Pricing and the Rx Police State* (25¢); etc. Books: *Consumers Union Reviews Classical Recordings* ($3.50; *see* entry 427); *Consumer Education: Its New Look* ($2); *The Consumers Union Report on Life Insurance* ($2; *see* entry 313); *Health Guide for Travelers* (75¢), etc. Films: *Consumerism: Let the Seller Beware* (color; sound; 16 mm; 22 min., rent $10).

The Cooperative League of the USA. 1828 L St. N.W., Washington, D.C. 20036. Stanley Dreyer, President. (202) 872-0550.
Established: 1916.

A national federation of 104 regional, state, and local active and associate members and 188 family or individual members. Approximately 20 million families belong through membership in local groups. Interests of member groups span housing, insurance, credit, consumer goods and services, rural electrification, group health, farm marketing and supply, students, education, and travel. CLUSA represents member interests before congressional committees and federal agencies; helps member groups maintain professional competence and communicate with its own members and with the public. Provides speakers; produces and distributes pamphlets and books; represents the U.S. cooperative movement in the International Cooperative Alliance and other groups. Periodical: *KONSUM* (bimonthly). Pamphlets: *Co-op Depot Manual* ($3.25); *Co-op Stores and Buying Clubs; Credit Union Dynamics* ($1.95); *Economics of the Credit Union*($2.75); *Ours! How to Organize a Consumer Cooperative* (95¢); *Food Buying Groups* (45¢), etc.

Council of Better Business Bureaus. 1150 17 St. N.W., Washington, D.C. 20036. Elisha Gray II, Chairman. John W. Macy, Jr., President. (202) 467-5200.
Established: 1912 (1970 consolidation of National Better Business Bureau and the Association of Better Business Bureaus).

Provides standards of ethical business practices and self-regulation; acts against deceptive advertising and other fraudulent and misleading selling operations. Maintains information centers to provide information and handle consumer complaints. Composed of 138 U.S. bureaus, 12 Canadian bureaus, and four in other countries, the CBBB is supported by more than 125,000 businesses at a cost of approximately $12 million. Issues codes and standards in various fields, e.g., advertising, men's and boys' apparel advertising; auto sales, rental and leasing advertising. Established nine Consumer Councils providing communication between the BBBs, consumers, and the business community; conducts arbitration and has attracted 9,000 businesses to precommit to arbitration. Educational activities cover public service radio announcements, "Conversation for Consumers" (a ten-minute weekly radio program), and a variety of publications and newspaper columns ("Tips for Consumers from Your Better Business Bureau"). Pamphlets: Tip Sheets ($2 per 100) e.g., *Appliance Service; Bait and Switch; Buying by Mail; Buying on Time;* Information Series ($5.50 per 100) e.g., *Audio Products; Carpet and Rugs; Moving; Renting a Car; What Is a Better Business Bureau?; History and Tradition of the BBB*, etc.

Credit Union National Association, Inc. Box 431, Madison, Wis. 53701. Herb Wegner, Managing Director. (608) 241-1211.
Established: May 1970.

Nonprofit association of 51 credit union leagues and 27,693,294 credit union members. Any credit union league in the United States may belong. Represents the credit unions for legislative purposes; provides educational and informational materials; holds seminars. The unions offer financial counseling to members; many have consumer libraries. CUNA is a charter member of the Consumer Federation of America. Helped bring about passage of Truth-in-Lending Act. Periodicals: *Everybody's Money* (quarterly; $1); *Complaint Directory* (annual; $1). Pamphlets: *Consumer Facts* ($1.50); *Bibliography* ($1). Film: *Using Your Money* (film plus six slide shows and instructor's manual; (sale $285 to credit unions; $350 to others).

GET Consumer Protection, Inc. Box 355, Ansonia Sta., New York, N.Y. 10023. Janet Stebins, Executive Director. No telephone.
Established: July 1971.

Membership open to anyone wishing to volunteer to work for better services and rates from utilities in New York State. Volunteers appear and testify at public hearings. Handles consumer complaints for small charge. Provides educational materials on the gas, electric, and telephone companies. Has brought legal actions against the New York State Public Service Commission; forced Bell Telephone to produce pamphlet on single message units, and long distance credits; helped women get equal consideration on telephone deposits. Has rate of 85 percent success in settling complaints. Produced a *Consumer Training Program* to teach consumers about telephone charges and services. Produced pamphlets on energy uses of electric appliances. Pamphlets: *Consumer Training Program; Shedding "Light" on Electricity . . . What You Need to Know and Have Never Been Told* ($2.50; *see* entry 269).

Home Economics Education Association. 1201 16 St. N.W., Washington, D.C. 20036. Catherine A. Leisher, Professional Assistant. (202) 833-4138.
Established: 1927.

Approximately 3,000 home economics educators and others associated with or interested in home economics instruction in schools and colleges are members; dues are $5. An affiliate of the National Education Association, HEEA helps home economics educators promote understanding of family and community life, improve the quality of home economics instruction, and broaden the scope of the curriculum. It supplements existing services currently available to educators, cooperates with other associations in related fields, publishes materials of interest to teachers in the field. Periodical: *Newsletter.* Pamphlets: *Teacher's Guide to Financial Education* ($1); *Clothing for Young Men* ($2.50); *HEEPS* (Home Economics Education Packages), e.g., *Selection of Furniture* ($1.25); *The Family Budget* ($1.25); *The Budget as a Means to an End* ($1.25), etc.

L'Institut de Promotion des Intérêts de Consommateur (The Institute for the Promotion of Consumer Interests). 6000 est, boul. Métropolitain, Suite 108, Montreal, Que. H1S 1B2. Gilles Robert, Director. (418) 256-5545; 256-1524.
Established: June 11, 1969.

Membership open to all through subscription dues to magazine. Member of the American Council on Consumer Interests, this French-language organization is financed by Federation des Magazins Co-op (Federation of Store Cooperatives), their affiliates and members of the Cooprix. Educates and informs consumers about developments in the field; provides information on various consumer products; receives and handles consumer complaints; conducts research and publicizes results; takes actions within the eight branches in the Province of Quebec (Cooprix). Prepares materials, such as pamphlets and visual aids. Periodical: *Le Réveil du Consommateur* (*The Consumer's Awakening;* ten times a year; $6.50). Pamphlets: *Survivre Malgré Tout* (To Survive Despite All); *Recettes Hebdomadaires* (Weekly Recipes).

Insurance Consumers Union—Policyholders Protective Association, Inc. Box 16257, 4541 Office Park Dr., Jackson, Miss. 39206. John E. Gregg, Chairman. (601) 982-0236.
Established: July 1971.

Membership open to any individual, business firm, or corporation except insurance companies and their agents or employees. Currently has between 3,000 and 4,000 members. Donations are voluntary; members are asked to pay $25 a year (individuals and families) or $100 a year (organizations). Functions to educate consumers to buy insurance and negotiate claims wisely; represents consumers before insurance commissions, state legislatures, congressional committees; maintains national clearinghouse on insurance information; brings class actions and precedent-setting litigation in various courts. Recently provided consumers with access to the records of the Medical Information Bureau of Greenwich, Conn., to allow them to update and keep their records free of errors. Prepares weekly newspaper column "Premium Payer Be Damned." Periodical: *Guides to Health Insurance Buying and Collecting* (issued irregularly).

National Consumer Finance Association. 1000 16 St. N.W., Washington, D.C., 20036. Carl F. Hawver, Executive Vice-President. Donna G. Beavers, Coordinator, Consumer Affairs Center. (202) 638-1340.
Established: 1916.

Membership open to companies doing business in the consumer installment credit industry and related groups and associations. On February 1, 1971, NCFA established the Consumer Affairs Center to provide consumers with national representation on any type of inquiry or problem relating to the consumer installment credit industry. Handles and expedites complaints; assists consumer families with money and credit management problems; provides materials and guidance to social workers, ministers, teachers, and others who counsel in money and credit matters; provides information on the services offered by the industry. Pamphlets: *Methods of Stating Consumer Finance Charges* ($2); *Consumer Finance Rate Card; Family Budget Slide Guide* (10¢); *Family Budget Plan Worksheet* (2¢); *It's Your Money—$500 Bill* (3¢); *Money and Your Marriage* (35¢); *Sergeant Patsy Cartoons* (ten 8-by-10-inch B&W cartoons, $2), etc. Filmstrips: Money and Credit Management Series: *Your Money Matters* and *You Take the Credit* (80 and 79 frames, respectively; plus records, scripts, and teacher's guide; sale $40 for series package); *What Consumers Should Know about Truth in Lending* (92 frames; $10), etc.

National Consumers Congress. 1346 Connecticut Ave. N.W., Rm. 425, Washington, D.C. 20036. Ellen Zawel, President. (202) 833-9704.
Established: April 1973.

Membership open to all. Current membership approximately 4,000; $10 dues includes subscription to monthly newsletter. NCC is a grassroots organization concerned with inflation, distribution of wealth and power, marketplace manipulation, and government bias in decision making. Is establishing a national network of strong local action groups, providing them with information and support services. Represents consumer interests before Congress and federal agencies, e.g., USDA, FTC, and FDA. Concern has centered on antitrust, agricultural policies, supermarket practices, the structure of the meat and milk industries, and energy. Washington efforts have resulted in monthly meetings with the USDA for consumer input. Established a 12-city supermarket pilot program to promote consumer input in supermarket policies and practices. Has worked for a Bottlers' Bill and to lower beef and milk prices. Periodical: *Common Sense* (monthly; included with dues). Pamphlet: *Beef–One Year Later* ($1).

Public Interest Research Group. 2000 P St. N.W., Suite 711, Washington, D.C. 20036. Tom Stanton, Coordinator. (202) 833-9700.
Established: 1968.

A Nader organization, it aims to get government agencies to be more responsive to the public interest. Monitors work of various departments and agencies, e.g., Environmental Protection Agency, Department of Transportation–National Highway Traffic Safety Administration. Has investigated automobile safety and emission standards, pollution in various forms, federal meat and poultry inspection standards, etc. Established PIRGs in almost every state and coordinates their activities, publicizes results.

Women United for Action. 58 W. 25 St., New York, N.Y. 10010. Claudette Furlonge and Laurie Fierstein, Coordinators. (212) 989-1252.
Established: August 1972.

Membership open to all individuals; dues $2. All organizations except those representing business or government can become members for $10 dues. Currently has approximately 10,000 members. A nonprofit organization with 14 state chapters, it provides information on the food industry and food prices; organizes communities to bring all citizens together on a neighborhood level to fight for rights in the supermarket, against utilities, and for general welfare. Provides monthly information (through newspaper) on food, day care, welfare, housing, women's problems, and utility services. Holds community meetings and hearings on issues of consumer concern; initiated and participated in numerous picket lines, demonstrations, and boycotts. Organized the 1973 meat boycott in 14 states. Actively represents consumers legally and before legislative bodies. Initiated the New York State Commission for a Fair Milk Price; put out a study on milk prices and the milk industry in New York State. Periodical: *Women United* (monthly; $3). Pamphlets: *Operation Food Price Roll Back; Milk for Children, Not for Profits* ($1). Film: *We're Fed Up.*

U.S. State, County, and City Agencies

ALABAMA

STATE AGENCIES

Consumer Services—Office of the Attorney General. 669 S. Lawrence St., Montgomery 36104. William J. Baxley, Attorney General. Tom Brassell, Consumer Services Coordinator. (205) 269-7001.
Established: 1971.

Enforces different laws protecting consumers. (Alabama does not have a specific consumer protection law.) Resolves complaints. Each year recovers thousands of dollars from fraudulent concerns.

Governor's Office of Consumer Protection. 138 Adams Ave., Montgomery 36104. Annie Laurie Gunter, Consumer Protection Officer. (205) 269-7477.
Established: February 1972.

Acts as a clearing house for consumer complaints and promotes consumer education programs. Mediates and processes complaints; prepares and disseminates consumer information. Holds workshops, provides TV and radio spots and a weekly newspaper column "Of Consumer Interest." One staff member is an expert on rate cases involving utilities. Periodicals: *Office of Consumer Protection Monthly.* Toll-free telephone number: 1-(800) 392-5658.

ALASKA

STATE AGENCIES

Consumer Protection Section—Office of the Attorney General. 360 K St., Anchorage 99501. Norman C. Gorsuch, Attorney General. Stanley Howitt, Assistant Attorney General—Supervisor of Consumer Protection. (907) 279-0428.
Established: September 1972.

Enforces the Unfair Trade Practices and Consumer Protection Act (A.S. 45.50.471 *et seq.*) through court action, informal settlements, voluntary compliances, and injunctive relief. Has subpoena powers. Disseminates consumer fraud information. Recent successful activities include suits against itinerant boiler repairmen, magazines sales, etc., and voluntary compliance from air travel club. Preparing consumer information packet in cooperation with the University of Alaska Cooperative Extension Services. Periodicals: (planned for 1975). Pamphlets: *Where the Consumer Can Turn for Help in Alaska.*

Branch offices: 604 Barnette, Box 1309, *Fairbanks* 99701. (907) 452-1567; Pouch K, State Capitol, *Juneau* 99801. (907) 586-5391.

ARIZONA

STATE AGENCIES

Consumer Protection and Antitrust Division—Office of the Attorney General. 159 State Capitol Bldg., Phoenix 85007. Gary K. Nelson, Attorney General. William P. Dixon, Assistant Attorney General—Director, Consumer Protection. (602) 271-5510.

Enforces the Arizona Consumer Fraud Act (A.R.S. 44-1521, *et seq.*) covering all forms of deceptive trade practices. Has powers to investigate and prosecute. Authorizes county offices to enforce the law. Does not provide consumer materials.

COUNTY AGENCIES

Cochise County. Attorney's Office. Bisbee 85603. James K. Kerley, Deputy. (602) 432-2291.

Authorized delegate of the Arizona attorney general to enforce Consumer Fraud Act.

Pima County. Consumer Protection Division—Attorney's Office. 208 Lawyers Title Bldg., 199 N. Stone Ave., Tucson 85701. Robert C. Brauchli, Director. (602) 792-8688
Established: May 1973.

Enforces Arizona Consumer Fraud Act: investigates consumer complaints and attempts to resolve them; also initiates own investigations. Can order assurances of discontinuance, injunctions, and other relief; litigates. Conducts limited consumer education program. Recent assurances of discontinuance reached with bank advertising free services and illegal burglar alarm system advertising. Volunteers from the University of Arizona help staff of three attorneys and three investigators. Pamphlets: (currently being prepared for publication in 1975).

CITY AGENCIES

Tucson. Consumer Affairs Division—City Attorney's Office. Box 5547, 180 N. Meyer, 85703. Ronald M. Detrick, Assistant City Attorney. (602) 791-4886.
Established: February 1974.

Operates as a central agency for the receipt and processing of consumer complaints. Investigates and resolves complaints through civil and criminal litigation, administrative and nonjudicial remedies. Disseminates consumer information to the public; reviews local, state, and federal legislation and formulates recommendations for actions, including compliance and public educational programs. Coordinates activities with other public and private agencies providing consumer information and protection.

ARKANSAS

STATE AGENCIES

Consumer Protection Division—Office of the Attorney General. Justice Bldg., Little Rock 72201. Jim Guy Tucker, Attorney General. (501) 371-2007.
Established: July 1971.

Enforces the Arkansas Consumer Protection Act of 1971 covering all forms of deceptive or unfair trade practices. Serves as a central clearinghouse for complaints; investigates, enforces, or refers possible violations to other agencies or private organizations. Encourages business and industry to maintain high standards of honesty. Undertakes research in consumer affairs matters. Promotes consumer education, e.g., prepares weekly newspaper column "Consumer Alert" published in 60 newspapers across the state; monthly television show "Consumer Alert" (30 min.) seen on educational television; maintains speakers bureau. Organizes county consumer committees.

CALIFORNIA

STATE AGENCIES

Consumer Protection Unit—Office of the Attorney General. 600 State Bldg., Los Angeles 90012. Herschel T. Elkins, Deputy Attorney General, Consumer Protection Unit. (213) 620-2655.

Enforces the state consumer protection law covering all forms of deceptive trade practices. Engages in educational activities (pamphlet material, talks, films). Pamphlets: Information Pamphlet series (also available in Spanish), e.g., *On Guard—A Guide for the Consumer.* Films: Participated in the production of various FilmFair Communications films. The director Herschel Elkins, narrated *This Is Fraud* (*see* entry 249).

Branch office: 6000 State Bldg., *San Francisco* 94102. (415) 557-1646.

Department of Consumer Affairs. 1020 N St., Sacramento 95814. Patricia Gayman, Director. (916) 445-0660.
Established: July 1971.

Regulates over one million professionals by licensing and registration of over 100 occupations; represents consumers before the legislature and at hearings; prepares and disseminates consumer education materials; facilitates functioning of the market. Handles over 70,000 complaints yearly. Established the Division of Consumer Services "One-Stop Complaint Form." In 1972–1973 recovered over $2.75 million through complaint handling and consumer protection activities. Pamphlets: Consumer Affairs Education Series, e.g., *The Consumer and the Small Claims Court; "One Stop" Complaint Procedure; The Car You Care For!,* etc. Many pamphlets also in Spanish.

Branch offices: 107 S. Broadway, Rm. 7117, *Los Angeles* 90012. (213) 620-4360; 30 Van Ness Ave., *San Francisco* 94102. (415) 557-0966.

COUNTY AGENCIES

Del Norte County. Office of Consumer Affairs. 2650 Washington Blvd., Crescent City 95531. L. J. Garrett, Jr., Director. (707) 464-2716.

Los Angeles County. Consumer and Environment Protection Division—District Attorney's Office. 1800 Criminal Courts Bldg., Los Angeles 90012. Joseph P. Busch, District Attorney. (213) 974-3974.
Established: 1971.

Brings civil actions in large consumer protection cases. Authority by state statute. No educational materials published.

Orange County. Office of Consumer Affairs. 511 N. Sycamore St., Santa Ana 92701. M. S. Shimanoff, Director. (714) 834-6100.
Established: March 1972.

Investigates complaints of deceptive or unfair trade practices; protects and promotes consumer interests; mediates disputes; represents consumer interests before administrative and regulatory agencies, legislative bodies and judicial forums; conducts investigations, research, and studies; recommends amendments to consumer protection laws; refers violations of the law to appropriate agencies for enforcement. Handled 5,264 complaints (March 1972–December 1973) of which 2,513 were won outright and 1,613 were resolved through compromise. Periodical: *Consumer Newsletter* (to be published late 1974). Pamphlets: *Consumer Bulletin* (series of 25 bilingual, English-Spanish leaflets, e.g., on warranties, credit for married women, etc.)

Sacramento County. Consumer Protection Bureau. 816 H St., Rm. 104, Sacramento 95814. Leesa B. Speer, Director. (916) 454-2112.
Established: September 1972.

Mediates consumer complaints, educates and works on legislation helpful to consumers. Uses consumer protection trainees and specialists. Provides speakers for schools and community groups. Lobbies for consumer bills in the state legislature. Recently held mobile home hearings and conducted used car warranty survey. Periodical: *Newsletter* (issued irregularly, but at least six issues per year; $1).

San Bernardino County. Dept. of Weights and Measures and Consumer Affairs. 160 E. Sixth St., San Bernardino 92415. H. E. Sandel, Director. (714) 383-1411.
Established: February 1971.

Mediates specific complaints through personal contact, telephone and letters. Has no enforcement powers. Provides consumer education and counselling, coordinates activities with other agencies. Since inception, success rate of 88 percent in resolving complaints. Provides speakers for schools and organizations. Pamphlet: *Guide to Consumer Protection.* Other telephone numbers: Ontario area (714) 988-1355. Desert area (714) 256-1781.

San Diego County. Consumer Fraud Division–District Attorney's Office. 4001 Courthouse, 220 W. Broadway, San Diego 92112. M. James Lorenz, Deputy District Attorney. (714) 236-2474.
Established: 1970.

Investigates consumer complaints, prosecutes criminal and civil violations. Can enforce injunctions. Provides some consumer education. Recently instituted injunctions for alleged false advertising and unfair business practices against S. S. Kresge ($10,000), Earl Scheib ($60,000), and Consolidated Medical Systems ($30,000). Pamphlet: (one on consumer protection). Slides: (a series for use in educational programs).

Santa Clara County. Department of Weights, Measures and Consumer Affairs. 1555 Berger Dr., San Jose 95112. R. W. Horger, Director. (408) 299-2105. Established: July 1, 1970 (Consumer Affairs).

Enforces county and state laws, regulations and ordinances pertaining to consumer protection. Handles consumer complaints. Has public information program. Recently, the county adopted a new ordinance establishing a citizen consumer commission to work with the department and the Board of Supervisors in an advisory capacity. Periodical: *Newsletter* (monthly).

Santa Cruz County. Weights and Measures and Consumer Affairs. 640 Capitola Rd., Santa Cruz 95062. G. S. Anderson, Director. (408) 425-2054.

Stanislaus County. Office of Consumer Affairs. Box 3404, Modesto 95353. Rodney M. Stine, Coordinator. (209) 526-6211.

Investigates and follows up formal complaints, works with district attorney's office on criminal cases; refers other complaints to appropriate agencies; provides consumer education programs, such as workshops and lectures. In 1973, the Office handled 1,281 complaints. Disseminates materials prepared by state and federal bureaus. One investigator is available at all times to the Spanish-speaking community.

Ventura County. Department of Weights and Measures—Consumer Affairs. 608 El Rio Dr., Oxnard 93030. William H. Korth, Director. (805) 487-5511, ext. 4377. Established: June 15, 1971.

Receives, mediates, and refers complaints to appropriate agencies; informs consumers of small claims court procedures; assists in developing and conducting consumer education programs; disseminates information through the news media, displays, and pamphlets. Pamphlets: *A Guide to Consumer Protection; Full Value: Getting the Most for Your Shopping Dollar Through Correct Weights and Measures* (flyers on mail order sales, door-to-door sales, auto repairs, buying a used car, etc.).

CITY AGENCIES

Los Angeles. Bureau of Consumer Affairs. 848 City Hall, 200 N. Spring St. 90012. Fern Jellison, Director. (213) 485-4682. Established: January 1972.

Receives, investigates, and resolves written consumer complaints. Has subpoena powers; recommends filing of civil or criminal actions when violations occur. Works to promote ethical standards for business and consumers and to prevent unethical and illegal business practices. Established Senior Citizens' Consumer Protection Program to educate older people in ways to protect themselves from unconscionable trade practices. Also started an advertising verification program to uncover false and misleading advertisements. Volunteers are dispatched daily to business establishments to check truthfulness of advertising.

COLORADO

STATE AGENCIES

Office of Consumer Affairs—Department of Law. 112 E. 14 Ave., Denver 80203. John P. Moore, Attorney General. Susan L. Bishop, Consumer Affairs. (303) 892-3501.
Established: July 1969.

Enforces the Colorado Consumer Protection Act prohibiting deceptive and misleading trade practices, the Uniform Consumer Credit Code, which regulates consumer credit sales and loans and supervises lenders, and the Fair Trade Practices Act, which ensures competition by businesses. In the first half of 1974, recovered $150,000 for consumers by refunds, cancelled contracts and services performed. Other recent activities included the preparation of a legislative package on automobiles and a major educational effort on the mobile home industry. Statewide system of consumer protection encompases the attorney general's office, other regulatory agencies, and Colorado State University Cooperative Extension Services. Pamphlets: *A Fair Shake for Consumers and Responsible Businessmen; "The Rule of 78th;" Consumer's Checklist* (flyers on credit home improvement, repairmen, etc.) Some pamphlets available in Spanish. Slides: (being developed, in cooperation with CSU Extension Services).

COUNTY AGENCIES

Adams, Arapahoe, Boulder, Denver, and Jefferson counties. *See* Denver County.

Denver County. Metropolitan Denver District Attorney's Consumer Office. 655 S. Broadway, Denver 80209. Felicia Muftic, Executive Director. (303) 777-3072.
Established: March 1, 1974.

Under the direction of five district attorneys for the counties of Adams, Arapahoe, Boulder, Denver, and Jefferson. Investigates complaints, mediates, and brings criminal prosecution where violations of the Colorado Revised Statutes require. Most complaints settled by mediation. Particularly active and successful in the areas of odometer rollback and contractor fraud. Pamphlets: (being published, on the functions of this office and on contracts).

El Paso County. Consumer Fraud Division—District Attorney's Office. 303 S. Cascade, Suite B, Colorado Springs 80902. Bernard R. Baker, Chief Deputy District Attorney. (303) 473-3801.
Established: February 15, 1973.

The division was established to serve as an arbiter between business and consumers who have legitimate complaints. The division handles complaints on a civil basis for restitution (can issue injunctions); on a criminal basis, files actions in court. Carries out educational programs, disseminates consumer information materials. Recently, the division averaged $15,000 per month in restitutions. Pamphlets: *Consumer Fraud Booklet; Consumer Fraud Brochure.*

Pueblo County. Consumer Affairs Unit—District Attorney's Office. 320 W. Tenth St., Pueblo 81003. Libby McCraith, Consumer Affairs Officer. (303) 544-0075.
Established: November 1973.

Handles consumer complaints; mediates, and resolves disputes if possible; files criminal fraud charges; presents educational programs in county; participates in preparing legislative changes. Recently testified at automobile repair hearings in an attempt to get new auto repair legislation. Does not publish consumer materials.

CONNECTICUT

STATE AGENCIES

Department of Consumer Protection. State Office Bldg., Hartford 06115. Barbara B. Dunn, Commissioner. (203) 566-4206.
Established: 1959 (first agency of its type in the country).

Enforces legislation protecting consumers from injury by product use or merchandising deceit. Educates consumers on their rights and responsibilities. Six-member legal staff investigates complaints under Unfair Sales Practices Act. Enforcement is under Divisions of Food, Meat and Poultry, Drug, Commission of Pharmacy, Consumer Frauds, Weights and Measures, Boxing and Wrestling, and Consumer Education. Pamphlets: *What You Should Know about Toys* (also available in Spanish); consumer protection leaflets (also in Spanish); *$ Help*, etc. Toll-free telephone number 1-(800) 842-2649.

CITY AGENCIES

Middletown. Office of Consumer Protection. City Hall, 06457. Guy J. Tommasi, Director. (203) 347-4671.

DELAWARE

STATE AGENCIES

Consumer Protection Division—Office of the Attorney General. Public Bldg., Wilmington 19801. Jeffrey M. Winer, Deputy Attorney General. (302) 571-2450.
Established: 1967.

Investigates and prosecutes infractions of the criminal justice system covering all forms of deceptive trade practices.

Division of Consumer Affairs—Department of Community Affairs and Economic Development. 201 W. 14 St., Wilmington 19801. Francis M. West, Director. (302) 571-3250.
Established: November 1970.

Handles civil consumer complaints against Delaware firms; reviews and recommends consumer legislation and programs; engages in consumer education (in high schools and for private groups); refers unsettled complaints to appropriate agencies (*see* Consumer Protection Division, above). Recent successful activities include cease and desist order against major waterproofing firm, a study of the local swimming pool industry, consumer workshop for teachers. Periodical: *Consumer Alert* produced jointly with local AAUW (American Association of University Women). Pamphlet: *Make Use of Delaware Consumer Services.*

Branch offices:
Kent County. (302) 678-4000.
New Castle County. (302) 658-9251, ext. 442, 443.
Sussex County. (302) 856-2571.

DISTRICT OF COLUMBIA

Consumer Affairs Office—Government of the District of Columbia—Executive Office. 1407 L St. N.W., Washington, D.C. 20005. William B. Robertson, Director. (202) 629-2617.
Established: December 1973.

Investigates complaints of unfair or fraudulent trade practices and unsafe merchandise or services; enforces regulations and proposes new legislation; prepares consumer education materials; coordinates programs of all consumer organizations in the metropolitan area; handles referrals to other agencies. Recently sponsored Consumer Awareness Month. Runs a monthly consumer mobile van. Held teacher-parent workshop to develop consumer education curriculum guide; held conference on consumer food dollars, etc. Pamphlets: *Certificate of Guarantee Offering D.C. Consumers the Services of CAO;* flyers, e.g., *Consumer Tips for D.C. Homeowners, Please Read Me* (Contract), etc.

FLORIDA

STATE AGENCIES

Consumer Information Office—Office of the Comptroller. The Capitol, Tallahassee 32304. Fred O. Dickinson, Jr., Comptroller. Vernon Bradford, Director. (904) 488-1578; 488-5275.

Handles consumer complaints and inquiries concerning banking, securities, finance, abandoned property, credit cards, cemeteries, home repair contracts, trading stamps, and more. Periodicals: *CASH* (Consumer Advice on Spending Habits, quarterly.) Pamphlet: *Plan So Your Money Makes It.* Toll-free telephone number: (800) 342-3557.

Division of Consumer Affairs—Department of Agriculture. 106 W. Pensacola St., Tallahassee 32304. Doyle Conner, Commissioner. Robert J. Bishop, Director. (904) 488-2221.
Established: March 1, 1967 (Consumer Services Division).

Serves as a clearing house for consumer complaints. Investigates deceptive practices and other violations of the "Little FTC Act"; refers infractions to appropriate enforcing agencies. Provides consumer education through news columns and monthly newsletters. Recently investigated cases resulting in refunds to hundreds of victims of "free vacation" scheme; also refunds to victims of health spa which closed. Periodical: *What's Cooking of Consumer Interest* (monthly). Pamphlets: *What to Do . . . A Guide to Consumer Protection; The Florida Department of Agriculture and Consumer Services in a Nutshell;* Wise $hopper $eries, e.g., *$tretch Your Food Dollar*, *Buying Clothes*, *Fibers for Functional Fashion*, etc. Toll-free telephone number: (800) 342-2176.

Office of Consumer Protection and Fair Trade Practices—Department of Legal Affairs. The Capitol, Tallahassee 32304. Robert L. Shevin, Attorney General. Rod Tennyson, Consumer Counsel. (904) 488-4481.
Established: October 1, 1973.

Enforces Deceptive and Unfair Trade Practices Act, which prohibits "unfair methods of competition and unfair or deceptive acts or practices." Adjudicates complaints; issues cease and desist orders, injunctions, and restraining orders; oversees the activities of the Florida county offices. From October 1973 to June 1974 the office obtained 37 assurances of voluntary compliance and seven cases were adjudicated. Disseminates "The Comparison Shopper" (wheel device, for figuring cost per ounce in packages).

State Attorney's Office—Special Prosecutions. Suite 620 Broward County Courthouse, 201 S.E. Sixth St., Fort Lauderdale 33301. Philip J. Montante, Jr., Assistant State Attorney in Charge of Special Prosecutions Division. (305) 765-4216.

Plus the Department of Legal Affairs (noted above), Florida maintains 20 separate states attorneys. Of special note, the Special Prosecutions Office prosecuted the largest case (196 criminal counts) in the United States under the Deceptive and Unfair Trade Practices Act (D.U.T.P.).

COUNTY AGENCIES

Note: Each of Florida's 20 Judicial Districts has a state attorney operating within the State Attorney's Office (*see* state listings) to enforce the Deceptive and Unfair Trade Practices Act. All of these offices became effective at the same time as the law, i.e., October 1, 1973. As of September 1974, two counties had their own consumer protection departments.

Metropolitan Dade County. Consumer Protection Division—Office of County Manager. 1399 N.W. 17 Ave., 2nd fl., Miami 33125. John C. Mays, Director. (305) 377-5111.
Established: October 1, 1968 (as Trade Standards Division).

Receives and responds to all consumer complaints. Administers and enforces trade practice laws of the county. Has police powers for inspectors and penalties with trials in the Metropolitan Dade County Court. Provides information and materials promoting consumer education and protection. In 1973, 2,225 complainants were returned $242,915 in cash and merchandise refunds; violators of consumer laws were fined $7,820 in County Court in 25 cases initiated and developed by the office. Carried on extensive speaking engagements e.g., "At Your Service" (WKAT-Radio) "Money Tree" (TV-channel 2); various colleges in the area. Pamphlet: *How to Make Consumer Protection Complaints* (in Metropolitan Dade County).

Palm Beach County. Office of Consumer Affairs. 301 N. Olive Ave., West Palm Beach 33401. Alice C. Skaggs, Director. (305) 655-5200, ext. 566. Established: May 18, 1972.

Enforces the provisions of the Consumer Affairs Ordinance by mediation. The director also has cease and desist powers and can issue Assurances of Voluntary Compliance. (The state attorney's office has legal powers.) The office provides education and information to the citizens of the county. Held "Consumerama '74" at local shopping centers. Pamphlets: *Consumer Affairs Ordinance of Palm Beach County; Palm Beach County Office of Consumer Affairs Pamphlet.*

CITY AGENCIES

Jacksonville. Division of Consumer Affairs—Department of Human Resources. 220 E. Bay St., 32202. Thatcher Walt, Consumer Affairs Officer. (904) 355-0411, ext. 531.

St. Petersburg. Office of Consumer Affairs. 1 City Hall, 175 Fifth St. N., St., 33701. William M. Bateman, Jr., Director. (813) 893-7395. Established: July 1971.

Upholds the Uniform Trade Standards Ordinance. Has police powers to inspect and enforce violations concerning misleading advertising, weights and measures, and other consumer complaints. Pamphlets: St. Petersburg Consumer Protection Series (flyers), e.g., *10 Ways to Combat Consumer Fraud*, *Unlawful Bill Collection Practices*, *Automobile Repairs*, *Municipal Bonds*, etc. Consumer telephone number: 894-1392.

GEORGIA

STATE AGENCIES

Consumer Services—State Department of Human Resources. 618 Ponce De Leon Ave., N.E., Atlanta 30308. Jacqueline Lassiter, Program Director. (404) 894-5845. Established: July 1969.

No enforcement authority: carries out functions through mediation and education. Provides support for statewide WATS telephone counseling center; operates Field Services Unit which trains agencies; conducts research on consumer problems and remedies; produces and distributes educational materials to all interested parties and through the mass media. Recently received authority to act as consumer advocate before the Public Service Commission; with Augusta State College, produced "neighborhood" workshops. Maintains library of over 500 pamphlets, films, filmstrips, tapes, and cassettes on all consumer subjects. Pamphlets available free on request; all else distributed on a loan basis. Periodical: *Georgia Consumer News & Views* (monthly). Pamphlets: counseling and training manuals (free on request to residents; $5 and $2.50 to others). Other: *Buyer Beware* and *Spotlight: Product Safety and You* (weekly) columns free to news media. *Consumer Alerts*, as needed, free to news media.

CITY AGENCIES

Atlanta. Office of Consumer Affairs–City of Atlanta Community Relations Commission. City Hall Annex, 121 Memorial Dr., S.W., 30303. Muriel Mitchell Smith, Consumer Affairs Specialist. (404) 658-6310. Established: 1968.

Receives consumer complaints by telephone, mail, or in person. Investigates and negotiates for resolution; if mediation and arbitration do not work, refers complaints to appropriate agencies. Prepares consumer materials. Pamphlets: *Who to Call for Consumer Action in Atlanta; It's Your Court* (procedures for small claims court).

HAWAII

STATE AGENCIES

Office of Consumer Protection–Office of the Governor. Box 3767, Honolulu 96811. Walter T. Yamashiro, Director. (808) 548-2560. Established: July 8, 1969.

Enforces "Little FTC Act" prohibiting "unfair methods of competition and unfair or deceptive acts or practices"; mediates disputes between consumers and business; brings cases to court; refers complaints to proper offices. Recent successful activities: obtained injunction against owners of condominium unit; conducted hearings to determine how prescription drug costs can be reduced; held hearings to determine why cement prices increased 55 percent in six months. Pamphlets: *Consumer Protection Laws; The Free Gift.*

IDAHO

STATE AGENCIES

Consumer Protection Division–Office of the Attorney General. Statehouse, Boise 83720. W. Anthony Park, Attorney General. Wayne Meuleman, Deputy Attorney General. (208) 384-2400. established: March 12, 1971.

Enforces the Consumer Protection Act through investigation and resolution of complaints. Assurances of voluntary compliance and litigation are also used. Distributes consumer information. In March 1974, the attorney general's office joined the Cooperative Extension Service to provide consumer protection services (including consumer education) at the local level. Periodical: *Idaho Consumer News* (monthly newsletter; limited distribution).

ILLINOIS

STATE AGENCIES

Consumer Fraud and Protection Division–Office of the Attorney General. Northern division: 134 N. LaSalle St., Rm. 204, Chicago 60602. Howard R. Kaufman, Chief. (312) 793-3580. Southern division: 500 S. Second St., Springfield 62706. William J. Scott, Attorney General. George M. Schafer, Chief, Consumer Fraud and Protection Division. (217) 782-1090. Established: July 24, 1961.

Protects against fraud, unfair methods of competition, and unfair or deceptive acts or practices in the conduct of any trade or commerce; educates consumers through speeches, seminars, radio and TV appearances. Works by conciliation, informal and formal hearings, and court litigation. Has injunctive and subpoena powers. In the past five years, the office has saved consumers over $6,368,000. Pamphlets: *Retail Sales Installment Act; Consumer Fraud & Protection Act; Motor Vehicle Installment Act.*

Branch offices:
- 6 W. Downer Pl., *Aurora* 60507. (312) 892-3550.
- 50 Raupp Blvd., *Buffalo Grove* 60090. (312) 537-4260.
- 134 N. LaSalle St., Rm. 204, *Chicago (Loop)* 60602. (312) 793-3580.
- 4750 N. Broadway, Rm. 216, *Chicago (Northside)* 60640. (312) 769-3742.
- 1104 N. Ashland Ave., *Chicago (Northwest)* 60622. (312) 793-5638. (Spanish).
- 7906 S. Cottage Grove, *Chicago (Southside)* 60619. (312) 488-2600.
- 203 S. Cicero Ave., *Chicago (Westside)* 60644. (312) 379-1195.
- 800 Lee St., *Des Plaines* 60016. (312) 824-4200.
- State Attorney's Office, 150 Dexter Court, 2nd fl., *Elgin* 60120. (312) 584-3142.
- 901 Wellington St., *Elk Grove* 60007. (312) 439-3900.
- 71 N. Ottawa St., *Joliet* 60434. (815) 727-5391.
- 501 W. Lake St., *Maywood* 60153. (312) 344-7700.
- 6300 N. Lincoln Ave., *Morton Grove* 60053. (312) 967-4100.
- 231 S. Civic Dr., *Schaumburg* 60172. (312) 894-3141.
- 5127 Oakton, *Skokie* 60076. (312) 674-2522.
- 214 Madison St., *Waukegan* 60085. (312) 623-2470.

COUNTY AGENCIES

Cook County. Fraud and Consumer Complaint Division—State's Attorney's Office, 303 Chicago Civic Center, Chicago 60602. Ronald S. Samuels, Director. (312) 443-8425.
Established: 1952.

Handles complaints through informal legal hearings on nonviolent crime; mediates and prosecutes violations. Approximately 85 percent of cases have been closed and satisfied. Pamphlet: *Cheated?: A Guide on How to Protect Yourself Whenever You Buy* (available in Spanish).

CITY AGENCIES

Chicago. Department of Consumer Sales and Weights and Measures. City Hall, 121 N. LaSalle St., 60602. Jane Byrne, Commissioner. (312) 744-4092.

Park Forest. Consumer Protection Commission. 200 Forest Blvd., 60466. Norman M. Dublin, Chairman. (312) 748-1112.
Established: January 1973.

Provides mediation of consumer complaints by ombudsman. Conducts consumer studies; provides educational programs. Recently conducted studies of generic and brand-name drugs and of contracts and warranties.

INDIANA

STATE AGENCIES

Consumer Protection Division—Office of the Attorney General. 219 State House, Indianapolis 46204. Theodore L. Sendak, Attorney General. Roland D. Mather, Director, Consumer Protection Division. (317) 633-6276; 633-6496.
Established: September 3, 1971.

Under Public Law 367, receives, reviews, investigates, mediates, and resolves legitimate consumer complaints; acts as a clearing house for complaints, and refers problems to related agencies. Has power to seek court injunctions to prevent companies from engaging in deceptive practices. Pamphlet: *Consumer Protection in Indiana.* Toll-free telephone number: (800) 382-5516.

COUNTY AGENCIES

Lake County. Consumer Protection Division—Prosecutor's Office. Hammond Courthouse, 232 Russell St., Hammond 46320. Henry Kowalczyk, Prosecutor. Carol Tyler, Consumer Protection Assistant. (219) 886-3621.
Established: September 1, 1971.

Protects consumers against fraud and deception by receiving, investigating, and helping resolve consumer complaints of a possible criminal nature. Helps enforce consumer statutes, e.g., theft by deception, home solicitation sales, deceptive practices, false advertising. By November 1974 almost $60,000 had been returned to Lake County consumers in the form of refunds or contract cancellations. Pamphlets: *Don't Be Gypped; Consumer Education and Protection for Lake Co., Indiana; Avoid Excessive Interest Charges.* Maintains office in Gary: Courthouse, 15 W. Fourth St. (219) 886-3621.

CITY AGENCIES

Gary. Office of Consumer Affairs. 1100 Massachusetts Ave. 46407. Brian Nelson, Director. Rodney Pace, Assistant Director. (219) 886-3155.

Investigates consumer complaints involving fraud and deceptive practices; provides consumer information; undertakes consumer research studies.

IOWA

STATE AGENCIES

Consumer Protection Division—Iowa Department of Justice. 220 E. 13 Court, Des Moines 50319. Richard C. Turner, Attorney General. Julian B. Garrett, Assistant Attorney General. (515) 281-5926.
Established: July 1, 1965.

Through enforcement powers under Iowa Consumer Fraud Act and Iowa Subdivided Land Sales Act, protects consumers against deception and misrepresentation of goods or services. The Iowa Consumer Credit Code helps those with interest rate or debt collection problems; Iowa Subdivided Land Sales Act protects against unscrupulous land developers of out-of-state land. Also upholds three-day cooling-off law dealing with door-to-door sales. Between January and April 1974, received 2,124 complaints, closed 1,619, recovered $612,869 for consumers. Pamphlets: *Iowa Consumer Fraud Act; Iowa Subdivided Land Sales*

Act; Consumer Protection at the State Level (study). Provides the media with news releases dealing with litigation cases or public warnings.

KANSAS

STATE AGENCIES

Consumer Protection Division–Office of the Attorney General. State Capitol, Topeka 66612. Vern Miller, Attorney General. Lance W. Burr, Chief, Consumer Protection Division. (913) 296-3751.
Established: 1973.

Protects buyers from fraud and deception under Kansas Buyer's Protection Act and the 1973 Kansas Consumer Protection Act (K.S.A. Supp. 50-623, *et sq.*). Enforcement is through investigation and prosecution. Also provides some consumer education. Recent successful activities: 1973 investigations and other legal actions netted Kansas consumers $283,620; the office also processed 4,129 complaints and closed 3,934. Periodical: *Kansas Consumer Advocate* (bimonthly).

COUNTY AGENCIES

Johnson County. Consumer Protection Division–District Attorney's Office. Box 728, Olathe 66061. William P. Coates, Jr., Assistant District Attorney. (913) 782-5000, ext. 318.
Established: January 1973.

Operating under the Kansas Consumer Protection Act, has both civil and criminal jurisdiction over consumer frauds, e.g., misleading advertising, bait and switch, door-to-door sales contracts which omit three-day cancellation clause, referral sales, phony appliance or car repairs, home improvement frauds, business opportunity investment frauds, and "low-balling" techniques. The office has subpoena power. Resolves complaints through arbitration or court actions. Recently prepared programs for Overland Park CableVision and WHB on consumers' rights. Maintains regular speaking engagements. Periodical: *Consumers, Every One* (monthly newsletter).

Sedgwick County. Consumer Protection Division–District Attorney's Office. 525 N. Main, Wichita 67203. Jack N. Williams, Director. (316) 268-7405.

Operating under powers derived from the Kansas Consumer Protection Act and related state civil and criminal statutes, handles complaints, initiates actions on fraudulent businesses, and proposes new legislation. Initiated proposal for nationwide disclosure in selling flood-damaged cars. Investigated phony business opportunity advertisements in county newspapers. Prepared two-minute TV program, "Consumer Scene," presented on Sunday Evening News–KAKE-TV. Publishes excellent pamphlets. Periodical: *The Consumer Protection Newsletter* (monthly). Pamphlets: *Help Yourself! A Handbook on Consumer Fraud; Help Yourself Mr. Businessman!*

CITY AGENCIES

Topeka. Consumer Protection Division–City Attorney's Office. 215 E. Seventh St., 66603. Douglas S. Wright, Assistant City Attorney. (913) 235-9261, ext. 205.
Established: July 1973.

Receives complaints and files suits for violations of the Topeka Consumer Protection Ordinance. Checks all weighing and measuring devices and enforces Weights and Measures Ordinance. Legal action is both civil and criminal and includes restitution for consumers, restraining orders against use of deceptive practices, civil penalties, and suits for misdemeanors. Provides information to citizens on consumer related problems. By July 1974, the office had over $8,000 returned to consumers. Pamphlet: *Some Facts You've Always Wanted to Know about Door-to-Door Peddlers, Canvassers and Solicitors in Topeka but Didn't Know Who to Ask.*

KENTUCKY

STATE AGENCIES

Division of Consumer Protection—Office of the Attorney General. Rm. 34 State Capitol, Frankfort 40601. Ed W. Hancock, Attorney General. Robert V. Bullock, Assistant Attorney General. (502) 564-6607.
Established: June 16, 1972.

Enforces the Kentucky Consumer Protection Act through coordination of all Kentucky consumer protection activities; provides consumer education programs, and works as a clearinghouse for consumer information in the state; promotes new consumer legislation; intervenes in rate-making cases in behalf of consumer interests. Pamphlet: *Kentucky's Consumer Protection Laws.* Film: *The Bad Apple* (free loan). Toll free telephone number: 1-(800) 372-2960.

COUNTY AGENCIES

Jefferson County. Consumer Protection Department. 401 Old Louisville Trust Bldg., 208 S. Fifth St., Louisville 40202. David R. Vandeventer, Director. (502) 581-6280.
Established: January 1974.

Mediates complaints and refers unresolved complaints to the Consumer Court; provides consumer information pamphlets; issues periodic news releases to local media; drafts and enforces consumer protection regulations. The department has not yet produced its own educational materials.

CITY AGENCIES

Louisville. Office of Consumer Affairs. 400 S. Sixth St., 40202. Minx M. Auerbach, Director. (502) 582-2206.
Established: July 1, 1974.

Mediates complaints, enforces existing city ordinances through the Police Department. Set up Neighborhood Consumer Councils for mediation and education. Also provides speakers, flyers, press releases for educating consumers. Working toward getting own powers of enforcement. Pamphlet: *Are You a Foxy Consumer?* (flyer).

LOUISIANA

STATE AGENCIES

Consumer Protection and Commercial Fraud Prosecution Unit—Department of Justice. 234 Loyola Bldg., 7th fl., New Orleans 70112. William J. Guste,

Jr., Attorney General. Peter Everett IV, State Director. (504) 529-1636. Established: July 1972.

Investigates and prosecutes unfair and deceptive acts or practices which violate the Louisiana Unfair Trade Practices and Consumer Protection Law, Act 759 (R.S. 51:1401-1418). Also enforces numerous additional consumer-oriented statutes, e.g., Louisiana Anti-Trust Act, Odometer Act, Rent Deposit Return Act, etc. Has subpoena power. Can institute court actions: restraining orders, injunctions, and judgments (including monetary restitution). Recently obtained injunction and restitution against vending machine distributor; also against firms and individuals engaged in fraudulent practices in home improvement, land development, auto repairs, swimming pool construction, referral sales, etc.

Branch offices:

Mid-Louisiana region. 1885 Wooddale Blvd., Suite 1208, *Baton Rouge* 70806. (504) 389-7228.

Northern region. 106 Henry Beck Bldg., *Shreveport* 71101. (301) 425-7493.

Southern region (same address as main office).

Governor's Office of Consumer Protection. Box 44091, Capitol Sta., Baton Rouge 70804. Charles W. Tapp, Director. (504) 389-7483. Established: 1972.

Enforces the Unfair Trade Practices and Consumer Protection Law, Act 759 (R.S. 51:1401–1418) by handling complaints through mediation and investigations. Provides a clearinghouse for information and materials; prepares and disseminates consumer information, e.g., weekly column sent to all newspapers in the state, and takes part in speaking engagements and consumer workshops. Pamphlets: *Crib Safety; Tenant's Rights; Buyers' and Owners' Guide to Mobile Homes; Right-of-Way to Car Care;* etc. Book: *Directory for Consumers* ($3.50). Audiovideo tape: *Know Your Auto: An Inside Look at Your Car.* Toll-free telephone number: (800) 272-9868.

COUNTY AGENCIES

East Baton Rouge Parish. Consumer Protection Center. 1779 Government St., Baton Rouge 70802. Roberta Madden, Director. (504) 344-8506. Established: July 1, 1972.

Handles complaints through investigation and mediation; conducts pricing research (using volunteers); provides educational program in schools and churches, to civic groups, and through the media; testifies for the consumer interest before various boards, commissions, and legislative bodies. Recently helped organize three local consumer groups and two outside the county; held a successful 12-state conference for low-income consumers. Produced 50 five-minute, reel-to-reel recordings on consumer topics (for use in the center's educational programs). The director serves on the Product Safety Advisory Council, U.S. Consumer Product Safety Commission. Periodical: *Lemon Aid* (monthly newsletter). Pamphlets: *Comparative Grocery Price Survey; Clue to Solving Consumer Problems; Don't Be Ripped Off, Be Tipped Off* (a consumer bibliography for teachers).

Jefferson Parish. Consumer Protection and Commercial Frauds Division—District Attorney's Office, Courthouse Annex, Gretna 70053. Ernest E. Barrow II, Director. (504) 367-6611, ext. 441.

CITY AGENCIES

New Orleans. Office of Consumer Affairs. 1W-12 City Hall, 1300 Perdido St., 70112. Nell Weekley, Director. (504) 586-4441.
Established: March 8, 1972.

Mediates complaints; acts as consumer advocate before regulatory bodies and legislature; provides information and educative service through media campaigns, public service announcements, newspaper articles, speaking engagements; conducts research in cooperation with local colleges and universities. Held Preventive Auto Maintenance Clinics; produced film on preventive auto maintenance (for rent and sale); six public service announcements (also for sale). Periodical: *Consumergrams* (issued irregularly). Pamphlets: *Preventive Auto Maintenance Pamphlet; Shopping for Food* (including October 1973 New Orleans Grocery Price Survey).

MAINE

STATE AGENCIES

Consumer Fraud Division—Office of the Attorney General. State House, Augusta 04330. Jon A. Lund, Attorney General. John E. Quinn, Assistant Attorney General. (207) 289-3716.
Established: 1970.

Enforces Maine Unfair Trade Practices Act and other consumer related legislation through investigation (including voluntary compliance and litigation). Recently issued court decrees halting unfair trade practices which resulted in restitution of funds to consumers. Provides no educational materials.

MARYLAND

STATE AGENCIES

Consumer Protection Division—Office of the Attorney General. 1 S. Calvert St., Baltimore 21202. Francis B. Burch, Attorney General. John N. Ruth, Jr., Assistant Attorney General and Chief, Consumer Protection Division. (302) 383-3700.
Established: June 1, 1967.

Protects against all forms of deceptive trade practices ("Little FTC Act"—Alternative #2) through investigations of complaints, ordering of cease and desist agreements, seeking of court injunctions, helping to provide restitution. Also educates consumer through news releases, pamphlets, speakers programs. Prepared award-winning 80-topic radio program, "Buyer Be Aware," in cooperation with WBAL, Baltimore, in 1968, that is still distributed and available to other states. Pamphlet: *Don't Get Ripped Off: The Attorney General's Crook Book.*

Branch office: 5112 Berwin Rd., *College Park* 20740. (301) 474-3500. Also maintains monthly scheduled trips to the following seven offices in the state: Concentrated Employment Program, 100 W. 23 St., *Baltimore;* 2nd fl, City Hall, *Cumberland;* 1st fl. Court House, *Easton;* JAG Office, *Fort Meade;* 2nd fl. Court House, *Hagerstown;* 2nd fl. Court House, *Salisbury;* Social Security Administration, *Woodlawn.*

COUNTY AGENCIES

Ann Arundel County. Board of Consumer Affairs. 403 Arundel Center, Annapolis 21404. Collen Bell, Administrator. (301) 268-4300, ext. 346.

Baltimore County. Consumer Fraud Division—State Attorney's Office. 204 County Courthouse, Baltimore 21202. Gerald Glass, Chief.

Montgomery County. Office of Consumer Affairs. 24 S. Perry St., Rm. 200, Rockville 20850. Barbara B. Gregg, Executive Director. (301) 340-1010. Established: December 1971.

Investigates and mediates individual complaints; conducts in-depth investigations when patterns of fraud appear. Issues subpoenas, fines ($500 per violation), and court orders enjoining businesses from engaging in deceptive or unconscionable trade practices. Cooperates with area businesses to promote good consumer-business relations; educates consumers by disseminating publications, holding speaking engagements, and public hearings. The office speaks for consumers before various agencies and legislative bodies and drafts and supports corrective consumer legislation. It has closed thousands of complaints since January 1972—most resolved in favor of consumers with thousands of dollars of credits and refunds obtained. Pamphlets: *Consumer Tips* (series of nine flyers); *Consumer Bibliography* (of Montgomery County Public Libraries); *Your Day in Court.*

Prince George's County. Consumer Protection Commission. County Courthouse, Upper Marlboro 20870. Polly W. Craghill, Executive Director. (301) 627-3000, ext. 561.
Established: February 1, 1970.

County ordinance empowers the commission to investigate complaints, initiate own investigations, hold hearings, issue subpoenas and cease and desist orders, order restitution of monies and/or property, initiate criminal or equitable court proceedings, revoke licenses. Uses volunteer investigators plus regular staff. Drafts corrective legislation. Between 75 percent and 80 percent of all cases are settled amicably. Carries out a program of information and education. Produces "Get Smart," weekly releases for county newspapers. Pamphlet: *Your Voice in the Marketplace.*

MASSACHUSETTS

STATE AGENCIES

Consumer Protection Division—Department of the Attorney General. 167 State House, Boston 02133. Robert H. Quinn, Attorney General. Herbert Goodwin, Assistant Attorney General and Chief, Consumer Protection Division. (617) 727-8400.
Established: 1968 (Consumer Protection Division).

The only state agency empowered to take legal action on behalf of Massachusetts consumers. Under the Consumer Protection Act, Chapter 93A, the attorney general enforces legal actions against "unfair business practices." Also develops consumer protection legislation and prepares consumer information materials. More than 20,000 consumer complaints are handled each year; over $800,000 saved. Recent actions included suits against supermarkets for violations of unit pricing laws; landlord-tenant cases, violations of mobile home law, swimming pool frauds, etc. Periodicals: *News Briefs* (bimonthly); *Consumer News* (weekly column). Pamphlets: *Consumer Protection Act; Consumer Fraud Is Not a Dirty Trick: It's Against the Law; What to Do Now* (for widows and widowers); *Consumer Information Leaflets* (eight flyers on consumer protection laws in Massachusetts). Nine regional offices: Fall River, Framingham, Hyannis, Lawrence, New Bedford, Pittsfield, Roxbury, Springfield, and Worcester.

Consumers' Council. 100 Cambridge St., Boston 02202. Paul Gitlin, Executive Secretary. (617) 727-2605.
Established: 1964.

Part of the Executive Department of the Commonwealth of Massachusetts, the council acts as consumer advocate, provides educational materials, coordinates consumer services, proposes consumer legislation, and prepares consumer studies. Periodicals: *Consumers' Council News* (issued irregularly).

Executive Office of Consumer Affairs. 100 Cambridge St., Rm. 905, Boston 02202. John R. Verani, Secretary of Consumer Affairs. Margot P. Kosberg, Director, Consumer Complaint Division. (617) 727-7755; 727-8000.

The office has no legal enforcement powers, and resolves complaints primarily by the fact that it is a state agency. Investigates frauds; maintains data processing complaint system; produces pamphlets on energy consumption. Promoted voluntary appliance labeling program. Pamphlets: *How You Can Conserve Energy in the Long Run; How You Can Save Energy This Winter; What to Do in an Energy Emergency; A Guide to Efficient Home Cooling.*

COUNTY AGENCIES

Franklin and Hampshire counties. Consumer Protection Agency–District Attorney's Office. Courthouse, North Hampton 01060. Joan Weston, Director. (413) 586-0992.

CITY AGENCIES

Boston. Consumer's Council. 721 City Hall, 02201. Richard A. Borten, Executive Director. (617) 722-4100, ext. 236.
Established: November 1968.

Investigates and resolves disputes with help of 11 investigators, trained as paralegal professionals in 36-hour course. They work in 14 "Little City Halls" throughout the city and are backed up by an attorney. Cases requiring court action can be referred to state enforcement agencies. Also conducts research on matters of consumer interest and provides consumer education programs. During the 1973–1974 energy crisis, assisted 500 families in finding heating oil to meet their needs. Also conducted home heating oil price and availability study. Issued 140-page two-year study of cable television, recommending that at present cable TV not be developed for the city.

Fitchburg. Consumer Protection Service. 455 Main St., 01420. Claudette Howe. (617) 345-1946.

Lowell. Consumer Advisory Council. City Hall, 01852. Owen F. Matthews, Administrative Assistant. (617) 454-8821.

MICHIGAN

STATE AGENCIES

Consumer Protection and Antitrust Division—Office of the Attorney General. Law Bldg., Lansing 48902. Frank J. Kelley, Attorney General. Edwin M. Bladen, Assistant Attorney General in Charge, Consumer Protection and Antitrust Division. (517) 373-1152.

Enforces "Little FTC Act" (Alternative # 3) which prohibits a variety of deceptive trade practices. Handles consumer complaints by investigation and prosecution. Has power to initiate civil law suits. Provides consumer education; proposes new consumer legislation. Periodical: *Consumer Fraud Newsletter* (monthly). Toll-free telephone number: 1-(800) 292-2431.

Consumers Council. 414 Hollister Bldg., Lansing 48933. Polly Gibson, Chairperson. James Hunsucker, Acting Director. (517) 373-0947. Established: 1966.

Handles consumer complaints by mediation; provides information and education through publication of bulletins, newsletter, press releases, media appearances, and public speaking engagements; proposes legislation on consumer bills and testifies before legislative hearings; investigates and reports on long- and short-term consumer research projects. Recent successful activities: worked for passage of legislation to prohibit sex and marital status discrimination in granting credit to women, to lift ban on prohibition of substitution of generically equivalent prescription drugs, to provide new franchise regulations, etc. Periodicals: *Consumer News & Views* (bimonthly); annual report; *Summary of Michigan Consumer Protection Legislation* (2nd ed. 1974); educational bulletins (issued irregularly). Pamphlets: *How to Sue Someone in Small Claims Court; You Can Stand Up to Unfair Business; Guide for Installment Buying.*

COUNTY AGENCIES

Bay County. Consumer Protection Unit. Prosecutor's Office. County Bldg., Bay City 48706. Paul N. Doner, Assistant Prosecutor. (517) 893-3594. Established: May 1, 1973.

Receives, investigates, mediates, and/or prosecutes consumer complaints within the county. Does not produce any educational materials.

Genesee County. Consumer Fraud Unit—Attorney's Office. 105 Courthouse, Flint 48502. Paul G. Miller, Jr., Chief. (313) 766-8890.

Jackson County. Prosecuting Attorney's Office. 464 County Bldg., Jackson 49201. David L. Bresler, Assistant Prosecuting Attorney. (517) 787-3800.

Washtenaw County. Consumer Action Center—200 County Bldg., Ann Arbor 48108. John P. Knapp, Director. (313) 665-4451.
Established: January 1972.

Funded by Law Enforcement Assistance Administration for 1972–1973 and 1974–1975. Mediates noncriminal complaints, prosecutes consumer fraud cases, prepares information on consumer matters, and educates consumers for self-protection. Recently participated in toy safety project and a volunteer training program. The organization evolved from an all-volunteer student-founded group to a division of county government. Since 1973 processed 867 complaints to completion, answered 5,000 inquiries, saved $60,000 for consumers. Pamphlets: *Consumer Protection: A Handy Consumer Reference; The Small Claims Court in Washtenaw County; Pocket Guide to Choosing a Vocational School; Free and Inexpensive Consumer Publications; Fair Credit Reporting: A Checklist for Consumers,* etc.

MINNESOTA

STATE AGENCIES

Consumer Protection Division—Office of the Attorney General. 102 State Capitol Bldg., St. Paul 55155. Warren Spannaus, Attorney General. William H. Kuretsky, Special Assistant Attorney General. (612) 296-3353.

Enforces Minnesota consumer protection statutes by formal court proceedings and assurances of voluntary discontinuance. Recently placed permanent injunction against a bulk meat dealer involved in bait and switch tactics. The office does not publish educational materials.

Office of Consumer Services. 5th fl. Metro Square Bldg. St. Paul 55101. Sherry Chenoweth, Director. (612) 296-4517.
Established: 1971.

Enforces consumer laws in cooperation with the attorney general's office in areas involving consumer fraud, toy safety, collection agencies, and octane rating postings. Also conducts research, proposes legislation, provides public information, and handles complaints. In summer 1974 the office engaged in a study of unit pricing and open dating. Pamphlets: (being prepared for distribution in 1975).

COUNTY AGENCIES

Hennepin County. Citizen Protection Division—Attorney's Office. 248 Court House, Minneapolis 55415. Floyd B. Olson, Chief. (612) 348-4528.
Established: December 1973.

Mediates disputes and enforces the state consumer laws in the civil area. The office is also responsible for prosecution of criminal violations. Has power to seek injunctions. Carries on educational programs. Pamphlet: *Fraud—The Target Is You.*

CITY AGENCIES

Minneapolis. Consumer Affairs Division—Department of Inspections. City Hall, 55415. John G. Gustafson, Director. (612) 348-2080.

St. Paul. Office of Consumer Affairs. 179 City Hall, Saint Paul 55102. Robert W. Mattson, Director. (612) 298-4567.
Established: January 1973.

Receives and mediates individual consumer complaints. Has power to subpoena witnesses and documents for formal hearings. The office initiates special investigations of problem areas. Has authority to levy civil fines of $300 per violation of ordinance. Drafts and supports consumer protection ordinances in the City Council. Introduced "raincheck" and home repair ordinances; investigated warranty on Chevrolet Vega resulting in warranty extension and refunds. The office is planning to have staff members specialize in different areas of consumer concerns. Pamphlets: Tips for the Cautious Consumer Series, e.g., *Buying a Car, Bulk Meat Buying, At the Grocery, Money for Rent; Consumer Tips for the Young Adult; Consumer Tips for the Senior Citizen.*

MISSISSIPPI

STATE AGENCIES

Consumer Protection Division—Department of Justice. Justice Bldg., Jackson 39205. A. F. Summer, Attorney General. Marshall G. Bennett, Assistant Attorney General and Chief, Consumer Protection Division.
(601) 354-7130.
Established: July 1, 1974.

Protects public from unfair and deceptive trade practices; provides public education programs. Files injunctions to stop unfair practices and refers other actions to appropriate agencies. Although the division was established in 1974, the legislature did not fund it, and consequently, the division operates under some limitations. It does not provide any educational materials at this time.

MISSOURI

STATE AGENCIES

Consumer Protection Division—Office of the Attorney General. Box 899, Jefferson City 65101. John C. Danforth, Attorney General. Harvey M. Tettlebaum, Assistant Attorney General and Chief Counsel, Consumer Protection Division. (314) 751-3321.
Established: 1967.

Prevents and enjoins fraudulent activities in connection with sales of merchandise to consumers. Recent successful activities include injunctions against National Food Stores and Ohio Merchandising Corp. Provides no educational materials.

Branch offices: 431 State Office Bldg., 615 E. 13 St., *Kansas City* 64106. (816) 274-6686; 705 Olive St., Suite 1323, *St. Louis* 63101. (314) 241-4760.

Consumer Services—Division of Insurance. 515 E. High St., Jefferson City 65101. Edward G. Farmer, Jr., Director. Ron Schollmeyer, Supervisor, Consumer Services. (314) 751-4126.

Investigates and mediates complaints involving insurance claims and policyholder service. Provides consumer extension programs in various cities on policyholder information. A consumers' guide is currently being completed and scheduled for distribution in 1975.

Branch offices: 615 E. 13 St., *Kansas City* 64106; 225 S. Meramec, *St. Louis* 63105.

COUNTY AGENCIES

Green County. Prosecuting Attorney's Office. 206 County Court House, Springfield 65802. Clyde P. Angle, Attorney in Charge. (417) 869-3581.

CITY AGENCIES

Kansas City. Office of Consumer Affairs. 11th fl. City Hall 64106. Robert L. Feder, Director. (816) 274-1638.
Established: November 1971.

Enforces Kansas City consumer protection ordinance pertaining to misrepresentation and unlawful practices in consumer transactions. Investigates and mediates complaints. Develops consumer education pamphlets, brochures, etc. for students and teachers. In affiliation with the University of Missouri at Kansas City held home improvement classes taught by community volunteers. In cooperation with the Kansas City chapter of the National Home Improvement Council the office created the 1974 HOMEE Project on prime time television: a competition between area home improvement contractors in eight categories of remodeling, to share buying information and remodeling ideas with consumers. During 1974 the office's Prosecution and Litigation Panel also resolved problems in the employment agency industry. Pamphlet: *Remodeling or Improving Your Home?: Ten Tips from the Office of Consumer Affairs.*

MONTANA

STATE AGENCIES

Consumer Affairs Division—Department of Business Regulation. 805 N. Main St., Helena 59601. Dick M. Disney, Administrator. (406) 449-3163.
Established: July 1, 1973.

Enforces the Montana Unfair Trade Practices and Consumer Protection Act (1973) through investigation and mediation of complaints and issuance of injunctions and subpoenas. Between July 1973 and June 1974, the division handled 536 cases, closed 422, and recovered $37,364. It does not prepare or disseminate consumer educational materials.

COUNTY AGENCIES

Lewis and Clark County. Consumer Protection Division—Attorney's Office. Court House, Helena 59601. Thomas E. Kirwin, Director. (406) 442-4550.

Silver Bow County. Consumer Protection Division—Attorney's Office. Butte 59701. Robert J. Harper, Director. (406) 792-2383.
Established: March 1973.

Protects consumers against unfair trade practices under the provisions of the Montana Unfair Trade Practices and Consumer Protection Act of 1973; assists consumers in the marketplace; sponsors and endorses corrective legislation.

NEBRASKA

STATE AGENCIES

Consumer Protection and Antitrust Division—Office of the Attorney General. State Capitol, Lincoln 68509. Clarence A. J. Meyer, Attorney General. Calvin E. Robinson, Assistant Attorney General, Consumer Protection Division. (402) 471-2211.

Does not enforce a general consumer protection law; refers complaints and inquiries to appropriate agencies. Provides no consumer education.

COUNTY AGENCIES

Douglas County. Consumer Fraud Division—Attorney's Office. 312 Service Life Bldg., Omaha 68102. Arthur S. Raznick, Director. (402) 444-7625. Established: March 1, 1973.

Investigates, mediates, and conciliates consumer complaints; prosecutes violations; drafts legislation; and provides educational services to the consumers of Douglas County. Does not publish materials.

NEVADA

STATE AGENCIES

Consumer Affairs Division—Department of Commerce. 219 Collett Bldg., 1111 Las Vegas Blvd. S., Las Vegas 89104. Rex Lundberg, Commissioner. (702) 385-0344.
Established: July 1, 1973.

The primary office for mediation and investigation of consumer complaints, the division investigates deceptive trade practices and false advertising, attends public hearings to present the consumer viewpoint, and provides consumer education. The office is a liaison with federal agencies and as such conducted a safe toy program in the state. About 70 percent of all complaints are resolved for consumers with refunds of monies and/or exchanges of faulty services and materials. Does not currently publish educational materials. Toll-free telephone number: 1-(800) 992-0900.

Branch office: 325 Nye Bldg., 201 S. Fall St., *Carson City* 89701. (702) 882-7874.

Consumer Protection Division—Office of the Attorney General. Supreme Court Bldg., Carson City 89701. Robert List, Attorney General. Elliott A. Sattler, Deputy Attorney General for Consumer Affairs. (702) 885-4170. Established: January 1971.

Enforces Nevada Revised Statutes on behalf of the state and the Consumer Affairs Division of the Nevada Department of Commerce. Recently obtained trial court verdicts and consent decrees concerning false advertising, unfair and deceptive trade practices, and pyramid selling.

COUNTY AGENCIES

Clark County. District Attorney's Office. County Court House, Las Vegas 98101. Jeffrey A. Silver, Deputy. (702) 386-4011.

Washoe County. Consumer Fraud Unit—District Attorney's Office. Box 34, Reno 89504. Peter Holden. (702) 785-4253.
Established: June 1972.

Processes complaints involving business transactions in Washoe County; refers violations to deputy district attorney for court action; drafts new legislation for consumer protection. Pamphlet: *What You Should Do . . . To Avoid Being Cheated, When You Have Been Cheated.*

NEW HAMPSHIRE

STATE AGENCIES

Consumer Protection Division—Office of the Attorney General. Statehouse Annex, Concord 03301. Warren B. Rudman, Attorney General. Richard V. Wiebusch, Chief, Consumer Protection.
Established: 1970.

Enforces New Hampshire's "Little FTC Act" prohibiting various deceptive practices. Investigates, negotiates, and litigates cases; proposes consumer legislation; and provides some education for citizens of the state. Does not publish any consumer materials.

NEW JERSEY

STATE AGENCIES

Division of Consumer Affairs—Department of Law and Public Safety. 1100 Raymond Blvd., Rm. 504, Newark 07102. Douglas J. Harper, Acting Director. (201) 648-3537.
Established: May 6, 1971.

One of the strongest consumer protection departments in the country, it promulgates rules and regulations necessary to protect consumer interests (by fall 1974 ten such laws had been promulgated, e.g., Deceptive Mail Order Practices, Motor Vehicle Advertising Practices. Investigates and enforces the Consumer Fraud Act (N.J.S.A. 56:8-1-20) and specific state statutes governing the Office of Weights and Measures, the Bureau of Securities, the Legalized Games of Chance Control Commission, and the Charitable Registration Section. Mediates many complaints; provides educational programs; coordinates work of division with other agencies. Provides Consumer Affairs Local Assistance (CALA) programs (*see* listing, below). Pamphlets: *The Consumer Fraud Act; To Buy or Not to Buy; When Buying a House; Be Sure Before You Sign!; Speak Up! When You Buy a Car; The New Jersey State Division of Consumer Affairs Is Ready to Protect You Against Fraud and Unconscionable Business Practices,* etc.

Federal, State and Local Programs—Division of Consumer Affairs. 1100 Raymond Blvd., Newark 07102. Ruth S. Ballou, Coordinator. (201) 648-3537.

Established the Consumer Affairs Local Assistance (CALA) Officer Program in 95 municipalities and six counties in the state which extends services at minimal cost. Most officers are volunteers, appointed by respective municipalities and counties. Refers complaints needing legal action to the division.

COUNTY AGENCIES

Atlantic County. Office of Consumer Affairs. 25 Dolphin Ave. and Shore Rd., Northfield 08232. H. Frank Fife, Director. (609) 646-6626.

Burlington County. Office of Consumer Affairs. 54 Grant St., Mount Holly 08060. James McGivney, Director. (609) 267-3300, ext. 259, 364.
Established: October 10, 1972.

Investigates consumer complaints under the powers of the New Jersey Consumer Fraud Act. Mediates, negotiates, and/or arbitrates with business community. Schedules and implements administrative hearings for violators. Initiates class actions. A 1,000-member volunteer corps compiles data. The office drafts new legislation. Successfully closed 98 percent of the almost 2,000 complaints filed. Started a weekly two-way radio program, conducted by Freeholder Catherine Costa on WJJZ. Held federal trade hearings on swimming pools. Provides sales tax information for contractors, floor covering dealers, etc.

Camden County. Office of Consumer Affairs. 606 Commerce Bldg., 1 Broadway, Camden 08103. Barbara P. Berman, Director. (609) 964-8700, ext. 277.
Established: October 1970.

The office has no judicial powers; it investigates and settles complaints, referring those requiring judicial action to the New Jersey Office of Consumer Protection, private attorneys, or Small Claims Court. Provides educational material to consumers; recommends legislation for consumer protection. Recently exposed fraudulent discount on dinner plan; provided educational program for consumer purchasing new homes, took part in a swimming pool investigation for the Federal Trade Commission. Pamphlets: *Wise Up! Know Your Camden County Office of Consumer Affairs; Make Your Meat Dollar Go Further; 10 Helpful Hints Offered Complaining Consumers; Be a Cautious Consumer* (consumer education series).

Cumberland County. Office of Weights and Measures and Consumer Protection. 800 E. Commerce St., Bridgeton 08302. George S. Franks, Superintendent. William L. Watson, Assistant Superintendent. (609) 451-8000, ext. 296.
Established: November 1972.

Investigates, evaluates, and mediates disputes. Makes referrals to local office of the CALA coordinator (*see New Jersey State Agencies*—Federal, State and Local Programs—Division of Consumer Affairs). Recently organized electronic repair service people to provide self-policing. Currently organizing the county's automobile dealers. As part of educational program, disseminates federal and state materials, many of them in Spanish, and will be buying films for programs in 1975.

Ocean County. Consumer Affairs Department. 129 Hooper Ave., Toms River 08753. Hazel S. Gluck, Supervisor. (201) 244-2121, ext. 424. Mailing address: Box 191, Toms River 08753.
Established: December 1973.

Empowered by the New Jersey Division of Consumer Affairs and laws of the state to investigate and mediate complaints between consumers and the business community. Provides educational and informational material from federal and state levels and produces own materials. Answers consumer questions regarding consumer laws. Recently put up an information booth at the county fair and conducted a consumer survey; published handbook on the department; planning to publish handbook for senior citizens. Public information column "Consumer Be Aware" prepared and sent to news media in county periodically. Pamphlet: *Ocean County Department of Consumer Affairs Handbook.*

CITY AGENCIES

See New Jersey State Agencies—**Federal, State and Local Programs—Division of Consumer Affairs.**

NEW MEXICO

STATE AGENCIES

Consumer Protection Division—Office of the Attorney General. Box 2246, Santa Fe, 87501. David Norvell, Attorney General. Charmaine Crown, Director. (505) 827-5237.
Established: 1967.

Enforces Unfair Trade Practices Act. Adjudicates consumer complaints; takes legal action on behalf of consumers. Has power to issue injunctions and levy civil penalties up to $5,000 per violation; has subpoena powers. Provides consumer education: seminars, lectures, speeches, and materials. From July 1971 to July 1973 received 3,034 complaints, resolved 2,189, recovered $163,328. Recently prepared and disseminated land subdivision questionnaire following 1973 land subdivision law. Periodical: *Consumer Protection* (monthly).

COUNTY AGENCIES

Bernalillo County. Consumer Protection Division—Office of the District Attorney. Rm. 215 County Courthouse, Albuquerque 87101. Viola Pena, Director. (505) 766-4341.
Established: January 1973.

Handles written consumer complaints through mediation, informal hearings, or referral to Small Claims or Magistrate's Court or appropriate agencies. In the first year of operation, almost $65,000 returned to consumers and over $18,000 in fraudulent or misleading contracts canceled. The director of the New Mexico Consumer Protection Division is available for counseling and guidance one day a week. In addition, trial and administrative attorneys regularly assist the division.

NEW YORK

STATE AGENCIES

Bureau of Consumer Frauds and Protection—Department of Law. Louis J. Lefkowitz, Attorney General. Barnett Levy, Assistant Attorney General. 2 World Trade Center, New York 10047. (212) 488-7450. Frank Pantalone, Assistant Attorney General. The Capitol, Albany 12224. (518) 474-5481. Established: October 1, 1957.

Enforces 14 state consumer protection laws covering all forms of deceptive trade practices (e.g., tenant security deposits, unordered merchandise, unsolicited credit cards, garnishees). Prepares legislation, mediates complaints, promotes education, acts as clearing house for industry and government. In 1973 prepared new program, "Educating the Educators"; established program of compliance reports on all court judgments and assurances of discontinuance; closed over 33,000 complaints resulting in the restitution of $2,465,390 to the public. Periodical: *Consumer Action* (quarterly). Pamphlets: *ABC's of Careful Buying; A Guide for Today's Consumer;* Be a Cautious Consumer (series), etc. Film: *The Fine Art of Fraud* (free loan).

Branch offices:

403 Metcalf Bldg., *Auburn.* (315) 253-9765.
44 Hawley St., *Binghamton.* (607) 773-7826.
65 Court St., *Buffalo.* (716) 842-4393.
48 Cornelia St., *Plattsburgh.* (518) JO1-1980.
2 Catherine St., *Poughkeepsie.* (914) 452-7760.
65 Broad St., *Rochester.* (716) 454-4540.
333 E. Washington St., *Syracuse.* (315) 473-8433.
207 Genesee St., *Utica.* (315) 797-6120, ext. 234.
317 Washington St., *Watertown.* (315) 782-0100.

Consumer Protection Board—Executive Department. 99 Washington Ave., Albany 12210. Peter M. Pryor, Chairman and Executive Director. (518) 474-8583. Established: 1970.

Refers consumer complaints and resolves about 700 per month. Uses complaints as basis for investigations and research for legislation and testimony at hearings. Drafts and lobbies for consumer legislation; is state liaison with U.S. Consumer Product Safety Commission; provides monthly newsletter, pamphlets, media announcements, state fair exhibits, speakers. Recently participated in Hazardous Toy Survey with C.P.S.C.; provided refunds to consumers of $30,000 between January and July 1974. In 1974 received authority to intervene in the public's behalf before the Public Service Commission in utility rate cases. Periodicals: *New York State Consumer* (monthly); Annual Report; Legislative Summary. Pamphlets: *Consumer Action; Dollars and $ense in the Energy Crisis; How to Complain; Who Is Available to Help; Buying on Time;* etc.

Branch office: New York State Office Bldg., 270 Broadway, *New York* 10017. (212) 488-5320.

COUNTY AGENCIES

Erie County. Consumer Fraud Bureau—District Attorney's Office. 25 Delaware Ave., Buffalo 14202. Franklin A. Stachowiak, Chief. (716) 852-6424.

Kings County. Consumer Frauds and Economic Crimes Bureau—District Attorney's Office. Municipal Bldg., 210 Joralemon St., Brooklyn 11201. Eugene Gold, District Attorney. Stephen R. Taub, Assistant District Attorney in Charge. (212) 643-5100.
Established: September 1, 1973.

Protects consumers through enforcement of the criminal statutes of the state and city. Investigates and initiates criminal proceedings. Also mediates and attempts to settle disputes in noncriminal transactions. Recently indicted 15 home improvement contractors on charges of larceny and other frauds in selling and performance practices and credit arrangements. Also seized over 8,000 deceptively labeled wristwatches. Pamphlets: *Be an Educated Consumer—Outsmart the Swindlers* (flyer).

Monroe County. Office of Consumer Affairs. 410-C County Office Bldg., Rochester 14614. Anthony Dambra, Director. (716) 454-7200.

Nassau County. District Attorney's Office. 262 Old Country Rd., Mineola 11501. William Cahn, District Attorney. (516) 535-4800.
Established: 1966.

Prosecutes commercial frauds. Recent indictments covered educational, charitable, welfare, and banking frauds. No educational materials available.

Nassau County. Office of Consumer Affairs. 160 Old Country Rd., Mineola 11501. James E. Picken, Commissioner. (516) 535-3100.
Established: June 9, 1967.

Local Law #2-1970 empowers the Commissioner of Consumer Affairs to hold conferences with offending vendors and accept assurances of discontinuance or to recommend prosecution by the county attorney. Investigates and mediates other consumer-vendor disputes; eliminates deceptive business practices; educates people to protect themselves. The office has taken action to end misleading advertising, nondelivery of merchandise, faulty workmanship, etc. Through its Weights and Measures Division, the office also licenses home improvement contractors, inspects commercial scales, packaged commodities, gas pumps, and fuel oil meters. Has speaker series, "How to Avoid Consumer Fraud"; assists consumer education teachers in county with resource materials and presentations; sends "Consumermobile" trailer throughout county visiting schools, shopping centers, and housing projects. Periodical: *News 'n' Cues for Nassau County Consumers.* Pamphlets: *How You Can Save Fuel and Money Too; If It's Not Fair, It's Our Affair; How to Avoid Home Improvement Problems,* etc. Senior Citizen Hot Line: (516) 535-3282.

Branch offices: Elmont, Freeport, Hempstead, Inwood, and Roosevelt in the County Cooperative Centers or in E.O.C. (Economic Opportunity Commission) offices.

Oneida County. Consumer Advocate. County Office Bldg., 800 Park Ave., Utica 13501. Virginia Gallagher, Consumer Advocate. (315) 798-5076.

Onondaga County. Office of Consumer Affairs. 634 James St., Syracuse 13203. Erik P. Dressler, Director. (315) 477-7911; 477-7971.
Established: January 1973.

Protects consumers through the authority of the Onondaga County Consumer Protection Code. Investigates and mediates consumer complaints; provides consumer education through mass media presentations, formal and informal speaking engagements, and personal interviews by staff personnel. Carries out product safety monitoring program in store surveys and inspections. Provides weekly press releases for radio and TV. Helps consumers find reputable businesses by checking its own records, those of the Syracuse Better Business Bureau, the attorney general's office and the Syracuse Consumer Affairs Unit. In the first ten months of 1973 returned over $47,000 to consumers (more than the office's budget).

Orange County. Office of Consumer Affairs and Weights and Measures. 99 Main St., Goshen 10924. James A. Van Zetta, Director. (914) 294-5822.
Established: November 1970.

Enforcement is through the New York State Agriculture and Markets Law and other laws pertaining to fraud and false and deceptive advertising. Handles complaints; inspects all weighing and measuring devices in the county; inspects all packages sold at retail for labeling, pricing, and quantity accuracy. Maintains information file on businesses with poor business practices. Advises consumers on purchases. Provides education through speaking engagements, newspaper articles, and radio programs.

Rensselaer County. Department of Weights and Measures and Consumer Affairs. 399 Whiteview Rd., Troy 12180. Donald W. Binck, Sealer. (518) 283-2115.

Rockland County. Office of Consumer Protection. County Office Bldg., New Hempsted Rd., New City 10956. James Farkas, Sealer-Coordinator. (914) 638-0500, ext. 395.

Suffolk County. Department of Consumer Affairs. County Center, Veterans Memorial Hwy., Hauppauge 11787. James J. Lack, Commissioner. (516) 979-3100.
Established: January 1, 1974.

Enforcement through Suffolk County Consumer Protection Act and the Unfair Trade Practices Act. Has subpoena powers. Handles and settles amicably many consumer complaints; handles all problems relating to weights and measures; licenses plumbers, electricians, and persons engaged in the home improvement field. Engages in consumer education at all age levels. Currently preparing 14 pamphlets on consumer tips. Plans for 1975 include purchase of films and/or filmstrips.

Westchester County. District Attorney's Office. Court House, 111 Grove St., White Plains 10601. Carl A. Vergari, District Attorney. (914) 682-2160.

Assists public with wide spectrum of consumer problems; prosecutes individuals and/or corporations violating consumer laws in the consumer frauds section. Recent prosecutions involved charity frauds, home repair schemes, odometer rollbacks, etc. No educational materials.

Westchester County. Division of Weights and Measures and Consumer Affairs. 38 Brockway Pl., White Plains 10601. Kenneth W. Hale, Sealer. (914) 949-1951.
Established: 1968.

Enforces General Business Law, Agriculture and Markets Law, Penal Law, Civil Practice Act; mediates many cases; assesses fines. No educational materials prepared.

Westchester County. Office of Consumer Affairs. County Office Bldg., 148 Martine Ave., White Plains 10601. Sharon Enea and Susan Korn, Co-Coordinators. (914) 682-2842.
Established: January 1974.

A volunteer agency, it receives and processes complaints; resolves some by mediation; refers violations to appropriate agencies. Provides consumer information and speakers to groups. Educational materials are planned when the office is granted official status.

CITY AGENCIES

Glen Cove. Weights and Measures and Consumer Affairs. City Hall, Bridge St., 11542. Norbert Stemcosky, Sealer of Weights and Measures and Director of Consumer Affairs. (516) 676-2000, ext. 31.

Enforces all ordinances pertaining to weights and measures in Glen Cove under the regulations of the New York State Department of Agriculture and Markets. No educational materials.

Huntington. Town of Huntington Consumer Protection Board. 227 Main St., 11743. Larry Gabor, Chairman. (516) 421-1000, ext. 232.
Established: October 19, 1971.

Resolves and mediates complaints. Has power to subpoena. Promotes local, county, state, and federal consumer legislation. Holds hearings and conferences. Develops educational programs for consumers, e.g., occasional newsletters, pamphlets, press releases, speakers for civic, social, and service organizations. Helped coordinate activities on Long Island to press for passage of the Consumer Protection Agency on the federal level. Resolved complaints of consumers when Huntington mail order business became defunct. Periodical: *Consumer Protection Board Newsletter* (issued occasionally). Pamphlets: *How to Keep the Fuel Shortage from Hitting Home; Home Improvement Contractors Must Be Licensed* (flyer); *To: The Parents of Huntington's Children* (toys).

Islip. Consumer Protection Section—Town Attorney's Office. 655 Main St., 11751. Fred L. Hageman, Investigator. (516) 581-8000.

Mt. Vernon. Weights and Measures and Consumer Affairs. Police Headquarters, Roosevelt Sq., 10550. Stefano J. Pedone, Superintendent. (914) 558-6000, ext. 27.

Enforces laws pertaining to weights and measures of the New York State Department of Agriculture and Markets. Does not produce consumer education materials.

New Rochelle. Consumer Affairs Committee. City Hall, North Ave., 10801. Joan Semenza, Chairman. (914) 632-2021, ext. 218.
Established: July 13, 1970.

A 15-member volunteer committee appointed by the mayor and city council. Mediates complaints; lobbies for effective consumer protection laws in Albany. Success rate for complaints is approximately 95 percent. Currently preparing a study for purpose of licensing general home improvement contractors. Prepares no educational materials.

New Rochelle. Weights and Measures and Consumer Protection. City Hall, 10801. Alfred Santoro, Sealer. (914) 632-2021, ext. 324.
Established: 1971.

Enforces laws of the New York State Department of Agriculture and Markets. Issues violations and brings unresolved cases to court. Does not produce educational materials.

New York. Department of Consumer Affairs. 80 Lafayette St., 10013. Eleanor Guggenheimer, Commissioner. (212) 566-2020.
Established: 1968.

One of the largest and most effective consumer agencies in the country. Responsible for enforcing all laws relating to weights and measures, advertising, sales of goods and services, licenses and permits. Inspects restaurants and other shops for sanitary conditions; checks on unit pricing. Has power to enforce its decisions by denying, suspending, or revoking licenses and by fining licensees. Handles over 100,000 complaints per year. Has staff of investigators and lawyers. Conducts weekly food price surveys. Plans and recommends legislation, conducts research, and develops programs for consumer education and protection. Provides speakers, slide talks, films, pamphlets. Disseminates information by radio programs on WCBS and WNYC, and by newspaper and magazine articles. Branch offices are located in Manhattan, Queens, and the Bronx. Pamphlets: *Wise Up! Know Your Department of Consumer Affairs; Do's and Don'ts for Consumers; Where to Go for Consumer Information and Action,* etc. Consumer complaint telephone number: (212) 964-7777.

Schenectady. Bureau of Consumer Protection. 206 City Hall, 12305. D. A. Massaroni, Administrative Officer. (518) 377-3381, ext. 357.

Suffern. Town of Ramapo Consumer Protection Board. Town Hall, Rte. 59, 10901. Joan Weissman, Chairman. (914) 357-5100, ext. 57.
Established: 1972.

Investigates and resolves consumer complaints. Holds hearings; has the power of subpoena. Refers complaints not under Ramapo jurisdiction to proper agencies. Recently, the County of Rockland, in cooperation with the Consumer Protection Board, established a "Raincheck" law, a price posting law, and a Home Improvement Contractor Licensing Law.

Syracuse. Consumer Affairs Unit—Department of Law. 420 City Hall, 13224. Howard R. Messing, Director. (315) 473-3240.
Established: December 1971.

Handles consumer complaints under the Consumer Protection Code of the City of Syracuse. Conducts research. Provides consumer education to the community. Periodical: *CAU Newsletter.*

Yonkers. Office of Consumer Protection. 316 City Hall, 10701. Michael N. Brilis, Sealer of Weights and Measures. (914) 965-0707.
Established: March 1971 (Consumer Protection Division).

Enforces New York State Agriculture and Markets laws and the consumer protection and weights and measures laws of Yonkers. The sealer has power to give summonses and notices of violations. Checks all scales in stores; checks gas pumps and all other weights and measures. Handles all consumer complaints. Provides information on buying products and services. Provides speakers to civic and other groups. Between January and August 1974, collected $1,700 in fines, settled 595 complaints satisfactorily, obtained $10,139 in refunds for consumers. Pamphlets: *Better Look Twice (For Newlyweds; For Senior Citizens)*; flyer: *Better Look Twice (Contracts).*

NORTH CAROLINA

STATE AGENCIES

Consumer Protection Division—Office of the Attorney General. Box 629, Raleigh 27602. Robert Morgan, Attorney General. James L. Blackburn, Assistant Attorney General. (919) 829-7741.
Established: 1969.

Enforces "Little FTC Act" prohibiting "unfair methods of competition and unfair or deceptive acts or practices." Mediates and investigates complaints; brings civil suits against fraudulent individuals or businesses. Provides consumer education. Has prepared 60-second public affairs spots currently broadcast on seven commercial television stations in state, and 10-, 20-, and 30-second spots aired on 67 radio stations. Recently brought suits against a children's talent agency, a debt adjusting firm, and 11 freezer beef companies. Periodical: *Consumer Protection News* (monthly; $1 per year). Pamphlets: *Consumer Remedies in North Carolina; How to Use Magistrate's Court to Resolve Small Claims.*

NORTH DAKOTA

STATE AGENCIES

Consumer Fraud Division—Office of the Attorney General. State Capitol, Bismarck 58501. Allen B. Olson, Attorney General. Curtis B. Hansen, Supervisor, Consumer Fraud Division. (701) 224-2210.
Established: 1965 (Consumer Fraud Division).

Enforces North Dakota Consumer Fraud Law (Chapter 51-15) through legal actions to enjoin fraudulent activities, files criminal complaints, and promotes informal settlements. Between January and August 1974, received 863 complaints, recovered $996,768.26 for consumers. No educational materials prepared at present.

State Laboratories and Consumer Affairs. Box 937, Bismarck, 58505. Ailsa Simonson, Director. (701) 224-2485.
Established: 1903.

The major consumer protection agency for the state, it acts as a clearinghouse for consumer complaints and is a liaison with the U.S. Consumer Product Safety Commission. Inspects establishments and test products to make sure they conform to sanitary and health standards. (Products include food, drugs, cosmetics, feeds, fertilizers, and petroleum products.) The department investigates complaints, develops educational materials, and publishes a newsletter. Periodicals: *North Dakota Consumer* (monthly); *Food and Drug Bulletin; Feeds, Fertilizer and Pesticides Bulletin; Petroleum Products and Anti-freeze Bulletin.* Pamphlets: *Give Your Children Playtime Fun with Safety; Everything You Never Thought to Ask about the State Laboratories Department Because You Didn't Know It Existed.*

OHIO

STATE AGENCIES

Consumer Frauds and Crimes Section—Office of the Attorney General. 30 E. Broad St., Suite 1541, Columbus 43215. William J. Brown, Attorney General. Robert H. Olson, Jr., Section Chief. (614) 466-8760.
Established: 1962.

Enforces Ohio's consumer protection laws through injunctions, mediation, assurances of voluntary discontinuance, and consent judgments; also can order restitutions of monies. Disseminates information to public regarding legal activities. Recently litigated final court orders requiring consumer restitution; obtained 25 consent orders providing $2.4 million in reimbursement to Ohio consumers. Periodical: *Consumer Frauds & Crimes Information Bulletin* (quarterly). Pamphlet: *Consumer Protection and the Law.*

Consumer Protection Division—Department of Commerce. 33 N. Grant Ave. Columbus 43215. Diane R. Liff, Chief. (614) 466-8760.
Established: July 14, 1972.

Resolves complaints; investigates industry practices and possible frauds; promulgates rules regulating consumer transactions; conducts public hearings; prepares and distributes consumer education materials, e.g., newspaper stories, public service announcements, etc. Division recently completed in-depth investigation of mobile home industry. A guide will soon be ready for publication and distribution. Periodicals: *Consumer Protection Bulletin* (bimonthly). Pamphlets: *Credit Warning; Hotline Brochure; Anticipating Home Improvement; Auto Repairs* (all available with consumer protection rules in "Consumer Protection Kit"). Also ten leaflets, e.g., *Facts about Air Conditioning, Small Claims Court,* etc. Film: 26-min. color documentary loaned to classes, organizations, and Ohio TV stations. Toll-free telephone number: 1-(800) 282-1960.

COUNTY AGENCIES

Lake County. Prosecuting Attorney's Office. County Court House, Painesville, 44077. Marvin R. Plasco, Assistant Prosecuting Attorney. (216) 352-6281, ext. 281.

Montgomery County. Fraud Section–Prosecuting Attorney's Office. 41 N. Perry St., Dayton 45406. Jeffrey E. Froelich, Assistant Prosecutor. (513) 228-5126.
Established: November 1973.

Investigates and prosecutes major criminal frauds under the provisions of the Ohio Criminal Code. No educational materials.

CITY AGENCIES

Akron. Weights and Measures and Consumer Protection. 69 N. Union St., 44304. Anthony J. Ladd, Superintendent. (216) 375-2612.
Established: March 23, 1971.

Enforces City Ordinance No. 187-1971. Receives, investigates, and refers complaints to the Director of Law for legal action. Encourages fair business practices. Recommends legislation. Provides consumer education programs and materials. In 1973, resolved over 300 complaints involving over $173, 842. Prepared slides on department activities for use in talks. Pamphlets: *The Third Man* (flyer on the department).

Cleveland. Office of Consumer Affairs. City Hall, 44114. Herman Kammerman, Director. (216) 694-3200.

Columbus. Department of Community Services–Consumer Affairs. 220 Greenlawn Ave., 43223. Dorothy S. Teater, Program Administrator. (614) 461-7397.
Established: 1969.

Inspects and protects all weights and measures; provides consumer information programs; investigates complaints. Recently held a "Consumerama" in a shopping mall. No educational material published by the department.

Dayton. Bureau of Consumer Affairs. 101 W. Third St., 45402. James Gardner, Consumer Advocate. (513) 225-5048; 225-5574.

Toledo. Consumer Protection Agency. 565 N. Erie St., 43624. Thomas E. Fought, Chief Inspector. (419) 255-1500, ext. 451.
Established: April 18, 1973.

Enforces the Toledo Municipal Code, Article VII-Consumer Sales Practices Act, which protects against fraudulent sales practices. No educational materials published. Consumer Hot Line: (419) 244-6897.

OKLAHOMA

STATE AGENCIES

Consumer Protection Division–Office of the Attorney General. Suite 112 State Capitol, Oklahoma City 73105. Larry Derryberry, Attorney General. James R. Barnett, Assistant Attorney General. (405) 521-3921.
Established: September 1, 1972.

Enforces the Oklahoma Consumer Protection Act, which prohibits certain deceptive practices and advertising. Handles complaints. Attorney general has subpoena powers and may seek injunctive relief on behalf of the state. Recent successful mediation on behalf of a number of consumers, i.e., certain businesses have agreed to stop various advertising practices. Pamphlet: *Oklahoma Consumer Protection Act.*

Department of Consumer Affairs. 3033 N. Walnut, Oklahoma City 73105. Patrick C. Ryan, Administrator. (405) 521-3921.
Established: May 1969.

Supervises, investigates, and enforces various state laws related to interest rates and credit, in particular the Uniform Consumer Credit Code.

Governor's Advisor on Consumer Affairs. 3033 N. Walnut, Oklahoma City 73105. Beverly S. Stapleton, Advisor. (405) 521-3653.
Established: July 1, 1969.

This department is state designee for the U.S. Consumer Product Safety Commission. Regulates Uniform Consumer Credit Code, Sex Discrimination Act, Consumer Product Safety Act. Pamphlet: *Debtor's Rights–Lender's Rights.*

OREGON

STATE AGENCIES

Consumer Officer–Department of Agriculture. Agriculture Bldg. Salem 97310. Jane Wyatt, Consumer Officer. (503) 378-8298.
Established: 1971

Enforces the Oregon Food Law; educates and acts as a central office for handling complaints on foods and food-related problems; works on legislative matters pertaining to food. Educates and informs through seminars throughout the state, meetings, class lectures, university forums, etc. Periodical: *Consumer Protection* (bimonthly).

Consumer Protection Division–Department of Justice. 1133 S.W. Market St., Portland 97201. R. Lee Johnson, Attorney General. James L. Carney, Chief Counsel. (503) 229-5522.
Established: July 1, 1971.

Investigates complaints under the Deceptive Trade Practices Act involving misleading, fraudulent, or misrepresented transactions of consumer goods and services, real estate matters, franchises, distributorships, and other similar business opportunities involving illegal trade practices. Prepares and disseminates public service announcements for newspapers and radio stations throughout the state.

Consumer Services Division–Department of Commerce. Commerce Bldg. Salem 97310. Wanda Merrill, Administrator. (503) 378-4320.
Established: October 1, 1971.

Coordinates consumer services of various Oregon departments and agencies; furthers consumer education. The division has no legal powers. It handles complaints by referral, mediation, and persuasion. Acts as central clearinghouse for complaints filed with all agencies; testifies at hearings, and advises the state in matters affecting consumer interests at the executive and legislative levels. Periodical: (prepares monthly newsletter for the Chambers of Commerce). Pamphlets: *Where to Go for a Specific Complaint; Consumer Services Division;* bibliographies of pamphlets on the home, health, food, nutrition, etc.

COUNTY AGENCIES

Jackson County. Consumer Protection Service–District Attorney's Office. Court House, Medford 97501. Ronald K. Lango, Chief Investigator. (503) 779-1379.
Established: January 1972.

Handles all consumer complaints except those relating to insurance. Most complaints resolved informally, but the office has power to file Notice of Unlawful Trade Practice. Conducts talks and prepares newspaper articles on matters of consumer interest. Does not publish pamphlets.

Multnomah County. Consumer Protection Department–District Attorney's Office. 600 County Courthouse, Portland 97204. Roger G. Weidner, Deputy District Attorney and Director, Consumer Protection Department. (503) 248-3162.
Established: 1971.

Enforces the Unlawful Trade Practices Act by enjoining unlawful practices in the county and through the use of assurances of voluntary compliance. Recent successful activities include the assurance of voluntary compliance from a major home builder and remodeler. No educational materials prepared.

PENNSYLVANIA

STATE AGENCIES

Bureau of Consumer Protection–Department of Justice. 23A S. Third St., Harrisburg 17101. Israel Packel, Attorney General. Joel Weisberg, Director. (717) 787-9717.
Established: December 17, 1968.

Enforces the Unfair Trade Practices and Consumer Protection Law; handles complaints, investigates, mediates, and if necessary, takes legal action. Prepares and distributes consumer education programs and materials; assists in the preparation of consumer protection legislation; cooperates with local, state, and federal consumer agencies. Between January and June 1974, received 13,894 cases, closed 12,630 cases, and saved $1,087,703. Also hosted two-day workshop of consumer educators from around the country. Periodical: *Consumer News and Views* (monthly except January). Pamphlets: *Signing a Contract; Stretch Your Dollar; Renting an Apartment; How to Sue in District Justice Court*, etc.

Regional offices:
133 N. Fifth St., *Allentown* 18102 (Lehigh Valley office).
919 State St., Rm. 203, *Erie* 16501.
25 S. Third St., *Harrisburg* 17101.
342-44 N. Broad St., *Philadelphia* 19102.
1405 State Office Bldg., 300 Liberty Ave., *Pittsburgh* 15222 (Downtown office).
Hill House Center, 1835 Centre Ave., *Pittsburgh* 15219 (Hill District office).
402 Connell Bldg., 129 N. Washington Ave., *Scranton* 18503.
51 Public Square, *Wilkes-Barre* 18701.

Office of Consumer Affairs—Department of Agriculture. 2301 N. Cameron St., Harrisburg 17120. Tom Imswiller, Chief. (717) 787-5428.

Enforces very strict food and drug regulations. Empowered to inspect, test, seize, and destroy. Prepares consumer education materials. Branch offices: Evans City, Harrisburg (two offices), Hollidaysburg, Lansdale, Linden, Meadville, Tunkhannock.

COUNTY AGENCIES

Allegheny County. Bureau of Consumer Affairs. Jones Law Bldg., Pittsburgh 15219. Jean Ann Fox, Director. (412) 355-5402.
Established: February 1971.

Mediates complaints, publicizes investigations, lobbies for legislation on the state level, and prepares consumer information. The staff of five handles approximately 350 complaints each month. Recently held a seminar on buying a house in cooperation with the Board of Realtors and the community college. Lends film on free loan to school groups in the county. Pamphlets: Be a Cautious Consumer (leaflet series, e.g., tips on buying upholstered furniture, carpeting, appliances, used cars, etc.).

Bucks County. Department of Consumer Protection. Courthouse Annex, Broad and Union Sts., Doylestown 18901. Betsey G. Mikita, Manager.
(215) 348-2911, ext. 496.
Established: July 1, 1972.

Mediates consumer complaints, inspects all weights and measures. Acts as area business practices watchdog. Has consumer education program.

Butler County. Consumer Protection/Public Safety. Municipal Bldg., Butler 16045. David H. Stegner, Commissioner. (412) 287-6701.

Delaware County. Consumer Affairs. Office of Public Information. 2nd fl. Toal Bldg., Media 19063. Carl E. Rothenberger, Director. (215) 891-2430.

Lackawanna County. Department of Transportation, Environment and Consumer Affairs. 8th fl. News Bldg., Scranton 18503. William F. O'Hara, Director. (717) 342-8366.

Lancaster County. Consumer Protection Commission. County Court House, Lancaster 17602. Thomas J. Sheaffer, Executive Director. (717) 299-4222. Established: May 1972.

Investigates and mediates complaints when possible. Has program for educating consumers. In cases of actual fraud, the district attorney's office prosecutes.

Montgomery County. Department of Consumer Affairs. County Court House, Norristown 19404. Betty B. Linker, Director. (215) 275-3000, ext. 228. Established: January 1, 1973.

Aids and protects consumers; informs consumers about unethical, false, and fraudulent practices involving purchases, merchandise, services, and advertising; mediates disputes; refers criminal violations to county district attorney's office. Supplies speakers, initiates consumer education programs, and distributes consumer education materials. Pamphlet: *Consumer Protection.*

Philadelphia County. Frauds Bureau–District Attorney's Office. 666 City Hall, Philadelphia 19107. R. L. Brown, Head of Division. (215) 686-2110.

Investigates and prosecutes violations of the Pennsylvania criminal laws, also some civil fraud laws through the Consumer Complaint Division and Consumer Fraud Division. No educational materials.

CITY AGENCIES

Philadelphia. Consumer Service. 143 City Hall, 19107. Thomas McIntosh, Director. (215) 686-2798.

Handles consumer complaints and provides information on consumer services. Refers violations to the district attorney's office and to other appropriate agencies.

PUERTO RICO

Department of Consumer Affairs. Box 13934, Santurce 00908. Federico Hernandes Denton, Secretary. (809) 725-7555. Established: April 1973.

Defends and implements consumer rights; restrains inflationary trends; establishes and inspects price controls of goods and services. Maintains educational services, e.g., money management and credit counseling. Established CESCO (Educative Center for Consumer Services), which advises consumers by telephone, personal interviews, and correspondence. Coordinates and organizes seminars, workshops, radio and TV programs, and educational campaigns. Plans to start an interagency mobile exhibit explaining consumer services. Provides slides documenting the department's work: price controls, weights and measures, rent control, consumer education, etc. Pamphlets (all in Spanish): *Como Economizer Gasolina; ¿Que Es La Organización de Consumidores de Puerto Rico?;* etc.

RHODE ISLAND

STATE AGENCIES

Consumer Affairs Division—Office of the Attorney General. 250 Benefit St., Providence 02903. Richard J. Israel, Attorney General. Norma Goldberg, Assistant Attorney General. (401) 831-6850.
Established: 1970.

Investigates and prosecutes violations of the Rhode Island Deceptive Trade Practices Act. Complaints must be made in writing. In 1974, investigated bait and switch and other fraudulent business practices. Does not publish educational materials.

Consumers Council. 365 Broadway, Providence 02909. Edwin P. Palumbo, Executive Director. (401) 277-2764.
Established: 1966.

Protects the interests and safety of consumers by mediating and resolving complaints, testifying before state and federal agencies, conducting statewide education programs (particularly in the school system), engaging in speaking engagements, discussion groups, and related activities; administering nonprofit credit counseling service. The executive director is the designated coordinator for product safety activities in cooperation with the U.S. Consumer Product Safety Commission. Pamphlets (flyers): *Rhode Island Small Claims Court Procedure; Pros and Cons of Consolidation Loans; 10 Rules for Successful Spending/Saving; Consumer's Quick Credit Guide*, etc. Films: loans films made by other agencies and organizations, e.g., *The Poor Pay More; The Owl Who Gives a Hoot.*

SOUTH CAROLINA

STATE AGENCIES

Consumer Protection Agency—Office of the Governor. Columbia 29211. Judy S. Hodgens, Coordinator, Office of Citizen Service.
Established: January 1, 1975.

Office of the Attorney General. Box 11549, Columbia 29211. Daniel R. McLeod, Attorney General. Patricia O. Brehmer, Assistant Attorney General for Consumer Protection. (803) 758-3970.

Enforces the South Carolina Unfair Trade Practices Act. Investigates complaints, seeks injunctive relief; has subpoena powers. Will work in cooperation with the newly created Consumer Protection Agency (*see* listing, above). Does not produce consumer materials.

SOUTH DAKOTA

STATE AGENCIES

Consumer Protection Division—Office of the Attorney General. State Capitol Bldg., Pierre 57501. Kermit A. Sande, Attorney General. R. Van Johnson Assistant Attorney General. (605) 224-3215.
Established: July 1, 1971.

Chief law enforcement agency in state with authority to stop unfair and deceptive sale practices and act as legal counsel for various state agencies. Represents consumers before courts of law, litigates deceptive trade practice and consumer protection cases, represents consumers before governmental bodies, educates consumers. Works through court decisions, voluntary assurances of compliance, and mediated settlements. Recently settled several bulk meat sale cases. Pamphlet: *Consumer Alert.*

TENNESSEE

STATE AGENCIES

Office of Consumer Affairs—Department of Agriculture. Box 40627, Melrose Sta., Nashville 37204. Betty R. Tenpenny, Director. (615) 741-1461.

Tennessee does not have a consumer protection law. This department sets standards for foods, drugs, cosmetics, hazardous substances, food establishments, and weights and measures. Has powers to inspect, test, seize, and destroy. Toll-free telephone number: 1-(800) 342-8385.

TEXAS

STATE AGENCIES

Consumer Protection Division—Office of the Attorney General. Box 12548, Capitol Sta., Austin 78711. John L. Hill, Attorney General. Joe K. Longley, Chief, Consumer Protection Division. (512) 475-3288.
Established: 1968.

Investigates, mediates, and litigates violations of the Texas Deceptive Trade Practices and Consumer Protection Act. The attorney general's office shares concurrent jurisdiction for bringing injunctions with county and district attorneys. Protects and educates consumers about false, misleading, and deceptive business practices. Represents consumers before the legislature. Worked for passage of the D.T.P.C.P.A. Processed 4,932 complaints and recovered over $240,445 in 1973; between January 1974 and April 1974 processed 2,970 complaints and recovered over $173,188. Periodical: *Consumer Alert* (weekly column). Maintains six branch offices with 23 Assistant Attorneys General in Austin, Dallas, El Paso, Houston, Lubbock, San Antonio.

Office of Consumer Credit Commissioner. Box 2197, Austin 78767. Sam Kelley, Commissioner. (512) 475-2111.
Established: 1967.

Regulates consumer credit, loans, retail transactions, and deceptions. Maintains educational program. Pamphlets: *Before You Sign on the Dotted Line . . . ; Your Good Name Is Worth Money* (also available in Spanish).

COUNTY AGENCIES

Culberson and Hudspeth counties. *See* El Paso County.

El Paso County. Special Crimes and Consumer Fraud Division—District Attorney's Office. 401 City-County Bldg., El Paso 79901. Stephen S. Ash, Director. (602) 543-2860.
Established: March 1, 1972.

Receives, investigates, and arbitrates consumer complaints; seeks restraining orders, temporary and permanent injunctions, court orders for restitution of money and property. Prosecutes consumer fraud cases (in conjunction with state attorney general). Represents consumer interests before administrative, regulatory, and legislative agencies. Recently enforced warranty provisions on automobiles; recovered money on GAC and Horizon Corp. land contracts. Pamphlets: *El Paso Area Consumer* (leaflet).

Harris County. Consumer Fraud Division–District Attorney's Office. 301 San Jacinto, Houston 77002. C. H. Duvall, Assistant District Attorney. (713) 228-8311, ext. 501.

Tarrant County. Consumer Fraud Division–District Attorney's Office. 200 W. Belknap, Fort Worth 76102. Jack J. Ball, Jr. (817) 334-1603.
Established: November 1972.

Investigates and prosecutes cases of fraud or deception which constitute criminal activities. Has 97 percent disposition rate for restitution in cases of criminal offenses. Pamphlets: *Consumer Fraud; Consumer Complaints.*

CITY AGENCIES

Austin. Consumer-Vendor Affairs Office–City Department of Law. Municipal Bldg., 78767. Jan Kubicek. (512) 477-6511.

Dallas. Department of Consumer Affairs. 108 City Hall, 75201. Charles H. Vincent, Director. (214) 744-1133.
Established: October 1, 1972.

Investigates and prosecutes deceptive business practices covering auto repairs, electronic repairs, home solicitation, charitable solicitation, weights and measures, mail order sales, coin operated vending machines, etc. During first year of operation, handled 10,561 complaints, filed and prosecuted 95 court cases and won 94, and recovered $121,069.68 for consumers. Pamphlets: *What Auto Repair Law?; Tune in a Better Picture with the City of Dallas Electronic Repairs Ordinance; Who Cares if You Get Cheated?; The Home Solicitation Ordinance.*

Fort Worth. Consumer Affairs and Weights and Measures Division. 1800 University Dr., Rm. 218, 76107. Richard H. Aughinbaugh, Director. (817) 335-7211, ext. 209.
Established: October 1, 1972.

Enforces various city ordinances and Texas laws. Investigates complaints, renders assistance, and provides information to consumers on matters of misrepresentation and deceptive and fraudulent trade practices. Information and assistance is also given to consumers in public utility rates and service matters. As of October 1, 1974, the division handles Charitable Solicitation Applications. No educational materials published.

UTAH

STATE AGENCIES

Consumer Protection Division—Office of the Attorney General. 236 Capitol Bldg., Salt Lake City 84114. Vernon B. Romney, Attorney General. William T. Evans, Assistant Attorney General. (801) 328-5261, ext. 71. Established: September 1970.

Enforces the Utah Uniform Consumer Sales Practices Act. Investigates and resolves consumer complaints and problems. Files complaints in court and follows through for citizens of the state. Both the attorney general's office and the Department of Commerce can enforce consumer laws in Utah. No educational materials.

Department of Financial Institutions. 10 W. Broadway, Suite 331, Salt Lake City 84101. W. S. Brimhall, Commissioner. (801) 328-5461. Established: 1913.

Administers laws governing banks, building and loan associations, industrial loan corporations, and credit unions. Administers the Utah Uniform Consumer Credit Code. No consumer materials published.

VERMONT

STATE AGENCIES

Consumer Fraud Division—Office of the Attorney General. Box 981, 200 Main St., Burlington 05401. Kimberly B. Cheney, Attorney General. Howard Goldberg, Assistant Attorney General in Charge. (802) 864-0111.

Investigates, mediates, and litigates cases under the Vermont Consumer Fraud Law; educates the public, drafts legislation, promulgates consumer fraud rules. Drafted and secured the passage of mobile homeowners' "bill of rights" and three-day "cooling off" period for home solicitation sales. Began radio-TV public service announcements in July 1974. Pamphlet: *The Mobile Homeowner's Bill of Rights.*

COUNTY AGENCIES

Chittenden County. Economic Crime Division—State Attorney's Office. 39 Pearl St., Burlington 05401. Patrick J. Leahy. (802) 863-2865. Established: September 1973.

An investigative unit which checks on white-collar crime. Has power to prosecute and convict economic crime offenders under consumer fraud rules and regulations of the State of Vermont. Recent investigations covered discount prices in discount stores, the fat content of hamburgers, and a gas saving device. The division is a project of the National District Attorney's Association.

VIRGINIA

STATE AGENCIES

Division of Consumer Counsel—Office of the Attorney General. Supreme Court Bldg., Richmond 23219. Andrew P. Miller, Attorney General. Douglas S. Wood, Assistant Attorney General. (804) 770-3518. Established: 1970.

Represents the interests of Virginia consumers by appearing before governmental commissions, agencies, etc., to be heard on their behalf and to investigate matters relating to such appearances; makes studies related to enforcing the consumer laws of the Commonwealth, and recommends legislation. The Attorney General has the power to investigate and bring actions in the name of the Commonwealth to enjoin certain unfair trade and sales practices. Works closely with state of Virginia Office of Consumer Affairs–Department of Agriculture (*see* listing, below).

Office of Consumer Affairs–Department of Agriculture and Commerce.
Box 1163, Richmond 23209. Roy L. Farmer, Director, (804) 770-2042.
Established: 1970.

Virginia's main consumer protection agency. It coordinates programs and responsibilities of all departments and agencies; promotes consumer education in cooperation with the Department of Education; serves as a clearinghouse for complaints of illegal, fraudulent, deceptive, or dangerous practices; refers complaints to proper agencies for appropriate actions; maintains records of complaints and their disposition. Pamphlet: *Guide to Consumer Services.* Toll-free telephone number: 1-(800) 552-9963.

Branch office: 7309 Arlington Blvd., Suite 300, *Falls Church* 22042. (703) 573-1286.

COUNTY AGENCIES

Arlington County. Consumer Protection Commission. 2049 15 St., N., Arlington 22201. Charles E. Hammond, Executive Director. Audrey Ghizzoni, Chairman.
Established: September 1971.

Mediates and conciliates. The commission is an advisory body dealing in policy recommendations and in reviewing possible legislation. It has no enforcement powers. It has jurisdiction over marketplace arbitrators (Arlington citizens who are trained and volunteer their services). Mediation efforts have helped consumers with home improvements, auto and TV repairs. Enabling legislation is now being considered in the home improvement and auto repair fields based on this activity. No educational material published.

Fairfax County. Consumer Protection & Public Utilities Commission.
4100 Chain Bridge Rd., Fairfax 22030. Fred K. Kramer, Director (703) 691-3214.
Established: March 11, 1974 (reorganized).

Originally established in June 1972 as Consumer Protection and Public Utilities Commission. Solicits, investigates, and responds to complaints by mediation and legal means; develops consumer education and information programs; recommends legislation; represents consumers before legislative and regulatory bodies. Recently passed legislation allows actions to enjoin for specific violations through the offices of the county attorney and Commonwealth attorney. Among other activities, concluded a home buyers and condominium study, developed an arbitration procedure, intervened in rate increase cases concerning utilities. Pamphlets: *Fairfax County Consumers . . . We're Here to Help You;*

Tips for Buying Toys; Home Improvements . . . If You Can't Do It Yourself; Home Shoppers Check List; Consumer Arbitration Rules of Procedure.

CITY AGENCIES

Newport News. Office of Consumer Affairs and Weights and Measures. City Hall, 2400 Washington Ave., 23607. Jack L. Davis, Supervisor. (804) 247-8616; 247-8618.
Established: July 1, 1973 (Consumer Affairs).

Enforces state laws on consumer affairs and city ordinances on weights and measures. Handles all types of consumer complaints; inspects all weighing and measuring devices for accuracy as well as all prepackaged commodities. Settles disputes by mediation or civil suits. Among other activities, recently brought suit against a supermarket for short weighing; recovered funds for consumer in a civil suit on a used washing machine. Prepares educational materials. Pamphlets: *Consumer Affairs Office; Selected Consumer Protection Laws.*

Norfolk. Division of Consumer Protection—Department of Community Improvement. 804 City Hall Bldg., 23501. Martin D. Greenwell, Chief. (804) 441-2821.
Established: 1973.

Protects consumers against unfair or deceptive trade practices, including misrepresented weights and measures, by handling and mediating complaints and referring violations to appropriate law enforcement agencies. Cooperates with the Better Business Bureau and other organizations for better business-consumer relations. Collects data for drafting legislation and consumer education programs. Prepares and distributes consumer-merchant literature and press releases; participates in group discussions and speaking engagements. Pamphlets: *Selected Consumer Protection Laws/Consumer Advocate Comments; Care Labels; Consumer Concerns and What to Do about Them; Protection for the Elderly; What to Do if You Have Been Dealt with Unfairly; 10 Ways to Combat Consumer Fraud;* etc.; There Is a Law in Virginia (flyer series, on sale of motor vehicles by licensed dealers, unsolicited goods, etc.).

Virginia Beach. Bureau of Consumer Protection. Municipal Center, 23456. J. N. McClannan. (804) 427-4421.

WASHINGTON

STATE AGENCIES

Consumer Protection Division—Office of the Attorney General. 1266 Dexter Horton Bldg., Seattle 98104. Slade Gorton, Attorney General. John H. Bright, Sr., Assistant Attorney General. (206) 464-7744.
Established: 1961.

Enforces the Fair Business Practices—Consumer Protection Act (Chapter 19.86 RCW). Investigates, processes complaints, and takes court actions; issues injunctions and accepts assurances of discontinuance. Also enforces other laws: Fair Trade, Unfair Practices, Weights and Measures, Unsolicited Merchandise, etc. Prepares and proposes consumer legislation, e.g., a bill for unit pricing, the establishment of a Consumer Protection Agency. The department handles over 35,000 complaints per year, litigates 30–40 suits. By September 1974, had returned over $4 million for the year. Periodical: *Newletter* (quarterly). Pamphlet: *Consumer Alert.* Toll-free telephone number: 1-(800) 552-0700.

Branch offices:
- Temple of Justice, *Olympia* 98504. (206) 753-6200.
- Central District, 1316 E. Pike, *Seattle* 98122. (206) 464-6684.
- Old National Bank Bldg., *Spokane* 99200. (509) 456-3123.
- 1502 Tacoma Ave., *Tacoma* 98402. (206) 593-2904.

COUNTY AGENCIES

King County. Consumer Fraud Division—District Attorney's Office. County Court House. 554 S. King, Seattle 98104. Eugene Anderson, Assistant District Attorney. (206) 344-7350.

CITY AGENCIES

Seattle. Division of Consumer Affairs. 107 Municipal Bldg., 98104. Virginia Galle, Director of Licenses and Consumer Affairs. Charles Ehlert, Assistant Director of Consumer Affairs. (206) 583-6060.
Established: November 1973.

Enforces Seattle's Consumer Protection Ordinances, including consumer fraud. Investigates cases, mediates between business and consumers, refers violations to Seattle police, corporation counsel, or county prosecutor. Also prepares educational materials and conducts research for future consumer legislation. In July 1974, promoted campaign to deter consumer fraud by preventive advertising of laws, e.g., Peddler's and Solicitor's Ordinance and False Advertising Law. Conducted the campaign using brochures, transit advertising, radio announcements, and talks to interested groups. Pamphlets: *What You Should Know about Unlicensed Peddlers; False Advertising Is Against the Law; Consumer Problems? Inquire Within; Here's How Small Claims Court Can Work for You; Shopping by Mail—Is the Temptation Worth the Risk?* (flyer).

WEST VIRGINIA

STATE AGENCIES

Consumer Protection Division—Department of Agriculture. State Capitol Bldg., Charleston 25305. C. Harold Amick, Director. (304) 348-2226.
Established: 1964.

Enforces 12 agriculture laws on purity and quality of food production, processing and storage; maintains education program; disseminates information through materials and speaking engagements. Enforces laws through the services of 14 field inspectors and West Virginia's Laboratory Services Division. Pamphlet: *Protecting Our Food.* Others: "The Food We Eat" (20-min. program on state food laws and the work of the C.P.D.); "Food Buying and Marketing" (30 min., with slides, visuals, and printed materials). The department also has 2 X 2 color slides on consumer subjects for loan of up to three days.

Office of the Attorney General. State Capitol Bldg. Charleston, 25305. Chauncey H. Browning, Jr., Attorney General. James S. Arnold, Assistant Attorney General. (304) 348-3377.

The office of the attorney general enforces the West Virginia Consumer Credit and Protection Act which became effective September 1, 1974.

CITY AGENCIES

Charleston. Consumer Protection Department. Box 2749, City Bldg., 25330. Jane H. Theiling, Director. (304) 348-8172.
Established: June 5, 1972 (activated January 2, 1973).

Handles consumer complaints by mediation, brings cases involving up to $300 in claims to the Magistrate's Court or takes appropriate legal actions. Educates and protects consumer through educational materials and programs; newspaper articles (monthly front-page article in City Section of *Charleston Gazette*), weekly 15-minute radio show on WCAW, six three-minute consumer hotline tapes on WTIP-AM/FM. Gives approximately two speeches a week to school and service groups. The director is on the Governor's Advisory Commission for Mobile Home Building Standards and a member of the nine-member implementation task force for the organization of the National Association of Consumer Protection Administrators.

WISCONSIN

STATE AGENCIES

Bureau of Consumer Protection—Department of Agriculture. 801 W. Badger Rd., Madison 53713. Thomas D. Crist, Jr., Director. (608) 266-7221.
Established: July 1963.

Mediates consumer complaints; refers others to proper agencies for enforcement; has "Little FTC Act" authority to promulgate rules regulating trade practices. Can issue letters of assurance, special orders, and injunctions. Promulgated rules related to door-to-door solicitation, mobile home parks, food plans, referral selling, etc. Does not produce educational materials.

Governor's Council for Consumer Affairs. 16 N. Carroll, Rm. 415, Madison 53703. Martin J. Schreiber, Lieutenant Governor, Chairman. James S. Fosdick, Director. (608) 266-3104.
Established: March 1972.

Serves as focal point for citizen complaints; advocates and coordinates agency actions; reviews and evaluates existing activities and proposes changes to the legislature; recommends new state and/or local activities, and reviews the impact of federal legislation on state activities. Successfully lobbied for Mobile Home Standards and Warranty Act which went into effect January 1, 1974. Planning to produce pamphlets on consumer services and mobile homes in 1975.

Office of Consumer Protection—Department of Justice. State Capitol, Madison 53702. Robert W. Warren, Attorney General. Camille Haney, Consumer Affairs Coordinator. (608) 266-1852.
Established: March 1970.

Wisconsin's chief law enforcement agency, it has independent enforcement authority in the consumer fraud area; acts as legal counsel for various agencies in the state in other consumer protection matters. The office has broad injunctive authority in such areas as lotteries, unfair trade practices, and usurious sales. Acts as a clearinghouse for complaints; refers complaints to appropriate agencies. Develops consumer information program and materials. Pamphlets: Consumer Fact Sheets (series of eight, e.g., *State Agency Jurisdiction for Consumers, 10 Ways to Combat Consumer Fraud*): *Consumer Alert; Knock Knock* (door-to-door sales); *Be Sure before You Sign!; Speak Up! When You Buy a Car;* etc.

Branch office: State Office Bldg., 819 N. Sixth St., *Milwaukee* 53706. (414) 933-1104.

WYOMING

STATE AGENCIES

Consumer Affairs Division–Office of the Attorney General. Supreme Court Bldg., Cheyenne 82002. Clarence A. Brimmer, Attorney General. J. Leo DeHerrera, Special Assistant (307) 777-7775.
Established: January 1, 1973.

Handles consumer complaints as authorized under the Wyoming Consumer Protection Act (40:102-113), which prohibits unfair and deceptive practices in the sale of goods and services to individuals, prohibits referral sales, grants three-day cooling-off period in home solicitation sales, etc. Also enforces Multi-Level and Pyramid Distributorship Act and Anti-Trust Statutes. January-September 1974, handled over 250 complaints. Pamphlet: *Wyoming Consumer Protection Manual.*

State Examiner. Supreme Court Bldg., Cheyenne 82002. Dwight D. Bonham, State Examiner. (307) 777-7797.
Established: July 1, 1971.

Administers Uniform Consumer Credit Code; responsible for the regulation of all state financial organizations, e.g., savings and loans, banks, finance companies, sales finance companies. Pamphlet: *Know Your Legal Credit Rights and Remedies.*

Canadian Agencies

NATIONAL AGENCIES

Department of Consumer and Corporate Affairs. Place du Portage, Ottawa-Hull, Ont. K1A 0C9. André Ouellet, Minister. C. M. Bolger, Acting Assistant Deputy Minister. (613) 997-2862. Complaints: (613) 997-2211.
Established: 1967.

The department enforces approximately 20 laws dealing with various facets of consumer protection, among them misleading advertising, consumer loan interest, product safety, textile labeling, and weights and measures. The Field Operations Service inspects weights and measures, electricity and gas measurement, and a wide range of meat, fish, and agricultural products (sold in retail stores) for quality and grade standards. The department investigates complaints and refers violations to Canada's Department of Justice. It holds discussions with provincial agencies charged with consumer protection; proposes consumer legislation. It conducts many educational programs and produces a great variety of informational materials, such as periodicals, pamphlets and fact sheets; conducts multimedia advertising on radio, television, and in print. Currently producing a series of 13 weekly, half-hour television shows entitled "It's up to You" that feature participants learning to make wise consumer decisions. Disseminates safety information through pension and family allowance check envelopes. Periodical: *Consumer Contact* (monthly; 11 times a year). Pamphlets: *A Law for Consumer Purchases; Stop! and Save a Life* (hazardous product symbols); *Fibre and Fibre Facts; Look at That Label!; Metrification: A Guide for Consumers; Keep Your Family Safe; Think Safety—Be Safe*, etc.

Regional offices: Vancouver, Winnipeg, Toronto, Montreal, and Halifax; plus 34 district offices.

PROVINCIAL AGENCIES

Alberta. Consumer Affairs. 9915 108 St., 7th fl., Edmonton T5K 2G8. D. E. L. Keown, Director. V. A. Kapoor, Consumer Affairs Officer. (403) 429-7155. Established: April 1, 1973.

Liaison with business and governmental organizations; disseminates information; investigates consumer complaints and inquiries (complaints must be in writing). Refers complaints outside department's jurisdiction to appropriate agency. Handles approximately 5,000 complaints per year; 75 percent satisfactorily resolved. By fall 1974 the unit was handling about 500 telephone inquiries per month. Periodical: *Alberta Consumer Affairs Newsletter* (five issues a year). Pamphlets: *What Does Consumer Affairs Mean to You?* (others in developmental stages).

Branch office: J. J. Bowlen Bldg. *Calgary* (403) 261-6107.

British Columbia. Department of Consumer Services. Parliament Bldgs., Victoria V8V 1X4. Phyllis F. Young, Minister. (604) 387-3797. Established: 1973.

Recommends and introduces legislation to protect consumers and encourage responsibility of all parties in consumer transactions; investigates complaints and alleged illegal selling practices under the direction of the Trade Practices Branch. Established debtor counseling under Debtor Assistance Division; established and developed educational services. Recently helped pass Trade Practices Act, Personal Information Reporting Act, and Debtor Assistance Act. Prepares press releases as required. Pamphlets: *The Trade Practices Act and You; Personal and Confidential* (The Personal Information Reporting Act); assorted flyers.

Manitoba. Consumers' Bureau—Office of the Rentalsman. 210 Osborne St. N., Winnipeg R3C OV8. John E. Mason, Associate Deputy Minister, Consumer Affairs. (204) 956-1010.
Established: January 2, 1970.

Enforces the Consumer Protection Act by receiving, investigating and mediating consumer complaints; licensing bonded collection agents, vendors, and direct sellers; ensuring that consumer law requirements are met; conducting research into consumer problems; providing information and educational programs; cooperating with other agencies and groups interested in consumer problems; reporting to the government on matters affecting Manitoba concerns. Periodical: *Counter-Points* (five issues a year). Pamphlets: *The Consumer Protection Act; For an Honest Deal; 62 Questions, 62 Answers for Manitoba Landlords and Tenants; What You Don't Know . . . Can Hurt You!; A Government Service at Work for You;* etc. Films: *Questions and Answers for Manitoba Landlords and Tenants* (11 min.; available for loan): *The Law and Consumer Protection* (20 min., color; for bureau information programs); *The Law and Financing* (20 min., color; for bureau information programs); *Buyer Beware, Seller Take Care* (20 min., color; for bureau information programs). Toll-free telephone number: 1-(800) 262-8844.

New Brunswick. Consumer Bureau—Department of Provincial Secretary. 564 Queen St., 2nd fl., Fredericton E3B 5H1. Omer Leger, Provincial Secretary. H. H. D. Cochrona, Deputy Minister. (506) 453-2659.
Established: July 1967.

Investigates and mediates registered consumer complaints; informs consumers about provincial consumer legislation; advises the public on general consumer matters; provides information and educational programs, cooperates with other agencies and groups interested in consumer problems. Administers nine acts, e.g., Cost of Credit Disclosure Act, Direct Sellers Act, Collection Agencies Act, Unconscionable Transactions Relief Act. Periodical: *Facts & Views* (quarterly). Pamphlets: *Know Your Salesman; It's Your Money; Here're Facts for Consumers;* (some pamphlets are available in French).

Newfoundland. Consumer Affairs Division—Department of Provincial Affairs and Environment. 2nd fl. Elizabeth Towers, Elizabeth Ave., St. John's. R. J. Barter, Director. (709) 753-2140.
Established: 1968.

Administers and investigates consumer complaints and inquiries concerning six laws: Direct Sellers Act, Consumer Protection Act, Real Estate Trading Act, Credit Reporting Agencies Act, Collection Agencies Act, Unsolicited Goods and Credit Cards Act. Provides educational materials and programs. Pamphlets: *New Year Resolutions for Wise and Thrifty Shoppers; What Can I Do—The Direct Sellers Act; Real Estate.*

Nova Scotia. Consumer Services Bureau—Department of Provincial Secretary. Box 998, Halifax B3J 2X3. A. G. Cunning, Director. (902) 424-4479.
Established: 1968.

Administers nine consumer laws covering retail credit, loans, financing, contracts, services, collection harassment, consumer reporting, misleading advertising, high-pressure salesmanship, referral and pyramid selling, real estate transactions, and door-to-door selling.

Branch offices:
5639 Spring Garden Rd., 2nd fl., *Halifax*. (902) 424-5631.
11 Commercial St., *Middleton*. (902) 825-3429.
502 Maritime Bldg., Provost St., *New Glasgow*. (902) 752-0975.
Provincial Bldg., Prince St., *Sydney*. (902) 564-8424.

Ontario. Consumer Protection Bureau, Business Practices Division–Ministry of Consumer and Commercial Relations. 555 Yonge St., Toronto M4Y 1Y7. S. B. Turner, Director. D. V. Goudy, Registrar. (416) 965-6471.
Established: 1966 (as Department of Financial and Commercial Affairs).

Enforces the Consumer Protection Act covering door-to-door sales and true interest rates and ten other laws covering motor vehicle dealers, automobile fraud, sale of real estate, etc. Handles and investigates complaints. Proposes legislation. Produces educational materials including a film on fraud and a series of 13 pamphlets on facets of consumer protection. Pamphlets: *Consumer Protection Act and How It Helps You the Consumer; Consumer Reporting Act and How It Helps You; Using Credit Wisely; Tips for Senior Citizens; Getting a Mortgage; Buying a Franchise*; etc.

Prince Edward Island. Consumer Services Division–Department of Provincial Secretary. Box 2000, Charlottetown C1A 7N8. M. B. Fitzpatrick, Director. (902) 894-3824.
Established: 1967.

Enforces laws pertaining to credit information, conditional sales, warranties and guaranties, door-to-door sales, insurance, real estate, collection agencies, and landlord-tenant rules. Provides free credit counseling and a debt liquidation plan. Has a 75–80 percent success record in settling disputes. Does not publish educational materials.

Quebec. Office de la Protection du Consommateur. 201 est, boul. Crémazie, Montreal H2M 1L2. Niquette Delage, Director. (514) 381-8555.
Established: July 1971.

Enforces the Consumer Protection Act, receives complaints, and investigates infractions of regulations; protects, educates, and informs consumers on matters of consumer protection; carries out studies and makes recommendations respecting consumer protection; promotes and subsidizes the establishment and development of consumer protection services or agencies and cooperates with them; cooperates with various departments and governmental bodies in Quebec and coordinates their work; cooperates with national government and with governments of other provinces concerning consumer protection. Has monthly periodicals; prepares pamphlets; has film in French only.

Branch offices:
663, boul. St-Joseph, *Hull*. (819) 770-9004.
800, Place d'Youville, *Quebec*. (418) 643-8652.
134 est, rue St-Germain, *Rimouski*. (418) 724-6692.
740 ouest, rue Galt, *Sherbrooke*. (819) 567-8903.
863, rue St-Pierre, *Trois-Rivières*. (813) 374-2424.

Saskatchewan. Department of Consumer Affairs. 1753 Cornwall St., Regina S4P 2K1. Ed Tchorzewski. (306) 525-8791.
Established: June 1972.

Investigates consumer complaints, supervises all consumer affairs in the province; assesses consumer legislation and recommends new legislation or amendments to existing laws; disseminates information on consumer matters.

III. NEWSPAPERS

U.S. newspapers are arranged geographically by state, Canadian newspapers, geographically by province. Within each state or province, entries are alphabetical by city.

Syndicated columnists are listed alphabetically by name.

U.S. Newspapers

ALABAMA

Birmingham Post-Herald. 2200 Fourth Ave. N., Birmingham 35202. (205) 325-2326. "Action Line." Bill Mylius. 5/wk. All complaints must be submitted in writing. Column also features a short article each day on new products, hazardous products, federal publications of interest to consumers, and/or companies which have committed fraudulent acts.

ALASKA

Anchorage Daily Times. Box 40, Anchorage 95510. (907) 297-5622. "Action Line." 5/wk. Complaints not accepted by phone. "Tell It To Bud." 5/wk.

ARIZONA

The Arizona Daily Star. Box 26807, 4850 S. Park Ave., Tucson 85726. (602) 294-4433. "The Ombudsman." Dale Parris. 2/wk.

Tucson Daily Citizen. Box 26767, Tucson 85726. (602) 294-4433. "Action, Please!" Robert C. McCormick. 4/wk. Also special articles on such topics as tenants rights, warranty problems, finance charges, Social Security benefits, etc.

ARKANSAS

Arkansas Democrat. Capitol Ave. at Scott St., Little Rock 72203. (501) 372-6226. "Answer Please." Julie Baldridge. 7/wk.

CALIFORNIA

The Fresno Bee. Fresno 93786. (209) 268-5221. "Fact Finder." Howard Miller, ed. 2/wk.

The Hanford Sentinel. Box 9, 418 W. Eighth St., Hanford 93230. (209) 582-0471. "Question Box." Ruth Gomes. 1/wk. General column having some material related to consumer affairs. Consumer topics also covered in "At Home and Abroad" and "Of Commerce and Careers."

Independent Press-Telegram. Box 230, 604 Pine Ave., Long Beach 90844. (213) 432-3451. "Action Line." Paul Wallace. 7/wk.

Herald-Examiner. Box 2416, Terminal Annex, Los Angeles 90051. (213) 748-1212. "Answer Line." Warren Morrell. 7/wk.

Oakland Tribune. Box 509, Oakland 94604. (415) 645-2000. "Action Line." Clifford Pletschet. 6/wk.

Oroville Mercury. Oroville 95965. (916) 533-3131. "Action." Don Shaffer. Appears irregularly.

Star-News. Bin 46, Pasadena 91109. (213) 796-0311. "Action Line." Harry Bortin. 5/wk.

Paso Robles Press. 1212 Pine St., Paso Robles 93446. (805) 238-0330. Dorothy Reddick, Consumer ed. 1/wk.

Progress-Bulletin. Box 2708, 300 S. Thomas St., Pomona 91766. (714) 622-1201. "Action Line." Peggy Gonzales. 3/wk.

Redwood City Tribune. Box 5188, Redwood City 94063. (415) 365-3111. "Action Line." Otto Tallent. 6/wk.

Salinas Californian. Box 1091, Salinas 93901. (408) 424-2221. "Action Desk." Staff. 6/wk.

Evening Tribune. Box 191, San Diego 92112. (714) 299-4470. "Action Line." Scott Stewart. 6/wk.

San Jose Mercury-News. 750 Ridder Park Dr., San Jose 95190. (408) 287-1222. "Action Line." Andy Bruno. 6/wk.

COLORADO

Colorado Springs Sun. 103 W. Colorado Ave., Colorado Springs 80902. (303) 633-3881. "Action Line." Charles Saad. 6/wk.

The Daily Reporter-Herald. Box 59, Cleveland Ave. & Fifth St., Loveland 80537. "Around the Valley." John Pfeiffenberger. 1/wk.

CONNECTICUT

The News-Times. 333 Main St., Danbury 06810. (203) 744-5100. "Letters for Action." Grace Wells. 1/wk. Phone messages accepted; letters preferred. When inquiries are heavy, an occasional midweek column is run.

The Hartford Times. 10 Prospect St., Hartford 06101. (203) 249-8211, ext. 336. "Dear George." Cynthia Kallman, ed. 7/wk.

The Meriden Record. Crown St. Sq., Meriden 06450. (203) 235-1661. "Dear Gus." Rick Judd. 1/wk.

DISTRICT OF COLUMBIA

The Washington Post. 1150 15 St. N.W., Washington, D.C. 20005. (202) 223-6000. "The Ombudsman." Robert C. Maynard. Morton Mintz, Consumer writer. (Information received from secondary sources.)

FLORIDA

Boca Raton News. Box 580, Boca Raton 33432. (305) 395-8300. "The Helper." Julia Fitzpatrick with Peter Pepinsky, Business ed. 5/wk. "Consumer Ask." University of Florida Extension Service. 1/wk. "Buyer's Billboard." M. Conlon (UPI).

Gainesville Sun. 101 S.E. Second Pl, Gainesville 32601. (904) 373-3366. "Action Line." Anon. 7/wk. Sunday consumer page, some syndicated features.

Jacksonville Journal. Box 1949, 1 Riverside Ave., Jacksonville 32201. (904) 791-4374. "Call Box." Helen Bates. 6/wk.

Lakeland Ledger. Box 408, Lakeland 33802. (813) 688-6011. "Action Line" Bobbie Rossiter. 5/wk. "Claim Check." June Erlick. 1/wk., plus an average of six additional articles.

The Miami Herald. 1 Herald Pl., Miami 33101. (305) 379-0764. "Action Line." Anne S. Baumgartner. 7/wk. Molly Sinclair, Consumer writer.

The Miami News. Box 615, Miami 33152. (305) 358-6397. Consumer column. Harry Haigley. 1/wk. Also daily material, tests of advertising claims, consumer commentary.

Palm Beach Post. 2751 S. Dixie Hwy., West Palm Beach 33602. (305) 833-7411. Barbara Somerville, Consumer ed. 1/wk.

St. Petersburg Times. 490 First Ave. S., St. Petersburg 33701. (813) 893-8111. "Watch This Space." Victor Livingston, Michael Marzella. 1/wk. (tests advertising claims). Also national and local consumer coverage to help consumers cope in the marketplace.

Sarasota Herald-Tribune. Drawer 1719, Sarasota 33578. (813) 958-7755. "Hotline." Sharon Tucker. 7/wk.

Tallahassee Democrat. Box 990, Tallahassee 32302. (904) 877-6141. "Action Line." Anon. 6/wk.

GEORGIA

The Valdosta Daily Times. Box 968, Valdosta 31601. (912) 242-8000. "Times Line." Becky Capotosti. 5/wk.

IDAHO

The Idaho Statesman. Box 40, 1200 N. Curtis Rd., Boise 83707. (208) 376-2121. "Action Post." Betsy Beck. 6/wk. "Save a Buck." (Reader suggestions on how to save money.)

Lewiston Morning Tribune. 505 C St., Lewiston 83501. (208) 743-9411. "Action Forum." Mary Jane O'Connell. 2–3/wk.

ILLINOIS

The Herald. Paddock Publications, Inc., Box 280, Arlington Heights 60006. (312) 394-2300. Monica Wilch Perin, Consumer Interest ed. 1/wk.

The Herald, Buffalo Grove. *See* **The Herald,** Arlington Heights.

Chicago Tribune. 435 N. Michigan Ave., Chicago 60611. (312) 222-3006. Consumer features: Christine Winters. 1/wk. Consumer stories also featured in Sunday "Lifestyle" and daily "Tempo."

The Commercial-News. 17 W. North St., Danville 61832. (217) 446-1000. "Action!" Dale Foster. 3–4/wk.

The Herald, Des Plaines. *See* **The Herald,** Arlington Heights.

Dixon Evening Telegraph. 113–115 Peoria Ave., Dixon 61021. (815) 284-2222. Robert H. Nellis, Consumer ed. 4/wk.

Daily Courier-News. 300 Lake St., Elgin 60120. (312) 741-1800. "Do Line." Leroy S. Clemens. 3/wk.

The Herald, Elk Grove. *See* **The Herald,** Arlington Heights.

The Herald, Mount Prospect. *See* **The Herald,** Arlington Heights.

The Daily Times. 110 W. Jefferson St., Ottawa 61350. (815) 433-2000, ext. 44. "Times Ticker." Joan Hustis. 1/wk.

The Herald, Palatine. *See* **The Herald,** Arlington Heights.

Peoria Journal-Star. 1 News Plaza, Peoria 61601. (309) 688-2411. Ted Newberg, Consumer Interest ed. Frequency varies with need.

Rockford Morning Star. Box 1088, Rockford 61105. (815) 962-4433, ext. 219. "Help." Eileen Peterson. 5/wk.

The Herald, Rolling Meadows. *See* **The Herald,** Arlington Heights.

The Herald, Schaumburg. *See* **The Herald,** Arlington Heights.

The State Journal Register. 313 S. Sixth St., Springfield 62701. (217) 544-5711. "J-R Line." Jeff Nelson. 2/wk.

The Herald, Wheeling. *See* **The Herald,** Arlington Heights.

INDIANA

Daily Herald-Telephone. Box 909, 1900 S. Walnut St., Bloomington 47401 (812) 332-4401. "Hot Line." Bill Schrader. 6/wk. Consumer page every Thursday.

Brazil Daily Times. Brazil 47834. (812) 446-2216 "Times-line." Chuck Crabb. Appears infrequently. "Dateline: Clay County." Appears infrequently.

The Journal-Gazette. 600 W. Main St., Fort Wayne 46802. (219) 423-3311. "Action Line." Roger L. Mosher, Assistant City ed. 2/wk.

The Indianapolis Star. 307 N. Pennsylvania St., Indianapolis 46206. (317) 633-1198. Richard D. Lennis, Consumer Interest ed. 2/wk.

The Kokomo Tribune. 300 N. Union St., Kokomo 46901. (317) 459-3121, ext. 202. "Action Line." Joanne Lack. 1/wk.

Lafayette Journal and Courier. 217 N. Sixth St., Lafayette, 47901. (317) 742-4011. "Help!" Paul N. Janes. 5/wk.

LaPorte Herald-Argus. 701 State St., LaPorte 46350. (219) 362-2161. "H-Action." D. Reed Eckhardt. 1/wk.

The Lebanon Reporter. 117 E. Washington St., Lebanon 46052. (317) 482-5400. "Live Wire." Jane Cassell, City ed. 1/wk. "Keep Smiling." Jeanne Hill. 1/wk.

The Pharos-Tribune & Press. 517 E. Broadway. Logansport 46947. (219) 753-7511. "Answer Line." Margo Coffman. 1/wk.

South Bend Tribune. South Bend 46626. (219) 233-6161. "Action Line." Gayle Zubler. 5/wk.

IOWA

Sioux City Journal. Box 118, Sioux City 51102. (712) 255-8991. "Action." Dianne Rose. 1/wk.

Waterloo Daily Courier. 501 Commercial St., Waterloo 50704. (319) 234-3551. Phyllis Singer, Consumer Interest ed. 1/wk.

KANSAS

The Manhattan Mercury. Osage at N. Fifth St., Manhattan 66502. (913) 776-8805. "Action Line." Lynn Pickett. 1/wk. Special consumer stories when need arises.

Topeka Capital-Journal. Sixth and Jefferson, Topeka 66607. (913) 357-4421, ext. 231. "Let's Ask." Ruth Martin. 1/wk.

KENTUCKY

The Louisville Times. 525 W. Broadway, Louisville 40202. (502) 582-4641. Les Whiteley, Consumer ed. 1/wk. (about advertising). Also consumer investigatory stories, general features.

The Messenger. Box 529, Madisonville 42431. (502) 821-6833. "Hot Line." Ernest R. Vaughn, ed. Appears irregularly.

LOUISIANA

Morning Advocate/State-Times. Baton Rouge 70821. (504) 383-1111. "Action, Please." Donna Lynch. 5/wk.

The States-Item. 3800 Howard Ave., New Orleans 70140. (504) 821-1727. "Ask A. Labas." Anon. 6/wk. "Louisiana Consumers' League Says." Tom Soniat, New Orleans Better Business Bureau. 1/wk.

Shreveport Journal. 222 Lake St., Box 1110, Shreveport 71130. (318) 221-5263. "Action Line." Robin B. Goodwin. 6/wk.

MARYLAND

The Evening Sun. Calvert & Centre Sts., Baltimore 21203. (301) 539-7745. "Direct Line." David F. Woods. 5/wk.

The Herald-Mail. 25–31 Summit Ave., Hagerstown 21740. (301) 733-5890, ext. 54. "Action Line." Terry Leyh. 5/wk.

MASSACHUSETTS

Boston Globe. 135 Morrissey Blvd., Boston 02107. (617) 929-2990. "Ask the Globe." Edward W. Quill. 7/wk.

The Christian Science Monitor. 1 Norway St., Boston 02115. Washington Bureau: 910 16 St. N.W., Washington, D.C. 20006. (202) 785-4400. Lucia Mouat, Consumer ed. 1/wk. (Washington Bureau).

Greenfield Recorder. Box 273, Greenfield 01301. (413) 772-0261. Walentyna Pomasko, Consumer Interest ed. 2/wk.

The Evening News. 25 Elm St., Southbridge 01551. (617) 764-4325. "Consumer's Corner." Linda Megathlin. 1/wk. Consumer features run irregularly. Food price index. 1/mo.

MICHIGAN

The Ann Arbor News. 340 E. Huron St., Ann Arbor 48106. (313) 665-7721. "Action Please!" Jody Vellucci. 2–3/wk. Occasional feature articles.

Detroit Free Press. 321 W. Lafayette Blvd., Detroit 48231. (313) 222-5996. Trudy Lieberman, Consumer Affairs ed. Appears irregularly.

The Detroit News. 615 Lafayette Blvd., Detroit 48231. (313) 222-6000. "Contact 10." James M. Lycett. 7/wk.

The Grand Rapids Press. Press Plaza, Vandenberg Center, Grand Rapids 49502. (616) 451-8484. "Pinch Hitter." Michael R. Grant, ed. 3/wk.

The Daily News. Greenville 48838. (616) 754-5943; 754-5641. "Do Line." Martha Higbie. 1/wk.

Jackson Citizen Patriot. 214 S. Jackson St., Jackson 49204. (517) 787-2300. "Action, Please!" Martha Cotton. 7/wk.

Kalamazoo Gazette. 401–5 S. Burdick St., Kalamazoo 49003. (616) 345-3511. James Stommen, Consumer reporter. Appears irregularly.

Petoskey News–Review. 319 State St., Petoskey 49770. (616) 347-2544. Betty Bader, Consumer ed. 1–2/wk.

The Oakland Press. Box 1037, Pontiac 48056. "Oakland Hotline." Corenna Aldrich. 6/wk. Inquiries by mail only. Not primarily a consumer column, but handles complaints and services as consumer advocate.

MINNESOTA

Worthington Daily Globe. 300 11 St., Worthington 56187. (507) 376-4121. Robert Cashel, Consumer reporter. Appears irregularly.

MISSISSIPPI

Greenwood Commonwealth. Box 549, Greenwood 38930. (601) 453-5312. "Do." Frank T. Long. Column frequency not given.

Vicksburg Post. Box 951, Vicksburg 39180. (601) 636-4545. "Keeping Posted." Charles Faulk. 1/wk.

MISSOURI

The Columbia Daily Tribune. Columbia 65201. (314) 449-3811. "Action Line." Margaret Taylor. 7/wk. "Us Poor Folks." Margaret Taylor.

The Mexico Ledger. Box 8, Mexico 65265. (314) 581-1111. "Action Line Answers." James Sterner. Appears irregularly.

News/Leader & Press. 651 Boonville, Springfield 65801. (417) 869-4411. "Action." Katie Dark. 1/wk. Other consumer features include Whole Earth Almanac, local and business news.

NEBRASKA

North Platte Telegraph. Box 370, 315 E. Fifth, North Platte 69101. (308) 532-6000. "Action Line." Sharron Hollen. 1/wk. Toll free telephone number: (800) 662-2910.

York Daily News-Times. Fourth & Platte, York 68467. (402) 362-4478. "Gripe Pipe." Anon. Less than once per week.

NEW JERSEY

Asbury Park Press. Press Plaza, Asbury Park 07712. (201) 774-7000. "Troubleshooter." Jack Hastings. 7/wk.

Courier-Post. Camden 08101. (609) 663-6000. Rich Bergeman, Consumer ed. 1/wk.

The Daily Advance. 87 E. Blackwell St., Dover 07801. (201) 366-3000. "Action Line." Gertrude Lauenstein. 5/wk.

The Record. 150 River St., Hackensack 07602. (201) 646-4190. "Action Line." Lani Luciano. 3/wk. "Of Consuming Interest." Edward J. Gorin. 1/wk. (201) 646-4191. Carol Knopes, Consumer writer. (201) 646-4180.

The Herald-News. 988 Main Ave., Passaic 07055. (201) 777-6000. "Speak Up." Sally Trussell, ed. 5/wk. Publish **Speak Up Directory** (25¢).

The Evening Times. 500 Perry St., Trenton 08605. (609) 659-7500. "Action Line." H. Arthur Smith III. 6/wk.

The News Tribune. Box 9, 1 Hoover Way, Woodbridge 07095. (201) 442-7603. "Action Line." Renae Kasper. 5/wk. "Consumer Notes" and "Action Line Specials" 2/wk.

NEW MEXICO

Albuquerque Journal. Drawer J, Albuquerque 87103. (505) 842-2361. "Journal Action Line." G. Ward Fenley and Louise Miller. 6/wk. Recording phone: (505) 842-2362.

NEW YORK

The Knickerbocker News/Union-Star. Albany 12201. "Action Line." Irene Keeney, ed. 6/wk. Questions by mail only.

The Citizen-Advertiser. 25 Dill St., Auburn 13021. "That's a Good Question." (Vacant). 6/wk. (315) 253-5311.

The Press. Vestal Pkwy. E., Binghamton 13902. (607) 798-1331. "Ask Us for Help." Ed Barrett. 6/wk. Spinoffs on consumer-business pages.

The Sun-Bulletin. Vestal Pkwy. E., Binghamton 13902. (607) 798-1333. "Action Line." Connie Kellam. 6/wk.

Buffalo Evening News. 1 News Plaza, Buffalo 14240. (716) 849-4444; 849-4419. "NEWSpower." Richard Christian. 6/wk. Newspaper produces guides, pamphlets, and other materials which are free of charge to consumers.

Elmira Star-Gazette. 201 Baldwin St., Elmira 14902. (607) 734-5151. "Consumer Scene." Salle Richards. 1/wk.

The Ithaca Journal. 123 W. State St., Ithaca 14850. (607) 272-2321. "Help." Monica Glover. 1/wk.

Union-Sun and Journal. 459–491 S. Transit St., Lockport 14094. (716) 533-3811. "Action Line." Charles J. Wellner. 1/wk. "Consumers Report." Appears irregularly.

The Times Herald/Record. 40 Mulberry St., Middletown 10940. (914) 343-2181, ext. 135. "Action." Jean Kaufman. 2/wk.

The Daily News. 220 E. 42 St., New York 10017. (212) 883-1122. "Listen, Bess . . . ." Bess Myerson. 2/wk. (Syndicated.)

The New York Times. 229 W 43 St., New York 10036. (212) 556-1234. "Consumer Notes." Frances Cerra and Will Lissner. 6/wk., or other consumer features.

Niagara Gazette. 310 Niagara St., Niagara Falls 14302. (716) 282-2311. "HELP." Rebecca Irving. 3/wk.

Democrat & Chronicle. 55 Exchange St., Rochester, 14614. (716) 232-7100. "Help!" Kay Fish. 6/wk. "Help Yourself." Kay Fish. 1/wk.

The Times Record. Broadway and Fifth Ave., Troy 12181. (518) 272-2000. "Hot Line." Frank Sherry. 5/wk.

Utica Observer-Dispatch. 221 Oriskany Plaza, Utica 13503. (315) 792-5037. "Help!" Mary Kendrick. 4/wk.

NORTH CAROLINA

The Charlotte News. Box 360, 600 S. Tryon St., Charlotte 28233. (704) 374-7262. "Call Quest." Bill Weisner. 6/wk. Judy Gaultney and Lib Golding, Consumer columnists.

The Charlotte Observer. Box 2138, 600 S. Tryon St., Charlotte 28233. (704) 375-8635; 374-7338. "Tell-It Line." Jerry H. Simpson, Jr. 7/wk. "Eating Out in the Piedmont." 1/wk. Jack Horan, Consumer reporter.

The Durham Sun. 115–19 Market St., Durham 27702. (919) 682-1317. "Sun Dial." Tom Beavers. 6/wk. Questions and answers on all topics—including consumer affairs.

The Fayetteville Observer. Box 849, Fayetteville 28302. (919) 485-2121, ext. 239. "Live Wire." Jan Van Dine. 6/wk.

Greensboro Daily News/Record. Box 20848. Greensboro 27402. (919) 273-8611, ext. 374. "Hot Line." Elizabeth Swindell. 6/wk. Reader surveys approximately 3/mo.; feature articles when warranted.

The Robesonian. 121 W. Fifth St., Lumberton 28358. (919) 739-4322. "Action Line." Lolita Huckaby. 2/wk.

The Raleigh Times. 215 S. McDowell St., Raleigh 27602. (919) 828-5733. "HOTLINE." Phineas R. Fiske. 6/wk.

Salisbury Post. Box 1160, Salisbury 28144. (704) 636-4231. "Zeroing In." Mary Jane Park. 1/wk.

The Sentinel. Box 3159, Winston-Salem 27102. (919) 723-1011. "Answer Man." Bill Williams. 5/wk.

NORTH DAKOTA

Grand Forks Herald. Box 998, Grand Forks 58201. (701) 775-4211. Marilyn Hagerty, Consumer ed. 3/wk.

OHIO

Beacon Journal. 44 E. Exchange St., Akron 44328. (216) 375-8080. "Action Line." Anon. 7/wk.

Ashland Times-Gazette. Box 128, Ashland 44805. (419) 324-3564, ext. 35. "Question Mart." Jane Swartz. 1/wk.

The Cincinnati Enquirer. 617 Vine St., Cincinnati 45201. (513) 241-8005. "Bick's Action Line." Dwight Bicknell. 6/wk.

The Cleveland Press. 901 Lakeside Ave., Cleveland 44114. (216) 623-1111. "Action Line." Richard Fansler. 6/wk.

The Plain Dealer. 1801 Superior Ave., Cleveland 44114. (216) 523-4295. Electronic recorder phone: (216) 523-4870. "P.D.Q.—Plain Dealer Quickline." John Huth, ed. 7/wk. "P.D. Heartline." 2–3/wk. (on Social Security). (Syndicated.)

The Journal Herald. Fourth and Ludlow Sts., Dayton 45401. (514) 222-2866; 223-1111, ext. 358. "Action Line." William Wild. 6/wk. "Consumer Watch." Ann Heller. 1 or more/wk.

The Crescent-News. Box 249, Defiance 43512. (419) 784-5441. "Action Line." Dave Rhamy. 1/wk.

The Journal News. Court St. and Journal Sq., Hamilton 45012. (513) 863-8281. "Action Line." James Newton. 7/wk.

The Journal. 1657 Broadway, Lorain 44052. (216) 245-6901. "Hot Line." Joanne Deubel. 4/wk. "Watchdog for Buyers." 1/wk.

News Journal. 70 W. Fourth St., Mansfield 44901. (419) 524-2417. "Hot Line." Anne Miller. 7/wk.

Niles Times. 35 W. State St., Niles 44446. (216) 652-5841. "Here's Your Answer." Lloyd R. Stoyer. 1/wk.

The Blade. Box 399, Toledo 43691. (419) 259-7376. "ZIP Line." Ren Rieger, ed. 7/wk. "Mary's ZIP Line." 1/wk. (women). "Auto ZIP Line." 1/wk. (autos).

The News-Herald. Box 351, 38879 Mentor Ave., Willoughby 44094. (216) 942-2103. "Hot Line." Peggy Brumagin. 7/wk.

OKLAHOMA

Tulsa Daily World. Box 1770, Tulsa 74102. (918) 583-5804. "Action Line." Phil Mulkins. 5/wk.

OREGON

The Mail Tribune. Box 1108, Medford 97501. (503) 779-1411. "I'd Like to Know." Earl H. Adams. 1/wk.

PENNSYLVANIA

Call-Chronicle. Sixth and Linden Sts., Allentown 18105. (215) 433-4241. "Consumer Comment." Charlyne Markonyi, Consumer ed. 4/wk. Also "Marketbasket" and "FDA Recall Report."

News-Tribune. Beaver Falls 15010. (412) 846-2560. Pam Franko, Family ed. Consumer information as the need arises.

The Bethlehem Globe-Times. 202 W. Fourth St., Bethlehem 18016. (215) 867-7571, ext. 235. "Action Line." Dolores Caskey. 2/wk.

Bradford Era. 43 Main St., Bradford 16701. (814) 368-3173. "Round the Square." Staff. 6/wk.

The Courier-Express. Courier-Express Bldg., Dubois 15801. (814) 371-4200, ext. 38. "Jottings." M. L. Bloom. 3/wk.

Ellwood City Ledger. 835 Lawrence Ave., Ellwood City 16117. (412) 758-7529. "Action Line." C. R. Moser. 1/wk.

Erie News-Times. Box 400, 205 W. 12 St., Erie 16512. (814) 456-8531. "Newsbeats Action." Doug Rieder. 5/wk.

The Philadelphia Inquirer. 400 N. Broad St., Philadelphia 19101. (215) 854-2586. "Consumer News." Richard Pothier. 2/wk. Frequent general stories.

Pottsville Republican. 111–117 Mahantongo St., Pottsville 17901. (717) 622-2345. "Action Line." Catharine Bright. 2/wk.

Reading Eagle. Box 582, Reading 19603. (215) 373-4221, ext. 275. Carole F. Reber, Consumer reporter.

RHODE ISLAND

The Sun. 56 Main St., Westerly 02891. (401) 596-7791. Charles W. Utter, Consumer ed. Appears irregularly.

SOUTH DAKOTA

Rapid City Journal. Box 450. Rapid City 57701. (605) 342-0280. "Action Line." Sally Farrar. 1/wk.

Watertown Public Opinion. Watertown 57201. (605) 886-6903. "Action Line." Gordon Garnes. 1/wk.

TENNESSEE

Bristol, Tenn. See **Herald-Courier**, Bristol, Va.

Greeneville Daily Sun. Greeneville 37743. (615) 638-4181. "Searchlight." John M. Jones, Jr. 1/wk. "Dear Consumer." (Syndicated column by Virginia Knauer, Special Assistant to the President for Consumer Affairs.)

Commercial Appeal. 495 Union Ave., Memphis 38101. (901) 526-3311. "Action Please." Sally Wright. 4/wk. Christine Arpe, Consumer Affairs ed. 1/wk. (901) 526-8811.

TEXAS

The Abilene Reporter-News. Box 30, Abilene 79605. (915) 673-4271. "Action Line." Ellie Rucker. 5/wk.

Cleburne Times-Review. Box 1620, Cleburne 76031. (817) 645-2441. "Howdy Folks!" John Butner. 6/wk.

Caller-Times. Box 9136, Corpus-Christi 78408. (512) 884-2011, ext. 206. "Action Line." Lynn Pentony. 7/wk.

The Dallas Times Herald. Box 5445, Dallas 75222. (214) 744-6249. "Action Line." Mae Graves, ed. 6/wk.

The Fort Worth Press. Press Bldg., Fifth and Jones, Fort Worth 76101. (817) 336-2626. "Action Desk." Marvin Garrett. 6/wk.

The Houston Post. 4747 Southwest Freeway, Houston 77001. (713) 621-7242. "Action Line." Leslie Sowers. 7/wk.

The News. Box 789, Port Arthur 77640. (713) 985-5541. "Box 7-8-9." Ellen Corbello. 6/wk.

San Antonio Express. Box 2171, San Antonio 78297. (512) 225-7411. "Action/Express" Anon. 7/wk.

UTAH

The Deseret News. Box 1257, 34 E. First S., Salt Lake City 84110. "Do-It Man." John E. McCormick. 5/wk.

VIRGINIA

Herald-Courier. Box 678. Bristol 24201. (703) 669-2181. "Hot Line." Helen Mitchell. 2/wk.

The Free Lance-Star. Box 617, Fredericksburg 22401. (703) 373-5000. "Action Line." Earl M. Copp, Jr. 5/wk.

Ledger-Star. Norfolk 23501. (804) 446-2265. "Hot Line Spinoffs." Rome Scott. 7/wk.

WASHINGTON

The Daily News. Port Angeles 98362. (206) 452-2345. "Ask Capt. Clallam." Donald V. Paxson. Appears irregularly.

The Seattle Times. Box 70, Seattle 98111. (206) 622-0300, ext. 239. "Troubleshooter." Dick Moody. 6/wk. Janet Horne, Consumer reporter. Appears irregularly.

WISCONSIN

Press-Gazette. 435 E. Walnut, Green Bay 54305. (414) 435-4411. Robert Woessner, Consumer ed. As need arises.

The Milwaukee Journal. Journal Sq., Milwaukee 53201. (414) 224-2364. "Ask the Journal." Hyman Chester. 6/wk. Mildred Freese, Consumer writer. Column 1/wk; stories daily.

Canadian Newspapers

ALBERTA

Edmonton Journal. Edmonton T5J 2S6. (403) 425-9120. "Counterpoints." Nancy Clegg Buck. 4/wk.

BRITISH COLUMBIA

The Province. 2250 Granville St., Vancouver V6H 3G2. (604) 732-2497. "Action Line." R. A. Chatelin. 6/wk.

MANITOBA

The Brandon Sun. Brandon R7A 5Z6. (204) 727-2452. "Question Period." John Mayhew. 3/wk.

The Winnipeg Tribune. Box 7000, Winnipeg R3C 3B2. (204) 985-4609. "Spotlight." Marjorie Gilles. 5/wk. "Buyers' Forum." 1/wk.

ONTARIO

The London Free Press. Box 2280, London N6A 4G1. (519) 679-1111. "Sound Off." Gordon Sanderson. 5/wk.

The Times-Journal. 16–18 Hincks St., St. Thomas N5P 3W6. (519) 631-6120. "Dial-Log." L. J. Beavis. 6/wk. Reader opinion feature; consumer problems handled occasionally.

The Toronto Star. 1 Yonge St., Toronto M5E 1E6. (416) 367-2000. "Star Probe." Rod Goodman. 6/wk.

Syndicated Columnists

Dave Goodwin. "Insurance for Consumers." 5/wk. Dave Goodwin & Assoc., Box 6661, Surfside, Fla. 33154. (305) 531-0071. Feature runs in **Miami Beach Sun-Reporter**, etc.

Eliot Janeway. "Ask Janeway"; "Janeway's View." 4/wk. Chicago Tribune-New York News Syndicate. 220 E. 42 St., New York, N.Y. 10017. (212) 249-8833. Features run in **Chicago Tribune** and about 100 other newspapers.

Sidney Margolius. "For the Consumer." 2/wk. Women's News Service. 220 E. 42 St., New York, N.Y. 10017. (212) 682-3020. Feature runs in **Philadelphia Bulletin, Washington Star, Boston Globe** and about 50 other newspapers. Also syndicated once a week by **The Machinist** to about 100 labor papers.

Martha Patton. "Money in Your Pocket." 3/wk. Chicago Tribune-New York News Syndicate. 220 E. 42 St., New York, N.Y. 10017. (212) 249-8833. Originates on the financial page of the **Chicago Tribune**; syndicated to 100 newspapers in the United States and Canada.

Sylvia Porter. "Your Money's Worth." 5/wk. Publishers Hall Syndicate. 30 E. 42 St., New York, N.Y. 10017. (212) 682-5560. Runs in **Washington Post, New York Post, San Francisco Chronicle** and 343 other newspapers in the United States and Canada.

Arthur E. Rowse. "Consumer Contact." 2/wk.; "HELP-MATE." 1/wk. Consumer News, Inc., Rm. 813, National Press Bldg., Washington, D.C. 20004. (202) 737-1190. Appears in **Chicago Sun Times, Baltimore Sun,** plus several dozen others.

Merryle Stanley Rukeyser. "Everybody's Money." 3/wk. B. H. Simon Syndicate. Old Mamaroneck Rd., Suite 6C, White Plains, N.Y. 10605. (914) 761-7868. Appears in **The Home** (Norwalk, Conn.) and many other syndicate papers.

Peter Weaver. "Mind Your Money." Frequency unknown. Weaver Communications. 661 National Press Bldg., Washington, D.C. 20004. Syndicated through King Features to **Washington Post, Los Angeles Times,** many others.

Betty Yarmon. "Family Finance." 1/wk. 35 Sutton Pl., New York, N.Y. 10022. (212) 755-3487. Syndicated through Women's News Service to **Long Island Press** and over 40 others.

DIRECTORY OF PUBLISHERS

Abbey Press
St. Meinrad, Ind. 47577
(812) 356-6649

Academic Media
14852 Ventura Blvd.
Sherman Oaks, Calif. 91403
(213) 981-8101

Acropolis Books, Ltd.
Colortone Bldg.
2400 17th St. N.W.
Washington, D.C. 20009
(202) DU7-6800

Adams Press
30 W. Washington St.
Chicago, Ill. 60602
(312) 236-3838

Addison-Wesley Publishing Co, Inc.
Jacob Way
Reading, Mass. 01867
(617) 944-3700

AIMS Instructional Media Services, Inc.
P.O. Box 1010
Hollywood, Calif. 90028
(213) 386-3066

Allyn & Bacon, Inc.
470 Atlantic Ave.
Boston, Mass. 02210
(617) 482-9220

American Council on Consumer Interests
238 Stanley Hall
University of Missouri
Columbia, Mo. 65201
(314) 882-7836

American Enterprise Institute
1150 17th St. N.W.
Washington, D.C. 20036
(202) 296-5616

American Home Economics Assn.
2010 Massachusetts Ave. N.W.
Washington, D.C. 20036
(202) 833-3100

American Institute for Economic Research
Division St.
Great Barrington, Mass. 01230
(413) 528-0140

American Optometric Assn.
7000 Chippewa St.
St. Louis, Mo. 63119
(314) 832-5770

American Photographic Book Publishing Co., Inc.
E. Gate & Zeckendorf Blvds.
Garden City, N.Y. 11530
(516) 248-2233

American Public Health Assn.
1015 18th St. N.W.
Washington, D.C. 20036
(202) 467-5000

Apex Piano Publishers
2621 S. Eighth St.
Sheboygan, Wis. 53081
(414) 458-4489

Arbor House Publishing Co., Inc.
757 Third Ave.
New York, N.Y. 10017
(212) 832-3810

Arco Publishing Co., Inc.
219 Park Ave. S.
New York, N.Y. 10003
(212) OR3-6600

Arlington House, Inc.
81 Centre Ave.
New Rochelle, N.Y. 10801

Atheneum Publishers
122 E. 42 St.
New York, N.Y. 10017
(212) 661-4500

Aurora Publishers Inc.
118 16th Ave. S.
Nashville, Tenn. 37219
(615) 254-5842

Avant-Garde Media, Inc.
251 W. 57 St.
New York, N.Y. 10019
(212) LT1-2000

Avi Publishing Co.
P.O. Box 831
Westport, Conn. 06880
(203) 227-0534

Award Books
235 E. 45 St.
New York, N.Y. 10017
(212) MU3-3000

Ballantine Books, Inc.
201 E. 50 St.
New York, N.Y. 10022
(212) 751-2600

Bantam Books, Inc.
666 Fifth Ave.
New York, N.Y. 10019
(212) 765-6500

Barnes & Noble Books
10 E. 53 St.
New York, N.Y. 10022
(212) 593-7000

Beacon Press
25 Beacon St.
Boston, Mass. 02108
(617) 742-2110

Belmont-Tower Books, Inc.
185 Madison Ave.
New York, N.Y. 10016
(212) 679-7707

Benchmark Films
145 Scarborough Rd.
Briarcliff Manor, N.Y. 10510
(914) 762-3838

The Benjamin Co., Inc.
485 Madison Ave.
New York, N.Y. 10022
(212) 759-6920

Charles A. Bennett Co., Inc.
809 W. Detweiller Dr.
Peoria, Ill. 61614
(309) 691-4454

Channing L. Bete Co., Inc.
45 Federal St.
Greenfield, Mass. 01301
(413) 774-2301

Blue Goose, Inc.
Educational Dept.
P.O. Box 46
Fullerton, Calif. 92632
(714) 879-1520

The Bobbs-Merrill Co., Inc.
4300 W. 62 St.
Indianapolis, Ind. 46206
(317) 291-3100

Books For Better Living
21322 Lassen St.
Chatsworth, Calif. 91311
(213) 882-5900

The Boxwood Press
183 Ocean View Blvd.
Pacific Grove, Calif. 93950
(408) 375-9110

Branden Press, Inc.
221 Columbus Ave.
Boston, Mass. 02116
(617) 267-7471

Brigham Street House
5899 S. State St., Suite 15
Salt Lake City, Utah 84107
(801) 262-3338

William Brose Productions, Inc.
3168 Oakshire Dr.
Hollywood, Calif. 90068
(213) 851-5822

William C. Brown Co., Publishers
2460 Kerper Blvd.
Dubuque, Iowa 52001
(319) 588-1451

Brownstone Publishers, Inc.
149 E. 81 St.
New York, N.Y. 10028
(212) 687-4555

Bureau of National Affairs, Inc.
1231 25th St. N.W.
Washington, D.C. 20037
(202) 223-3500

Camaro Publishing Co.
P.O. Box 90430
Los Angeles, Calif. 90009
(213) 837-7500

Canfield Press
850 Montgomery St.
San Francisco, Calif. 94133
(415) 989-9000

Career Institute, Inc.
555 E. Lange St.
Mundelein, Ill. 60060
(312) 566-5400

Caveat Emptor
556 U.S. Hwy. 22
Hillside, N.J. 07205

Celestial Arts
231 Adrian Rd.
Millbrae, Calif. 94030
(415) 692-4500

Chancellor Press
See Dell Publishing Co., dist.

Charterhouse Books, Inc.
750 Third Ave.
New York, N.Y. 10017
(212) 661-1700

The Chatham Press, Inc.
15 Wilmot Lane
Riverside, Conn. 06878
(203) 637-4313

Child Welfare League of America
67 Irving Place
New York, N.Y. 10003
(212) 254-7410

Citizens' Advisory Committee on
Environmental Quality
1700 Pennsylvania Ave. N.W.
Washington, D. C. 20006
(202) 223-3040

P. F. Collier, Inc.
866 Third Ave.
New York, N.Y. 10022
(212) 935-2000

Commerce Clearing House, Inc.
4025 W. Peterson Ave.
Chicago, Ill. 60646
(312) CO7-9010

Consumer Action Now
30 E. 68 St.
New York, N.Y. 10021
(212) 628-2295

Consumer Age Press
P.O. Box 279
Syracuse, N.Y. 13214
(315) 446-6262

Consumer Federation of America
1012 14th St. N.W.
Washington, D.C. 20005
(202) 737-3732

Consumer Information Center
Public Documents Distribution Center
Pueblo, Colo. 81009
(303) 544-5277

Consumer News, Inc.
National Press Bldg.
529 14th St. N.W.
Washington, D.C. 20004
(202) 737-1190

Consumers' Alliance
P.O. Box 160
Christopher St. Sta.
New York, N.Y. 10014

Consumers' Assn. of Canada
251 Laurier Ave. W., Rm. 801
Ottawa, Ont. KlP 5Z7
(613) 238-4840

Consumers League of New Jersey
22 Church St.
Montclair, N.J. 07042
(201) 744-6449

Consumers' Research, Inc.
Washington, N.J. 07882
(201) 689-3300

Consumers Union of the U.S., Inc.
256 Washington St.
Mount Vernon, N.Y. 10550
(914) 664-6400

Cornerstone Library, Inc.
630 Fifth Ave.
New York, N.Y. 10020
(212) CI6-1350

Council on the Environment of New York City
New York City Health Services Admin.
51 Chambers St.
New York, N.Y. 10007
(212) 566-0990

Coward, McCann & Geoghegan, Inc.
200 Madison Ave.
New York, N.Y. 10016
(212) 883-5500

Thomas Y. Crowell Co.
666 Fifth Ave.
New York, N.Y. 10019
(212) 489-2200

Crown Publishers, Inc.
419 Park Ave. S.
New York, N.Y. 10016
(212) MU5-8550

Dafran House Publishers, Inc.
42 W. 39 St.
New York, N.Y. 10018
(212) 564-6760

The John Day Co., Inc.
257 Park Ave. S.
New York, N.Y. 10010
(212) 533-9000

Dell Publishing Co., Inc.
1 Dag Hammarskjold Plaza
New York, N.Y. 10017
(212) 832-7300

Deseret Book Co.
P.O. Box 659
Salt Lake City, Utah 84110
(801) 328-8191

The Dial Press
1 Dag Hammarskjold Plaza
New York, N.Y. 10017
(212) 832-7300

Dodd, Mead & Co.
79 Madison Ave.
New York, N.Y. 10016
(212) 685-6464

Dolphin
See Doubleday & Co., Inc.

Dorrance & Co.
1617 J. F. Kennedy Blvd.
Philadelphia, Pa. 19103
(215) 568-3553

Doubleday & Co., Inc.
Garden City, N.Y. 11530
New York Office: 277 Park Ave.
New York, N.Y. 10017
(212) 953-4516

Dow Jones Books
P.O. Box 300
Princeton, N.J. 08540
(609) 452-2000

Drake Publishers, Inc.
381 Park Ave. S.
New York, N.Y. 10016
(212) 679-4500

E. P. Dutton & Co., Inc.
201 Park Ave. S.
New York, N.Y. 10003
(212) 674-5900

Economic Education Bulletin
See American Institute for Economic Research

Emporium Publications, Inc.
28 Sackville St.
Charlestown, Mass. 02129
(617) 241-9549

Enterprise Publications
230 Park Ave., Suite 410
New York, N.Y. 10017
(212) 679-3600

Essandess Special Editions
630 Fifth Ave.
New York, N.Y. 10020
(212) CI5-6400

Exposition Press, Inc.
50 Jericho Turnpike
Jericho, N.Y. 11753
(516) 997-9050

F.O.S.G. Publications
P.O. Box 95
Oradell, N.J. 07649
(201) 265-3680

Faber and Faber
See Transatlantic Arts, dist.

Farnsworth Publishing Co., Inc.
78 Randall Ave.
Rockville Centre, N.Y. 11570
(516) 536-8400

Farrar, Straus & Giroux, Inc.
19 Union Sq. W.
New York, N.Y. 10003
(212) 741-6900

Fawcett World Library
1515 Broadway
New York, N.Y. 10036
(212) 869-3000

Federal-State Reports, Inc.
2201 Wilson Blvd.
Arlington, Va. 22201
(202) 525-4950

Frederick Fell Publishers, Inc.
386 Park Ave. S.
New York, N.Y. 10016
(212) 685-9017

FilmFair Communications
10900 Ventura Blvd.
Studio City, Calif. 91604
(213) 985-0244

Financial Publishing Co.
82 Brookline Ave.
Boston, Mass. 02215
(617) 262-4040

Fleet Press Corp.
160 Fifth Ave.
New York, N.Y. 10010
(212) 243-6100

Follett Publishing Co.
1010 W. Washington Blvd.
Chicago, Ill. 60607
(312) 666-5858

Food and Drug Admin.
U.S. Dept. of Health, Education and Welfare
5600 Fishers Lane
Rockville, Md. 20852
(301) 443-3380

The Free Press
866 Third Ave.
New York, N.Y. 10022
(212) 935-2000

Friends of the Earth
See Ballantine Books, dist.

Funk & Wagnalls, Inc.
55 E. 77 St.
New York, N.Y. 10021
(212) 734-5502

Gale Research Co.
Book Tower
Detroit, Mich. 48226
(313) 961-2242

Gambit, Inc.
53 Beacon St.
Boston, Mass. 02108
(617) 523-8205

Garden Way Publishing Co.
Charlotte, Vt. 05445
(802) 425-2171

GET Consumer Protection
P.O. Box 355
Ansonia Sta.
New York, N.Y. 10023

Goodnews Publishing Co.
7576 Freedom, N.W.
Canton, Ohio 44720
(216) 494-7040

Goodyear Publishing Co., Inc.
15113 Sunset Blvd.
Pacific Palisades, Calif. 90272
(213) 459-2733

Grossman Publishers
625 Madison Ave.
New York, N.Y. 10022
(212) 755-4330

Gulf Publishing Co.
P.O. Box 2608
Houston, Tex. 77001
(713) 529-4301

H. P. Books
P.O. Box 50640
Tucson, Ariz. 85703
(602) 888-2150

Hanover Books
See Quick Fox, dist.

Harcourt Brace Jovanovich, Inc.
757 Third Ave.
New York, N.Y. 10017
(212) 572-5000

Harian Publications
1000 Prince St.
Greenlawn, N.Y. 11740
(516) AN1-2980

Harper & Row Publishers, Inc.
10 E. 53 St.
New York, N.Y. 10022
(212) 593-7000

Hart Publishing Co., Inc.
15 W. Fourth St.
New York, N.Y. 10012
(212) 260-2430

Hawthorn Books, Inc.
260 Madison Ave.
New York, N.Y. 10016
(212) 725-7740

Health Research Group
2000 P St. N.W.
Washington, D.C. 20036
(202) 872-0320

Holbrook Press, Inc.
470 Atlantic Ave.
Boston, Mass. 02210
(617) 482-9861

Holt, Rinehart and Winston, Inc.
383 Madison Ave.
New York, N.Y. 10017
(212) MU8-9100

Houghton Mifflin Co.
2 Park St.
Boston, Mass. 02107
(617) 423-5725

Hurricane House
See Trend Publications, dist.

Indiana University Audio-Visual Center
Bloomington, Ind. 47401
(812) 337-8087

Indiana University Press
Tenth & Morton Sts.
Bloomington, Ind. 47401
(812) 337-4203

Infact Systems
20 Boylston St.
Boston, Mass. 02116

Information Resources Press
2100 M St. N.W., Suite 316
Washington, D.C. 20037
(202) 293-2605

International Publications Service
114 E. 32 St.
New York, N.Y. 10016
(212) 685-9351

Interstate Commerce Commission
12 St. & Constitution Ave. N.W.
Washington, D.C. 20423
(202) 343-4761

The Interstate Printers & Publishers, Inc.
19 N. Jackson St.
Danville, Ill. 61832
(217) 446-0500

Journal Films, Inc.
909 W. Diversey Pkwy.
Chicago, Ill. 60614
(312) LA5-6561

Keats Publishing, Inc.
212 Elm St.
New Canaan, Conn. 06840
(203) 966-8721

The Kiplinger Washington Editors, Inc.
1729 H St. N.W.
Washington, D.C. 20006
(202) 298-6400

Robert R. Knapp
P.O. Box 7234
San Diego, Calif. 92107
(714) 788-1666

Alfred A. Knopf, Inc.
201 E. 50 St.
New York, N.Y. 10022
(212) 751-2600

Law-Arts Publishers, Inc.
453 Greenwich St.
New York, N.Y. 10013
(212) 925-4978

Learning Systems Co.
1818 Ridge Rd.
Homewood, Ill. 60430
(312) IN8-9200

J. B. Lippincott Co.
E. Washington Sq.
Philadelphia, Pa. 19105
(215) WA5-4100

Liveright
386 Park Ave. S.
New York, N.Y. 10016
(212) 683-2050

The M.I.T. Press
28 Carleton St.
Cambridge, Mass. 02142
(617) 253-5646

McGraw-Hill, Inc.
1221 Ave. of the Americas
New York, N.Y. 10020
(212) 997-1221

David McKay Co., Inc.
750 Third Ave.
New York, N.Y. 10017
(212) 661-1700

Macmillan, Inc.
866 Third Ave.
New York, N.Y. 10022
(212) 935-2000

Macrae Smith Co.
225 S. 15 St.
Philadelphia, Pa. 19102
(215) KI5-4270

Major Appliance Consumer Action
Panel
20 N. Wacker Dr.
Chicago, Ill. 60606
(312) 236-3165

Media & Consumer Foundation
P.O. Box 850
Norwalk, Conn. 06852
(203) 972-0441

Charles E. Merrill Publishing Co.
1300 Alum Creek Dr.
Columbus, Ohio 43216
(614) 258-8441

Julian Messner
1 W. 39 St.
New York, N.Y. 10018
(212) CI5-6400

Mixed Media
See J. B. Lippincott, dist.

Money Management Institute
Household Finance Corp.
Prudential Plaza
Chicago, Ill. 60601
(312) 944-7174

Moody Press
820 N. LaSalle St.
Chicago, Ill. 60610
(312) 329-4343

William Morrow & Co., Inc.
105 Madison Ave.
New York, N.Y. 10016
(212) 889-3050

Nash Publishing Corp.
9255 Sunset Blvd.
Los Angeles, Calif. 90069
(213) 272-9624

National Assn. of Secondary School
Principals
1904 Association Dr.
Reston, Va. 22070
(703) 860-0200

National Automobile Dealers Used Car Guide Co.
2000 K St. N.W.
Washington, D.C. 20006
(202) 337-6000

National Underwriter Co.
420 E. Fourth St.
Cincinnati, Ohio 45202
(513) 721-2140

The New American Library Inc.
1301 Ave. of the Americas
New York, N.Y. 10019
(212) 956-3800

New Jersey Dept. of Community Affairs
Office of Legal Services
363 W. State St.
Trenton, N.J. 08625
(609) 292-2121

North Carolina Dept. of Natural and Economic Resources
P.O. Box 27687
Raleigh, N.C. 27611

W. W. Norton & Co., Inc.
500 Fifth Ave.
New York, N.Y. 10036
(212) 354-5500

Oceana Publications, Inc.
Dobbs Ferry, N.Y. 10522
(914) 693-1320

Old-House Journal Co.
199 Berkeley Place
Brooklyn, N.Y. 11217
(212) 636-4514

101 Productions
834 Mission St.
San Francisco, Calif. 94103
(415) 495-6040

Pantheon Books, Inc.
201 E. 50 St.
New York, N.Y. 10022
(212) PL1-2600

Paperback Library
See Warner Paperback Library

Parker Publishing Co.
West Nyack, New York 10994
(201) 947-1000

Pendulum Press, Inc.
Academic Bldg.
Saw Mill Rd.
West Haven, Conn. 06516
(203) 933-2551

Pennsylvania Dept. of Insurance
Harrisburg, Pa. 18503
(717) 787-4049

Pergamon Press, Inc.
Maxwell House
Fairview Park
Elmsford, N.Y. 10523
(914) 592-7700

Petersen Publishing Co.
8490 Sunset Blvd.
Los Angeles, Calif. 90069
(213) 657-5100

Pierian Press
P. O. Box 1808
Ann Arbor, Mich. 48106
(313) 662-1777

Pocket Books
630 Fifth Ave.
New York, N.Y. 10020
(212) CI5-6400

Popular Library
600 Third Ave.
New York, N.Y. 10016
(212) 661-4200

Popular Science
See E. P. Dutton, dist.

Praeger Publishers, Inc.
111 Fourth Ave.
New York, N.Y. 10003
(212) 254-4100

Prentice-Hall, Inc.
Englewood Cliffs, N.J. 07632
(201) 947-1000

Public Affairs Committee, Inc.
381 Park Ave. S.
New York, N.Y. 10016
(212) 683-4331

Publications International, Ltd.
3323 Main St. Skokie, Ill. 60076
(312) 676-3470

G. P. Putnam's Sons
200 Madison Ave.
New York, N.Y. 10016
(212) 883-5500

Pyramid Communications, Inc.
919 Third Ave.
New York, N.Y. 10022
(212) MU8-9215

Quadrangle/The New York Times Book Co.
10 E. 53 St.
New York, N.Y. 10022
(212) 593-7800

Quick Fox
33 W. 60 St.
New York, N.Y. 10023
(212) 246-0325

Random House, Inc.
201 E. 50 St.
New York, N.Y. 10022
(212) PL1-2600

Reader's Digest Assn.
Pleasantville, N.Y. 10570
(914) 769-7000

Henry Regnery Co.
114 W. Illinois St.
Chicago, Ill. 60610
(312) 527-3300

Research and Education Assn.
342 Madison Ave.
New York, N.Y. 10017
(212) 490-3222

Rodale Press
33 E. Minor St.
Emmaus, Pa. 18049
(215) 967-5171

The Ronald Press Co.
79 Madison Ave.
New York, N.Y. 10016
(212) MU3-9070

Rutgers University Cooperative Extension Service
New Brunswick, N.J. 08903
(201) 932-9306

S.O.S. Directory, Inc.
P.O. Box 96
Dearborn, Mich. 48121
(313) 563-5092

William H. Sadlier, Inc.
11 Park Place
New York, N.Y. 10007
(212) 227-2120

St. Martin's Press, Inc.
175 Fifth Ave.
New York, N.Y. 10010
(212) 674-5151

San Francisco Consumer Action
312 Sutter St.
San Francisco, Calif. 94108
(415) 982-0557

Saskatchewan Provincial Library
Bibliographic Services Div.
1352 Winnipeg St.
Regina, Sask. S4R 1J9
(306) 525-9847

Saturday Review Press
See E. P. Dutton, dist.

Charles Scribner's Sons
597 Fifth Ave.
New York, N.Y. 10017
(212) 486-2700

Serina Press
70 Kennedy St.
Alexandria, Va. 22305
(703) 548-4080

Sherbourne Press
1640 S. La Cienega Blvd.
Los Angeles, Calif. 90035
(213) 273-4833

Signet
See New American Library, Inc.

Simon & Schuster, Inc.
630 Fifth Ave.
New York, N.Y. 10020
(212) CI5-6400

South-Western Publishing Co.
5101 Madison Rd.
Cincinnati, Ohio 45227
(513) 271-8811

Sports Car Press
See Crown Publishers, dist.

Stamm Industries
471 W. South St.
Kalamazoo, Mich. 49006
(616) 343-5076

Stein & Day Publishers
7 E. 48 St.
New York, N.Y. 10017
(212) 753-7285

Lyle Stuart, Inc.
120 Enterprise Ave.
Secaucus, N.J. 07094
(201) 866-0490
New York Office: (212) 736-1141

SusAnn Publications
725 S. Central Expressway
Dallas, Tex. 75201
(214) 235-8707

Syracuse University Publications in Continuing Education
105 Roney Lane
Syracuse, N.Y. 13210
(315) 476-5541

J. P. Tarcher, Inc.
9110 Sunset Blvd.
Los Angeles, Calif. 90069
(213) 274-9331

Ten Speed Press
P.O. Box 4310
Berkeley, Calif. 94704
(415) 845-8414

Charles C Thomas, Publisher
301-27 E. Lawrence Ave.
Springfield, Ill. 62717
(217) 789-8980

Time, Inc.
Time & Life Bldg.
Rockefeller Center
New York, N.Y. 10020
(212) 556-3060

Time-Life Books
Time & Life Bldg.
Rockefeller Center
New York, N.Y. 10020
(212) JU6-1212

Tower Publications, Inc.
185 Madison Ave.
New York, N.Y. 10016
(212) 679-7707

Trail-R-Club of America
P.O. Box 1376
Beverly Hills, Calif. 90213
(213) 829-1721

Trailer Life Publishing Co.
23945 Craftsman Rd.
Calabasas, Calif. 91302
(213) 888-6000

Transatlantic Arts, Inc.
N. Village Green
Levittown, N.Y. 11756
(516) 735-4777

Trend Publications, Inc.
P.O. Box 2350
1306 W. Kennedy Blvd.
Tampa, Fla. 33601
(813) 251-1081

Trident Press
630 Fifth Ave.
New York, N.Y. 10020
(212) 245-6400

Charles E. Tuttle Co., Inc.
28 E. Main St.
Rutland, Vt. 05701
(802) 773-8930

United Consumer Service Corp.
466 Lexington Ave.
New York, N.Y. 10017
(212) 532-8840

U.S. Dept. of Agriculture
Office of Communication
Washington, D.C. 20250
(202) 447-5247

U.S. Dept. of Health, Education and Welfare
Office of Consumer Affairs
330 Independence Ave. S.W.
Washington, D.C. 20201
(202) 245-6877

U.S. Dept. of Housing and Urban Development
HUD Bldg.
451 Seventh St. S.W.
Washington, D.C. 20410
(202) 655-5280

U.S. Office of Consumer Affairs
See U.S. Dept. of Health, Education and Welfare, Office of Consumer Affairs

University of Illinois in Champaign
Audio-Visual Dept.
16 S. Oak St.
Champaign, Ill. 61820
(217) 333-1362

University of Oklahoma Press
1005 Asp Ave.
Norman, Okla. 73069
(405) 325-5111

Van Nostrand Reinhold Co.
450 W. 33 St.
New York, N.Y. 10001
(212) 594-8660

Vantage Press, Inc.
516 W. 34 St.
New York, N.Y. 10001
(212) 736-1767

Voice Over Books
200 Park Ave. S.
New York, N.Y. 10003
(212) 674-8666

Wadsworth Publishing Co., Inc.
Belmont, Calif. 94002
(415) 592-1300

Walker & Co.
720 Fifth Ave.
New York, N.Y. 10019
(212) 265-3632

Warner Paperback Library
75 Rockefeller Plaza
New York, N.Y. 10020
(212) 484-8000

Washington Square Press
630 Fifth Ave.
New York, N.Y. 10020
(212) CI5-6400

Franklin Watts, Inc.
730 Fifth Ave.
New York, N.Y. 10019
(212) 757-4050

The Westminster Press
Witherspoon Bldg.
Philadelphia, Pa. 19107
(215) 893-4400

Westover Publishing Co.
333 E. Grace St.
Richmond, Va. 23219
(804) 649-6500

John Wiley & Sons, Inc.
605 Third Ave.
New York, N.Y. 10016
(212) 867-9800

The H. W. Wilson Co.
950 University Ave.
Bronx, N.Y. 10452
(212) 588-8400

Woodall Publishing Co.
3520 Western Ave.
Highland Park, Ill. 60035
(312) 433-4550

Workman Publishing Co., Inc.
231 E. 51 St.
New York, N.Y. 10022
(212) 421-8050

Peter H. Wyden/Publisher
750 Third Ave.
New York, N.Y. 10017
(212) 661-1700

Yara Press
P.O. Box 99113
San Francisco, Calif. 94109

AUTHOR INDEX

Note: Listings refer to entry numbers not page numbers.

Aaker, David A., and George S. Day, eds. *Consumerism: Search for the Consumer Interest*, 115

Addison, Betty G., jt. auth. *See* Wingate, Isabel B., and Karen R. Gillespie

Baker, Jeffrey. *The Truth about Contact Lenses*, 199

Baldyga, Daniel G. *How to Settle Your Own Insurance Claim*, 300

Ballantine, Richard. *Richard's Bicycle Book*, 37

Banker, John C. *Personal Finances for Ministers*, 358

Bauer, Erwin. *The Sportsman on Wheels*, 450

Beasley, M. Robert. *Fell's Guide to Buying, Building and Financing a Home*, 291

Belth, Joseph M. *Life Insurance: A Consumer's Handbook*, 312

Berger, Robert, and Joseph Teplin. *Law and the Consumer*, 117

Berland, Theodore, and the Editors of Consumer Guide. *Rating the Diets*, 187

Bespaloff, Alexis. *Alexis Bespaloff's Guide to Inexpensive Wines*, 516

Better Business Bureau. *Consumer's Buying Guides: How to Get Your Money's Worth*, 57

Bianchi, Carl F. *How to File a Suit in the New Jersey Small Claims Division*, 326

Biddle, G. Vance. *To Buy or Not to Buy? That Is Only One of the Questions*, 292

Bingham, Harry H., jt. auth. *See* Cohen, Jerome B.

Biossat, Bruce. *What You've Got Coming in Medicare & Social Security*, 492

Bird, Jean. *Factory Outlet Shopping Guide*, 503. *See also* 502, 504, 505

Black, Hillel. *Buy Now, Pay Later*, 167

Blackwell, Kate, jt. auth. *See* Nader, Ralph

Blackwell, Kate, jt. ed. *See* Nader, Ralph, and Peter J. Petkas, eds.

Blair, Lorraine. *Answers to Your Everyday Money Questions*, 359

Blaustein, B. J., and Robert Gorman. *How to Have More Money to Spend*, 177

Blodgett, Richard E. *The New York Times Book of Money*, 360

Blum, Richard H. *A Commonsense Guide to Doctors, Hospitals and Medical Care*, 331. *See also* 341

Boggers, Louise. *Your Social Security Benefits*, 493

Bonnesen, Judith A., and Janet L. Burkley. *The Bargain Hunters Field Guide.* See *The Factory Outlet Bargain Book*

——. *The Factory Outlet Bargain Book*, 504

Boudreau, Eugene. *Buying Country Land*, 443

Bowman, George M. *How to Succeed with Your Money*, 361

Brake, John R., ed. *Farm and Personal Finance*, 362

Britton, Virginia. *Personal Finance*, 363

Brown, Jan. *Buy It Right: A Shopper's Guide to Home Furnishings*, 260

Browning, Frank, jt. auth. *See* Ramparts Magazine

Bruce, Ronald, ed. *The Consumer's Guide to Product Safety*, 437. *See also* 439, 441

Buckley, Joseph C. *The Retirement Handbook*, 476

Bureau of National Affairs. *ABC's of the Consumer Product Safety Act: The Law in Brief, Commission Directory, Text of Act, Consumer Product List*, 438

Burger, Robert E., and Jan J. Slavicek. *The Layman's Guide to Bankruptcy*, 33

Burke, Martin, jt. auth. *See* Moger, Byron, with Omar V. Garrison

Burkley, Janet L., jt. auth. *See* Bonnesen, Judith A.

Burns, Scott. *Squeeze It till the Eagle Grins: How to Spend, Save and Enjoy Your Money*, 364

Burton, Rulon T. *How to Get Out of Debt . . . and Stay Out*, 178

——. *SBS (Save before You Spend) Master Budget.* See *How to Get Out of Debt . . . and Stay Out*

Cameron, Allan G. *Food—Facts and Fallacies*, 221

Cannel, Elaine. *How to Invest in Beautiful Things without Being a Millionaire: How the Clever Consumer Can Outthink the Tastemakers*, 261

Caplovitz, David. *The Poor Pay More: Consumer Practices of Low-Income Families*, 168

Car/Puter. *Autofacts 1973*, 5

Carcione, Joe, and Bob Lucas. *The Greengrocer: The Consumer's Guide to Fruits and Vegetables*, 204

Carlson, Margaret Bresnahan, and Ronald G. Shafer. *How to Get Your Car Repaired without Getting Gypped*, 17. *See also* 15, 20

Carper, Jean, jt. auth. *See* Magnuson, Warren G.

Cassiday, Bruce. *The Best House for the Money*, 271

——. *How to Choose Your Vacation House*, 272

Center for Auto Safety. *Small on Safety: The Designed-In Dangers of the Volkswagen*, 23

Charell, Ralph. *How I Turn Ordinary Complaints into Thousands of Dollars: The Diary of a Tough Customer*, 53

Charters, Margaret. *Consumer Education Programming in Continuing Education*, 109

Chernik, Vladimir P. *The Claims Game*, 301

——. *The Consumer's Guide to Insurance Buying*, 302

Christy, George. *The Los Angeles Underground Gourmet*, 460

Citizens Board of Inquiry into Health Services for Americans. *Heal Your Self*, 332

Cobb, Betsy, and Hubbard H. Cobb. *Vacation Houses: What You Should Know before You Buy or Build*, 273

Cobb, Hubbard H. *The Dream House Encyclopedia.* See *How to Buy and Remodel the Older House*

——. *How to Buy and Remodel the Older House*, 286

Cobb, Hubbard H., jt. auth. *See* Cobb, Betsy

Cohen, Jerome B., assisted by Harry H. Bingham. *PLAID for Personal*

Finance. See *Programmed Learning Aid for Personal Finance*
——. *Programmed Learning Aid for Personal Finance*, 365
Cohen, Manuel F., jt. auth. *See* Stigler, George J.
Colby, C. B. *Today's Camping: New Equipment for Modern Campers*, 42
Coleman, B. D. *Money: How to Save It, Spend It and Make It*, 366
Collin, Richard H. *The New Orleans Underground Gourmet.* See *The Revised New Orleans Underground Gourmet*
——. *The Revised New Orleans Underground Gourmet*, 461
Collins, Thomas. *The Complete Guide to Retirement*, 477
Consumer Guide. *Auto Test*, 7
——. *Automobile Buying Guide*, 7
——. *Automobiles*, 7. *See also* 62
——. *Best Buys & Discount Prices*, 62. *See also* 63
——. *Bicycle Test Reports*, 39
——. *Camping and Backpacking Equipment Test Reports*, 43
——. *Fishing Equipment Test Reports*, 202
——. *Guns & Hunting Equipment Test Reports*, 254
——. *Photographic Equipment Test Reports*, 433. *See also* 62
——. *Previews*, 7
——. *Product Report*, 63. *See also* 62
——. *Ratings & Discount Prices.* See *Best Buys & Discount Prices*
——. *Ski Equipment Test Reports*, 491
——. *Stereo & Tape Equipment Test Reports*, 498
Consumer Guide Editors, jt. auths. *See* Berland, Theodore
Consumer Reports. *The Consumers Union Report on Life Insurance*, 313. *See also* 312
——. *The Medicine Show*, 188. *See also* 130
Consumer Reports Editors, jt. auth. *See* Consumers Union's Music Consultant
Consumers League of New Jersey. *New Jersey Consumer Protection Laws*, 161
Consumers Union's Music Consultant and the Editors of Consumer Reports. *Consumers Union Reviews Classical Recordings*, 427
Cook, Geri, jt. auth. *See* Patridge, Barbara
Cooley, Lee Morrison, jt. auth. *See* Cooley, Leland Frederick
Cooley, Leland Frederick, and Lee Morrison Cooley. *How to Avoid the Retirement Trap*, 478. *See also* 476
Corey, Will, jt. auth. *See* Wurlitzer, Randolph
Corr, Francis A. *Government Services for Consumers*, 122
Coulson, Robert. *How to Stay Out of Court*, 327
Cross, Jennifer. *The Supermarket Trap: The Consumer and the Food Industry*, 223. *See also* 236

Dacey, Norman F. *What's Wrong with Your Life Insurance*, 314
Day, George S., jt. auth. *See* Aaker, David A.
deBenedictus, Daniel J. *The Complete Real Estate Adviser*, 293
——. *The Family Real Estate Adviser.* See *The Complete Real Estate Adviser*
——. *How to Become a Real Estate Broker and Turn Your License into*

Big Money. See *The Complete Real Estate Adviser*

——. *Laws Every Homeowner and Tenant Should Know.* See *The Complete Real Estate Adviser*

——. *Practical Ways to Make Money in Real Estate.* See *The Complete Real Estate Adviser*

de Camp, Catherine Crook. *The Money Tree: A New Guide to Successful Personal Finance*, 367

de Caso, Jacques, jt. auth. *See* Pratt, James Norwood

De Forrest, Michael. *How to Buy at Auction*, 3

Denenberg, Herbert S. *A Shopper's Guide to Dentistry*, 185

——. *A Shopper's Guide to Health Insurance*, 309

——. *Shopper's Guide to Insurance: A Series of Tips on How to Shop and Save on Insurance*, 303

——. *A Shopper's Guide to Insurance on Mobile Homes (Pennsylvania)*, 322

——. *A Shopper's Guide to Lawyers*, 328

——. *Shopper's Guide to Pennsylvania Automobile Insurance*. 307

——. *Shopper's Guide to Straight Life Insurance*, 315

——. *Shopper's Guide to Surgery: Fourteen Rules on How to Avoid Unnecessary Surgery*, 333

——. *A Shopper's Guide to Term Life Insurance*, 316

——. *The Shopper's Guidebook to Life Insurance, Health Insurance, Auto Insurance, Homeowner's Insurance, Doctors, Dentists, Lawyers, Pensions, Etc.*, 69. *See also* 185, 309, 315, 316, 333

Dickens, Doris Lee. *You and Your Doctor*, 334

Dickerson, F. Reed, ed. *Product Safety in Household Goods*, 439. *See also* 437

——. *"Report on Product Safety: Household Goods."* See *Product Safety in Household Goods*

Di Cyan, Erwin, and Lawrence Hessman. *Without Prescription: A Guide to the Selection and Use of Medicines You Can Get Over-the-Counter without Prescription, for Safe Self-Medication*, 189

Difloe, Donna. *How to Buy Furniture*, 262

Dodge, Lowell, jt. auth. *See* Nader, Ralph, and Ralf Hotchkiss

Donaldson, Elvin F., and John K. Pfahl. *Personal Finance*, 368

Dorn, Sylvia O'Neill. *The Insider's Guide to Antiques, Art and Collectibles*, 48

Dorries, W. L., Arthur A. Smith, and James R. Young, *Personal Finance: Consuming, Saving and Investing*, 369

Dorst, Sally. *The New York Food Book*, 499

Dowd, Merle E. *How to Get More for Your Money in Running Your Home*, 255. *See also* 393

——. *How to Get Out of Debt and Stay Out of Debt*, 179. *See also* 70

——. *How to Live Better and Spend 20% Less*, 70. *See also* 405

Doyle, Patrick J. *Save Your Health & Your Money*, 335

Driscoll, James G. *Survival Tactics: Coping with the Pressure of Today's Living*, 123

Drury, Treesa Way, and William L. Roper. *Consumer Power*, 124

Ducovny, Amram M. *The Billion $ Swindle: Frauds against the Elderly*, 245

Duncan, Rodger Dean. *Teaching Your Child the Fiscal Facts of Life*, 408

Edmonds, I. G. *Minibikes and Minicycles for Beginners*, 413

Edwards, Marvin H. *Hazardous to Your Health*, 336

Ehrenreich, Barbara, jt. auth. *See* Health Policy Advisory Committee

Ehrenreich, John, jt. auth. *See* Health Policy Advisory Committee

Emanuel, W. D., and Leonard Gaunt. *How to Choose the Camera You Need*, 434

Engel, Lyle Kenyon. *The Complete Book of Mobile Home Living*, 352

——. *The Complete Book of Trailering*, 451

Epstein, Samuel S., and Richard D. Grundy, eds. *Consumer Health and Product Hazards—Chemicals, Electronic Products, Radiation*, 440

——. *The Legislation of Product Safety*, 440

Etcheson, Warren W., jt. auth. *See* Gaedeke, Ralph M.

Evans, Travers Moncure, and David Greene. *The Meat Book: A Consumer's Guide to Selecting, Buying, Cutting, Storing, Freezing and Carving the Various Cuts*, 205

Faber, Doris. *Enough! The Revolt of the American Consumer*, 158. *See also* 159

Fargis, Paul. *Consumer's Handbook*, 71

Ferguson, Mike, and Marilyn Ferguson. *Champagne Living on a Beer Budget: How to Buy the Best for Less*, 72. *See also* 80

Filaseta, Kathy, jt. auth. *See* Socolich, Sally

Finegan, Marcella E. *The Consumer and His Dollars: Workbook and Study Guide*, 96

Fitzsimmons, Cleo. *Consumer Buying for Better Living*, 73

Fletcher, Adele Whitely. *How to Stretch Your Dollar*, 74

Fogiel, Max. *How to Pay Lots Less for Life Insurance . . . and Be Covered for as Much and as Long as You Want*, 317

Ford, Norman D. *Where to Retire on a Small Income*, 479

Fortune Magazine Editors. *Consumerism: Things Ralph Nader Never Told You*, 126

Fowler, Glenn. *How to Buy a Home, How to Sell a Home*, 294

Frank, Arthur, and Stuart Frank. *The People's Handbook of Medical Care*, 337

Frank, Stuart, jt. auth. *See* Frank, Arthur

Franses, Jack. *European and Oriental Rugs for Pleasure and Investment*, 44

Friedman, Gil. *How to Buy and Sell a Used Car in Europe*, 25. *See also* 32

Fuller, John G. *200,000,000 Guinea Pigs: New Dangers in Everyday Foods, Drugs, and Cosmetics*, 127

Gaedeke, Ralph M., and Warren W. Etcheson. *Consumerism: Viewpoints from Business, Government, and the Public Interest*, 128

Gale, Ella. *$$$ and Sense: Your Complete Guide to Wise Buying*, 75. *See also* 130, 393

Garrett, Pauline G. *Consumer Housing*, 256

Garrison, Omar V., jt. auth. *See* Moger, Byron, and Martin Burke

Gartner, John. *All about Pickup Campers, Van Conversions and Motor Homes*, 452

Gaunt, Leonard, jt. auth. *See* Emanuel, W. D.

Geier, Arnold. *Life Insurance: How to Get Your Money's Worth*, 318

Giammattei, Helen, and Katherine Slaughter. *Help Your Family Make a Better Move*, 416. *See also* 393, 421

Gillespie, Karen R., jt. auth. *See* Wingate, Isabel B., and Betty G. Addison

Gillespie, Paul, and Miriam Klipper. *No-Fault: What You Save, Gain, and Lose with the New Auto Insurance*, 308

Gilmore, Forrest E. *How to Plan Now for Your Retirement*, 480

Glaser, Milton, and Jerome Snyder. *The Underground Gourmet*, 462

Glickman, Arthur P., jt. auth. *See* Randall, Donald A.

Goldbeck, Nikki, and David Goldbeck. *The Supermarket Handbook: Access to Whole Foods*, 224

Golde, Roger H. *Can You Be Sure of Your Experts?*, 442

Goldman, Danny, jt. auth. *See* James, Judy

Goldstein, Sue, and Ann Light. *The Underground Shopper*, 506

Gollin, James. *Pay Now, Die Later: What's Wrong with Life Insurance: A Report on Our Biggest and Most Wasteful Industry*, 319

Goodman, Emily Jane. *The Tenant Survival Book*, 323. *See also* 325

Goodwin, Dave. *Stop Wasting Your Insurance Dollars*, 304

Gordon, Leland J., and Stewart M. Lee. *Economics for Consumers*, 76

Gorman, Robert, jt. auth. *See* Blaustein, B. J.

Gourlie, John. *How to Locate in the Country: Your Personal Guide*, 417

Greene, David, jt. auth. *See* Evans, Travers Moncure

Gregg, John E. *The Health Insurance Racket and How to Beat It*, 310

Grey, Jonathan. *How to Get Out of Debt and Stay Out*, 180

Griffin, Al. *The Credit Jungle*, 170

——. *Motorcycles: A Buyer's and Rider's Guide*, 414

——. *Recreational Vehicles: A Buyer's & User's Guide*, 453

——. *So You Want to Buy a House*, 274

——. *So You Want to Buy a Mobile Home*, 353. *See also* 352

——. *So You Want to Buy a Motorboat: A Handbook for Prospective Owners, Describing and Evaluating Current Makes and Models*, 412

——. *So You'd Like to Buy an Airplane!*, 1

Grodner, Arlene, B., jt. auth. *See* Tuck, Miriam L.

Groll, Richard, jt. auth. *See* Ranney, George, Jr., and Edmond Parker

Groupe, Leonard M. *Going Broke and How to Avoid It*, 181

Groves, C. E. *How to Buy Cars at Top Discount*, 8. *See also* 12

Grozier, Mary, and Richard Roberts. *New York's City Streets*, 193

Gruenberg, Sidonie Matsner. *Your Child and Money*, 409

Grundy, Richard D., jt. ed. *See* Epstein, Samuel S.

Gulick, William. *Consumers' Guide to Prescription Prices*, 190

Gushee, Charles H., ed. *Cost of Personal Borrowing in the United States*, 169

Habeeb, Virginia. *MACAP's Handbook for the Informed Consumer*, 263

Halcomb, Ruth. *Money & the Working Ms.*, 370

Hamilton, Richard T. *The Great Confidence Games: Game 1—The Insurance Game*, 305

Harmer, Ruth Mulvey. *Unfit for Human Consumption*, 211

Harris, Gertrude. *Pots & Pans Etc.*, 264

Harris, Kenn. *Opera Recordings: A Critical Guide*, 428

Hastings, Paul, and Norbert Nietus. *Personal Finance*, 371

Hayes, Richard L. *How to Live Like a Retired Millionaire on Less than $250 a Month*, 481

Health Policy Advisory Committee (written for Health Pac by Barbara Ehrenreich and John Ehrenreich). *The American Health Empire: Power, Profits and Politics*, 338. *See also* 336

Heimerl, Ramon P. jt. auth. *See* Wilhelms, Fred T., and Herbert M. Jelley

Henkel, Stephen C. *Bikes: A How-to-Do-It Guide to Selection, Care, Repair, Maintenance, Decoration, Safety, and Fun on Your Bicycle*, 40

Herndon, Booton. *Satisfaction Guaranteed: An Unconventional Report to Today's Consumers*, 129

Herrmann, Robert O., jt. auth. *See* Jelley, Herbert M.

Hessman, Lawrence, jt. auth. *See* Di Cyan, Erwin

High Fidelity. *High Fidelity Record Annual.* See *Records in Review*

——. *Records in Review*, 429

Higson, James D. *The Higson Home Buyer's Guide*, 275

Hoffman, George C. *The Comstock Western Home Buyer's Guide*, 276

Holcombe, Melinda, jt. auth. *See* Thal, Helen M.

Hopkins, Robert. *I've Had It: A Practical Guide to Moving Abroad*, 418

Hotchkiss, Ralf, jt. auth. *See* Nader, Ralph, and Lowell Dodge

Hoyt, Edwin P. *Your Health Insurance: A Story of Failure*, 311

Hull, Clinton. *How to Choose, Buy and Enjoy a Motor Home, Van Camper, Tent-Top or Tent*, 454

Humphrey, Clifford C. *Back to the Bike*, 41

Hunter, Beatrice Trum. *Consumer Beware! Your Food and What's Been Done to It*, 212. *See also* 236

——. *Fact/Book on Food Additives and Your Health*, 213

Hunter, Mark, jt. auth. *See* Meyer, Martin J.

Interstate Commerce Commission. *Summary of Information for Shippers of Household Goods*, 419

Jackson, Charles R. *How to Buy a Used Car*, 26

Jacobsen, Charles W. *Check Points on How to Buy Oriental Rugs*, 45. *See also* 44

Jacobson, Michael F. *Eater's Digest: The Consumer's Factbook of Food Additives*, 214

James, Judy, and Danny Goldman. *Nothing New: A Guide to the Fun of Second-Hand Shopping in Los Angeles and Surrounding Areas*, 507

Janeway, Eliot. *What Shall I Do with My Money?*, 372. *See also* 373

——. *You and Your Money: A Survival Guide to the Controlled Economy*, 373

Jelley, Herbert M., jt. auth. *See* Wilhelms, Fred T., and Ramon P. Heimerl

Jelley, Herbert M., and Robert O. Herrmann. *The American Consumer: Issues and Decisions*, 78. *See also* 102, 104

Jenney, George. *How to Rob a Bank without a Gun*, 488

Johnson, Thomas A. *Dollar Power*, 374

——. *A Place to Live*, 257

Kahn, E. J., Jr., jt. auth. *See* Kahn, Joseph P.

Kahn, Joseph P., and E. J. Kahn, Jr. *The Boston Underground Gourmet*, 463. *See also* 470, 471

Kallet, Arthur, and F. J. Schlinck. *100,000,000 Guinea Pigs. See* Fuller, John G. *200,000,000 Guinea Pigs*

Kaplan, Melvin James. *Out of Debt through Chapter 13*, 182

Karr, James N. *The Condominium Buyer's Guide: What to Look for—and Look Out for—in Resort, Residential and Commercial Condominiums*, 49. *See also* 50

Kemp, Judy Lynn. *The Supermarket Survival Manual*, 225

Kennedy, Edward M. *In Critical Condition: The Crisis in America's Health Care*, 339

Kime, Robert E. *Health: A Consumer's Dilemma*, 340

King, John W. *Save Money and Grow Rich*, 79

Kinney, Cle, jt. auth. *See* Kinney, Jean

Kinney, Jean, and Cle Kinney. *How to Find and Finance a Great Country Place*, 444

——. *How to Get 20 to 90% Off on Everything You Buy*, 80

Kirk, John. *How to Manage Your Money*, 375

Klamkin, Charles. *How to Buy Major Appliances*, 265

——. *If It Doesn't Work, Read the Instructions: The Electrical Appliance Jungle*, 266

Klein, David, and Marymae Klein. *Supershopper: A Guide to Spending and Saving*, 81. *See also* 94

Klein, Marymae, jt. auth. *See* Klein, David

Klipper, Miriam, jt. auth. *See* Gillespie, Paul

Klotz, S. D. *Guide to Modern Medical Care*, 341. *See also* 331

Kneass, Jack. *How to Buy Recreational Vehicles*, 455

——. *How to Select a Car or Truck for Trailer Towing*, 456

Kramer, Amihud. *Food and the Consumer*, 226

Kratz, Carole, and Albert Lee. *The Coupon Way to Lower Food Prices*, 227

Kunnes, Richard. *Your Money or Your Life: Rx for the Medical Market Place*, 342

Laas, William. *Lawyers Title Home Buying Guide*, 295

Lane, Sylvia, jt. auth. *See* Phillips, E. Bryant

J. K. Lasser Tax Institute. *J. K. Lasser's Managing Your Family Finances*, 376. *See also* 393

——. *Your Guide to Social Security and Medicare Benefits*, 494

J. K. Lasser Tax Institute, and Sam Shulsky. *Investing for Your Future*, 482

Lee, Albert. *The ASC Guide to Best Buys in Used Cars*, 27

Lee, Albert, jt. auth. *See* Kratz, Carole

Lee, Albert, and John D. Weimer. *How to Get Good and Honest Auto Service*, 19

Lee, Mary Price. *Money & Kids: How to Earn It, Save It and Spend It*, 410

Lee, Stewart M., jt. auth. *See* Gordon, Leland J.

Leibenderfer, John E. *Planning Your Financial Independence*, 377

Leinwald, Gerald, ed. *The Consumer*, 130

Lewis, James, ed. *The Consumer's Fight-Back Book*, 131

Lewis, Roz. *The Little Restaurants of Los Angeles*, 464

Lewis, Roz, and Joe Pierce. *The Little Restaurants of San Francisco*, 464

Light, Ann, jt. auth. *See* Goldstein, Sue

Linder, Bertram L., and Edwin Selzer. *You the Consumer*, 82

Longgood, William. *The Poisons in Your Food*, 215

Lucas, Bob, jt. auth. *See* Carcione, Joe

McCarthy, Albert, et al. *Jazz on Record: The First 50 Years 1917–1967*, 430

McClellan, Grant S., ed. *The Consuming Public*, 132

McClure, John A. *Meat Eaters Are Threatened*, 206

McDaniel, Joseph M., Jr., jt. auth. *See* Meyer, Martin J.

McGarrah, Rob. "It's Time Consumers Knew More about Their Doctors," 343

McKay, Quinn G., and William A. Tilleman. *Money Matters in Your Marriage*, 378

McKenna, H. Dickson. *A House in the City: A Guide to Buying and Renovating Old Row Houses*, 287. *See also* 290

McTaggart, Aubrey C., and Howard L. Slusher, consulting ed. *The Health Care Dilemma*, 344

Magnuson, Warren G., and Jean Carper. *The Dark Side of the Marketplace: The Plight of the American Consumer*, 133

Maloney, Richard F., ed. "Annuities from the Buyer's Point of View," 2

——. "Life Insurance from the Buyer's Point of View," 320

Margolius, Sidney. *The Consumer's Guide to Better Buying*, 83

——. *Family Money Problems*, 379

——. *The Great American Food Hoax*, 229. *See also* 230, 236

——. *A Guide to Consumer Credit*, 171

——. *Health Foods: Facts and Fakes*, 230

——. *How to Finance Your Home*. 277

——. *How to Make the Most of Your Money*, 183

——. *How to S-t-r-e-t-c-h Your M-o-n-e-y*, 380

——. *The Innocent Consumer vs. the Exploiters*, 134. *See also* 130

——. *The Responsible Consumer*. 135

Marine, Gene, and Judith Van Allen. *Food Pollution: The Violation of Our Inner Ecology*, 216

Markovich, Alexander. *How to Buy a New or Used Car*, 9. *See also* 26

Markstein, David L. *Manage Your Money and Live Better: Get the Most from Your Dwindling Dollars*, 381

Marwick, Charles S., jt. auth. *See* Placere, Morris N.

Massee, William E. *An Insider's Guide to Low-Priced Wines*, 517. *See also* 518

——. *McCall's Guide to the Wines of America.* See *Massee's Guide to Wines of America*

——. *Massee's Guide to Wines of America*, 518. *See also* 517

Matthews, Douglas. *Sue the B*st*rds: The Victim's Handbook*, 329

Mehr, Robert I. *PLAID for Principles of Insurance.* See *Programmed Learning Aid for Principles of Insurance*

——. *Programmed Learning Aid for Principles of Insurance*, 306

Mendelson, Mary Adelaide. *Tender Loving Greed: How the Incredibly Lucrative Nursing Home "Industry" Is Exploiting America's Old People and Defrauding Us All*, 423

Meyer, Martin J. *Martin Meyer's Moneybook*, 84

Meyer, Martin J., and Joseph M. McDaniel, Jr. *Don't Bank on It!*, 489. *See also* 84, 405, 488

Meyer, Martin J., and Mark Hunter. *How to Turn Plastic into Gold: A Revolutionary New Way to Make Money and Save Money Every Time You Buy Anything—with Credit Cards*, 172. *See also* 84

Meyers, Jerome I. *Wipe Out Your Debts and Make a Fresh Start*, 34

Miller, Erston V., and James I. Munger. *Good Fruits and How to Buy Them*, 207

Mintz, Morton. *By Prescription Only*, 191

——. *The Therapeutic Nightmare.* See *By Prescription Only*

Moger, Byron, and Martin Burke, with Omar V. Garrison. *How to Buy a House*, 278

Monefeldt, Jess. *How to Buy or Sell a Home*, 296

Moolman, Valerie. *How to Buy Food*, 232

Moral, Herbert R. *Buying Country Property*, 445

Morgan, Jean, jt. auth. *See* Wasserman, Paul

Morganstern, Stanley. *Legal Protection for the Consumer*, 162

Mumey, Glen A. *Personal Economic Planning*, 385

Munger, James I., jt. auth. *See* Miller, Erston V.

Murray, Barbara B., ed. *Consumerism—the Eternal Triangle: Business, Government and Consumers*, 137

Murray, Robert W., Jr. *How to Buy the Right House at the Right Price*, 279. *See also* 271

Musson, Noverre. *The National Directory of Retirement Residences: Best Places to Live when You Retire*, 483

Nadel, Mark V. *The Politics of Consumer Protection*, 163

Nader, Ralph. *Beware*, 441. *See also* 437

——. *Unsafe at Any Speed: The Designed-In Dangers of the American Automobile*, 24. *See also* 14, 23, 130

Nader, Ralph, ed. *The Consumer and Corporate Accountability*, 138

Nader, Ralph, and Kate Blackwell. *You and Your Pension*, 426

Nader, Ralph, Ralf Hotchkiss, and Lowell Dodge. *What to Do with Your Bad Car: An Action Manual for Lemon Owners*, 14. *See also* 15, 29, 146

Nader, Ralph, Peter J. Petkas, and Kate Blackwell, eds. *Whistle Blowing: Report of the Conference on Professional Responsibility*, 139

Natella, Arthur A., jt. auth. *See* Schoenfeld, David

National Commission on Product Safety. *Hearings and Final Reports.*

See Bruce, Ronald, ed. *The Consumer's Guide to Product Safety*

National Observer. *The Consumer's Handbook: 100 Ways to Get More Value for Your Dollars*, 88

Neal, Charles. *Sense with Dollars*, 386

Nelson, Edward A., jt. auth. *See* Rodda, William H.

Nelson, Roger H. *Personal Money Management: An Objectives and Systems Approach*, 387

New York Magazine Editors, jt. auth. *See* Scharlatt, Elisabeth Lohman

New York Public Library, jt. auth. *See* U.S. Office of Consumer Affairs

Nielsen, Jackie, jt. auth. *See* Nielsen, Jens

Nielsen, Jens, and Jackie Nielsen. *How to Save or Make Thousands When You Buy or Sell Your House*, 297

Nietus, Norbert, jt. auth. *See* Hastings, Paul

Niss, James F. *Consumer Economics*, 388

Nuccio, Sal. *The New York Times Guide to Personal Finance*, 389

Null, Gary. *Body Pollution*, 217

Nulsen, David. *All about Parks for Mobile Homes and Recreational Vehicles*, 356. *See also* 354

Nulsen, Robert H. *How to Buy Trailers, Mobile Homes, Travel Trailers, Campers*, 457

——. *Mobile Home Manual*, 354. *See also* 456, 457

Olney, Ross R. *How to Keep Your Car Running, Your Money in Your Pocket, and Your Mind Intact*, 20

Omohundro, Delight Dixon. *How to Win the Grocery Game: A Proven Strategy for Beating Inflation*, 234

Oppenheim, Irene. *The Family as Consumers*, 90

O'Toole, Edward T. *Family Guide to Financial Security.* See *How to Gain Financial Independence*

——. *How to Gain Financial Independence*, 390

Pagino, Edmond J., Jr. *Car Purchase and Maintenance*, 29

Parker, Edmond, jt. auth. *See* Ranney, George, Jr., and Richard Groll

Patridge, Barbara. *Bargain Hunting in L.A. and Surrounding Areas*, 508. *See also* 503, 507

Patridge, Barbara, and Geri Cook. *Bargain Hunting in L.A.: Including 150 Listings in the San Fernando Valley and Orange County*, 508. *See also* 504, 507

Paulson, Morton C. *The Great Land Hustle*, 449

Perl, Lila. *The House You Want: How to Find It, How to Buy It*, 280

Peterson, Mary Bennett. *The Regulated Consumer*, 142. *See also* 126

Petkas, Peter J., jt. ed. *See* Nader, Ralph, and Kate Blackwell, eds.

Pfahl, John K., jt. auth. *See* Donaldson, Elvin F.

Phillips, E. Bryant, and Sylvia Lane. *Personal Finance*, 391

Pierce, Joe, jt. auth. *See* Lewis, Roz

Placere, Morris N., and Charles S. Marwick. *How You Can Get Better Medical Care for Less Money*, 346

Planck, Carolyn, jt. auth. *See* Planck, Charles

Planck, Charles, and Carolyn Planck. *How to Double Your Travel Funds*, 513

Poriss, Martin. *How to Live Cheap but Good*, 91

Pratt, James Norwood, and Jacques de Caso. *The Wine Bibber's Bible*, 519

Pratt, Richard Putnam, jt. auth. *See* Smith, Carlton

Price, Irving. *Buying Country Property: Pitfalls and Pleasures*, 446

Pucci, P. G. *The Housewife's Handy Guide to Meat Shopping*, 208

Quinn, Jim. *Word of Mouth: A Completely New Kind of Guide to New York City Restaurants*, 466

Rabell, Paquita. *More Dollars for Your Cents*, 392

Rader, Barbara. *The Long Island Underground Gourmet*, 467

Raines, Margaret. *Consumers' Management*, 92

——. *Managing Livingtime.* See *Consumers' Management*

Rainey, Jean. *How to Shop for Food*, 235

Ramparts Magazine with Frank Browning. *In the Marketplace: Consumerism in America*, 144

Rand, Abby. *How to Get to Europe and Have a Wonderful Time*, 514

Randall, Donald A., and Arthur P. Glickman. *The Great American Auto Repair Robbery: A Report on a Ten-Billion Dollar National Swindle and What You Can Do about It*, 15

——. *The Great American Auto Repair Robbery* (cassette recording), 16

Randall, Robert W. *Consumer Purchasing*, 93

Ranney, George, Jr., Edmond Parker, and Richard Groll. *Landlord and Tenant*, 324

Read, R. B. *The San Francisco Underground Gourmet*, 468

Reader's Digest Editors. *How to Live on Your Income*, 393

Reddin, W. J. *The Money Book*, 394

Reiner, Laurence E. *Buy or Build? The Best House for You*, 281

Revere, Paul. *Dentistry and Its Victims*, 186

Richmond, Doug. *All about Minibikes*, 415

Robbins, William. *The American Food Scandal: Why You Can't Eat Well on What You Earn*, 236. *See also* 223

Roberts, Eirlys. *Consumers*, 159

Roberts, Richard, jt. auth. *See* Grozier, Mary

Rodale, J. I., and staff. *Our Poisoned Earth and Sky*, 194

Rodda, William H., and Edward A. Nelson. *Managing Personal Finances*, 395

Rogers, Donald I. *How to Beat Inflation by Using It*, 396

——. *Save It, Invest It, and Retire*, 484

Rolling Stone Editors. *The Rolling Stone Record Review*, 431

Roper, William L., jt. auth. *See* Drury, Treesa Way

Rosefsky, Robert S. *Frauds, Swindles, and Rackets*, 247

——. *The Ins and Outs of Moving: A Common Sense Guide to an Easy, Thrifty Move*, 420

Rosenbloom, Joseph. *Consumer Action Guide.* See *Consumer Complaint Guide*

——. *Consumer Complaint Guide*, 54. *See also* 157

Ross, Donald K. *A Public Citizen's Action Manual*, 145

Routh, Thomas A. *Choosing a Nursing Home: The Problems and Their Solutions*, 424

Rubin, Cynthia, jt. auth. *See* Rubin, Jerome

Rubin, Jerome, and Cynthia Rubin. *Boston Dining Out: A Guide to Dining in Boston*, 469. *See also* 470, 471

——. *Boston Lunching Out: A Guide to Lunching in Boston*, 470. *See also* 471

——. *The Real Boston Underground Dining*, 471. *See also* 469, 470

Rubin, Leona. *How to Defend Yourself at Auctions*, 4

Ruina, Edith. *Moving: A Common-Sense Guide to Relocating Your Family*, 421

Russcol, Herbert. *Guide to Low-Priced Classical Records*, 432

Rutberg, Sidney. *Ten Cents on the Dollar or the Bankruptcy Game*, 35

San Roman, Peter. *Travel at ½ the Price*, 515

Sanford, David. *Who Put the Con in Consumer?*, 146

Saunders, Rubie. *Smart Shopping and Consumerism*, 94

Scaduto, Anthony. *Getting the Most for Your Money: How to Beat the High Cost of Living*, 95. *See also* 397

——. *Handling Your Money*, 397

Scharlatt, Elisabeth Lohman, and the Editors of New York Magazine. *How to Get Things Done in New York*, 500

——. *The Passionate Shopper*, 501. *See also* 499

Scher, Les. *Finding and Buying Your Place in the Country*, 447. *See also* 448

Scherer, John L. *All about Mobile Homes*, 355

Schlick, D. P. *Modern Oriental Carpets: A Buyer's Guide*, 46

Schlink, F. J., *100,000,000 Guinea Pigs*, jt. auth. *See* Fuller, John C. *200,000,000 Guinea Pigs: New Dangers in Everyday Foods, Drugs, and Cosmetics*

Schmeckel, Carl D. *The Piano Owners Guide*, 435. *See also* 436

Schmidt, Henry. *The Retirement Handbook*, 476

Schoenfeld, David, and Arthur A. Natella. *The Consumer and His Dollars*, 96

Schorr, Daniel. *Don't Get Sick in America*, 347. *See also* 336

Schottland, Charles I. *The Social Security Program in the United States*, 495

Schrag, Philip G. *Counsel for the Deceived: Case Studies in Consumer Fraud*, 147

Schroeder, Henry A. *The Poisons around Us: Toxic Metals in Food, Air and Water*, 195

Seaver, Jacqueline. *Fads, Myths, Quacks—and Your Health*, 350

Selzer, Edwin, jt. auth. *See* Linder, Bertram L.

Shafer, Ronald G., jt. auth. *See* Carlson, Margaret Bresnahan

Shapiro, Andrew O., jt. auth. *See* Striker, John M.

Sheldon, Roy. *Know the Ins and Outs of Condominium Buying*, 50

Shell, Adeline Garner. *Supermarket Counter Power*, 237

Shortney, Joan Ranson. *How to Live on Nothing*, 98

Shulsky, Sam, jt. auth. *See* J. K. Lasser Tax Institute

Sifarkis, Carl. *175 Money Saving Tips for Every Car Owner*, 11

Slaughter, Katherine, jt. auth. *See* Giammattei, Helen

Slavicek, Jan J., jt. auth. *See* Burger, Robert E.

Slusher, Howard L., consulting ed. *See* McTaggart, Aubrey C.

Smith, Arthur A., jt. auth. *See* Dorries, W. L., and James R. Young

Smith, Carlton, and Richard Putnam Pratt. *The Time-Life Book of Family Finance*, 398

Snyder, Jerome, jt. auth. *See* Glaser, Milton

Socolich, Sally, and Kathy Filaseta. *Bargain Hunting in the Bay Area: Including San Francisco, the East Bay, the Peninsula, San Jose and Surrounding Areas*, 510

Solomon, Goody L. *The Radical Consumer's Handbook*, 148

Sprecher, Daniel, ed. *Directory of Government Agencies Safeguarding Consumer and Environment*, 151

Springer, John L. *Consumer Swindlers and How to Avoid Them*, 248

——. *Financial Self-Defense*, 399

Stamm, Gustav W. *How to Buy a Piano*, 436

Stamm, Martha, jt. auth. *See* Stanforth, Deirdre

Stanforth, Deirdre, and Martha Stamm. *Buying and Renovating a House in the City: A Practical Guide*, 289

Steinberg, Harry, jt. auth. *See* White, Jack, and Gary Yanker

Stern, Gloria. *How to Start Your Own Food Co-Op*, 220

Stigler, George J., and Manuel F. Cohen. *Can Regulatory Agencies Protect the Consumer?*, 164

Stillman, Richard J. *Guide to Personal Finance: A Lifetime Program of Money Management*, 400

Stone, Bill. *So You're Going to Buy a Used Sports Car*, 30

Stover, William R. *What You Should Know before Buying a Condominium*, 51

Striker, John M., and Andrew O. Shapiro. *Super Tenant: New York City Tenant Handbook: Your Legal Rights and How to Use Them*, 325

Sullivan, George. *The Boom in Going Bust: The Threat of a National Scandal in Consumer Bankruptcy*, 36. *See also* 401

——. *Do-It-Yourself-Moving: All You Need to Know to Save Money by Moving Your Own Household Belongings*, 422

——. *The Dollar Squeeze and How to Beat It*, 401

Swartz, Edward M. *Toys that Don't Care*, 512

Swatek, Paul. *The User's Guide to the Protection of the Environment*, 196

Teplin, Joseph, jt. auth. *See* Berger, Robert

Thal, Helen M., with Melinda Holcombe. *Your Family and Its Money*, 402

Thomas, Sarah M., and Bernadine Weddington. *A Guide to Sources of Consumer Information*, 152

Till, Anthony. *What You Should Know before You Buy a Car*, 12. *See also* 26

——. *What You Should Know before You Have Your Car Repaired*, 21

Tilleman, William A., jt. auth. *See* McKay, Quinn G.

Tolf, Robert W. *Florida Trend's Guide to Florida Restaurants*, 472. *See also* 473

——. *100 Best Restaurants of Florida*, 473

Townsend, Clair, project director. *Old Age: The Last Segregation: Ralph Nader's Study Group Report on Nursing Homes*, 425. *See also* 483

Troelstrup, Arch W. *The Consumer in American Society: Personal and Family Finance*, 99

Trzyna, Thaddeus C., ed. *Directory of Consumer Protection and Environmental Agencies*, 153

Tuck, Miriam L., and Arlene B. Grodner. *Consumer Health*, 351

Ullman, James Michael. *How to Hold a Garage Sale*, 251

Unger, Maurice A., and Harold A. Wolf. *Personal Finance*, 403

U.S. Department of Agriculture. *Consumers All: The Yearbook of Agriculture, 1965*, 100. *See also* 66, 71

——. *Food for Us All: The Yearbook of Agriculture, 1969*, 238. *See also* 232, 240

——. *Handbook for the Home: The Yearbook of Agriculture, 1973*, 101

U.S. Department of Housing and Urban Development. *Wise Home Buying*, 282

U.S. News and World Report. *How to Buy Real Estate*, 298

——. *Social Security and Medicare Simplified*, 497

U.S. Office of Consumer Affairs. *An Approach to Consumer Education for Adults*, 113

——. *Directory of State, County, and City Government Offices*, 154. *See also* 157, 237

——. *Forming Consumer Organizations*, 155

——. *Guide to Federal Consumer Services*, 156. *See also* 157

——. *State Consumer Action–Summary '72*, 166

——. *Suggested Guidelines for Consumer Education: Grades K–12*, 114. *See also* 113

U.S. Office of Consumer Affairs and New York Public Library. *Consumer Education Bibliography*, 108

Van Allen, Judith, jt. auth. *See* Marine, Gene

Vogts, Alfred. *How to Buy a Condominium*, 52

Wagstaff, Lanny. *The Little Restaurants of San Diego*, 464

Waldo, Myra. *Myra Waldo's Restaurant Guide to New York City and Vicinity*, 474. *See also* 466

Warmke, Roman F., et al. *Consumer Economic Problems*, 102

Wasserman, Paul, and Jean Morgan, eds. *Consumer Sourcebook*, 157

Watkins, Art. *Building or Buying the High-Quality House at the Lowest Cost*, 283. *See also* 285, 405

——. *Dollars and Sense: A Guide to Mastering Your Money*, 405. *See also* 489

——. *The Homeowner's Survival Kit: How to Beat the High Cost of Owning and Operating Your Home*, 259

——. *How to Avoid the Ten Biggest Home-Buying Traps*, 284. *See also* 283, 285, 405

——. *How to Judge a House*, 285. *See also* 283

Weathersbee, Bonnie, jt. auth. *See* Weathersbee, Christopher

Weathersbee, Christopher, and Bonnie Weathersbee. *The Intelligent Consumer: How to Buy Food, Clothes, Cars, Vacations, Houses, Appliances at the Least Cost to Yourself and the Environment*, 197

Weddington, Bernadine, jt auth. *See* Thomas, Sarah M.

Wehringer, Cameron K. *When and How to Choose an Attorney*, 330

Weimer, John D., jt. auth. *See* Lee, Albert

Weiss, Mark. *501 Valuable Tips and Free Materials for Motorists*, 13

Weissler, Paul. *How to Buy Services and Parts for Your Car*, 22

Wellford, Harrison. *Sowing the Wind: A Report from Ralph Nader's Center for Study of Responsive Law on*

Food Safety and the Chemical Harvest, 218. *See also* 236

West, David A., and Glenn L. Wood. *Personal Financial Management*, 406

White, Jack, Gary Yanker, and Harry Steinberg. *The Angry Buyer's Complaint Directory*, 56

Wicka, Sunny. *Garage Sale Shopper: A Complete Illustrated Guide for Buyers and Sellers*, 252

Wilder, Rex. *The Macmillan Guide to Family Finance*, 407

Wilhelms, Fred T., Ramon P. Heimerl, and Herbert M. Jelley. *Consumer Economics*, 104. *See also* 78

Wilkes, John. *How to Buy a Used Volkswagen in Europe, Keep It Alive and Bring It Home!*, 32. *See also* 25

Wilkes, Joy, and Paul Wilkes. *You Don't Have to Be Rich to Own a Brownstone*, 290

Wilkes, Paul, jt. auth. *See* Wilkes, Joy

Will, Charles A. *Does It Make Sense?*, 321

Williams, Lawrence P. *How to Avoid Unnecessary Surgery*, 348

Williamson, Ellen. *Spend Yourself Rich*, 105

Wilson, Patricia. *Consumer Guide to Used and Surplus Home Appliances and Furnishings*, 270

Wingate, Isabel B., Karen R. Gillespie, and Betty G. Addison. *Know Your Merchandise*, 106

Winter, Ralph K., Jr. *The Consumer Advocate Versus the Consumer*, 149

Winter, Ruth. *Beware of the Food You Eat*, 219

——. *How to Reduce Your Medical Bills*, 349

——. *Poisons in Your Food.* See *Beware of the Food You Eat*

Wise, Sidney Thomas. *Invest and Retire in Mexico*, 485

Wolf, Harold A., jt. auth. *See* Unger, Maurice A.

Wood, Glenn L., jt. auth. *See* West, David A.

Woods, Eugene. *How to Retire in Mexico*, 486

Wren, Jack. *Home Buyer's Guide*, 299

Wright, Carlton E. *Food Buying*, 239

Wurlitzer, Randolph, and Will Corey. *How to Get the Most for Your Food Dollar*, 240

Yanker, Gary, jt. auth. *See* White, Jack, and Harry Steinberg

Yeadon, Anne, and David Yeadon. *Hidden Restaurants: Northern California*, 475

——. *Hidden Restaurants: Southern California*, 475

Yeadon, David, jt. auth. *See* Yeadon, Anne

Young, James R., jt. auth. *See* Dorries, W. L., and Arthur A. Smith

Young, Jean, and Jim Young. *The Garage Sale Manual: A Guide to Alternative Economics–Buying, Selling & Trading*, 253

——. *People's Guide to Country Real Estate*, 448

Young, Jim, jt. auth. *See* Young, Jean

TITLE INDEX

Note: Listings refer to entry numbers not page numbers. Magazines are designated by an asterisk (*); films by a dagger (†).

ABC's of the Consumer Product Safety Act: The Law in Brief, Commission Directory, Text of Act, Consumer Product List, Bureau of National Affairs, 438

**ACCI Newsletter*, 116

The ASC Guide to Best Buys in Used Cars, Albert Lee, 27

. . . About Sunglasses, 198

Alexis Bespaloff's Guide to Inexpensive Wines, Alexis Bespaloff, 516

All about Minibikes, Doug Richmond, 415

All about Mobile Homes, John L. Scherer, 355

All about Parks for Mobile Homes and Recreational Vehicles, David Nulsen, 356. *See also* 354

All about Pickup Campers, Van Conversions and Motor Homes, John Gartner, 452

The American Consumer: Issues and Decisions, Herbert M. Jelley and Robert O. Herrmann, 78. *See also* 102, 104

The American Food Scandal: Why You Can't Eat Well on What You Earn, William Robbins, 236. *See also* 223

The American Health Empire: Power, Profits and Politics, Health Policy Advisory Committee, 338. *See also* 336

The Angry Buyer's Complaint Directory, Jack White, Gary Yanker, and Harry Steinberg, 56

*"Annuities from the Buyer's Point of View," Richard F. Maloney, ed., 2

Answers to Your Everyday Money Questions, Lorraine Blair, 359

An Approach to Consumer Education for Adults, U.S. Office of Consumer Affairs, 113

Auto Test, Consumer Guide, 7

Autofacts 1973, Car/Puter, 5

Automobile Buying Guide, Consumer Guide, 7

Automobiles, Consumer Guide, 7. *See also* 62

Back to the Bike, Clifford C. Humphrey, 41

Bargain Finder, 502

**Bargain Hunter.* See *S.O.S. Directory*

The Bargain Hunters Field Guide, Judith A. Bonnesen and Janet L. Burkley. *See The Factory Outlet Bargain Book*

Bargain Hunting in L.A. and Surrounding Areas, Barbara Patridge, 508. *See also* 504, 507

Bargain Hunting in L.A.: Including 150 Listings in the San Fernando Valley and Orange County, Barbara Patridge and Geri Cook, 508. *See also* 504, 507

Bargain Hunting in the Bay Area: Including San Francisco, the East Bay, the Peninsula, San Jose and Surrounding Areas, Sally Socolich and Kathy Filaseta, 510

Best Buys & Discount Prices, Consumer Guide, 62. *See also* 63

The Best House for the Money, Bruce Cassiday, 271

Beware, Ralph Nader, 441. *See also* 437

Beware of the Food You Eat, Ruth Winter, 219

Bicyle Test Reports, Consumer Guide, 39

Bikes: A How-to-Do-It Guide to Selection, Care, Repair, Maintenance, Decoration, Safety, and Fun on Your Bicycle, Stephen C. Henkel, 40

The Billion $ Swindle: Frauds against the Elderly, Amram M. Ducovny, 245

Body Pollution, Gary Null, 217

The Boom in Going Bust: The Threat of a National Scandal in Consumer Bankruptcy, George Sullivan, 36. *See also* 401

Boston Dining Out: A Guide to Dining in Boston, Jerome Rubin and Cynthia Rubin, 469. *See also* 470, 471

Boston Lunching Out: A Guide to Lunching in Boston, Jerome Rubin and Cynthia Rubin, 470. *See also* 471

The Boston Underground Gourmet, Joseph P. Kahn and E. J. Kahn, Jr., 463. *See also* 470, 471

†*Brand Names and Labeling Games*, 241

Break the Banks!: A Shopper's Guide to Banking Services, 487

Building or Buying the High-Quality House at the Lowest Cost, Art Watkins, 283. *See also* 285, 405

†*The Bunco Boys—And How to Beat Them!*, 244

Buy It Right: A Shopper's Guide to Home Furnishings, Jan Brown, 260

Buy Now, Pay Later, Hillel Black, 167

Buy or Build? The Best House for You, Laurence E. Reiner, 281

†*Buying an Automobile.* See *Consumer Education: Buying an Automobile*

Buying and Renovating a House in the City: A Practical Guide, Deirdre Stanforth and Martha Stamm, 289

Buying Country Land, Eugene Boudreau, 443

Buying Country Property, Herbert R. Moral, 445

Buying Country Property: Pitfalls and Pleasures, Irving Price, 446

The Buying Guide for Fresh Fruits, Vegetables, Herbs and Nuts, 203

Buying Guide Issue. See *Consumer Reports*

†*Buying in a Supermarket.* See *Consumer Education: Buying in a Supermarket*

By Prescription Only, Morton Mintz, 191

Camping and Backpacking Equipment Test Reports, Consumer Guide, 43

**CAN: Consumer Action Now*, 118

Can Regulatory Agencies Protect the Consumer?, George J. Stigler and Manuel F. Cohen, 164

Can You Be Sure of Your Experts?, Roger H. Golde, 442

**Canadian Consumer*, 58. *See also* 265

Car Purchase and Maintenance, Edmond J. Pagino, Jr., 29

**Caveat Emptor: The Consumer Protection Monthly*, 119

Champagne Living on a Beer Budget: How to Buy the Best for Less, Mike Ferguson and Marilyn Ferguson, 72. *See also* 80

Changing Times: The Kiplinger Magazine, 59. *See also* 393

Check Points on How to Buy Oriental Rugs, Charles W. Jacobsen, 45. *See also* 44

†*A Chemical Feast*, 210

Child Welfare League of America Standards for Day Care Service. See *Guidelines for Day Care Service*

Choosing a Nursing Home: The Problems and Their Solutions, Thomas A. Routh, 424

Citizen Action Guide to Energy Conservation, 192

The Claims Game, Vladimir P. Chernik, 301

A Commonsense Guide to Doctors, Hospitals and Medical Care, Richard H. Blum, 331. *See also* 341

Complete Bicycle Book: Buyer's Guide, 38

The Complete Book of Mobile Home Living, Lyle Kenyon Engel, 352

The Complete Book of Trailering, Lyle Kenyon Engel, 451

The Complete Guide to Retirement, Thomas Collins, 477

The Complete Real Estate Adviser, Daniel J. deBenedictus, 293

The Comstock Western Home Buyer's Guide: A Manual for House Inspection, George C. Hoffman, 276

The Condominium Buyer's Guide: What to Look for—and Look Out for—in Resort, Residential and Commercial Condominiums, James N. Karr, 49. *See also* 50

**Le Consommateur Canadien.* See *Canadian Consumer*

The Consumer, Gerald Leinwald, ed., 130

Consumer Action Guide. See *Consumer Complaint Guide*

The Consumer Advocate Versus the Consumer, Ralph K. Winter, Jr., 149

The Consumer and Corporate Accountability, Ralph Nader, ed., 138

The Consumer and His Dollars, David Schoenfeld and Arthur A. Natella, 96

The Consumer and His Dollars: Workbook and Study Guide, Marcella E. Finegan, 96

Consumer Beware! Your Food and What's Been Done to It, Beatrice Trum Hunter, 212. *See also* 236

**Consumer Bulletin.* See *Consumers' Research Magazine*

Consumer Bulletin Annual. See *Handbook of Buying Issue (Consumers' Research Magazine)*

Consumer Buying for Better Living, Cleo Fitzsimmons, 73

Consumer Class Action Legislation, 160

**Consumer Close-Ups*, 120

Consumer Complaint Guide, Joseph Rosenbloom, 54. *See also* 157

Consumer Economic Problems, Roman F. Warmke, et al., 102

Consumer Economics, James F. Niss, 388

Consumer Economics, Fred T. Wilhelms, Ramon P. Heimerl, and Herbert M. Jelley, 104. *See also* 78

Consumer Education: A Bibliography, 107

Consumer Education Bibliography, U.S. Office of Consumer Affairs and New York Public Library, 108

†*Consumer Education: Buying an Automobile*, 6

†*Consumer Education: Buying in a Supermarket*, 222

**Consumer Education Forum*, 116

†*Consumer Education: Maintaining an Automobile*, 18

Consumer Education Programming in Continuing Education, Margaret Charters, 109

**The Consumer Educator*, 60

**The Consumer Gazette*, 61

Consumer Guide to Used and Surplus Home Appliances and Furnishings, Patricia Wilson, 270

Consumer Health, Miriam L. Tuck and Arlene B. Grodner, 351

Consumer Health and Product Hazards—Chemicals, Electronic Products, Radiation, Samuel S. Epstein and Richard D. Grundy, eds., 440

Consumer Housing, Pauline G. Garrett, 256

The Consumer in American Society: Personal and Family Finance, Arch W. Troelstrup, 99

**Consumer Information: An Index of Selected Federal Publications of Consumer Interest*, 64

Consumer Living. See *The American Consumer: Issues and Decisions*

**Consumer New$week*, 121

Consumer Power, Treesa Way Drury and William L. Roper, 124

Consumer Problems. See *The Consumer in American Society: Personal and Family Finance*

Consumer Problems and Personal Finance. See *The Consumer in American Society: Personal and Family Finance*

**Consumer Product Information.* See *Consumer Information: An Index of Selected Federal Publications of Consumer Interest*

Consumer Purchasing, Robert W. Randall, 93

**Consumer Reports*, 65. *See also* 27, 58, 62, 148, 263, 265, 427

Consumer Sourcebook, Paul Wasserman and Jean Morgan, eds., 157

Consumer Swindlers and How to Avoid Them, John L. Springer, 248

Consumerism: Search for the Consumer Interest, David A. Aaker and George S. Day, eds., 115

Consumerism—the Eternal Triangle: Business, Government and Consumers, Barbara B. Murray, ed., 137

Consumerism: Things Ralph Nader Never Told You, Fortune Magazine Editors, 126

Consumerism: Viewpoints from Business, Government, and the Public Interest, Ralph M. Gaedeke and Warren W. Etcheson, 128

Consumers, Eirlys Roberts, 159

Consumers All: The Yearbook of Agriculture, 1965, U.S. Department of Agriculture, 100. *See also* 66, 71

Consumer's Buying Guides: How to Get Your Money's Worth, Better Business Bureau, 57

A Consumer's Directory of Prince George's County Doctors. See *Supplement to Medical Economics Reprint on A Consumer's Directory of Prince George's County Doctors*

The Consumer's Fight-Back Book, James Lewis, ed., 131

The Consumer's Guide to Better Buying, Sidney Margolius, 83

The Consumer's Guide to Insurance Buying, Vladimir P. Chernik, 302

Consumers' Guide to Prescription Prices, William Gulick, 190

The Consumer's Guide to Product Safety, Ronald Bruce, ed., 437. *See also* 439, 441

Consumer's Handbook, Paul Fargis, 71

The Consumer's Handbook of Better Living, 66. *See also* 71

The Consumer's Handbook: 100 Ways to Get More Value for Your Dollars, National Observer, 88

**Consumers Index to Product Evaluations and Information Sources*, 67

Consumers' Management, Margaret Raines, 92

**Consumers' Research Magazine*, 68. *See also* 58, 77, 263, 265

The Consumers Union Report on Life Insurance: A Guide to Planning and Buying the Protection You Need, Consumer Reports, 313. *See also* 312

Consumers Union Reviews Classical Recordings, Consumers Union's Music Consultant and the Editors of Consumer Reports, 427

The Consuming Public, Grant S. McClellan, ed., 132

Contact Lenses: . . . a vital role in vision care, 200

Cost of Personal Borrowing in the United States, Charles H. Gushee, ed., 169

Counsel for the Deceived: Case Studies in Consumer Fraud, Philip G. Schrag, 147

The Coupon Way to Lower Food Prices, Carole Kratz and Albert Lee, 227

Credit-Cardsmanship. See *How to Turn Plastic into Gold: A Revolutionary New Way to Make Money and Save Money Every Time You Buy Anything—with Credit Cards*

The Credit Jungle, Al Griffin, 170

The Dark Side of the Marketplace: The Plight of the American Consumer, Warren G. Magnuson and Jean Carper, 133

Dentistry and Its Victims, Paul Revere, 186

Directory of Consumer Protection and Environmental Agencies, Thaddeus C. Trzyna, ed., 153

Directory of Government Agencies Safeguarding Consumer and Environment, Daniel Sprecher, ed., 151

Directory of State and Local Government and Non-Government Consumer Groups, 150

Directory of State, County, and City Government Offices, U.S. Office of Consumer Affairs, 154. *See also* 157, 237

Do-It-Yourself-Moving: All You Need to Know to Save Money by Moving Your Own Household Belongings, George Sullivan, 422

Does It Make Sense?, Charles A. Will, 321

Dollar Power, Thomas A. Johnson, 374

The Dollar Squeeze and How to Beat It, George Sullivan, 401

Dollars and Sense: A Guide to Mastering Your Money, Art Watkins, 405. *See also* 489

$$$ and Sense: Your Complete Guide to Wise Buying, Ella Gale, 75. *See also* 130, 393

Don't Bank on It!, Martin J. Meyer and Joseph M. McDaniel, Jr., 489. *See also* 84, 405, 488

Don't Get Sick in America, Daniel Schorr, 347. *See also* 336

The Dream House Encyclopedia. See *How to Buy and Remodel the Older House*

Eater's Digest: The Consumer's Factbook of Food Additives, Michael F. Jacobson, 214

Economics for Consumers, Leland J. Gordon and Stewart M. Lee, 76

Enough! The Revolt of the American Consumer, Doris Faber, 158. *See also* 159

European and Oriental Rugs for Pleasure and Investment, Jack Franses, 44

**FDA Consumer*, 125

**FDA Consumer Memo.* See *FDA Consumer*

Fact/Book on Food Additives and Your Health, Beatrice Trum Hunter, 213

The Factory Outlet Bargain Book, Judith A. Bonnesen and Janet L. Burkley, 504

**The Factory Outlet Newsletter*, 505

Factory Outlet Shopping Guide, Jean Bird, 503. *See also* 502, 504, 505

Fads, Myths, Quacks—and Your Health, Jacqueline Seaver, 350

The Family as Consumers, Irene Oppenheim, 90

Family Guide to Financial Security. See *How to Gain Financial Independence*

Family Money Problems, Sidney Margolius, 379

The Family Real Estate Adviser. See *The Complete Real Estate Adviser*

Farm and Personal Finance, John R. Brake, ed., 362

**Federal Register.* See *OCA Consumer News*

Fell's Guide to Buying, Building and Financing a Home, M. Robert Beasley, 291

Financial Self-Defense, John L. Springer, 399

Finding and Buying Your Place in the Country, Les Scher, 447. *See also* 448

Fishing Equipment Test Reports, Consumer Guide, 202

501 Valuable Tips and Free Materials for Motorists, Mark Weiss, 13

Florida Trend's Guide to Florida Restaurants, Robert W. Tolf, 472. *See also* 473

Food and the Consumer, Amihud Kramer, 226

Food Buying, Carlton E. Wright, 239

Food—Facts and Fallacies, Allan G. Cameron, 221

Food for Us All: The Yearbook of Agriculture, 1969, U.S. Department of Agriculture, 238. *See also* 232, 240

†*Food Labeling: Understanding What You Eat*, 242. *See also* 243

Food Pollution: The Violation of Our Inner Ecology, Gene Marine and Judith Van Allen, 216

†*Foot in the Door*, 246. *See also* 249

Forming Consumer Organizations, U.S. Office of Consumer Affairs, 155

Frauds, Swindles, and Rackets: A Red Alert for Today's Consumers, Robert S. Rosefsky, 247

The Garage Sale Manual: A Guide to Alternative Economics—Buying, Selling & Trading, Jean Young and Jim Young, 253

Garage Sale Shopper: A Complete Illustrated Guide for Buyers and Sellers, Sunny Wicka, 252

The Gerber Report. See *Hazardous to Your Health*

Getting the Most for Your Money: How to Beat the High Cost of Living, Anthony Scaduto, 95. *See also* 397

Going Broke and How to Avoid It, Leonard M. Groupe, 181

Good Fruits and How to Buy Them, Erston V. Miller and James I. Munger, 207

Government Services for Consumers, Francis A. Corr, 122

The Great American Auto Repair Robbery (cassette recording), Donald A. Randall and Arthur P. Glickman, 16

The Great American Auto Repair Robbery: A Report on a Ten-Billion Dollar National Swindle and What You Can Do about It, Donald A. Randall and Arthur P. Glickman, 15

The Great American Food Hoax, Sidney Margolius, 229. *See also* 230, 236

The Great Confidence Games: Game 1 —the Insurance Game, Richard T. Hamilton, 305

The Great Land Hustle, Morton C. Paulson, 449

The Greengrocer: The Consumer's Guide to Fruits and Vegetables, Joe Carcione and Bob Lucas, 204

A Guide for Evaluating Consumer Education Programs and Materials, 110

A Guide to Consumer Credit, Sidney Margolius, 171

Guide to Federal Consumer Services, U.S. Office of Consumer Affairs, 156. *See also* 157

Guide to Low-Priced Classical Records, Herbert Russcol, 432

Guide to Modern Medical Care, S. D. Klotz, 341. *See also* 331

Guide to Personal Finance: A Lifetime Program of Money Management, Richard J. Stillman, 400

A Guide to Sources of Consumer Information, Sarah M. Thomas and Bernadine Weddington, 152

Guidelines for Day Care Service, 176

Guns & Hunting Equipment Test Reports, Consumer Guide, 254

Handbook for the Home: The Yearbook of Agriculture, 1973, U. S. Department of Agriculture, 101

**Handbook of Buying Issue* (*Consumers' Research Magazine*), 77. *See also* 62, 68

Handling Your Money, Anthony Scaduto, 397

Hazardous to Your Health, Marvin H. Edwards, 336

Heal Your Self, Citizens Board of Inquiry into Health Services for Americans, 332

Health: A Consumer's Dilemma, Robert E. Kime, 340

The Health Care Dilemma, Aubrey C. McTaggart and Howard L. Slusher, consulting ed., 344

Health Foods: Facts and Fakes, Sidney Margolius, 230

The Health Insurance Racket and How to Beat It, John E. Gregg, 310

Hearings and Final Reports, National Commission on Product Safety. *See The Consumer's Guide to Product Safety,* Ronald Bruce, ed.

Help Your Family Make a Better Move, Helen Giammattei and Katherine Slaughter, 416. *See also* 393, 421

HELPs (Home Economics Learning Packages), 111

Hidden Restaurants: Northern California, Anne Yeadon and David Yeadon, 475

Hidden Restaurants: Southern California, Anne Yeadon and David Yeadon, 475

High Fidelity Record Annual. See *Records in Review*

The Higson Home Buyer's Guide, James D. Higson, 275

Home Buyer's Guide, Jack Wren, 299

Home Economics Learning Packages. *See HELPs*

The Homeowner's Survival Kit: How to Beat the High Cost of Owning and Operating Your Home, Art Watkins, 259

A House in the City: A Guide to Buying and Renovating Old Row Houses, H. Dickson McKenna, 287. *See also* 290

The House You Want: How to Find It, How to Buy It, Lila Perl, 280

The Housewife's Handy Guide to Meat Shopping, P. G. Pucci, 208

How I Turn Ordinary Complaints into Thousands of Dollars: The Diary of a Tough Customer, Ralph Charell, 53

How to Avoid the Retirement Trap, Leland Frederick Cooley and Lee Morrison Cooley, 478. *See also* 476

How to Avoid the Ten Biggest Home-Buying Traps, Art Watkins, 284. *See also* 283, 285, 405

How to Avoid Unnecessary Surgery, Lawrence P. Williams, 348

How to Beat Inflation by Using It, Donald I. Rogers, 396

How to Become a Real Estate Broker and Turn Your License into Big Money. See *The Complete Real Estate Adviser*

How to Buy a Condominium, Alfred Vogts, 52

How to Buy a Home, How to Sell a Home, Glenn Fowler, 294

How to Buy a House, Byron Moger and Martin Burke, with Omar V. Garrison, 278

How to Buy a New or Used Car, Alexander Markovich, 9. *See also* 26

How to Buy a Piano, Gustav W. Stamm, 436

How to Buy a Used Car, Charles R. Jackson, 26

How to Buy a Used Volkswagen in Europe, Keep It Alive and Bring It Home!, John Wilkes, 32. *See also* 25

How to Buy and Remodel the Older House, Hubbard H. Cobb, 286

How to Buy and Sell a Used Car in Europe, Gil Friedman, 25. *See also* 32

How to Buy at Auction, Michael De Forrest, 3

How to Buy Cars at Top Discount, C. E. Groves, 8. *See also* 12

How to Buy Food, Valerie Moolman, 232

How to Buy Furniture, Donna Difloe, 262

How to Buy Major Appliances, Charles Klamkin, 265

How to Buy or Sell a Home, Jess Monefeldt, 296

How to Buy Real Estate: Profits and Pitfalls, U.S. News and World Report, 298

How to Buy Recreational Vehicles, Jack Kneass, 455

How to Buy Services and Parts for Your Car, Paul Weissler, 22

How to Buy the Right House at the Right Price, Robert W. Murray, Jr., 279. *See also* 271

How to Buy Trailers, Mobile Homes, Travel Trailers, Campers, Robert H. Nulsen, 457

How to Choose, Buy and Enjoy a Motor Home, Van Camper, Tent-top or Tent, Clinton Hull, 454

How to Choose the Camera You Need, W. D. Emanuel and Leonard Gaunt, 434

How to Choose Your Vacation House, Bruce Cassiday, 272

How to Defend Yourself at Auctions, Leona Rubin, 4

How to Double Your Travel Funds, Charles Planck and Carolyn Planck, 513

How to File a Suit in the New Jersey Small Claims Division, Carl F. Bianchi, 326

How to Finance Your Home, Sidney Margolius, 277

How to Find and Finance a Great Country Place, Jean Kenney and Cle Kinney, 444

How to Gain Financial Independence, Edward T. O'Toole, 390

How to Get Good and Honest Auto Service, Albert Lee and John D. Weimer, 19

How to Get More for Your Money in Running Your Home, Merle E. Dowd, 255. *See also* 393

How to Get Out of Debt and Stay Out, Jonathan Grey, 180

How to Get Out of Debt . . . and Stay Out, Burton T. Rulon, 178

How to Get Out of Debt and Stay Out of Debt, Merle Dowd, 179. *See also* 70

How to Get the Most for Your Food Dollar, Randolph Wurlitzer and Will Corey, 240

How to Get Things Done in New York, Elisabeth Lohman Scharlatt and the Editors of New York Magazine, 500

How to Get to Europe and Have a Wonderful Time, Abby Rand, 514

How to Get 20 to 90% Off on Everything You Buy, Jean Kinney and Cle Kinney, 80

How to Get Your Car Repaired without Getting Gypped, Margaret Bresnahan Carlson and Ronald G. Shafer, 17. *See also* 15, 20

How to Have More Money to Spend, B. J. Blaustein and Robert Gorman, 177

How to Hold a Garage Sale, James Michael Ullman, 251

How to Invest in Beautiful Things without Being a Millionaire: How the Clever Consumer Can Outthink the Tastemakers, Elaine Cannel, 261

How to Judge a House, Art Watkins, 285. *See also* 283

How to Keep Your Car Running, Your Money in Your Pocket, and Your Mind Intact, Ross R. Olney, 20

How to Live Better and Spend 20% Less, Merle E. Dowd, 70. *See also* 405

How to Live Cheap but Good, Martin Poriss, 91

How to Live Like a Retired Millionaire on Less than $250 a Month, Richard L. Hayes, 481

How to Live on Nothing, Joan Ranson Shortney, 98

How to Live on Your Income, Reader's Digest Editors, 393

How to Locate in the Country: Your Personal Guide, John Gourlie, 417

How to Make the Most of Your Money, Sidney Margolius, 183

How to Manage Your Money, John Kirk, 375

How to Pay Lots Less for Life Insurance . . . and Be Covered for as Much and as Long as You Want, Max Fogiel, 317

How to Plan Now for Your Retirement, Forrest E. Gilmore, 480

How to Reduce Your Medical Bills, Ruth Winter, 349

How to Retire in Mexico, Eugene Woods, 486

How to Rob a Bank without a Gun, George Jenney, 488

How to Save or Make Thousands When You Buy or Sell Your House, Jens Nielsen and Jackie Nielsen, 297

How to Select a Car or Truck for Trailer Towing, Jack Kneass, 456

How to Settle Your Own Insurance Claim, Daniel G. Baldyga, 300

How to Shop for Food, Jean Rainey, 235

How to Start Your Own Food Co-Op, Gloria Stern, 220

How to Stay Out of Court, Robert Coulson, 327

How to Stretch Your Dollar, Adele Whitely Fletcher, 74

How to S-t-r-e-t-c-h Your M-o-n-e-y, Sidney Margolius, 380

How to Succeed with Your Money, George M. Bowman, 361

How to Turn Plastic into Gold: A Revolutionary New Way to Make Money and Save Money Every Time You Buy Anything—with Credit Cards, Martin J. Meyer and Mark Hunter, 172. *See also* 84

How to Win the Grocery Game: A Proven Strategy for Beating Inflation, Delight Dixon Omohundro, 234

How You Can Get Better Medical Care for Less Money, Morris N. Placere and Charles S. Marwick, 346

If It Doesn't Work, Read the Instructions: The Electrical Appliance Jungle, Charles Klamkin, 266

In Critical Condition: The Crisis in America's Health Care, Edward M. Kennedy, 339

In the Marketplace: Consumerism in America, Ramparts Magazine with Frank Browning, 144

**Información para el Consumidor*. See *Consumer Information*

The Innocent Consumer vs. the Exploiters, Sidney Margolius, 134. *See also* 130

The Ins and Outs of Moving, Robert S. Rosefsky, 420

The Insider's Guide to Antiques, Art and Collectibles, Sylvia O'Neill Dorn, 48

An Insider's Guide to Low-Priced Wines, William E. Massee, 517. *See also* 518

The Intelligent Consumer: How to Buy Food, Clothes, Cars, Vacations, Houses, Appliances at the Least Cost to Yourself and the Environment, Christopher Weathersbee and Bonnie Weathersbee, 197

Invest and Retire in Mexico, Sidney Thomas Wise, 485

Investing for Your Future, J. K. Lasser Tax Institute and Sam Shulsky, 482

*"It's Time Consumers Knew More about Their Doctors," Rob McGarrah, 343

I've Had It: A Practical Guide to Moving Abroad, Robert Hopkins, 418

Jazz on Record: The First 50 Years 1917–1967, Albert McCarthy et al, 430

**The Journal of Consumer Affairs*, 116

Know the Ins and Outs of Condominium Buying, Roy Sheldon, 50

Know Your Merchandise, Isabel B. Wingate, Karen R. Gillespie, and Betty G. Addison, 106

†*Label Logic*, 243

Landlord and Tenant, George Ranney, Jr., Edmond Parker and Richard Groll, 324

J. K. Lasser's Managing Your Family Finances, J. K. Lasser Tax Institute, 376. *See also* 393

Law and the Consumer, Robert Berger and Joseph Teplin, 117

Laws Every Homeowner and Tenant Should Know. See *The Complete Real Estate Adviser*

Lawyers Title Home Buying Guide, William Laas, 295

The Layman's Guide to Bankruptcy, Robert E. Burger and Jan J. Slavicek, 33

Legal Protection for the Consumer, Stanley Morganstern, 162

The Legislation of Product Safety, Samuel S. Epstein and Richard D. Grundy, eds., 440

Life Insurance: A Consumer's Handbook, Joseph M. Belth, 312

*"Life Insurance from the Buyer's Point of View," Richard F. Maloney, ed., 320

Life Insurance: How to Get Your Money's Worth, Arnold Geier, 318

The Little Restaurants of Los Angeles, Roz Lewis, 464

The Little Restaurants of San Diego, Lanny Wagstaff, 464

The Little Restaurants of San Francisco, Roz Lewis and Joe Pierce, 464

The Long Island Underground Gourmet, Barbara Rader, 467

The Los Angeles Underground Gourmet, George Christy, 460

MACAP's Handbook for the Informed Consumer, Virginia Habeeb, 263

McCall's Guide to the Wines of America. See *Massee's Guide to Wines of America*

The Macmillan Guide to Family Finance, Rex Wilder, 407

†*Magical Disappearing Money,* 228

†*Maintaining an Automobile.* See *Consumer Education: Maintaining an Automobile*

Manage Your Money and Live Better: Get the Most from Your Dwindling Dollars, David L. Markstein, 381

Managing Livingtime. See *Consumers' Management*

Managing Personal Finances, William H. Rodda and Edward A. Nelson, 395

Martin Meyer's Moneybook, Martin J. Meyer, 84

Massee's Guide to Wines of America, William E. Massee, 518. *See also* 517

The Meat Book: A Consumer's Guide to Selecting, Buying, Cutting, Storing, Freezing and Carving the Various Cuts, Travers Moncure Evans and David Greene, 205

Meat Eaters Are Threatened, John A. McClure, 206

**Media & Consumer,* 136

The Medicine Show, Consumer Reports, 188. *See also* 130

**Minibike Guide Magazine.* See *Minibikes and Minicycles for Beginners*

Minibikes and Minicycles for Beginners, I. G. Edmonds, 413

Mobile Home Manual, Robert H. Nulsen, 354. *See also* 456, 457

**Mobile/Modular Living Magazine.* See *Woodall's Mobile Home & Parks Directory*

Modern Oriental Carpets: A Buyer's Guide, D. P. Schlick, 46

**Money,* 382

Money & Kids: How to Earn It, Save It and Spend It, Mary Price Lee, 410

Money & the Working Ms., Ruth Halcomb, 370

The Money Book, W. J. Reddin, 394

Money: How to Save It, Spend It and Make It, B. D. Coleman, 366

Money Management Booklet Library, 85

Money Management: Children's Spending, 411

Money Management: It's Your Credit—Manage It Wisely, 173

Money Management: Reaching Your Financial Goals, 383

Money Management: Your Automobile Dollar, 10

Money Management: Your Clothing Dollar, 47

Money Management: Your Equipment Dollar, 267

Money Management: Your Food Dollar, 231

Money Management: Your Health and Recreation Dollar, 345

Money Management: Your Home Furnishings Dollar, 268

Money Management: Your Housing Dollar, 258

Money Management: Your Savings and Investment Dollar, 490

Money Management: Your Shopping Dollar, 86

Money Matters in Your Marriage, Quinn G. McKay and William A. Tilleman, 378

†*The Money Tree*, 384

The Money Tree: A New Guide to Successful Personal Finance, Catherine Crook de Camp, 367

**Moneysworth*, 87

More Dollars for Your Cents, Paquita Rabell, 392

Motorcycles: A Buyer's and Rider's Guide, Al Griffin, 414

Moving: A Common-Sense Guide to Relocating Your Family, Edith Ruina, 421

Myra Waldo's Restaurant Guide to New York City and Vicinity, Myra Waldo, 474. *See also* 466

**N.A.D.A. Official Used Car Guide*, 28

The National Directory of Retirement Residences: Best Places to Live When You Retire, Noverre Musson, 483

New Jersey Consumer Protection Laws, Consumers League of New Jersey, 161

The New Orleans Underground Gourmet. See *The Revised New Orleans Underground Gourmet*

The New York Food Book, Sally Dorst, 499

The New York Times Book of Money, Richard E. Blodgett, 360

The New York Times Guide to Dining Out in New York, 465. *See also* 466

The New York Times Guide to Personal Finance, Sal Nuccio, 389

New York's City Streets, Mary Grozier and Richard Roberts, 193

No-Fault: What You Save, Gain, and Lose with the New Auto Insurance, Paul Gillespie and Miriam Klipper, 308

Nothing New: A Guide to the Fun of Second-Hand Shopping in Los Angeles and Surrounding Areas, Judy James and Danny Goldman, 507

†*Nutritional Quackery*, 233

**OCA Consumer News*, 140

**OCA Consumer Register*. See *OCA Consumer News*

**Of Consuming Interest*, 141

Old Age: The Last Segregation: Ralph Nader's Study Group Report on Nursing Homes, Clair Townsend, project director, 425. *See also* 483

**The Old-House Journal*, 288

†*On Your Own*, 112

100 Best Restaurants of Florida, Robert W. Tolf, 473

100,000,000 Guinea Pigs, Arthur Kallet and F. J. Schlinck. *See 200,000,000 Guinea Pigs: New Dangers in Everyday Foods, Drugs, and Cosmetics*, John G. Fuller

175 Money Saving Tips for Every Car Owner, Carl Sifarkis, 11

138 Ways to Beat the High Cost of Living, 89

Opera Recordings: A Critical Guide, Kenn Harris, 428

Our Poisoned Earth and Sky, J. I. Rodale and staff, 194

Out of Debt through Chapter 13, Melvin James Kaplan, 182

The Passionate Shopper, Elisabeth Lohman Scharlatt and the Editors of New York Magazine, 501. *See also* 499

Pay Now, Die Later: What's Wrong with Life Insurance: A Report on Our Biggest and Most Wasteful Industry, James Gollin, 319

People's Guide to Country Real Estate, Jean Young and Jim Young, 448

The People's Handbook of Medical Care, Arthur Frank and Stuart Frank, 337

Personal Economic Planning, Glen A. Mumey, 385

Personal Finance, Virginia Britton, 363

Personal Finance, Elvin F. Donaldson and John K. Pfahl, 368

Personal Finance, Paul Hastings and Norbert Nietus, 371

Personal Finance, E. Bryant Phillips and Sylvia Lane, 391

Personal Finance, Maurice A. Unger and Harold A. Wolf, 403

Personal Finance: Consuming, Saving and Investing, W. L. Dorries, Arthur A. Smith and James R. Young, 369

Personal Finances for Ministers, John C. Banker, 358

Personal Financial Management, David A. West and Glenn L. Wood, 406

Personal Money Management: An Objectives and Systems Approach, Roger H. Nelson, 387

**Photographic Equipment Test Reports,* Consumer Guide, 433. *See also* 62

The Piano Owners Guide, Carl D. Schmeckel, 435. *See also* 436

A Place to Live, Thomas A. Johnson, 257

PLAID for Personal Finance. See *Programmed Learning Aid for Personal Finance*

PLAID for Principles of Insurance. See *Programmed Learning Aid for Principles of Insurance*

Planning Your Financial Independence, John E. Leibenderfer, 377

The Poisons around Us: Toxic Metals in Food, Air and Water, Henry A. Schroeder, 195

Poisons in Your Food. See *Beware of the Food You Eat*

The Poisons in Your Food, William Longgood, 215

The Politics of Consumer Protection, Mark V. Nadel, 163

†*The Poor Pay More,* 143

The Poor Pay More: Consumer Practices of Low-Income Families, David Caplovitz, 168

Pots & Pans Etc., Gertrude Harris, 264

Practical Ways to Make Money in Real Estate. See *The Complete Real Estate Adviser*

Previews, Consumer Guide, 7

Product Report, Consumer Guide, 63. *See also* 62

Product Safety in Household Goods, F. Reed Dickerson, ed., 439. *See also* 437

Programmed Learning Aid for Personal Finance, Jerome B. Cohen assisted by Harry H. Bingham, 365

Programmed Learning Aid for Principles of Insurance, Robert I. Mehr, 306

A Public Citizen's Action Manual, Donald K. Ross, 145

The Radical Consumer's Handbook, Goody L. Solomon, 148

Rating the Diets, Theodore Berland and the Editors of Consumer Guide, 187

Ratings & Discount Prices. See *Best Buys & Discount Prices*

†*Read before You Write*, 174

The Real Boston Underground Dining, Jerome Rubin and Cynthia Rubin, 471. *See also* 469, 470

Records in Review, High Fidelity, 429

Recreational Vehicles: A Buyer's & User's Guide, Al Griffin, 453

The Regulated Consumer, Mary Bennett Peterson, 142. *See also* 126

*"Report on Product Safety: Household Goods." *See Product Safety in Household Goods*

The Responsible Consumer, Sidney Margolius, 135

The Retirement Handbook, Joseph C. Buckley, 476

The Revised New Orleans Underground Gourmet, Richard H. Collin, 461

Richard's Bicycle Book, Richard Ballantine, 37

The Rolling Stone Record Review, Rolling Stone Editors, 431

SBS (Save before You Spend) Master Budget. See *How to Get Out of Debt . . . and Stay Out*

S.O.S. Directory, 509

The San Francisco Underground Gourmet, R. B. Read, 468

Satisfaction Guaranteed: An Unconventional Report to Today's Consumers, Booton Herndon, 129

Save It, Invest It, and Retire, Donald I. Rogers, 484

Save Money and Grow Rich, John W. King, 79

Save Your Health & Your Money, Patrick J. Doyle, 335

Sense with Dollars, Charles Neal, 386

**Service: USDA's Report to Consumers*, 97

Shedding "Light" on Electricity . . . What You Need to Know and Have Never Been Told, 269

A Shopper's Guide to Dentistry, Herbert S. Denenberg, 185

A Shopper's Guide to Health Insurance, Herbert S. Denenberg, 309

Shopper's Guide to Insurance, Herbert S. Denenberg, 303

A Shopper's Guide to Insurance on Mobile Homes (Pennsylvania), Herbert S. Denenberg, 322

A Shopper's Guide to Lawyers, Herbert S. Denenberg, 328

Shopper's Guide to Pennsylvania Automobile Insurance, Herbert S. Denenberg, 307

Shopper's Guide to Straight Life Insurance, Herbert S. Denenberg, 315

Shopper's Guide to Surgery: Fourteen Rules on How to Avoid Unnecessary Surgery, Herbert S. Denenberg, 333

A Shopper's Guide to Term Life Insurance, Herbert S. Denenberg, 316

The Shopper's Guidebook to Life Insurance, Health Insurance, Auto Insurance, Home-owner's Insurance, Doctors, Dentists, Lawyers, Pensions, Etc., Herbert S. Denenberg, 69. *See also* 185, 309, 315, 316, 333

Ski Equipment Test Reports, Consumer Guide, 491

Small on Safety: The Designed-In Dangers of the Volkswagen, Center for Auto Safety, 23

Smart Shopping and Consumerism, Rubie Saunders, 94

So You Want to Buy a House, Al Griffin, 274

So You Want to Buy a Mobile Home, Al Griffin, 353. *See also* 352

So You Want to Buy a Motorboat: A Handbook for Prospective Owners, Describing and Evaluating Current Makes and Models, Al Griffin, 412

So You'd Like to Buy an Airplane!, Al Griffin, 1

So You're Going to Buy a Used Sports Car, Bill Stone, 30

Social Security and Medicare Explained—Including Medicaid, 496

Social Security and Medicare Simplified, U.S. News & World Report, 497

The Social Security Program in the United States, Charles I. Schottland, 495

Some North Carolina Manufacturing Firms with Outlet Stores, 511

Sowing the Wind: A Report from Ralph Nader's Center for Study of Responsive Law on Food Safety and the Chemical Harvest, Harrison Wellford, 218. *See also* 236

Spend Yourself Rich, Ellen Williamson, 105

The Sportsman on Wheels, Erwin Bauer, 450

Squeeze It till the Eagle Grins: How to Spend, Save and Enjoy Your Money, Scott Burns, 364

State Consumer Action—Summary '72, U.S. Office of Consumer Affairs, 166

**Stereo & Tape Equipment Test Reports,* Consumer Guide, 498

Stop Wasting Your Insurance Dollars, Dave Goodwin, 304

*Sue the B*st*rds: The Victim's Handbook,* Douglas Matthews, 329

Suggested Guidelines for Consumer Education: Grades K–12, U.S. Office of Consumer Affairs, 114. *See also* 113

Summary of Information for Shippers of Household Goods, Interstate Commerce Commission, 419

Super Tenant: New York City Tenant Handbook: Your Legal Rights and How to Use Them, John M. Striker and Andrew O. Shapiro, 325

Supermarket Counter Power, Adeline Garner Shell, 237

The Supermarket Handbook: Access to Whole Foods, Nikki Goldbeck and David Goldbeck, 224

The Supermarket Survival Manual, Judy Lynn Kemp, 225

The Supermarket Trap: The Consumer and the Food Industry, Jennifer Cross, 223. *See also* 236

Supershopper: A Guide to Spending and Saving, David Klein and Marymae Klein, 81. *See also* 94

Supplement to Medical Economics Reprint on A Consumer's Directory of Prince George's County Doctors, 343

Survival Tactics: Coping with the Pressure of Today's Living, James G. Driscoll, 123

Teaching Your Child the Fiscal Facts of Life, Rodger Dean Duncan, 408

Telegripe Complaint Kit, 55

Ten Cents on the Dollar or the Bankruptcy Game, Sidney Rutberg, 35

The Tenant Survival Book, Emily Jane Goodman, 323. *See also* 325

*Tender Loving Greed: How the Incredibly Lucrative Nursing Home "Industry" Is Exploiting America's

Old People and Defrauding Us All, Mary Adelaide Mendelson, 423
The Therapeutic Nightmare. See *By Prescription Only*
†*There Is a Law against It,* 165
†*This Is Fraud,* 249
The Time-Life Book of Family Finance, Carlton Smith and Richard Putnam Pratt, 398
To Buy or Not to Buy? That Is Only One of the Questions, G. Vance Biddle, 292
Today's Camping: New Equipment for Modern Campers, C. B. Colby, 42
†*Tommy's First Car,* 31
Toys That Don't Care, Edward M. Swartz, 512
Trailer Life's Recreational Vehicle Campground and Services Guide, 458
Travel at ½ the Price, Peter San Roman, 515
The Truth about Contact Lenses, Jeffrey Baker, 199
20 Ways Not to Be "Gypped," 250
200,000,000 Guinea Pigs: New Dangers in Everyday Foods, Drugs, and Cosmetics, John G. Fuller, 127

The Underground Gourmet, Milton Glaser and Jerome Snyder, 462
The Underground Shopper, Sue Goldstein and Ann Light, 506
Unfit for Human Consumption, Ruth Mulvey Harmer, 211
**U.S. Consumer.* See *Consumer New$week*
Unsafe at Any Speed: The Designed-In Dangers of the American Automobile, Ralph Nader, 24. *See also* 14, 23, 130
The User's Guide to the Protection of the Environment, Paul Swatek, 196
†*Using Money Wisely,* 404

Vacation Houses: What You Should Know before You Buy or Build, Betsy Cobb and Hubbard Cobb, 273

What Shall I Do with My Money?, Eliot Janeway, 372. *See also* 373
What to Do with Your Bad Car: An Action Manual for Lemon Owners, Ralph Nader, Ralf Hotchkiss, and Lowell Dodge, 14. *See also* 15, 29, 146
What to Expect in Vision Care, 201
What You Should Know before Buying a Condominium, William R. Stover, 51
What You Should Know before You Buy a Car, Anthony Till, 12. *See also* 26
What You Should Know before You Have Your Car Repaired, Anthony Till, 21
What You've Got Coming in Medicare & Social Security, Bruce Biossat, 492
What's Wrong with Your Life Insurance, Norman F. Dacey, 314
When and How to Choose an Attorney, Cameron K. Wehringer, 330
Where to Pick-Your-Own Fruits and Vegetables in New Jersey, 209
Where to Retire on a Small Income, Norman D. Ford, 479
Whistle Blowing: Report of the Conference on Professional Responsibility, Ralph Nader, Peter J. Petkas, and Kate Blackwell, eds., 139
Who Put the Con in Consumer?, David Sanford, 146
†*Why Do You Buy?,* 103
The Wine Bibber's Bible, James Norwood Pratt and Jacques de Caso, 519
Wipe Out Your Debts and Make a Fresh Start, Jerome I. Meyers, 34
Wise Home Buying, U.S. Dept. of Housing and Urban Development, 282

Without Prescription: A Guide to the Selection and Use of Medicines You Can Get Over-the-Counter without Prescription, for Safe Self-Medication, Erwin Di Cyan and Lawrence Hessman, 189

Woodall's Mobile Home & Parks Directory, 357. *See also* 356

Woodall's Trailering Parks and Campgrounds Directory, 459

Word of Mouth: A Completely New Kind of Guide to New York City Restaurants, Jim Quinn, 466

You and Your Doctor, Doris Lee Dickens, 334

You and Your Money: A Survival Guide to the Controlled Economy, Eliot Janeway, 373

You and Your Pension, Ralph Nader and Kate Blackwell, 426

You Don't Have to Be Rich to Own a Brownstone, Joy Wilkes and Paul Wilkes, 290

You the Consumer, Bertram L. Linder and Edwin Selzer, 82

Your Child and Money, Sidonie Matsner Gruenberg, 409

†*Your Credit is Good . . . A Film about Paying Later,* 175

Your Family and Its Money, Helen M. Thal with Melinda Holcombe, 402

Your Guide to Social Security and Medicare Benefits, J. K. Lasser Tax Institute, 494

Your Health Insurance: A Story of Failure, Edwin P. Hoyt, 311

Your Money or Your Life: Rx for the Medical Market Place, Richard Kunnes, 342

†*Your Right to a Hearing,* 184. *See also* 249

Your Social Security Benefits, Louise Boggers, 493

SUBJECT INDEX

Note: Listings refer to entry numbers not page numbers.

Airplanes, 1

Annuities, 2. *See also* Insurance, Life; Pensions; Retirement

Appliances. *See* Household Equipment and Furnishings

Auctions, 3–4

Automobiles, 5–13. *See also* Insurance, Automobiles

Automobiles—Complaints, 14. *See also* Consumer Complaints

Automobiles—Frauds, 15–16. *See also* Frauds

Automobiles—Maintenance and Repairs, 17–22

Automobiles—Safety, 23–24

Automobiles—Used, 25–32

Banking Services. *See* Savings and Thrift

Bankruptcy, 33–36. *See also* Credit; Debts

Bicycles, 37–41

Cameras. *See* Photographic Equipment

Camping Equipment, 42–43

Carpets, 44–46. *See also* Household Equipment and Furnishings

Clothing, 47. *See also* Stores and Services

Collecting, 48

Complaints. *See* Consumer Complaints

Condominiums, 49–52. *See also* Houses—Buying; Landlords and Tenants

Consumer Complaints, 53–56. *See also* Consumer Protection; Consumer Protection—Directories

Consumer Education, 57–106. *See also* Consumer Protection; specific topics, e.g., Food; Medical Care

Consumer Education—Bibliographies, 107–108

Consumer Education—Study and Teaching, 109–114

Consumer Organizations. *See* Consumer Protection—Directories

Consumer Protection, 115–149. *See also* Consumer Education; specific topics, e.g., Automobiles—Frauds; Food—Adulteration and Protection; Product Safety

Consumer Protection—Directories, 150–157

Consumer Protection—History, 158–159

Consumer Protection—Laws and Legislation, 160–166

Contact Lenses. *See* Eye Care

Credit, 167–175. *See also* Debt

Day Care, 176

Debt, 177–184. *See also* Bankruptcy; Credit

Dental Care, 185–186. *See also* Medical Care; Professional Services

Diets, 187

Doctors. *See* Medical Care; Professional Services

Drugs, 188–191. *See also* Medical Care

Electricity. *See* Environment; Household Equipment and Furnishings

Environment, 192–197. *See also* Food–Adulteration and Protection; Product Safety

Eye Care, 198–201

Finance, Personal. *See* Money Management

Fishing Equipment, 202

Food (Fruits, Herbs, Meats, Nuts, Vegetables), 203–209. *See also* Stores and Services

Food–Adulteration and Protection, 210–219. *See also* Environment

Food–Cooperatives, 220

Food–Industry and Trade, 221–240

Food–Labeling, 241–243

Frauds, 244–250. *See also* Automobiles–Frauds; Consumer Protection; Medical Care–Frauds; Real Estate–Frauds

Furnishings. *See* Household Equipment and Furnishings

Garage Sales, 251–253

Guns and Hunting Equipment, 254

Health Care. *See* Dental Care; Eye Care; Insurance, Health; Medical Care; Nursing Homes

Health Foods. *See* Food-Industry and Trade

Health Insurance. *See* Insurance, Health

Home Ownership and Maintenance, 255–259. *See also* Houses–Buying

Household Equipment and Furnishings, 260–270. *See also* Carpets; Stores and Services

Houses–Buying, 271–285. *See also* Condominiums; Real Estate

Houses–Buying and Renovating, 286–290

Houses–Buying and Selling, 291–299. *See also* Real Estate

Housing. *See* Condominiums; Home Ownership and Maintenance; Houses –Buying; Mobile Homes; Real Estate

Hunting Equipment. *See* Guns and Hunting Equipment

Insurance, 300–306

Insurance, Automobile, 307–308

Insurance, Health, 309–311. *See also* Medical Care; Social Security and Medicare

Insurance, Life, 312–321

Insurance, Mobile Homes, 322

Kitchen Utensils. *See* Household Equipment and Furnishings

Landlords and Tenants, 323–325

Lawyers. *See* Legal Services; Professional Services

Legal Services, 326–330. *See also* Professional Services

Life Insurance. *See* Insurance, Life

Loans. *See* Credit

Medical Care, 331–349. *See also* Dental Care; Drugs, Eye Care; Insurance, Health; Nursing Homes; Professional Services

Medical Care–Frauds, 350–351. *See also* Frauds

Medicare. *See* Social Security and Medicare

Minibikes. *See* Motorcycles and Minibikes

Mobile Homes, 352–355. *See also* Insurance, Mobile Homes; Recreational Vehicles

Mobile Homes–Parks, 356–357

Money Management, 358–407

Money Management–by Children, 408–411

Mortgages. *See* Credit; Houses—Buying
Motorboats, 412
Motorcycles and Minibikes, 413–415
Moving, 416–422
Music. *See* Phonograph Recordings; Pianos; Stereo and Tape Equipment

Nursing Homes, 423–425. *See also* Medical Care

Pensions, 426. *See also* Retirement
Personal Finance. *See* Money Management
Pharmaceuticals. *See* Drugs
Phonograph Recordings, 427–432
Photographic Equipment, 433–434
Physicians. *See* Medical Care; Professional Services
Pianos, 435–436
Product Safety, 437–441. *See also* Consumer Protection; specific topics, e.g., Toys
Professional Services, 442. *See also* Dental Care; Legal Services; Medical Care

Real Estate, 443–448. *See also* Houses—Buying; Houses—Buying and Selling
Real Estate—Frauds, 449. *See also* Frauds
Recordings. *See* Phonograph Recordings
Recreation. *See* Airplanes; Bicycles; Camping Equipment; Fishing Equipment; Guns and Hunting Equipment; Mobile Homes; Motorboats; Motorcycles and Minibikes; Recreational Vehicles; Skiing Equipment; Stereo and Tape Equipment; Travel
Recreational Vehicles, 450–457. *See also* Airplanes; Bicycles; Camping Equipment; Mobile Homes; Motorboats; Motorcycles and Minibikes
Recreational Vehicles—Campgrounds, 458–459
Restaurants, 460–475
Retirement, 476–486. *See also* Annuities; Money Management; Nursing Homes; Social Security and Medicare
Rugs. *See* Carpets

Savings and Thrift, 487–490. *See also* Money Management
Shopping. *See* Food; Food—Industry and Trade; Stores and Services
Skiing Equipment, 491
Small Claims Courts. *See* Legal Services
Social Security and Medicare, 492–497. *See also* Insurance, Health; Medical Care; Retirement
Stereo and Tape Equipment, 498
Stores and Services, 499–500
Stores and Services—Discount and Secondhand, 501–511
Surgery. *See* Medical Care

Tenants. *See* Landlords and Tenants
Toys, 512. *See also* Consumer Protection; Product Safety
Travel, 513–515

Wines, 516–519